Preventing School Failure

Preventing School Failure

Tactics for Teaching Adolescents

Second Edition

Thomas C. Lovitt

pro·ed
An International Publisher

8700 Shoal Creek Boulevard
Austin, Texas 78757-6897
800/897-3202   Fax 800/397-7633
Order online at http://www.proedinc.com

© 2000, 1991 by PRO-ED, Inc.
8700 Shoal Creek Boulevard
Austin, Texas 78757-6897
800/897-3202   Fax 800/397-7633
Order online at http://www.proedinc.com

Library of Congress Cataloging-in-Publication Data

Lovitt, Thomas C.
    Preventing school failure : tactics for teaching adolescents /
Thomas C. Lovitt. — 2nd ed.
        p.   cm.
    Includes bibliographical references and indexes.
    ISBN 0-89079-824-9 (alk. paper)
    1. Dropouts—United States—Prevention.   2. Handicapped
youth—Education—United States.   3. Special education—United
States.   I. Title.
LC146.6   .L68   2000
371.2'1973—dc21

                                                        99-27076
                                                        CIP

This book is designed in Frutiger and New Century Schoolbook.

Executive Editor: James R. Patton
Production Director: Alan Grimes
Production Coordinator: Dolly Fisk Jackson
Managing Editor: Chris Olson
Art Director: Thomas Barkley
Designer: Jason Crosier
Print Buyer: Alicia Woods
Preproduction Coordinator: Chris Anne Worsham
Staff Copyeditor: Martin Wilson
Project Editor: Debra Berman
Publishing Assistant: Jason Morris

Printed in the United States of America

1   2   3   4   5   6   7   8   9   10   03   02   01   00   99

To Sequoia Dendron Gigantium

Contents

◆ ◆ ◆ ◆ ◆ ◆ ◆ ◆ ◆ ◆ ◆ ◆ ◆ ◆ ◆ ◆ ◆ ◆

Chapter 3

Chapter 4

Chapter 5

Chapter 6

Chapter 7

Chapter 8

Chapter 9
Participation ◆ 245

Chapter 10
Goals ◆ 263

Chapter 11
Peer-Mediated Instruction ◆ 277

Preface

The title of the first edition of this book was *Preventing School Dropouts*. It was my belief that if tactics in that volume were judiciously chosen and carefully arranged, many youth would be kept from exiting school before they were supposed to. However, because I now believe that many other adolescents, ones who were not actually headed in that direction but who were simply "serving time," also would be aided by these tactics, I have changed the title of this second edition to reflect this larger group and to mirror its broader mission—that is, preventing school failure. Many of the tactics in this edition should prove helpful to a wide range of youth, those classified as learning disabled, remedial, and at risk, as well as regular students who have avoided being classified.

The first edition of this book had a good run; I am pleased to send out its offspring. In the first edition there were 11 chapters and 120 tactics. The chapters were based on extensive surveys of teachers, asking about the characteristics of youth who are at risk. Although the tactics were organized in a reasonable way, I changed the arrangement in this second edition. In this edition there are 16 chapters and 134 tactics. I added chapters titled Homework, Adapting Materials, Testing and Grading, Peer-Mediated Instruction, Self-Management, and Parents. I eliminated the chapter titled Attitudes, although some of those tactics are incorporated into other chapters in this edition. My primary reason for the revised organization was to make the chapter titles more descriptive of the tactics they included.

I kept 83 tactics from the first edition and added 51 new ones. I edited all the original tactics, some of them rather significantly, and added new references when appropriate. Along with traditional journal and textbook references for the tactics, I cited several World Wide Web sites.

I removed the three appendixes from the first edition because most individuals with whom I spoke who had used that book did not refer to them. I added a brief introduction to each chapter to set the tone for the content and to introduce the tactics included.

I made several other changes in this edition, many of which were prompted by a recent, multiyear study of youth who are at risk or classified as disabled in high schools (Lovitt, 1995). My experiences teaching in the secondary teacher education program at the University of Washington, Seattle, in the past few years also urged me to consider certain changes. Other modifications in this volume were suggested by an extensive review of the first edition by Ellis and Larkin (1994).

The following are the most important of those revisions:

- Inclusion of several "how tos" in the Health chapter

- Clearer distinctions between study skills and basic skills

- A more detailed rationale for tactics in the Study Skills chapter

- Suggestions for current types of monitoring and evaluation

- More consideration for higher order processes and cognitive development
- Showing of interrelationships between several chapters and tactics in an attempt to get at the "bigger picture"
- Consideration of problems of grading, testing, and graduation
- Promotion of parents as advocates for their children

The format for the tactics is the same as it was in the first edition; that is, the information is divided into sections titled Background, Who Can Benefit, Procedures, Modifications and Considerations, and Monitor. Most users have found this framework to be acceptable. As for the tactics in the first edition, the ones in this volume are, to the extent possible, based on data. The original researchers have been cited, and their write-ups paraphrased, and in the process I believe their tactics are easier to implement.

References

Ellis, E. S., & Larkin, M. J. (1994). Preventing school dropouts: Tactics for at-risk, remedial, and mildly handicapped adolescents [Book Review]. *Remedial and Special Education, 15,* 189–197.

Lovitt, T. C. (1995). Curricular options and services for youth with disabilities. *Journal of Behavioral Education, 5,* 211–233.

Chapter 1
ATTENDANCE

♦ ♦ ♦ ♦ ♦ ♦ ♦ ♦ ♦ ♦ ♦ ♦ ♦ ♦ ♦ ♦ ♦ ♦ ♦ ♦

Included in this chapter on attendance are 15 tactics. Their purpose is to encourage youth to show up for school on time and to stay there once they arrive. Tardy individuals, especially those who are chronically late, annoy everyone and seem to think that others will always wait for them. When individuals skip classes, they miss out on the material presented, and if they are absent several days they are less likely to graduate.

On any given day in many city high schools, about 20% to 25% of students are absent. Needless to say, even with the best laid lesson plans, delivered by the most exciting and knowledgeable teachers, with all sorts of "cutting edge" technology, and all the rest, if students do not show up, then all that is available at school is lost. School is not like the famous baseball field claim that if you "build it they will come." It is more like the Woody Allen truism: "80% of success is simply showing up."

The first two tactics in this chapter are schoolwide activities, focusing on promoting attendance. The next two deal with punctuality. The fifth is concerned with the transition from middle school to high school, a crucial decision point for either dropping out or staying in school. The next tactic is addressed to substitute teachers because some students take advantage of them and skip classes. The following eight tactics offer approaches for dealing with attendance: arranging contingencies, setting contracts, using parents, setting up alternative educational environments, and others. The final tactic describes a program for keeping teenage mothers in school.

SCHOOLWIDE CHANGES: CHANGING ATTITUDES REGARDING EDUCATION

Background

The Changing Attitudes Regarding Education (CARE) program was designed to help educators become aware of students who are developing attitudes toward education that are not conducive to learning (Duval County Schools, 1986). It provides them with a way to intervene with these students to change their negative attitudes, and offers a range of preventive activities.

A team made up of an administrator, teachers, a counselor, and parents has the responsibility of taking referrals, proposing a plan of action for students who have been referred, and reviewing their progress. Anyone may refer a student to this team for intervention.

Who Can Benefit

Referrals for intervention by the CARE team target intermediate or middle school students displaying characteristics that have been observed in studies (Hess, Wells, Prindle, Liffman, & Kaplan, 1987) conducted with high school dropouts (e.g., low reading ability, above or below average age for class). The hope is that attempts to intervene with these youth who are at risk at an early age will prevent them from dropping out later on. (See Table 1.1 for a listing of characteristics of these youth.)

Table 1.1. Characteristics of Youth At Risk of School Failure or Dropout

Characteristics	Never				Always
I. Academic					
1. The student displays a low reading ability.	1	2	3	4	5
2. The student fails to achieve in regular schoolwork.	1	2	3	4	5
3. The student possesses either a low scholastic aptitude *or* average to high scholastic aptitude but with performance consistently below potential.	1	2	3	4	5
4. The student's grade level placement is below average age for grade.	1	2	3	4	5
II. School Patterns					
5. The student displays irregular attendance/frequent tardiness.	1	2	3	4	5
6. The student displays antagonism to faculty.	1	2	3	4	5
7. He or she causes discipline problems.	1	2	3	4	5
8. The student had a frequent change of schools.	1	2	3	4	5
III. Social					
9. There is little acceptance of student by school staff.	1	2	3	4	5
10. The student's friends are much younger or older.	1	2	3	4	5
11. He or she has few friends.	1	2	3	4	5
12. There is a marked difference in student from schoolmates in:					
a. size ☐					
b. interests ☐					
c. physique ☐					
d. social class ☐					
e. dress ☐					
f. personality development ☐					
13. The student participates in extra-curricular activities.	1	2	3	4	5
14. The student has a record of delinquency.	1	2	3	4	5

Table 1.1. *(Continued)*

Characteristics	Never				Always
IV. Family					
15. The student is not able to compete with, or is ashamed of, brothers and sisters.	1	2	3	4	5
16. The student has an unhappy/unstable family situation.	1	2	3	4	5
17. The parents of the student did *not* graduate from high school.	1	2	3	4	5
18. The student has a low socioeconomic status.	1	2	3	4	5
19. The family has an inability to afford the normal expenditures of schoolmates.	1	2	3	4	5
V. Health					
20. The student has a serious emotional or physical handicap.	1	2	3	4	5
21. The student has or has had chronic illness.	1	2	3	4	5

Note. From *CARE: Changing Attitudes Regarding Education* (pp. 3, 4) by Duval County Schools, 1986, Jacksonville, FL: Author. ERIC Document Reproduction Service No. ED 285 923. Reprinted with permission.

Procedures

Guidelines for the CARE Team

The following are suggestions for developing and running a CARE team:

1. (*Principal*) Appoint members of the CARE team: principal, a classroom teacher, guidance counselor, referring teacher, and parents.

2. Select a chairperson for the team.

3. Meet a minimum of once every 9 weeks to
   - Act on new referrals
   - Review current and previous cases

4. (*Recorder*) Complete individual reporting forms and log each case.

5. (*Counselor*) Flag cumulative record to make tracking possible, and place a copy of the individual report form in cumulative folder.

6. Initiate intervention.

7. Monitor and modify interventions as necessary.

Intervention for Project CARE

The purpose of Project CARE is to help students care about education and know that educators care about them. Students who have been identified as candidates for the program become members of Project CARE according to guidelines established by the team in their school. Following are suggestions for establishing the structure and function of this group:

1. Conduct monthly meetings with students of similar age to decide on and put together a project to show that they care about their school, education, and teachers.

2. Ask interested teachers to volunteer to meet with Project CARE students to coordinate the projects.

3. Support students' attempts to write and give a CARE skit for individual classes or the whole school.

4. Encourage students to write CARE thoughts and read them over the intercom.

5. Encourage students to welcome new students and take them on a tour of the school.

6. Give each student involved in the project a CARE button to identify them and instill a sense of pride.

Taking Individual Action

For students with academic difficulties, the following may be useful:

1. Provide assistance through appropriate referrals:
   - A homework assistance program
   - Volunteer tutor
   - Peer tutoring
   - Primary resource teacher
   - Special programs such as Title I

2. Set up counseling groups for work and study skills.

3. Write behavioral contracts with the referring teacher and student to improve daily work and study skills.

4. Conduct parent workshops to teach students ways to assist their children.

5. Use selective class scheduling.

Family Concerns

Divorce/Death/New Family

1. Provide individual and group counseling.

2. Give parents referral information such as family counseling services and homemaker services.

3. Establish parent education groups for parents with similar concerns.

Chronic/Serious Illness

1. Arrange for individual counseling.

2. Make referrals as needed:

- School social worker
- Parents regarding information on available services
- Home reinforcement services

Abuse or Neglect: Refer to home reinforcement services.

Unidentified Family Concerns: Request assistance from school social worker who can

1. Assess needs

2. Offer help with possible resources

Frequent School Changes

1. Assign a Big Brother or Big Sister to the referred student.

2. Formulate a plan, including

   - Early contact with counselor, principal, and other appropriate staff
   - Frequent follow-up in first weeks to alleviate the stress of change

3. Contact next school when student leaves about

   - Academic difficulties
   - Need for referral to outside agencies

Frequent Tardiness or Absence

1. Have a parent conference to explain need for attendance.

2. Engage the assistance of the school social worker, attendance officer, or others when appropriate.

Health Concerns

Uncertain Health Concern. Contact school nurse or school social worker to

1. Determine existence and nature of health problem

2. Assist parents in securing needed assistance

Cleanliness/Hygiene

1. Counsel with student.

2. Have parent conference.

3. Refer to nurse or social worker.

4. Refer to home reinforcement services if appropriate.

Chronic Illness

1. Conference with parents to learn about

   - Nature of the illness
   - Related limitations
   - Special needs

2. Counsel with student to help him or her deal with the illness and its effects.

3. Involve student in support or counseling groups with others who have chronic health concerns (e.g., diabetes or epilepsy).

4. Assist parents to get help through hospital or homebound programs.

5. Inform all school staff who have contact with the student about the nature and limitations of the illness.

Physical or Emotional Handicap

1. Make appropriate referrals:
   - Services available through the school
   - Hospital
   - Counseling services

2. Provide individual or group counseling.

3. Arrange for school presentations by mental or physical health organizations.

Interpersonal Relationship Concerns

Problems with Peer Group

1. Make staff members who work with the student aware of his or her situation, and work with them when dealing with behaviors such as tattling, teasing, and name calling.

2. Conduct classroom sessions on building interpersonal skills, acceptance of individual differences, and a cooperative classroom spirit.

3. Provide individual or group counseling on interpersonal relationships (i.e., how to develop friendships, finding a way to belong to the group).

4. Involve the student with problems as a "buddy" for a younger student who needs a friend.

5. Help student find
   - A hobby
   - A sport
   - A club
   - Music or art activities

6. Develop behavioral contracts with the students to help them change negative behaviors (e.g., fighting, bullying, teasing).

7. Refer to outside agencies if needed.

8. Ask parents to help plan cooperative efforts to provide youth with more positive interactions.

Problems with School Staff

1. Plan strategies with adults who work with the student to change the cycle of negative interactions.

2. Conduct workshops to help staff improve relationships with such students, including
   - Communication skills
   - Improving self-concept and positive discipline approaches

Modifications and Considerations

The CARE strategies have been recommended to give staff immediate ways to deal with students who are displaying negative attitudes toward school. Whenever possible, it would be more desirable to act early in each student's school experience to prevent these attitudes from developing at all.

Wood (1992, p. 106) noted the following factors that are crucial in understanding the attitudes of regular students toward students with disabilities:

1. Patterns of discriminatory behavior may actually be relatively normal patterns.

2. Teachers' attitudes toward students with disabilities may exist with or without labels. There are those who maintain that the most discriminated against youth are the overweight boys and girls.

3. Attitudes of students toward disabilities are significantly influenced by others with whom they relate.

Monitor

This program should be evaluated by keeping track of who is involved (students and faculty) and the time spent on the program, and by detailing the program's components that are involved. Beyond gathering these descriptive data, all (or at least representative) individuals involved in the program should be interviewed periodically to determine whether they are pleased with the progress or would recommend changes.

References

Duval County Schools. (1986). *CARE: Changing attitudes regarding education.* Jacksonville, FL: Author. (ERIC Documentation Service No. ED 285 923)

Hess, A. G., Jr., Wells, E., Prindle, C., Liffman, P., & Kaplan, B. (1987). "Where's Room 185?" How schools can reduce their dropout problem. *Education and Urban Society, 19*(3), 330–335.

Wood, J. W. (1992). *Adapting instruction for mainstreamed and at-risk students* (2nd ed.). Upper Saddle River, NJ: Merrill/Prentice-Hall.

STAYING IN SCHOOL: A SCHOOLWIDE PROGRAM

Background

The suggestions from this tactic can be applied in one of two ways: (a) as a checklist for a school's staff to consider as they evaluate their program (or lack of) for handling students at risk of failing or dropping out of school or (b) as an outline to follow in developing such a program.

The author of this material (Conrath, 1988), an educational consultant specializing in dropout prevention, recommended that, prior to evaluating an existing program or budgeting funds to set up a new one, three questions should be addressed: What makes a dropout prevention program effective? What makes teachers in dropout programs effective? What do probable dropouts need from adults and a dropout prevention program?

Who Can Benefit

Students from Grades K through 12 should be served by the type of program outlined here. These students are not "dumb"; often, they are simply discouraged. A program that acknowledges their feelings and deals with the factors that cause these students to fail will help more than will programs that provide watered-down curricula and "fun" activities to the exclusion of work that must be done to remain in school. Furthermore, the avoidance and hostility demonstrated by many students who are likely to become dropouts is exacerbated by anonymity. This approach seeks to avoid that by treating students personally.

Procedures

Program Effectiveness

Address the question, "What makes a dropout prevention program effective?" in the following ways:

1. Make the program part of a systemwide, K through 12 strategy.

   - Talk about dropout prevention in faculty meetings.

   - Involve all staff members.

   - Consider the program to be essential.

2. Identify which students will be best served by the program.

   - Place only those students in the program.

   - Do not overload it with all students who have special needs.

3. Clarify roles within the program.

   - Tell students precisely why they are in the program.

   - Establish the fact that the adults involved in the program are experienced professionals with the skills needed to help students.

   - Emphasize the seriousness of the situation, and that serious work will need to be done.

4. Expect students to live up to high ethical and intellectual standards.

   - Begin academic work at students' current levels of achievement, but do not water down the content.

   - Make no false assumptions about students in terms of lacking ability.

   - Do not give students insulting labels, such as "reluctant learners."

   - Refrain from patronizing students (i.e., giving "warm fuzzies" or inappropriate external rewards).

5. Teach discipline and responsibility.

   • Do not automatically expect students to possess and display these characteristics.

   • Understand the difference between teaching discipline and imposing obedience, and do not confuse the two.

6. Avoid treating students anonymously or impersonally.

   • Always acknowledge their presence or absence.

   • Demonstrate genuine concern for their well-being.

7. Present an alternative strategy for learning.

   • Require students to do real schoolwork.

   • Provide the kind of learning that students need to mature intellectually.

8. Locate the program in a place where students feel a sense of belonging.

   • Avoid putting it in classrooms that are used by other teachers whenever possible.

   • Give students an opportunity to develop a sense of ownership.

9. Balance the program between fitting into the total school program and having enough autonomy to allow the kinds of decisions teachers must make in order to assist students who are at risk.

10. Make strong efforts to help discouraged students see

    • The point of what they are being asked to do

    • How it will improve their lives

Teacher Effectiveness

Address the question, "What makes teachers in dropout prevention programs effective?" by selecting teachers who have the following qualities:

1. *Toughness* (ethical, emotional, and intellectual)

   • Can handle angry and confrontational students

   • Keep critical issues in focus

   • Can work with difficult youth day after day

2. *Compassion*

   • Understand the grimness of many students' lives

   • Are willing to spend time with students getting serious work done

3. *Professionalism*

   • Know why graduation from high school is important

   • Value, enjoy, and are willing to talk to youth about the pleasure and importance of learning

4. *Seriousness*

- Are clear about end results desired for students, and flexible about how to get them

- Believe in serious work and that all students are capable of doing it

- Know that the "I don't care" attitudes of students are for self-protection, and do not accept or put up with such attitudes

5. *Knowledge*

Are knowledgeable about

- Teaching and learning

- Learning styles

- Motivational theories and practice

- The reasons some youth become discouraged and defeated

6. *Creativity*

- Know many ways to introduce and explain new topics and ideas

- Persevere until all students "get it"

- Stimulate youth to think

7. *Authoritativeness*

- Lead through own expertise and sense of competence

- Do not constantly quote rules and regulations

8. *Sense of purpose*

- Have high ethical and intellectual expectations for themselves

- Act accordingly

- Know why they like teaching and why they are working with difficult youth

9. *Cultured competence*

- Wear education and culture with pride

- Use language effectively

- Enjoy knowledge and expertise

- Value own and students' cultural heritage

Student Needs

Answer the question, "What do probable dropouts need from adults and a dropout prevention program?"

1. Structure and predictability

- Provide a supportive structure.

- Make purposes and benefits of work clear.

2. Flexible means and consistent ends: Provide different approaches (traditional ones have not worked).

3. High ethical and intellectual expectations: Realize that these students are discouraged; they are not dumb.

4. "Do-able" academic work

   • Select work that provides intellectual challenges without academic threats.

   • Help students "catch up" in skills and self-image.

5. Contact with adults

   • Do not have youth work in isolation, setting their own pace.

   • Provide engagement with adults that students can trust and respect.

6. Adult leadership

   • Confront students with their behavior when they behave poorly.

   • Handle student confrontations with skill and compassion, not as ego threats or battles to be won.

7. Serious, useful schoolwork

   • Avoid busywork.

   • Be sure students know the use of the work they are doing.

8. Trust

   • Do not assume these students have chosen failure.

   • Help them learn to break the pattern.

9. Increased self-esteem: Provide opportunities for achievement in worthwhile endeavors.

Modifications and Considerations

These suggestions can be modified and expanded as needed for any setting or situation. The basic premise—that students who are at risk deserve a serious, dedicated approach to helping them succeed—must remain constant. Regular reevaluations of existing programs should be required, and compliance should be specified in detail. Districts may wish to incorporate suggestions on what makes teachers effective in this sort of program into the qualifications required in hiring them for such programs.

Monitor

The most important data to keep for a program such as this would be the number of dropouts. In addition to knowing the numbers, concerned individuals should follow up with and interview each dropout. Several questions should be asked of them. The two most obvious are "Why did you drop out?" and "What would it take for you to return?"

Reference

Conrath, J. (1988). Dropout prevention: Find out if your program passes or fails. *The Executive Educator, 10*(8), 15–16.

THREE TECHNIQUES TO REDUCE TARDINESS

Background

Young adults must learn to take responsibility for their own successes and failures. They must learn to accept responsibility for being in class on time, just as they must later report to work at the appointed hour. Chances are increased that the dependable, prompt individual will obtain and keep a job.

Who Can Benefit

This tactic is especially suitable for students characterized as at risk, because a prime characteristic of those youth is that they are often late for school. Regrettably, these are the students who can least afford to miss hours or even minutes of instruction. They need all the help they can get to stay in school, make acceptable grades, graduate, and move on to the world after high school.

Procedures

Three techniques are explained here to reduce tardiness. The following steps should be taken before any of them are introduced, however:

1. Explain your desire to eliminate tardiness. Inform students that you want to assist them to develop positive job skills. Remind them that all jobs have rules and responsibilities.

2. Inform the students that you are disappointed in them when they are tardy. Explain to the students that when they arrive at class on time they will be given something they want, but when they are tardy they will not receive the reward. Let them know that they are now in control of the situation, and that your job as the teacher is simply to record the attendance pattern accurately.

3. Be consistent. Explain clearly what you expect, what you will do, and what the consequences are for successful behavior. Keep an accurate record that is open and accessible to the students.

Daily Report Card

1. Develop a card such as that shown in Figure 1.1 or Figure 1.2. Negotiate with the students what reward they would receive for acceptable behavior. Rewards might include stereo time, free reading time, extra minutes of break time, or time to surf the net.

2. Require each student to take the card home each day. The parents can record the number of successful days and perhaps arrange a reward for acceptable behavior.

DAILY REPORT CARD—ATTENDANCE

Name _____ Date _____ Class _____

Attendance: ☐ on time   ☐ tardy

Teacher's initial _____

Figure 1.1. The Daily Report Card. From "Late Again? Three Techniques to Reduce Tardiness in Secondary Learning Handicapped Students," by J. O. Potthoff, 1979, *Teaching Exceptional Children, 11,* p. 146. Copyright 1979 by The Council for Exceptional Children. Reprinted with permission.

3. Drop this procedure when the student has been on time for an extended period.

Contract Card

1. Develop a contract similar to that shown in Figure 1.3 that specifies the behavior to be improved, how pupils intend to improve it, how success will be measured, the time requirements, and the reward.

2. Post the contract where students can see it and record their progress.

3. Select this technique for more difficult cases and for maintaining attendance over extended periods of time.

Grade-Point Credit

1. Award points for completed assignments. Give additional points each day the students come in on time.

DAILY REPORT CARD

Name _____ Date _____ Class _____

Attendance: ☐ on time   ☐ tardy

Classrom Behavior: ☐ good   ☐ OK   ☐ poor

Work/Participation: ☐ good   ☐ OK   ☐ poor

Comment _____

Teacher's initial _____

Figure 1.2. The Daily Report Card, expanded to include other behavioral areas. From "Late Again? Three Techniques to Reduce Tardiness in Secondary Learning Handicapped Students," by J. O. Potthoff, 1979, *Teaching Exceptional Children, 11,* p. 146. Copyright 1979 by The Council for Exceptional Children. Reprinted with permission.

DAILY INDIVIDUAL CONTRACT

Name _____ Date _____ Class _____

I would like to improve: _____

To improve I will: _____

This will be measured by: _____

Time limit: _____

Mon.	Tues.	Wed.	Thurs.	Fri.

Reward _____

Student signature _____

Teacher's signature _____

Figure 1.3. The Contract Card. From "Late Again? Three Techniques to Reduce Tardiness in Secondary Learning Handicapped Students," by J. O. Potthoff, 1979, *Teaching Exceptional Children, 11,* p. 147. Copyright 1979 by The Council for Exceptional Children. Reprinted with permission.

2. Post the number of points required to earn each grade on the board and explain this arrangement to the students.

3. Select this technique for students who need to be nudged not only to attend school but to get to work once they get there.

Modifications and Considerations

These techniques could be more or less complex, with more or fewer situations and different consequences written into any of the three.

The matter of showing up on time could be tied to a group activity in which a reward is granted to all individuals if they all arrive at school on time for a few days (or turn in acceptable assignments).

Monitor

Students could be encouraged to take on the responsibility of record keeping, or it could be the joint responsibility of the youth and the teacher. An ongoing graph or record of prompt attendance and performance could be displayed either privately or publicly.

Reference

Potthoff, J. O. (1979). Late again? Three techniques to reduce tardiness in secondary learning handicapped students. *Teaching Exceptional Children, 11,* 146–148.

ARRIVING ON TIME FOR CURRENT EVENTS

Background

This tactic was carried out by a seventh-grade social studies teacher because his fourth-period students were not getting to class on time (Ron Lehman, Einstein Middle School, Seattle, WA). Prior to this class was lunchtime, and many of the students were more motivated to eat and chat than to show up promptly for social studies.

Who Can Benefit

Students in a class where this procedure is used all benefit. The pupils who are chronically late profit in that they do not miss out on instruction, and those who are rarely late benefit because the tardy students do not disrupt them. Moreover, the instructor gains in that he or she no longer has to cajole, threaten, and lament.

Procedures

1. Inform students that they should show up on time. Identify the advantages to them personally and to the class generally for prompt arrival. Acknowledge the reality of the particular situation (e.g., that it is sometimes difficult to arrive at this class on time because it follows a lunch period, or some other situation).

2. Tell students that from now on a "current events program" will go into effect 10 minutes before the period begins. Say that, although they do not have to come to class that early, they should arrive as early as possible to earn extra credit.

3. Inform the students that they will be able to share current events with the class. (With some classes you may need to have a discussion about current events—what they are and where to find out about them.)

4. Appoint or elect a current events "counter." This person keeps a record of the students who contribute news items. At the end of the period, he or she informs the class as to how many total events were contributed and who gave them. Moreover, the counter keeps track of the contributions for a week and summarizes those data for the class on Friday. This person could be chosen by the teacher initially, and elected by the class later.

5. Call on students to offer news items. Ask students to give the source of their information and offer brief comments on their topic.

6. Inform the students, when current events are being offered at a reasonable rate, that they will get extra credit if they embellish on someone else's current event (i.e., give news that provides additional information on the topic).

7. Set up a redemption plan: For so many points (gained from their contributions), they will get something. This could be points toward their grade, minutes of time to socialize, or something else.

8. Segue smoothly into the topic of the day at the actual time for the class by offering a transition current event or two.

Modifications and Considerations

Some students might not be able to arrive at class during the 10 minutes before the start of the class, and will miss out on the current events program and the points to be gained from contributing. Take their reasons into account and offer an alternate way for them to keep up with the times and to earn points.
Several modifications of the program could be considered:

1. The source of the events could be specified. Students could be asked, for example, to contribute items from only the Internet or from a specified newspaper.

2. The subjects of the events could be specified and students could be asked to contribute material related to the topic of the day.

3. Students could be encouraged to elect not only the counter of events but also the person who calls on others to contribute. Alternatively, the counter and the caller could be earned positions; students would have to do certain things over a period of time in order to earn those responsibilities.

Monitor

The counter keeps daily records of who offered the current events. Those data could be analyzed to show the frequency of contributions as a class, per day and week, and to show the times that each individual contributed.

 # TRANSITION FROM MIDDLE SCHOOL TO HIGH SCHOOL

Background

The transition from middle school to high school is rough for many students, but it can be especially difficult for youth who are disadvantaged or at risk. The *BRIDGE Curriculum Guide* developed by the Northwest Regional Educational Laboratory (1989) is designed to bridge that gap and to keep discouraged learners in school while enhancing their employability.

Who Can Benefit

Although this curriculum is designed for students who are disadvantaged and at risk, other youngsters could profit from such a program, because more students drop out of school at around the ninth grade than at any other time. The BRIDGE curriculum provides a structured sequence of activities designed for high school freshmen and sophomores.

Procedures

The activities in the BRIDGE curriculum revolve around skills that are seldom addressed in the standard high school curriculum. According to the program's author, "If students don't experience success right away, they may opt to leave. They often don't have the social skills and self-esteem to battle what can be a tough environment" (p. 3).

Students are recruited for the program during their last year of middle school. During the summer, prior to high school, they participate in a training and education program that consists of a half day of basic skills and life skills training and a half day of work experience.

During the school year they are involved with units of the BRIDGE curriculum, of which there are 18: self-esteem; self-responsibility; decision making; time management; conflict resolution; communication; peer relationships; career awareness; leadership; career goals and expectations; multicultural/multiethnic awareness; me, myself, and I; traditional and nontraditional roles; substance abuse; self-preservation; community resources; planning for summer; and using leisure time.

Each unit begins with an overview of the topic and responds to the question, "Why should I care about this topic?" Then relevant and provocative quotations are brought up for class discussion for each unit. A third component for all units is a listing of pertinent vocabulary. Some words in the self-esteem section are *goal, cooperate,* and *success,* and in the conflict resolution section are *aggressive, assertive, negotiate,* and *compromise.* The main focus of each unit (each runs for about 2 weeks) is a series of eight or so activities that include role plays, word jumbles, writing projects, discussions, and reading assignments. At the end of each unit, students are encouraged to reflect on what they learned and to think about ways to apply that information to their lives.

Modifications and Considerations

One adjustment in the management of this curriculum would be to involve a group of high school students in some of the summer sessions with the middle school youth and, later, as guides, mentors, or friends when the younger students enter high school.

Although not reviewed here, there is a second BRIDGE curriculum with 10 units: Back to school; The fear of success and the comfort of defeat; Say what?; I am my own leader; The company we keep; Dealing with difficult people; Twenty years to life; Traditions, rituals, beliefs; I can make a difference; and Crystal ball of the future.

Monitor

At the end of each unit, students have an opportunity to synthesize and reflect on what they learned and to think about ways to apply the new information to their lives. A summary of those thoughts would be informative. The true evaluation of this program, however, would come from interviews of youth, who have previously participated in the BRIDGE program, a few weeks after they begin high school. They should be asked what difficulties they are experiencing in their adjustment, how the program prepared them to cope with high school, and what more could be done in middle school to make the transition even smoother. Parents of these youth and a few of their high school teachers should also be interviewed to learn about their impressions of the BRIDGE program and the general process of transition.

Reference

BRIDGE curriculum guide. (1989). Prepared by the Northwest Regional Educational Laboratory for The Private Industry Council and the Portland Public Schools. (Available for $115.95 per volume, from The Private Industry Council, 720 SW Washington, Suite 250, Portland, OR 97205; 503/241-4600; For information or technical assistance, contact Andrea Baker at 503/275-9595)

PARENTAL INVOLVEMENT AND SUGGESTIONS FOR SUBSTITUTE TEACHERS

Background

This tactic is based on the idea that students will be influenced to attend classes if their parents encourage them to do so. Students in Suprina's (1979) study indicated that they would welcome family interest in their lives, and parents were receptive to comments about their children that were timely and indicated teachers' concern or interest.

Suprina (1979) also found that the best deterrent to absences was a stimulating class, even when the primary teacher is missing. Therefore, in addition to improving instruction and encouraging parental involvement, Suprina outlined activities for substitute teachers, because a survey of students indicated that they often skipped classes when substitutes took over.

Who Can Benefit

Surpina's study was conducted with students in a New York high school. Suggestions from that study are appropriate for students who are at risk or remedial. The recommended techniques would be especially helpful for substitute teachers.

Procedures

1. Identify students with frequent absences.
2. Ask them what they think about the class routine as it is, and what they would do to make it more interesting. These insights into stu-

dents' perceptions may help you to make changes that encourage their attendance.

3. Identify activities of interest to students that can be used later, when the class is managed by a substitute. Suggestions include scheduling video cassettes or CD-ROMs that are related to certain units; games (again related to specific units) that involve group or individual competition; portions of books or articles on various topics that could be read to the class, with suggested questions; and lists of current themes to bring up to the class with accompanying questions and statements.

4. Consider leaving the following for substitutes: a seating chart (perhaps including names of students who are and are not dependable); some recommended classroom management techniques; suggestions for introducing oneself; a simple map of the school; and names of people to call or go to for help (including phone numbers and room numbers).

5. Meet with parents and students together to address any special concerns and to explain the following guidelines, from Suprina's study:

   • Upon determining that an illegal absence has occurred, you will discuss it with the pupil and mail an illegal absence report to his or her home.

   • If a second illegal absence occurs, you will request a parent conference through the guidance or counseling office. At this conference the criteria necessary to maintain enrollment in the class are discussed and an agreement is signed by all concerned.

   • If continuous attendance is not maintained, the student will be permanently withdrawn from the class. It must be clearly understood that such action may delay the student's graduation from high school.

   • Students withdrawn from class are assigned to a restricted study hall during that class period. Cutting this study hall or other behaviors resulting in disciplinary problems are grounds for suspension.

Modifications and Considerations

An important part of this tactic is the parent conference that takes place following a second unexcused absence. At this conference, there should be discussion about the pupil's performance in class, attitudes, and efforts to get along in school. In Suprina's study, these meetings improved the relationships among the students, educators, and parents. Alternatively, the initial meeting could cover some of the same topics to establish rapport between those involved, without waiting for unexcused absences to stimulate a conference.

Parents could be encouraged to incorporate a reward system to ensure regular attendance. Rewards could be privileges, relief from household duties, or payments to savings accounts for special purchases.

Monitor

Attendance may be checked against a seating chart and recorded on a master list. This allows a substitute to take attendance quickly without having to call out names. Students can also keep track of their own attendance by checking off days on a calendar or on another form.

In addition to keeping those data, valuable information could be gathered from parents of absent-prone youth. Periodically they should be interviewed to determine what they were doing to keep their youth in school, particularly if they were successful. A compilation of those responses could be helpful to other parents and teachers, and counselors as well.

Reference

Suprina, R. N. (1979). Cutting down on student cutting. *National Association of Secondary School Principals, 63,* 27–31.

 SHOWING UP AND DOING THE ASSIGNMENTS

Background

The procedures explained here arose from necessity. Some years ago I was teaching an introductory course in special education to a class of about 50 undergraduates. It was the typical lecture–question–discussion type of class. All the students showed up for Session 1, but about 5 students were absent for Session 2, and about 10 missed Session 3. During those dates there was no attendance policy; I simply expected the students to attend class. When it became clear that clusters of them were finding other things to do, I knew it was time for a change.

Who Can Benefit

We all benefited from the following procedures. Certainly, I gained, for when the following steps were put in place, I didn't worry about attendance because most students came to class. The majority of students also benefited by showing up more regularly to the class. By consistently attending class, they were forced to keep up and had little need to cram during the final session or two.

Procedures

As I indicated, attendance was a problem. I had baseline data to support this; there was no need for further confirmation.

The following are the steps I took to set up and implement this procedure:

1. I announced that from this day forward I would give a brief test over the material that was to be covered on that day. Before class, the students were to read an assigned chapter from a textbook or an article or two. The readings formed the basis of the sessions: I asked questions about them; the students raised issues and questions; I or others responded to them; and I gave information from other, related sources.

2. I informed students that their scores on these tests and on the midterm and final examinations would be taken into account when determining their final grade.

3. I gave the test at various times. Sometimes I gave the test at the beginning of the period, and sometimes following the break in the middle of the 2½-hour class. If the test was given at the same time each session, some students would likely show up for it and then leave.

Modifications and Considerations

To further promote student attendance, you might give two or even three short tests on the same day, instead of only one. All or some tests could be considered when determining grades. Occasionally a double bonus test could be given. Another option would be to test only a few students each time. You could randomly select those who would be tested, and their scores (if they were in class to take the tests) could be folded into a group score. Yet another option would be to pair students. One of each pair would be required to respond to Items 1, 3, and 5 and the other to Items 2, 4, and 6. Their combined scores would be given to the pair, whether both of them attended class or not.

Monitor

This tactic is easy to monitor. You can keep data on how many students showed up for class before initiating the approach. Then, you gather data at each session to determine how the total number of the students was affected by the approach, and which students were especially influenced.

SCHOOL ORGANIZATION AFFECTS ATTENDANCE

Background

The ideas summarized for this tactic were taken from studies by Bryk and Thum (1989) and Guthrie, Long, and Guthrie (1989). Whereas most previous research on dropouts focused on their personal characteristics, these two studies gave attention to how aspects of school organization might contribute to reducing dropouts.

Who Can Benefit

Students identified as at risk would especially profit from the procedures and approaches described here. As those students were assisted, so then would their teachers and parents.

Procedures

Following are nine conclusions and recommendations from the two studies. I offer explanations for each and provide examples as to how it might be put into practice.

1. Small schools and reduced class size—A number of educators, such as Goodlad (1993), have called for smaller high schools of around

500 students. It is often impossible to reduce the size of schools, but it is possible to schedule students in more intimate groups by designing academies and "schools within schools." When units are decreased, the chances are greater that youth will know most of the others in their group and it will be easier for teachers to know them. Keep in mind that the real issue is not the size of the school or class, but rather that teachers interact more often and more positively with more students, especially those considered to be at risk. If school or class size is reduced and faculty do not take advantage of this opportunity to engage their students more often, then the school or the classes might as well have remained large.

2. Commonality in programs for students—Most educators agree that tracking is not a good idea (e.g., Goodlad, 1993; Oakes, 1985). Instead, the recommendation is to support the fullest inclusion of all children, including those with disabilities, those learning English as a Second Language (ESL), and remedial youth, in general education classes.

3. Less specialization of staff—Experts from the reviewed studies suggest that more school personnel should simply be teachers rather than counselors, school psychologists, social workers, and so on. They also propose that individuals with other qualifications who are on the school staff should teach rather than simply work with special types of children on special types of matters.

4. High performance standards—Numbers of educators support the notion that schools should expect a great deal of all students and should not lower their expectations for certain individuals for any reason.

5. Orderly social environment—It is important for children to know that they are safe when they come to school, that they are not in danger of being injured or robbed.

6. Perception of fair treatment of students—Most educators agree that the school's rules, reinforcements, punishments, reprimands, and benefits should be equally applied to all students.

7. Involved businesses, community, and parents—Businesses must come up with approaches that support students. They must discard large, depersonalized programs and search for ways to influence students' lives directly. Community agencies can get teenagers off the streets and back into schools or educational programs by offering counseling, tutoring, job training, health education, child care, and other services. Schools can take three general approaches to encourage parental involvement: inform parents of school routines and expectations, recruit parents to provide suggestions for school programs, and engage them in instructional activities.

8. Alternative schedules and sites—Schools should be transformed into community education facilities, and should be open evenings and weekends. Some class periods, especially science labs or art classes, should be scheduled for large amounts of time. Educators should offer instruction on weekends and during summers. Year-round schools should be considered. Moreover, schools should provide services for youth in

places other than regular school buildings. "Classes" could be held in churches, community centers, shopping malls, and local businesses.

9. Targeting of special populations—Certain types of youth may need special attention. Pregnant or parenting teenagers need counseling and prenatal and parent training. Students with limited English proficiency may need ESL classes. Students who have dropped out of school need information on options for getting back into school or obtaining a high school degree or equivalent.

Modifications and Considerations

No single recommendation offered here will by itself keep youth in schools. Schools must implement a package of changes that have been found in previous research to affect attendance and dropouts.

Monitor

Schools should keep data not only on the numbers of students who drop out of school for whatever reason, but on the students they attempt to bring back and, of those, the ones who actually return. Schools should not take the out-of-sight, out-of-mind approach to dropouts.

References

Bryk, A. S., & Thum, Y. M. (1989). *The effects of high school organization on dropping out: An exploratory investigation.* (Available from Center for Policy Research in Education, Eagleton Institute of Politics, Rutgers, The State University of New Jersey, New Brunswick, NJ 08901)

Goodlad, J. I. (1993). Access to knowledge. In J. Goodlad & T. Lovitt (Eds.), *Integrating general and special education* (pp. 1–22). Upper Saddle River, NJ: Merrill/Prentice-Hall.

Guthrie, L. F., Long, C., & Guthrie, G. P. (1989). *Strategies for dropout prevention.* (Available from Far West Laboratory for Educational Research and Development, 1855 Folsom Street, San Francisco, CA 94103.)

Oakes, J. (1985). *Keeping track: How schools structure inequality.* New Haven, CT: Yale University Press.

PEER GROUP SUPPORT PLUS REWARDS

Background

This tactic is based on the notion that if students are involved with their peers, they may be encouraged to attend class regularly. Certainly at the secondary level, youth *are* more reinforced by peers than by adults.

When students are chronically absent, dedicated teachers must take time from their packed schedules to explain, provide examples, and help students stay afloat. This individualized attention takes time that teachers could devote to other students, many of whom attend school regularly. A goal, therefore, is to cut down on preventable after-hours teaching.

Who Can Benefit

The 92 elementary students in Morgan's (1985) study were from lower socio-economic backgrounds, and many had records of excessive unexcused absences. After implementing the procedures he devised, marked improvement in daily attendance was noted for the pupils. Because the procedures are linked neither to a particular subject nor to a certain length of time, they can be applied to most situations at the secondary level with students characterized as remedial or at risk.

Procedures

The following steps can be administered by a teacher or a counselor.

1. Identify those pupils with poor attendance records.

2. Assign two other students who attend school regularly to work with each target pupil. If possible, identify triads of pupils who are good friends.

3. Explain to each trio that they have the opportunity to earn rewards by working together. Present these rules to the students: (a) If all three members attend school on a particular day, each member will earn one token. (b) If the target member is absent, no one receives a token. (c) If only the target pupil comes to school, he or she will get a token. (d) If he or she and one other mate show up, they will each receive a token. Earning tokens, therefore, is dependent on the behavior of the absent-prone pupil.

4. Set the requirements for exchanging tokens: For a certain number of tokens, students could earn privileges such as an extended lunch hour, a midday break, homework time in class, or granting of a reasonable request. When tokens are exchanged for one of those privileges, that should be indicated on the Attendance Rewards Chart (Figure 1.4). Pupils who attend school for a certain number of days could earn larger rewards (e.g., points toward a class party in celebration of their effort).

5. Give immediate reinforcement in the form of tokens every morning or at the beginning of the class period.

Modifications and Considerations

This tactic can be adopted for individual or total class attendance. In either case, a daily chart should be maintained that serves as an immediate source of feedback for the students.

One method of determining which rewards might be effective would be to question the students, who might have ideas for rewards that either they or other students would enjoy.

This tactic, as originally set up, provides two motivating factors: the prospect of immediate rewards and peer persuasion. Because the participation of individuals important to the target pupils is involved, the target student stands to learn the values of responsibility and working with others.

ATTENDANCE REWARDS CHART

Week of _____

Record date on which award was earned in correct space under group number. (Must be initialed by teacher.)

Rewards	Groups 1	2	3	4	5	6	7	8
Extended lunch period								
Midday break								
Class time for homework								
Personal request								
Class party								

Figure 1.4. Attendance Rewards Chart.

When setting up the triads—the target student and two pupils with better attendance records—the teacher may want to involve peers who are not necessarily friends of the target youngster, particularly for students who are at risk. Youth who are at risk often associate with similar students. Such an arrangement might provide an opportunity for them to acquire friends, at least acquaintances, who value school attendance.

Monitor

This technique can be evaluated by the data from the Attendance Rewards Chart. By calculating the number of times the triad earned rewards, you would learn about the effects of this tactic. If some groups never received a reward, a different technique should be arranged or a different combination of students should be formed. By studying the groups' choices of "rewarding" events, you would learn about their relative strengths. You also should keep data on the number of absences over a period of time.

Reference

Morgan, R. (1985). An exploratory study of three procedures to encourage school attendance. *Psychology in the Schools, 12,* 209–215.

CONTRACTS AND LOTTERIES

Background

For this tactic, students open up "bank accounts" for which they receive "funds" each day they attend class. In addition, students can deposit a small amount once a week and have a chance to win a large amount in a lottery. Epstein, Wing, Thompson, and Griffin (1980) found that both methods proved effective in increasing attendance and participation in an aerobic exercise program.

Who Can Benefit

Epstein et al.'s (1980) study was conducted with 41 female college students over two academic quarters. The interventions could be used for a variety of situations at the secondary school level, and would be particularly beneficial for youth characterized as remedial or at risk.

Procedures

Contracting

1. Determine which students might benefit from the intervention.
2. Develop an "account" form for each student, with places to indicate a beginning balance, deposits, withdrawals, and daily balance.
3. Translate the value of "money" into school supplies that students can earn.
4. Tell students that they will start out with a balance of 1 dollar, to which they can add 25 cents every day they come to class.
5. Inform students that they will lose 25 cents for each day they miss class.
6. Require students to balance their accounts at the end of each week. Allow them to either cash in their funds for school supplies or bring their balance forward to the next week.

Lottery

1. Inform students that at the end of each week, those who were present all 5 days are eligible to take part in the lottery.
2. Require eligible students to donate 25 cents on the day of the lottery.
3. Conduct the lottery by placing slips of paper with the students' names on them in a container. Ask a volunteer to draw a name.
4. Give the winning student the total amount that was in the lottery.

Modifications and Considerations

Epstein et al. (1980) suggested that the contracting option worked better than the lottery for initial attendance, but the lottery was more effective for maintaining attendance.

One way to increase the motivation for the bank account feature of this tactic would be to pay interest on money held in student accounts. The amounts given each day or for the beginning of the contracting program could, of course, be different from those suggested here. Furthermore, the amounts that students were allowed to place in the lottery could vary.

A way to enhance the effects of a lottery would be to hold it on random days of the week so that students would be less likely to skip class for fear of missing their chance of winning it. Several suggestions for dealing with absences are in a volume by Sprick and Howard (1995).

Monitor

As with other attendance programs, the most straightforward way to measure the success of the ideas presented here would be to acquire data, over time, on the number of absences and who was absent. The teacher or counselor should gather data prior to scheduling these techniques and during their involvement. Furthermore, the evaluator could determine the comparative effects of the techniques by relating the frequency of absences when contracting was in place to the frequency when the lottery was.

References

Epstein, L. H., Wing, R. R., Thompson, J. K., & Griffin, W. (1980). Attendance and fitness in aerobic exercise: The effects of contract and lottery procedures. *Behavior Modification, 4,* 465–479.

Sprick, R. S., & Howard, L. M. (1995). *The teacher's encyclopedia of behavior management.* Longmont, CO: Sopris West.

PRAISE AND REWARDS FOR ATTENDING

Background

The idea behind this tactic is that a combination of praise and rewards can improve attendance. Teachers or administrators do not ordinarily praise youngsters for showing up at school. They expect students to do so, and when they do not, teachers are disappointed and fuss at them for their nonattendance. In a study by VanSciver (1986), students who received rewards and praise for attendance had better attendance records than students who received lowered grades and suspensions for poor attendance.

Who Can Benefit

VanSciver's (1986) study was conducted with a sophomore class of approximately 100 students in a rural high school. This tactic could be arranged for urban schools and for middle schools as well as high schools.

Procedures

1. Explain the attendance improvement program to students. Inform them that copies of letters or awards received for good attendance will be included in their permanent files, and that future recommendations

to employers or colleges will include mention of those outstanding attendance records.

2. Send a letter containing the same information to the youths' parents.

3. Deliver a statement about the importance of good attendance on several occasions during the first period of the day. Vary the message from week to week, but always emphasize the fact that teachers and administrators appreciate the responsible and positive behaviors that students demonstrate by coming to school each day.

4. Post the names of students who had perfect attendance on the school bulletin board at the end of each month.

5. Call parents midway through the marking period to congratulate them if their son or daughter had a perfect attendance record.

6. Send congratulatory letters at the end of the marking period to students with perfect attendance.

7. Publish the names of these "perfect attenders" in the local newspaper.

8. Send similar congratulatory letters to students who maintained perfect attendance throughout the next marking period.

9. Award attendance certificates to students who had perfect attendance through two marking periods at a special school ceremony.

Modifications and Considerations

The length of time that students must maintain perfect attendance to receive recognition may be modified, depending on their previous attendance records. Students who have especially poor attendance records may benefit from more frequent congratulatory letters and phone calls to their parents. For students who have fairly good attendance records, the procedure described here should be adequate. But whatever the reinforcement schedule, it should not be too lean. As indicated earlier, teachers generally and mistakenly take good attendance for granted.

In addition to the previous procedures, an attendance contest was held between homerooms in VanSciver's study. T-shirts donated by a local car dealer were awarded to students in the homeroom that maintained the best overall attendance for each marking period. The shirts were printed in the school colors, and on the front was printed, "My homeroom maintained the highest daily attendance in the 1st (or 2nd) marking period of the 1984–85 school year." This proved to be a popular part of the attendance program.

Schedule special activities (e.g., social activities) on Mondays and Fridays, the worst days for absenteeism. School yearbooks, rings, or activity tickets could be distributed on those days as well.

The general tone of this tactic is positive; therefore, it should create an environment for many opportunities to model positive attitudes. One could hope that the positive approach used to increase attendance would also promote more attention to assignments, better grades, and better attitudes toward self, school, and community.

Monitor

Interview or provide questionnaires to students, teachers, and parents following the implementation of these techniques to learn which of the program's features were most effective. Certain aspects may be more effective for some youth than for others, and some practices more difficult or expensive to carry out than others. That information would be helpful in making future plans for increasing attendance.

Reference

VanSciver, J. (1986). Use rewards to boost student attendance (and public goodwill). *The Executive Educator, 6,* 22–23.

SOCIAL REWARDS FOR ATTENDING

Background

This tactic is designed to help students improve their school attendance by involving individuals who are important to them. Teacher cooperation is required for this tactic, because secondary students generally have several classes. Teachers who wish to initiate this tactic may begin by helping students design contracts that exchange attention (in the form of phone calls or special outings) from individuals who are important to them for attendance. Contracting is cost-free, takes little time to implement, and has been shown to be effective.

Who Can Benefit

Bizzis and Bradley-Johnson (1981) conducted a study with an 11th-grade girl who had a history of truancy and other problems. This tactic, which is based on naturally occurring rewards (attention from others), should be considered for chronically absent high school students. The rewards increase the likelihood that the positive results of an intervention will generalize to other situations.

Procedures

Design a chart on which students can record their hourly attendance (see example in Figure 1.5).

1. Define attendance as being present when the morning bell rings and remaining in school for all class periods.

2. Help each student create a contract between himself or herself and a partner of his or her choice who has agreed to participate in the project.

3. Incorporate telephone calls into the contracts by allowing students to call their designated partners at a specified time on days they arrived on time and attended every class.

ATTENDANCE CHART

Student _____

Class														Dates
English														
Social Studies														
Algebra I														
Study Hall														
Shop														
Computers														
Biology														
Checked by														
Call made?														

Comments:

_____

ATTENDANCE CHECK FOR _____

Class												Dates
Morning												
Afternoon												

Checked by _____
Locker # _____

Figure 1.5. Sample Attendance Chart.

4. Provide bonuses in the contract, such as outings with the student's partner for being in attendance a specified number of days in a row.

5. Instruct students to keep their attendance charts in their lockers and record a "yes" or "no" for whether they attended each class.

6. Encourage target students to ask a locker neighbor at school to keep a chart in his or her locker on which he or she records whether the target students were present at the beginning and end of each day.

7. Compare the target students' attendance records with those of the teachers and their school neighbors. Resolve any disagreements in these sets of data.

8. Renegotiate the contracts as attendance patterns change.

Modifications and Considerations

Something to consider when planning this technique is that target students might try to contact their partners even though they were absent. Steps should be taken so that the partner does not accept calls on days when the student is absent. A daily message for the partner could be left at his or her office or home, stating whether the target student was in attendance that day. This contact is easier in this day of cellular phones, Fax machines, and e-mail.

This tactic could be modified in a number of ways. The partners who are called could change from time to time. A number of partners could be identified as contacts. The partners could initiate the calls to the attending pupils rather than the other way around. Target pupils might be allowed to call someone long distance if they showed up for school several days in a row.

An important benefit from this approach could be the increased interaction of students with those with whom they contact. Their partners could be prompted to reinforce the pupils for good attendance, and converse with them about matters that are generally reinforcing. Yet another source of reinforcement and communication to be derived from this technique could be the attention of those who might answer the phone for the designated individual being called. Those individuals, like the partners, could be cued to reinforce the absent-prone students and spend a few moments talking with them before they call the designated persons to the phone.

Monitor

Data regarding the effects of this technique are available from the attendance chart. In fact, those data indicate the specific classes the student attended. It might be revealed that a student missed only certain of his or her classes from time to time but showed up regularly for others. That would be informative to the student's teachers and counselor. The person who was called could also keep data regarding when the call came, how long they chatted, and what they talked about. That information might be useful for future planning. If those conversations are recorded, they could be evaluated later.

Reference

Bizzis, J., & Bradley-Johnson, S. (1981). Increasing the school attendance of a truant adolescent. *Education and Treatment of Children, 4,* 149–155.

CONTINGENCY CONTRACTING PLUS GROUP COUNSELING

Background

This tactic is based on the notion that when two powerful and compatible approaches are combined, they will effectively reduce truancy.

Who Can Benefit

Students in the study by Hess, Rosenberg, and Levy (1990) were boys and girls with learning disabilities in an urban middle school. Targeted students were those who had from one to three unexcused absences per week for the 10 weeks prior to the treatment.

Procedures

Two components made up the treatment.

1. *Contingency contracts*—Students and teachers set individual contracts; they identified the responsibility of the student, the corresponding rewards, and the conditions under which the behaviors should occur. Following were rewards the students could select: pizza party, cash, school supplies, fast food certificates, CDs, or tape cassettes. The teacher set up the conditions for obtaining any of the prizes; that is, they must do x in order to get y.

2. *Group counseling*—Six group sessions, led by a school psychologist, were held during the 10-week treatment period. During these sessions students were given support in developing more appropriate beliefs toward school attendance. So-called irrational beliefs (e.g., "The teacher doesn't like me," "What's the use?") were confronted, and alternatives were selected. Following are activities common to each counseling session:

   • Members reviewed their school attendance for the week.

   • Students suggested solutions to remedy their truant behavior.

   • Students made oral commitments to improve attendance during the next week.

Modifications and Considerations

Some of the rewards listed would be acquired by individuals, whereas others would be granted to a group (i.e., the pizza party). It might be of interest to set up conditions whereby the educators learn about the relative merits of either procedure and the effects of the combined techniques.

Monitor

It is important to keep data on how often students show up for school, and whether they learn more by attending more regularly. In that regard, data could be kept on students' test scores and semester grades.

Reference

Hess, A. M., Rosenberg, M. S., & Levy, G. K. (1990). Reducing truancy in students with mild handicaps. *Remedial and Special Education, 11*(4), 14–19, 28.

SELF-RECORDING AND PUBLIC POSTING

Background

The idea behind this technique is that if young people keep their own records of attendance and performance, and if those records are publicly posted, they will be motivated to increase their attendance and improve their performance. A number of investigations have indicated that both these practices are motivating.

Who Can Benefit

The youngsters studied by McKenzie and Rushall (1974) were several boys and girls from 9 to 16 years of age who were members of a swim team. The concern of this study was that most of the swimmers had poor attendance records, and when they did come to practice, they often left early, did not complete their workouts, and in some instances, never entered the pool. Not surprisingly, the team came in near the bottom in most of their competitions.

Their coaches, in efforts to turn that situation around, became harsh disciplinarians for behavior problems rather than systematic trainers for swimming. As a result, the swimmers' attendance became even worse.

In the study, when self-management procedures (i.e., when swimmers monitored their own attendance and performance) and public posting of records were introduced, improvements in those behaviors were noted. As that happened, their coaches resumed their proper roles as instructors, and performance improved even more as did the team's morale.

This tactic would be suitable for most sports teams, such as volleyball, football, and basketball. It would also be appropriate for classes in which youth were engaged in cooperative activities, and everyone's performance influenced the reward or grade of everyone else.

Procedures

1. Record attendance and daily performance (e.g., laps per pupil) of each student before initiating the self-management and public posting procedures. (These are baseline data.)

2. Design a team chart on which every member's name is written. Assign a different color to each member, and instruct them all to chart the number of laps they swam each day (see Team Chart in Figure 1.6).

3. Provide each pupil with a colored marker that matches his or her color.

4. Determine individual goals for each student. They should be decided on by a trainer and each pupil.

5. Post the chart in plain view so that all team members can see the performances of all participants.

6. Raise students' goals periodically as they become more proficient and more motivated to succeed.

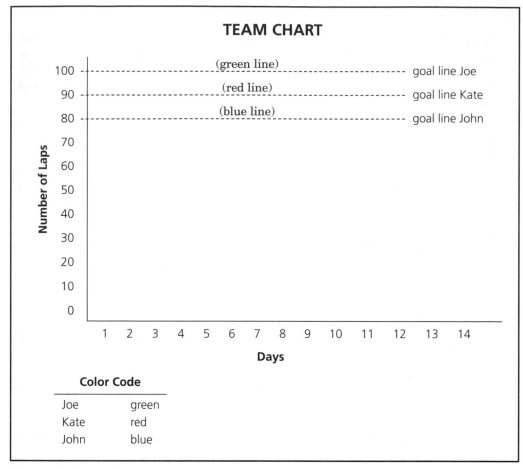

Figure 1.6. Team Chart.

7. Relate these attendance and performance gains with the team's performances in the various competitions.

8. Encourage the swimmers to record data on other features of their swimming program: weight training, running laps, other exercises, and measures of diet.

Modifications and Considerations

Self-recording and public posting were successful in McKenzie and Rushall's (1974) study, but in some instances it may be necessary to arrange a consequence for the improved behavior in addition to self-monitoring. In those situations, monitor the accuracy with which students self-recorded, and give them bonus points for counting reliably.

For some students, a public display of performance may be aversive. This could further deter them from coming to practice and participating in the exercises. Encourage them to keep their records privately at first, then if they become more comfortable with their progress, they could join in with the group.

Monitor

In this project, data on the number of laps swum each day for each student are kept on the Team Chart. As indicated in number 7 of the Procedures section, data should also be kept on the performances of team members at the various competitions. It is anticipated that a team would win more awards as the members become more disciplined.

Reference

McKenzie, T. L., & Rushall, B. S. (1974). Effects of self-recording on attendance and performance in a competitive swimming training environment. *Journal of Applied Behavior Analysis, 7,* 199–206.

 # STAYING IN SCHOOL: PROGRAM FOR MOTHERS AND TODDLERS

Background

The idea behind this project is to keep young married or unmarried mothers in school, either the high school they had been attending or some other place aligned with the school. The program outlined here is especially helpful for those mothers who have problems reading and perhaps need ideas for interacting with their children.

The information provided for these programs, where mothers and their youngsters go to school, is based on the federally supported program, Even Start.

Who Can Benefit

Young mothers who have trouble reading and have not graduated from high school would be assisted by this program. They would be instructed not only in reading and basic skills, but also in parenting skills. The youngsters of the mothers who participate in this program should also be assisted, because as their mothers learn to read and develop skills for parenting, the probability is increased that their mothers will read and interact more with them, and that will further their development.

Procedures

The following six goals are typical of an Even Start program:

1. Raise the educational level of the parents of preschool children through instruction in basic skills.

2. Increase developmental skills of preschool children to better prepare them for academic success.

3. Enhance the relationship of parents and children through planned, structured interactions.

4. Demonstrate to parents their power to affect their children's ability to learn.

5. Encourage early identification and treatment of physical or mental handicaps that may inhibit the children's learning ability.

6. Encourage identification and treatment of handicapping conditions in the adults that may inhibit their ability to care for their children.

The following is a plan for realizing some of those goals:

1. Recruit two groups of mothers who have reading problems and who have toddlers (about five pairs to a group).

2. Arrange for one group to come to the location (a school or some other community building) on Monday and Thursday, and the other to come on Tuesday and Friday, for 3 hours a visit.

3. Determine initially the mothers' and toddlers' levels of functioning. Ask the mothers to read orally a number of materials (e.g., newspapers, magazines, novels, recipes, bus schedules). For the toddlers, administer some of the items from a standard screening inventory, such as the *Developmental Assessment of Young Children* (Voress & Maddox, 1998).

4. Engage a teacher to work with the mothers as a group and another teacher to work with the toddlers for a 2-hour period. Instruct the mothers on aspects of functional reading and other basic skills. The instruction for the toddlers should be on standard preschool activities.

5. Pair the mothers with their toddlers for the final hour of the session. During that time, assist mothers to read and interact generally with their youngsters.

6. Give the mothers homework assignments for themselves and their toddlers at the end of each session. Encourage them to read books and newspapers at home and to read and interact with their toddlers. Show the mothers how to monitor the extent they carried out these assignments.

7. Go over the mothers' homework assignments when they return to the classroom for another session, prior to giving them the next assignment.

8. Help prepare the mothers to take the GED examinations as they become more proficient with reading and other basic skills.

9. Assist the mothers to take advantage of other services in the community (e.g., social and health agencies, libraries, emergency shelters, feeding programs).

Modifications and Considerations

Transportation and attendance are matters that must be taken into account when establishing projects such as the one explained here. Because some of the mothers may be a bit disorganized and not motivated to attend school, arrangements should be made to accommodate them. It may be necessary to pick them up. It may be advisable to place the centers in locations that are within walking distance of the mothers and their children.

Some projects of this type start off the sessions with a breakfast (or lunch). This is something to consider, because a good meal may be the key to their attendance.

Some of these programs are scheduled during the day and others are offered in the early evening. There are advantages and disadvantages to either, but the time of the sessions should be considered when arranging Even Start programs.

Monitor

There are three sets of curricula, objectives, and measures for this project. For the mothers, gather data on their reading (and perhaps other skills). Have them read from newspapers, TV guides, recipe books, training manuals, and other functional materials. Acquire data on oral reading rates and rates for retelling information from what they read, as a comprehension measure. Also, keep data on the extent they read at home and on the types of material they read.

For the toddlers, keep data on such behaviors as identifying objects, naming colors, counting and matching similar and dissimilar objects, arranging objects in sequence and in categories, and following directions.

With respect to interactions between mothers and their youngsters, keep data on some of the following: questions asked by the mothers; the extent they give praise, give examples, show, and tell; and the extent their toddlers ask questions.

Reference

Voress, J. K., & Maddox, T. (1998). *Developmental assessment of young children*. Austin, TX: PRO-ED.

Chapter 2
MOTIVATION

♦ ♦

Because Chapters 1 and 2 are the heart of this book, I have given them a lot of space. Attendance, the theme of Chapter 1, is of obvious importance. Students need to show up at school before any instruction can take place. Motivation, the theme of this chapter, is of vital importance to keep them at school and in a mood to learn.

Probably everyone would agree that all people can benefit from having motivation. However, not all youth have motivation, especially as it relates to school. It is generally easy to recognize whether a student is or is not motivated. A motivated student is someone who shows up for class, does most of the work on time, asks an intelligent question now and then, and generally has a reasonable attitude. An unmotivated student does not show up, does not do the work, and frequently claims to be bored. It is unclear, however, who is responsible for motivating students. Is it up to the teacher, the parent, someone else, or the student?

The 13 tactics in this chapter are intended to encourage youngsters to arrive at school, stay there and show up for classes, and learn something along the way. I selected a wide range and variety of approaches. One is a collection of ideas from psychologists, two are from the world of business, a couple rely on peers as motivators, two stress the idea of self-management, others are schoolwide changes that may affect motivation, and two deal with boredom.

☆ STRATEGIES FOR MOTIVATING STUDENTS TO LEARN

Background

The ideas from this piece are from material outlined by Brophy (1987) in his comprehensive review of studies on motivation.

Who Can Benefit

The most direct beneficiaries from these suggested motivational techniques would be those teachers who studied them and put them into practice. Subsequently, students with whom the practitioners have direct contact should benefit if recommended motivational techniques were arranged.

Procedures

One important theory to keep in mind in attempts to motivate youth, and the foundation of the ideas advanced here, is that "people do not invest effort on tasks that do not lead to valued outcomes, even if they know they can perform the tasks successfully, and they do not invest effort on even highly valued tasks if they are convinced that they cannot succeed no matter how hard they try" (Brophy, 1987, p. 43). What follows is a listing, by category, of 33 motivational strategies. I offer a brief explanation of each strategy, comment on a few of them, and, when appropriate, identify tactics described elsewhere in this book that emphasize the point being addressed.

Essential Preconditions

1. Supportive environment. Organize and manage the classroom so that students are encouraged and made to feel comfortable about taking academic risks.

2. Appropriate level of challenge/difficulty. Tasks should be neither too difficult nor too easy.

3. Meaningful learning objectives. Selected tasks should be worth developing.

4. Moderation/optimal use. Motivational attempts can be overdone; any particular strategy can lose its effectiveness if used too often.

Motivating by Maintaining Success Expectations

1. Program for success. Make certain that students achieve success consistently.

2. Teach goal setting, performance appraisal, and self-reinforcement skills. Help students set goals that can be achieved in a short period of time. (See tactics in Chapter 10, Goals.)

3. Help students to recognize linkages between effort and outcome. Arrange modeling, socialization, and feedback to make students aware that the amount and quality of effort they put into an activity determines, to a large extent, what they get out of it.

4. Provide remedial socialization. Among other approaches, use performance contracts with discouraged students. (See tactics in Chapter 8, Social Skills.)

Motivating by Supplying Extrinsic Incentives

1. Offer rewards for good (or improved) performance. These may include materials, activities, or symbolic or social consequences.

2. Structure appropriate competition. Carefully arrange activities that "pay off" for competitive arrangements, as well as for individual achievement and cooperative endeavors.

3. Call attention to the instrumental value of academic activities. Point out to students, whenever possible, that the knowledge or skills developed by academic tasks will enable them to meet their current needs,

provide them with "tickets" to social advancement, or prepare them for success in occupations or life generally. (See tactics in Chapter 8, Study Skills.)

Motivating by Capitalizing on Students' Intrinsic Motivation

1. Adapt tasks to students' interests. When possible, incorporate content that students find interesting. (See tactics in Chapter 14, Self-Management.)

2. Include novelty/variety elements. "Do not allow a steady diet of routine lessons followed by routine assignments to become the daily grind (Brophy, 1987, p. 44)."

3. Allow choices or autonomous decisions. When possible, offer students alternative ways to meet requirements.

4. Provide opportunities for students to respond actively. To the extent possible, provide students with opportunities to participate in projects, experiments, role-plays, simulations, educational games, and creative applications of what is being learned. (See tactics in Chapter 9, Participation.)

5. Provide immediate feedback to student responses. Set up a variety of ways to provide feedback and see that it is provided as soon as possible after students respond.

6. Allow students to create finished products. Students are likely to have a sense of accomplishment when they finish tasks. (This is one of the primary reasons that some secondary schools have moved from several short daily periods to fewer but longer ones.)

7. Include fantasy or simulation elements. Resort to fantasy or simulation when direct applications of the task to be learned are not possible.

8. Incorporate gamelike features into exercises. To some extent, transform ordinary activities into challenging puzzles or games. (This suggestion is perhaps based on the notion that many youth enjoy playing video-type games.)

9. Include higher level objectives and divergent questions. On occasion, include questions that address higher cognitive levels (e.g., application, analysis, synthesis, evaluation).

10. Provide opportunities to interact with peers. On occasion, build opportunities into whole-class activities by scheduling discussions, debates, role-plays, or simulations. (See the tactic titled Contingent Socialization later in this chapter.)

Strategies for Stimulating Student Motivation to Learn

1. Model interest in learning and motivation to learn. For example, share with students your interests in books, articles, and programs on subjects you teach.

2. Communicate desirable expectations and attributions about students' motivation to learn. Show students that you want them to be curious, to want to understand concepts, and to master skills.

3. Minimize students' performance anxiety during learning activities. "Structure most activities to promote learning rather than to evaluate performance" (Brophy, 1987, p. 47). (However, some anxiety probably is okay.)

4. Project intensity. Let students know that the lesson being introduced is important and they need to pay attention.

5. Project enthusiasm. Offer your reasons for believing the lesson is important and merits concentration.

6. Induce task interest or appreciation. When relevant, prompt students to note connections between the current activity and others, and mention immediate applications of the new lesson.

7. Induce curiosity or suspense. Place students in active problem-solving roles.

8. Induce dissonance or cognitive conflict. Counter students' thinking that they know everything there is to know about something.

9. Make abstract content more personal, concrete, or familiar. Promote personal identification with new content by using familiar examples and analogies.

10. Stimulate students to generate their own motivation to learn. Prompt students to ask questions about topics they would like to know about.

11. State learning objectives and provide advance organizers. Tell students exactly what they are supposed to get out of an activity.

12. Model task-related thinking and problem solving. Demonstrate problem-solving strategies for students. (See tactics in Chapter 3, Study Skills.)

Modifications and Considerations

Included previously is a "starter set" of strategies to select from in attempting to motivate students to acquire the knowledge and skills being taught. Other strategies should be sought and added to this motivational repertoire.

Lieber (1997) described ways in which businesses determine what motivates customers to buy. One approach is to encourage customers to explain what it is they like and dislike about certain products. Another approach is to follow customers as they use or consider using their product. Based on these explanations and observations, business folks learn what motivates customers to either buy or reject their products.

Idol and West (1993) identified and elaborated on the following five strategies for enhancing students' motivation: reduce social comparison, increase involvement in learning, focus on effort, promote beliefs in competence, and increase chances for success.

Monitor

Because the strategies noted here are general and not necessarily identified with specific situations, they are difficult to evaluate. One way to get a general idea of students' perceptions of how motivated they are would be to have them occasionally write brief essays on the topic.

References

Brophy, J. (1987, October). Synthesis of research on strategies for motivating students to learn. *Educational Leadership*, pp. 14–48.

Idol, L., & West, J. F. (1993). *Effective instruction of difficult-to-teach students*. Austin, TX: PRO-ED.

Lieber, R. B. (1997, February 3) Storytelling: A new way to get close to your customer. *Fortune*, pp. 102–108.

☆ DEALING WITH AESTHETICS: RENOVATING URBAN SCHOOLS

Background

The dismal picture of urban U.S. schools, particularly the high schools, is widely known: shattered windows and leaky roofs, malfunctioning plumbing and inadequate heating, crowded classrooms and noisy hallways, limited supplies and antiquated textbooks, spattered walls and dirty floors. Educators, psychologists, anthropologists, and architects have for some time recognized the effects of physical settings on production and learning.

For individuals to teach and learn, they need better environments than many of them now have. It is particularly important to renovate urban schools. Toward this end, according to Piccigallo (1989), two questions need consideration: To what degree can city youth be expected to believe that education is the principal route out of urban squalor and despair when society is either unable or unwilling to rescue the schools from similar conditions? And what message of self-worth and societal expectation does the abysmal physical state of inner-city schools convey to students who have no choice but to attend them or drop out?

Who Can Benefit

Everyone would benefit if schools were more aesthetically pleasing. The youth who are expected to show up, learn, and socialize would profit from more pleasant surroundings. Likewise, teachers would be more motivated to attend regularly and teach enthusiastically. Many teachers do not have adequate offices or places to prepare for teaching, faculty lounges are often unappealing and uncomfortable, and parking lots are frequently crowded and unsafe. Professionals in other occupations are rarely expected to function in such drab situations. Most parents also would be delighted if schools were more appealing. It cannot be too reinforcing for them when they visit schools to see the old and unkempt structures that house the future leaders of America.

Many youth who are at risk may be particularly motivated by school buildings, classrooms, and related facilities that are more appealing than their homes. Some inner-city youngsters rarely see buildings that are functional and beautiful. If schools were less dreary and dingy, they may feel like sanctuaries to many youth who are at risk.

Procedures

1. Attend to the interiors and exteriors of schools. As it is, many of the interior walls are barren (except for graffiti), and there are no flowers, paintings, or sculptures. Teachers in the home living, industrial arts, and art departments could have students help do something about this. In addition, businesses could be encouraged to provide money to repair or remodel schools. They could donate money for specific projects, which would bear their names. Contractors, developers, and builders could be persuaded to donate services for remodeling and repairing buildings.

2. Do something about the noise. Some noise could be overcome by carpeting a few rooms or hallways, staggering schedules so that students move from one location to another at different times, and placing a few hangings along hallways or in classrooms to absorb some of the noise (and at the same time to provide beauty).

3. Monitor the public address system. Much of what comes over the speakers in high schools is boring, threatening, or disruptive. Little that is entertaining or pleasing comes from the speakers. Teachers or students in the music, drama, and communication departments could see to it that more satisfying sounds came over the airwaves.

4. Attend to the school grounds. Contact architectural firms and landscape designers for ideas and plans for renovating and restructuring the school grounds.

Modifications and Considerations

Consider some of the decorative ideas that appear on the Home Garden Television Channel (HGTV). Although their programs are intended for homes and apartments, many of their suggestions would be suitable for schools and classrooms. Look for decorative ideas in magazines such as *Architectural Digest*. Visit schools and classrooms in other areas and take pictures of attractive settings. Much more attention could be paid to colors; to types of chairs, desks, shelves, and cabinets; to wall coverings (e.g., posters, tapestries, murals); and to floor coverings (e.g., carpets, throw rugs, hardwood, linoleum).

Monitor

Data of several types could be kept on the effects of improving school environments: numbers of dropouts and dropbacks (students who return to school after dropping out); teacher attendance; parent involvement with schools; parent, administrator, teacher, and student impressions of the physical plant; and involvement of business, industry, and community in the school.

Reference

Piccigallo, P. R. (1989). Renovating urban schools is fundamental to improving them. *Phi Delta Kappan, 70*, 402–406.

☆ MODIFYING THE CLASSROOM: EFFECTS ON ATTITUDES AND ACHIEVEMENT

Background

The physical environment of the classroom can affect students' motivation to learn just as the environment of a factory can affect workers' production. In most classrooms, the teacher stands at the front of the room and students sit at desks arranged in rows and columns. Seating arrangements can have a great impact on students' motivation and their interactions in a class. A number of other factors that can affect student behaviors—and hence comfort and motivation—include room lighting, colors, type of furniture, number of people in the room, and room temperature. Although some of those variables are easier to control than others, teachers should survey their situations from time to time to see that they are conducive to learning (Bassett & Smythe, 1979).

Who Can Benefit

Most people work better in environments that are comfortable, aesthetically pleasing, and nondistracting. It is hard to be productive, much less creative or enthusiastic, in surroundings that are dingy, crowded, and noisy. It is particularly important to arrange attractive environments at school for students who are at risk and remedial, who may come from homes that are drab, cluttered, and disorganized. There is the chance that some students would be motivated, hence more productive, if their classrooms were more attractive and pleasant.

Procedures

1. To make your classroom a more motivating place, examine the following features or conditions:

   - *Lighting*—Ask students if they would like any changes in lighting, if an option. Your pupils may prefer open window shades to those that are shut. Use natural lighting to balance fluorescent lights, as fluorescent lighting can put students to sleep more easily than regular lighting.

   - *Color*—Coordinate the colors in your classroom to increase school achievement, production, and morale and to lower absenteeism. Keep walls at the front and back a nondistracting, neutral tone. Place materials that are light and reflect sunlight opposite the windows. If your classroom is exposed to the north, use light-colored material on the walls to compensate for lack of the sun's rays.

   - *Overcrowding*—Brief periods of overcrowding have negative effects on individuals' moods and their satisfaction with tasks and the environment. If you have an overcrowded classroom, remove some furniture to create more open space. You may seem distant to students toward the rear of classes that are arranged by traditional rows and columns if you constantly teach from the front. Large classes often benefit from arranging seats in ways other than the ordinary row and column configuration.

- *Furniture*—Classroom seats are designed to last for many years and to make it easy for janitors to sweep around them. They are not designed for comfortable use 6 hours a day. Consider adding out-of-seat activities to your curriculum, especially in winter months and rainy periods.

- *Temperature*—Excessive heat has negative effects on pupils' moods, their impressions of the environment, and the assigned tasks. Use windows, fans, and/or air conditioning or heating to maintain a moderate temperature during extreme hot and cold weather.

- *Noise*—It may be possible to reduce the noise in your environment through simple changes: using a fan instead of an open window, appointing door monitors to shut the door when appropriate, or putting rubber pads or tennis balls on metal chair legs.

- *Attractiveness of surroundings*—Cover up parts of the room that are ugly with screens or fabrics. Tidy up those areas of the room that are messy. Transform "institutional" rooms to more attractive settings by adding travel posters, plants, and student artwork. Unattractive surroundings have a negative effect on pupils' moods and efforts.

2. Include in your examination of the classroom observations of student–teacher interactions. If the desks in your classroom are arranged in rows and columns, you might expect students in the center front to interact the most often. Observe students to determine whether those who sit outside the action zone participate. Do you tend to walk in the center front, the middle of the room, or around the perimeter? Use your observations and objectives to adjust the seating assignments and your movements until you get the type and frequency of student involvement you desire.

3. Match the seating pattern to the classroom activity:

- *Situation 1*—You may wish to minimize interactions between students in situations such as test taking or independent seatwork. Structure your environment in rows and columns to achieve this goal.

- *Situation 2*—You may want students to work in small groups. Plan for the least amount of distractions by pushing desks together so that students in each group are face to face with each other and away from other groups.

- *Situation 3*—If small groups of students are presenting a report to the class, you may want them to stand or sit at a table at the front of the room. Arrange seats for the other pupils in a large horseshoe or semicircle.

- *Situation 4*—For large group discussions, rearrange seats to maximize student involvement and minimize your role as controller of the discussion. Use a hollow rectangle or circular arrangement, and sit where you can assume leadership as the situation demands.

- *Situation 5*—If you use a film, slide, or overhead projector to show images on a screen at the front of the room and want students to interact with you, divide chairs into two lines along the sides of the room, leaving a wide aisle in the center, so that students can alternate between looking at the screen and at you as the activity dictates.

4. Allow students a few days to become adjusted to the changes before making your decisions about their continued use. Determine whether students participate to the extent you want, and evaluate their academic performances. Survey the pupils to see if they noticed or liked the changes.

Modifications and Considerations

Other changes could be made in classrooms to make them more conducive to learning. A number of good ideas for comfortable and attractive situations could be gathered by observing other classrooms or businesses, or by looking through magazines that focus on living and working environments.

Several interesting and practical suggestions with respect to classroom design are offered in Wood's (1992) book, *Adapting Instruction for Mainstreamed and At-Risk Students*. For example, she designed a "Checklist for Effective Classroom Environment," on which a respondent makes entries on four categories: wall areas, lighting, floors, and room area. Wood also offered suggestions on setting up learning stations.

Monitor

Data of two types should be gathered to evaluate the effects of any (particularly major) environmental change. One type has to do with pupils' production or achievement: Do the students, in general, learn more as a function of the change? The other type of data, which is probably related to the first, has to do with pupils' impressions of the changes. Students should be interviewed to determine these thoughts: Are they more comfortable? Do they interact more? Is it easier to attend? Do they learn more? Are they more inclined to come to school, at least to this class?

References

Bassett, R. E., & Smythe, M. (1979). *Communication and instruction*. New York: Harper & Row.

Wood, J. W. (1992). *Adapting instruction for mainstreamed and at-risk students* (2nd ed.). Upper Saddle River, NJ: Merrill/Prentice-Hall.

☆ ARRANGING PEER FORUMS TO MOTIVATE STUDENTS

Background

In this tactic Lewandowski (1989) established forums of student panelists who discussed a number of matters of importance to them. The underlying idea is that youth will listen to their peers when they discuss social and academic matters more than they will adults, and will be particularly impressed by youth who have turned their lives around.

Who Can Benefit

This tactic is appropriate for students characterized as remedial or at risk, and those who are turned off by school or generally not motivated. Lewandowski (1989) noted that the major lesson to be learned from this project is that success is the attainment of personal goals. According to the author, the most noted effects from this technique were on the panel members themselves. They gave advice about attitudes, accomplishments, self-concepts, and the need for education. Because of their responsibilities, the panelists believed that they must live up to their own advice.

Procedures

Preparation

1. Choose six students to serve on the panel. They should have a variety of abilities and experiences. Some of them may have experienced serious behavior problems in and out of school, others may have dealt successfully with drug or alcohol problems, and so forth. Panelists should be perceived as real people who have overcome problems familiar to other youth. In addition, they should meet as many of the following criteria as possible:

   • Be successful and interested in academics

   • Be involved and successful in extracurricular or out-of-school activities

   • Be well known and respected by other students

   • Be known to have overcome significant school problems

   • Be able to communicate their story

2. Obtain permission to proceed with the plan from administrators and parents.

3. Issue formal, written invitations to prospective panelists. State the purpose of the forum and explain why they were asked to participate.

4. Introduce the plan to all students. Point out that one goal is to become aware that real people with real problems can set reasonable goals and achieve them.

5. Prepare students by having them tell about problems they have at school or at home.

6. Prepare the panel members by asking them to think about what problems they had, how they dealt with them, what their goals are, and when they began setting these goals. Have them consider what kinds of positive advice they would offer about courses to take, attitudes to develop, and study strategies to learn.

Implementation

1. Seat the panel at a table in front of the classroom. Place a name card in front of each panel member, and provide a pitcher of water and glasses.

2. Moderate the panel and formally introduce each member.

3. Ask each member to comment briefly on a selected topic.

4. Open the floor to questions. You may have to ask the first one or two to get things going.

Follow-up

1. Send written thank-you notes to all participants.

2. Allow time for discussion the next day.

3. Refer back to the discussions that arose from the panel throughout the year, as appropriate occasions come up.

Modifications and Considerations

Teachers might invite graduates to come back and serve as panel members. They could talk about how their academic problems affected them on the job, in college, or at technical school. Most high school students are eager for information about what it is like "out in the world."

In setting up these situations, avoid putting the audience on the spot so that they feel they are being admonished. Point out that many of them may have a turn later as panelists. Students would probably feel more comfortable about this technique and more motivated to participate if they had a part in its structure.

For suggestions on how to deal with complex personal problems, ask students to tune in to expert, sensitive, talk show professionals. (Be aware, however, of the crackpots, for there are dozens of them.) Skilled professionals are adept at giving advice that is to the point, realistic, and sensitive to the nature of the problems.

Monitor

One way to monitor this procedure is to keep track of the interactions that develop between the panelists and between them and the audience. Another idea for evaluating the effects of the panel discussions would be to ask students (particularly those in the audience) to respond to a few items on a questionnaire or to write (without a structure) their comments about the event, and note their suggestions for future meetings.

Reference

Lewandowski, J. A. (1989, Spring). Using peer forums to motivate students. *Teaching Exceptional Children,* pp. 14–15.

⬚ INCREASING INTEREST IN SCHOOLS: IMMEDIATE APPLICATIONS

Background

The idea underlying this tactic is that most youth are unimpressed with much of the school's curriculum. They have a number of common complaints about schools and the subjects that are offered, but one that is heard often goes something like this: "What's the point in learning about this? I don't see any need to know this information." Teachers, in their efforts to convince students to attend to those subjects, tell students that in time they will need to know the information. Many students are unimpressed with that reason, and pay little attention to either the teacher or the subject.

Who Can Benefit

The students who should benefit most from this tactic—an attempt to explain the immediate gains from subjects that are taught—are those characterized as remedial or at risk (Zigmond, Sansone, Miller, Donahoe, & Kohnke, 1986). Many of those youth are motivated only by the immediate. They are totally unmoved by pleas to learn something for tomorrow, much less next month or next year. For them, the future is now. This activity should benefit teachers as well, because many of them need to carry out sessions of self-inquiry to assess the gains, immediate or otherwise, that can come from their instruction.

Procedures

Survey the content of your subject(s) and list carefully the arguments or rationales that can be offered to defend the relevancy of the material. In so doing, you may learn that some of the content is questionable in terms of its relevancy. Discuss the content of your course(s) and its merit with other teachers in your department. When fortified with justifications, present them to students in an effort to motivate them to take their courses more seriously. Following are several reasons that could be communicated to youth for needing skills taught at school:

1. To find a job and perform on a job

2. To assist in learning a more desirable skill

3. To be mainstreamed into a regular class

4. To stay in a regular class and not be sent to a special class

5. To enter some type of postsecondary training: vocational school, community college, 4-year college

6. To be accepted into the armed services

7. To complete the courses and earn the credits required for high school graduation

8. To pass the GED examination

9. To enjoy or participate in a desired leisure activity

10. To function like their more adept peers

11. To participate in extracurricular activities

12. To deal with parents and other adults

13. To help cope with stress

14. To be better able to live with others, particularly their family

Modifications and Considerations

The list of reasons provided is not exhaustive; parents, teachers, and citizens at large can think of many others. The justifications are greatly dependent on the subject taught. It is easier to make the case for immediate relevancy for home living and driver's education courses than it is for U.S. history and physical science.

Many of the suggestions for immediate application of content should come from students themselves. After your effort to bring your subject "back to the present," ask students to think of other rationales.

It would be a good idea to encourage some pupils—those who became more understanding and accepting of the course content because they saw how it fit into their immediate lives—to extend the period of gratification. Perhaps some of them could envision how certain content would benefit them in a week, a month, or even a year.

Counselors and administrators, as well as teachers, could be brought into this process. They too should be required to justify various subjects and their content.

The Seattle Times' "Guide to High Schools" (1996) contained a section highlighting ways to motivate youth to stay in school. Following are ideas that were mentioned several times: Distributive Education Clubs of America (DECA); partnerships with local theater groups; student exchanges with other countries; Future Business Leaders of America (FBLA); knowledge bowl; Natural Helpers; teen parenting classes; and Little Buddies program (athletes working with elementary-age children).

Monitor

After informing students how course content is immediately relevant, ask them to write out or discuss how they believe other specified content fits into their lives.

References

The Seattle Times. (1996, November 20). Guide to high schools. Seattle: Author.

Zigmond, N., Sansone, J., Miller, S. E., Donahoe, K. A., & Kohnke, R. (1986). *Teaching learning disabled students at the secondary school level: What research and experience say to the teacher of exceptional children* [Monograph]. Reston, VA: The Council for Exceptional Children.

☆ SELF-MANAGEMENT: IDENTIFYING ANTECEDENTS AND CONSEQUENCES OF BEHAVIOR

Background

The desire to change or improve one's own behavior and a willingness to be responsible for this effort are essential to the success of any attempt to self-manage. A positive introduction to the basic principles of self-management is the first, and possibly most important, step in the process. Students need to understand that, if they can manage their own behaviors, others will have less reason to control behaviors for them, which translates to greater independence. Most students are very motivated to self-manage.

This tactic provides guidelines for teaching students what self-management is and how to apply it to their own lives (Young, West, Smith, & Morgan, 1997). The main idea is to help them identify events that cause or trigger behaviors and anticipate the consequences or results of those behaviors.

Who Can Benefit

The increased freedom of choices available to individuals who manage their own behaviors can benefit adolescents in a number of ways. As they are given more opportunities to select activities and set goals they can achieve, they may develop stronger self-concepts and be more motivated by school and learning, all of which may combine to help them lead more successful and happier lives.

Apart from those personal gains, students who control their own behaviors responsibly will contribute to a more productive, focused classroom atmosphere, thus benefiting other students and their teachers as well. Later in life those independent adults will be better able to complete jobs satisfactorily with minimal supervision; hence more time and money can be spent on research and development rather than on training and repairing.

Procedures

Introduction

1. Set the tone for a positive learning experience.

   • Treat students as responsible persons.

   • Present the self-management program as a privilege, an opportunity to control one's own life.

   • Maintain a positive, interested attitude.

2. Define *self-management* and give examples of how it can be applied to students' lives.

3. Briefly trace the progression of control in all our lives.

   • *Young children*—virtually all behaviors are managed by adults

- *Adolescents*—a transition from management by adults to gradually assuming responsibility for themselves

- *Adults*—expected to manage their own behaviors in a responsible manner that does not infringe on the rights of others

- *All ages*—must learn to function within the range of rules and expectations of society

The ABCs of Behavior

1. Write on the board (or display on a poster) an explanation of the ABCs of Behavior:

   A = Antecedent: What happens to *trigger* your behavior

   B = Your Behavior: What you do or say

   C = Consequence: What happens as a result of your behavior

2. Present examples (see Examples of Antecedents, Behaviors, and Consequences in Table 2.1).

3. Ask students for personal examples of events that trigger certain behaviors, what the behaviors are, and what might result. Record their responses in the corresponding columns.

Discriminate and Predict

1. Present a lesson on how to discriminate between triggers (antecedent events) that cause students to act appropriately and triggers that cause them to act inappropriately (see Table 2.2).

   - Set up six columns, three under Positive (Triggers, Behaviors, Results) and three under Negative (Triggers, Behaviors, Results).

   - List three to five events (triggers) that would elicit positive results in the first column. (These steps correspond to those on the chart in Table 2.2.)

   - Record student responses to "What would you do if (<u>trigger</u>) happened?" in the second column.

   - List three to five triggers that would cause negative results to occur in the fourth column.

   - Record student responses next to each one in the fifth column.

2. Go back to the first two columns and discuss the probable results of each trigger and behavior pair. List student responses in the Positive Results column.

3. Repeat this procedure with the second set of triggers and behaviors. Record student responses in the Negative Results column.

4. Transfer the trigger in the fourth column to the first column immediately after students acknowledge the negative results of each inappropriate behavior, and elicit suggestions for more appropriate responses.

5. Discuss and list the positive results that might follow each amended behavior.

Table 2.1. Examples of Antecedents, Behaviors, and Consequences

("You," "Your," and "You're" refer to the student.)

Antecedents (Triggers)

1. Your friend keeps throwing paper wads at you during seatwork.
2. You're supposed to be at work by 3:30, but your friends always want you to hang out after school.
3. Your teacher gives you a book report assignment that's due in one week.
4. Your dad tells you that you have to baby-sit Friday night.
5. The girl that you want to go to the dance with asks you for help with homework after school.
6. You go out to the parking lot after school and find that you have a flat tire.
7. Your teacher gives an assignment that you don't understand.
8. One of your teachers announces that there will be a chapter test on Friday.
9. Your mom asks you to come home right after school to help her out.
10. You're walking down the hall and someone you don't get along with comes up behind you and shoves you.

Behaviors (Numbers in parentheses indicate "matching" antecedents.)

(9)   1. Even though your friends are going out for cokes, you go right home and help out.
(6)   2. You kick in your front fender and punch the side window, cracking it.
(2)   3. You get to work an hour late for five days in a row.
(5)   4. You go shopping with your friend because you'd rather do that than help her with school work.
(4)   5. You really want to go out, but you stay home as you've been asked to do.
(10)   6. You're really mad, but you just walk away from him or her.
(1)   7. You punch your friend and yell swear words at him.
(3)   8. You schedule your study time so that you work on your report a little each night and have enough time to rewrite it neatly the night before it is due.
(8)   9. You'd rather be out partying, but you decide to study each night between now and Friday.
(7) 10. You go to the teacher during seatwork time and ask for clarification on the assignment.

Consequences

(9)   1. Your mom really appreciates your help and offers to treat you and your girlfriend/boyfriend to a movie on Friday.
(4)   2. Your dad lets you borrow the car Saturday night and gives you $5.00.
(1)   3. Your teacher sends you to the principal's office.
(10)   4. The hall monitor sends the "other guy" to detention, but you're doing fine.
(6)   5. Instead of just having to change a flat tire, you have to come up with $100 for body work.
(3)   6. You get a B+ on your paper.
(8)   7. Even though you missed a couple of nights out, you ace the test.
(2)   8. Your boss fires you and you lose the income you were saving for a new car.
(7)   9. You are able to complete the assignment accurately and get a good grade.
(5) 10. When you ask her to go to the dance with you, she says, "Forget it!"

Note. From *Teaching Self-Management Strategies to Adolescents* (pp. 39–40), by K. R. Young, R. P. West, D. J. Smith, and D. P. Morgan, 1997, Longmont, CO: Sopris West. Copyright 1997 by Sopris West. Reprinted with permission.

Table 2.2. Predicting Consequences

Positive			Negative		
Triggers	**Behaviors**	**Results**	**Triggers**	**Behaviors**	**Results**
(Step 1b) Teacher asks class to work individually and quietly.	(Step 1c) You work on your own without talking.	(Step 2) You finish your work and are allowed to talk to friends for the last 5 minutes of class. You also have less homework.	(Step 1d) Your friend keeps throwing paper wads at you during seatwork.	(Step 1e) You think it's funny and start throwing paper wads back at him.	(Step 3) You both get sent to the principal's office. Because you missed the rest of class, you have more homework.

(To change *negative* to *positive* see Step 4, below.)

(Step 4 ————————-) Your friend keeps throwing paper wads at you during seatwork.	You ignore your friend and finish your work.	(Step 5) Your friend gets tired of bothering you and gets his work done, too, so you both have more time to have fun after school.

Note. These steps correspond to those in the Procedures section.

▶ **Example**

- *Trigger:* Your English teacher hands back a paragraph you wrote with several punctuation and capitalization errors underlined, and asks you to make corrections and recopy it in ink for tomorrow. She tells you to look it over now so you can ask questions about anything you do not understand.

- *Behavior:* You glance at the paper and stick it in your notebook, thinking you will get to it later. When you get home, you discover several errors you do not know how to correct.

- *Consequence:* You get a "zero" on the paper, and have to do it over again.

- *Ask the student to change the behavior:* You look over the paper in class, and ask for help on the errors you do not know how to correct. Once all the corrections have been made, you recopy it in ink, and turn it in on time the next day.

- *So that the consequence changes:* The teacher congratulates you for getting your work finished on time, and changes your F to a B.

6. Encourage students to employ self-talk statements to help make better choices (e.g., counting to 10, saying things like, "If I don't control myself,

someone else will," or "If I manage my own behavior, I will have more freedom to do what I want").

7. Repeat Steps 1 through 5 with new examples to provide additional practice in discriminating between events that are likely to trigger appropriate and inappropriate behaviors, and in predicting the consequences of those behaviors.

Role Plays and Discussions

1. Arrange for students to role-play a few ABC sequences (e.g., those listed in Table 2.1).

2. Discuss the concept of self-management as it relates to what students learned:

   • What the ABCs stand for

   • How the ABC arrangement can be applied to students' lives and those of others

   • The advantages to controlling one's own behavior

   • Ways to manage themselves so that others will not have to

Modifications and Considerations

Because the desire to change or improve one's own behavior is an important prerequisite to learning self-management, you should consider how each student in the class may react to the concept before introducing it to the group. If you anticipate that someone will respond negatively, it may be best to ask privately if he or she would like to participate, after explaining the basic notions of self-management to the student. If the response is negative, do not include the student in the instructional group.

Throughout this tactic there are opportunities to reinforce positive attitudes and to help students accept criticism. From the introduction on, the emphasis is on the positive aspects of self-management. During the "discriminate and predict" phase, students will have to deal with feedback from their negative responses. Since the next step is to rethink those negative responses and come up with positive alternatives, students will again be exposed to the concept of a positive attitude in practice.

Create lists similar to Table 2.1, and ask students to match up the 10 antecedents with the 10 behaviors and consequences. (The "matches" are indicated in parentheses.) They could also start with one set and predict events in the other two sets.

Monitor

As a determination of the degree to which students are able to apply these concepts, ask them to record examples of situations that occurred throughout their day that showed their awareness of events that triggered behaviors, their reactions, and the results of those actions.

Reference

Young, K. R., West, R. P., Smith, D. J., & Morgan, D. P. (1997). *Teaching self-management strategies to adolescents.* Longmont, CO: Sopris West.

☆ SELF-MANAGEMENT: SAVING A LIFE

Background

By learning to self-record important behaviors, an individual could save his or her own life. A number of self-recording tactics are described in other sections of this book, but the context in which self-recording is explained here—saving a life—should be the most motivating. This tactic primarily involves recording medical information.

Who Can Benefit

The tactics explained here should be appealing to most youth, particularly those said to be at risk or remedial, because they are generally the most critical about being "taught" things in school that are relevant. And what could be more relevant than saving one's own life? Youth who plan to enter the health care field would be especially interested in this tactic.

Procedures

Procedures for carrying out self-recording are rather simple: Pinpoint as precisely as possible the behaviors of concern; count the frequency with which those behaviors occur; chart those frequencies; and, if possible, establish aims or goals for those frequencies.

The remainder of this section is devoted to summaries of three instances in which individuals monitored extremely important behaviors of their own and, by doing so, helped themselves deal with a serious accident or disease.

Norman Cousins

When Cousins, a famous author and editor contracted a serious blood disorder, his doctors were unable to come up with a treatment for the problem, so Cousins (1977) took charge of his own care. He began taking measures and charting them on a number of vital functions: sedimentation rate, amount of blood sampled for diagnoses, and others. In addition, Cousins prescribed large doses of ascorbic acid and laughter. The latter was stimulated by watching old "Candid Camera" highlights. Careful records were maintained throughout a lengthy but successful period of rehabilitation.

Israel Goldiamond

In the mid-1960s, Goldiamond, a famous psychologist, was in an automobile accident and suffered a spinal injury. Following surgery he was unable to move any of his limbs and realized that if he was to improve he would have to take charge of his treatment. He began recording all the efforts of the doctors to aid him and, more important, set up his own exercise program and kept careful records of his movements. Although he never recovered fully, he became more mobile than he would have been without his own program.

Ken Campbell

In 1985 this Florida teacher wrote to me about being in a hospital following surgery to remove cartilage and its effect on his quadriceps muscles. He began exercising and imagining that he was charting the frequency of the movements. "I had no charts, was too doped up to draw a dot anyway, but thought chart. Within a day or so the movement hovered around 1 per minute. During the second day I increased to about 3 per minute. After a week I was up to around 80/90, any faster would not be exercise, nor control." After months of therapy and self-recording his behaviors, Campbell was back to normal.

Modifications and Considerations

Within a medical setting, it is important to monitor important behaviors of friends or loved ones, particularly when they are unable to do it for themselves. A friend told me that he once accompanied his wife to the hospital for minor surgery. Although he took along some reading materials, he also went with pencil, stopwatch, and chart paper in hand. When she returned to her hospital room following surgery, the data gatherer began recording her blood pressure readings, the rates her IVs were flowing, the frequencies of visits from doctors and nurses, and many other happenings. Over a period of 60 minutes, he had noted three "irregularities," and when he reported them to the head nurse, they were dealt with. My friend was not terribly upset by those events, because he was certain that she would have survived the mistakes; however, he was glad he had kept data.

Students could monitor a number of other types of events or circumstances that would be motivating for them. I will note only a few: the positive things you do for others; the number of exhilarating (or happy, pleasant) things that happen to you; the number of things you do that were written on your "to do" list.

Monitor

Teach students to acquire and record important medical data about themselves on events that are somewhat consistent over time: pulse, blood pressure, weight, temperature, type and amount of exercise, diet, sleep patterns. Those data could be charted across time by duration or frequency. They would serve individuals as benchmarks and would enable them to know when something might be going wrong. The data would also be useful for physicians in their attempts to prescribe treatment and in evaluating the effects of those treatments.

References

Cousins, N. (1977). Anatomy of an illness (as perceived by the patient). *Saturday Review, 5*(28), 4–6, 48–51.

Goldiamond, I. (1973, November). A diary of self-modification. *Psychology Today,* pp. 95–101.

⬚ LEARNING FROM BUSINESS: WHAT IT TAKES TO LIVE IN THE REAL WORLD

Background

The reason for including this tactic is that many adolescents are totally unaware of the expectations and realities of life outside school. When a group of high school students was asked what they wanted to do when they grew up, many of them did not have a thought, but they were uniformly adamant about not wanting to work in a local factory ("Learning," 1989). When asked why, they replied that the work was demeaning (not their word) and repetitive, although they did not really know what those workers did. Also, they had absolutely no idea what those workers earned or what their benefits were, or even what it would take to land a job at the factory. Many of the youth simply assumed that they could always get that type of job, when in reality it is doubtful that many of them could.

Who Can Benefit

The idea advanced in this tactic, to bring youth more in line with reality, would serve most adolescents, because the majority are not in touch with the world outside school. This tactic would be particularly helpful for youth described as at risk and remedial, or those who are apt to quit school and go out on their own, because it may shake them up when they find out what it takes to get along "out there." Possibly, when they know what is required, they will be more motivated to stay in school and better prepare themselves for life after high school.

Procedures

1. Ask the adolescents to identify something they really want, such as a car.

2. Ask them a few questions about the costs of purchasing and maintaining those things. As for a car: What will it cost? What about insurance and cost of license? Maintenance? Gasoline? Parking costs?

3. Design a few exercises for the youth so they seek out the answers to those questions.

4. Ask them about the cost of renting an apartment, since many of them are eager to move away from their parents. What about the monthly rent? What about the first and last months' rents? The damage

deposit? Utilities? Is there a garage for their car? How will they furnish the place? How would they locate an apartment in the first place?

5. As with the car, set up similar exercises to respond to these queries.

6. Ask them, once they know what it takes to live in their own place, about related matters: How much will their groceries cost? What about transportation costs, if they do not have a car? What about cleaning supplies and other incidentals to take care of their place?

7. Ask the big question. Now that they know a bit more about expenses in the real world, at least about cars and apartments, ask about how they intend to earn a living: How will they get a job? How much will they earn in their desired jobs (e.g., as a waitress or waiter, a rock musician, a gas station helper, a bricklayer, a plumber, a teacher, a preacher). Do they know what the requirements are to get those jobs?

Modifications and Considerations

All types of questions could be asked in an effort to assess how much adolescents understand reality. Ask them about Social Security, health care, the income tax process, insurance programs, investments, the stock market, laws and the courts, churches and religions, community organizations, meal preparation, home repairs, and so on. We would probably be disappointed by the answers of many so-called bright youth if they were given such "folk" assessments. We may be even more alarmed by the responses of individuals who are at risk.

When it comes to finding and keeping a job, there are three bedrock essentials, according to Rutledge (1997, p. 73):

1. An understanding that a good reputation is a major form of capital.

2. An ability to distinguish between people who are trustworthy and those who are not.

3. The realization that it is okay to fail, so long as you get back up, dust yourself off and try again.

Monitor

Pretest and posttest questions could be devised by teachers and parents to determine the effects of reality instruction. For example, prior to instructing youth to look up and calculate the costs of owning a car, simply ask them what it would take to buy and maintain a car. Readminister the assessment after they have compiled some facts and figures.

References

"Learning" [television program]. (1989, April). Sponsored by the Chrysler Corporation.

Rutledge, J. (1997, March 10). Teaching things that really matter. *Forbes,* p. 73.

⭐ LEARNING FROM BUSINESS: LIKERT'S MANAGEMENT SYSTEM

Background

After studying organizations of several types, Likert (1967) reached the conclusion that management approaches basically fall into four systems. These systems range from those that treat people poorly to those that treat them extremely well, with resulting productivity that correlates positively with the latter.

Likert's purpose in studying these systems was to help managers (teachers) embrace an approach that was the most motivating and resulted in the most production. Accordingly, he recommended that organizations rely, to the extent possible, on what he referred to as the System 4 approach. The advantage to involving such a system in business settings is that, as more human needs are satisfied, improved working relationships between workers and management will develop.

Although it may not be feasible to apply all of the elements of Likert's System 4 approach in schools, since it is based on economic rewards, there are components of that approach that can be incorporated (e.g., participation and involvement in goal setting, and up, down, and lateral communication).

Following is a summary of Likert's four styles of management, with special emphasis on motivation, the theme of this chapter.

- *System 1* (Treats people poorly)—Superiors show no confidence or trust of subordinates; subordinates do not feel free to discuss job matters with superiors; subordinates' ideas are seldom sought in dealing with job matters; subordinates are managed with threats, punishments, and occasional rewards; rank and file are given little opportunity to feel responsible and often behave in ways to defeat organizational goals; most decisions are made by high-level individuals; subordinates are often unaware of organizational problems; decisions that are made contribute little to subordinates' motivation.

- *System 2* (Treats people less poorly)—Superiors show condescending confidence and trust in subordinates; subordinates feel a bit less fear in discussing matters with superiors; subordinates' ideas and opinions are sometimes sought with respect to job matters; rewards and punishments are delivered to subordinates; subordinates feel relatively little responsibility for achieving organizational goals; policy decisions are made at the top, some decisions within prescribed framework are made at lower levels; subordinates are aware of a few organizational problems; decisions that are made about operations contribute little to workers' motivation.

- *System 3* (Treats people somewhat better)—Management extends a fair amount of confidence and trust to subordinates, but still desires to keep control of decisions; subordinates feel somewhat free to discuss job matters with their superiors; ideas and opinions are usually sought with respect to job problems; rewards and punishments are delivered along with some involvement of subordinates; substantial proportion of personnel, especially at high levels, feel responsibility for achieving organizational goals; broad policy and general decisions are made by top-level personnel and more specific decisions are made at lower levels; subordinates are moderately aware of organizational problems; workers contribute some decision making, which in turn enhances their motivation.

- *System 4* (Treats people quite well)—Management shows complete confidence and trust in subordinates in all matters; subordinates feel completely free to discuss job matters with their superiors; ideas and opinions are always sought when dealing with job matters; rewards based on participation are delivered, along with considerable group participation and involvement in setting goals, improving methods, and appraising progress; personnel at all levels feel responsibility for implementing and achieving organizational goals; decision making is widely done throughout the organization and well integrated through overlapping groups; subordinates are generally aware of most organizational matters and problems; subordinates contribute substantially to decision making, which in turn increases their general motivation.

Who Can Benefit

Students who freely express their ideas and concerns should be highly motivated by these procedures. Those who are not as glib and are perhaps alienated by schools should be motivated by these suggestions as well.

Procedures

Although a System 4 management style is most desirable, elements from both Systems 3 and 4 have been considered in offering the following suggestions.

1. Demonstrate confidence in students by allowing them to manage certain classroom procedures after they have been trained to do so (e.g., taking roll, checking papers, recording scores).

2. Provide time and opportunity for students to discuss their concerns about assignments and interactions with fellow students, teachers, administrators, and others with whom they are involved in the course of a school day, as these factors relate to their learning.

3. Identify clearly the benefits and rewards for productive academic and appropriate social behaviors, and establish fair and consistent consequences for unmet expectations and exceeded limits.

4. Define general school and specific classroom policies, but involve students in the decision-making process as to the applications of these policies to specific incidents and situations that affect individuals and certain groups.

5. Encourage students to set goals for themselves and for those school groups which they are a part of.

6. Keep students informed about new or revised policies and procedures, and encourage them to comment and discuss the feasibility and fair-

ness of those regulations through suggestion boxes, class meetings, letters to the editor of the school newspaper, and so forth.

7. Provide ample feedback on students' performance in all of these areas, and increase their levels of responsibility in as many ways as possible.

Modifications and Considerations

Unfortunately, many businesses (schools) have traditionally adopted management approaches that mirror the more negative and authoritarian elements of Systems 1 and 2. It will, therefore, take some time to make the necessary changes, so be prepared for a drop in the amount and quality of work, and possible increases in nonproductive behaviors in the short run. This commonly turns into increases in desired behaviors once workers (students) adjust, because when needs are satisfied, good working relationships between workers and management (students and teachers) develop, which tends to increase productivity.

In addition to Likert's strategy for motivating members of business organizations, Certo (1997) summarized a few others: *managerial communication,* which simply recommends that managers communicate well with organization members; *theory X–theory Y,* which operates from two sets of assumptions, *x* being negative beliefs about people and *y* representing positive assumptions that managers should strive for; *job design,* which might involve job rotation, job enlargement, or job enrichment; and *behavior modification,* which relies on positive and negative reinforcement and punishment.

Monitor

To monitor this program, students could be asked to survey a number of businesses and other organizations (e.g., their schools) with respect to Likert's four management systems. To do so, they might read about them, interview individuals from top management levels and others from middle management or entry levels, interview individuals who have dealt with these outfits, and so forth. Students might also be asked to list presumed advantages and disadvantages of the systems with respect to achieving short- and long-term objectives.

References

Certo, S. C. (1997). *Principles of modern management: Functions and systems* (7th ed.). Needham Heights, MA: Allyn & Bacon.

Likert, R. (1967). *The human organization: Its management and value.* New York: McGraw-Hill.

☆ BOREDOM: WHAT IT IS

Background

Boredom (or the absence of) is directly and indirectly related to motivation. It would seem that a person who is bored is not motivated. Boredom is a phenomenon that consumes the thinking of youth in secondary schools. Almost everything in which they are involved passes through a boredom screen.

The perception of being bored was mentioned dozens of times by students in the University of Washington teacher education program. After shadowing secondary students throughout an entire day, the university students reported that those students were bored much of the day. Moreover, the university students reported being equally bored getting through an entire day.

Most secondary teachers report that one of the most frequent expressions of adolescents as they appraise school activities is that they are bored. In fact, many of these students have a vast repertoire of ways to show and inform others about their boredom. In this first piece regarding boredom, I talk about what boredom is and how we think we know when it is happening.

Who Can Benefit

Students who are bored or say they are bored would surely benefit from this tactic in that they would at least have a better understanding of what boredom is. Because of anticipated student changes, teachers or parents might also benefit.

Procedures

The aims of this tactic are to point out the following:

- Boredom can be described and its symptoms are often observable.
- Almost everyone is occasionally bored.
- We know when we are bored and can often tell when others are bored.
- Most adolescents are bored more often than they were in grade school.
- Many youth say they are bored when they are not. Circumstances other than being bored prompt them to say they are bored.

The following discussion topics are suggested:

1. What is boredom? Ask students if they can define boredom. Have a student write the responses on the board. There will likely be some agreement and some disagreement as to what boredom is.

2. How do you know that boredom is happening? Ask students to describe how they feel when they are bored. Can they tell when their "mood" shifts from not being bored to being bored?

3. How do you act when you are bored? In most high school and university classes, a few students generally look bored. They may not actually be bored, but they appear to be. Many students have mastered looking bored: the slouch, the frown, the scowl, the vacant stare.

4. What do individuals say and how do they say it when bored? Many students have mastered this as well. Following are some things they say beyond informing others that they are bored: Why do we have to do this? We've done this before. I don't see any point in this!

5. Are you ever bored when you are by yourself or with your peers? It may be that adolescents are never bored, or never admit that they are

bored, when they are by themselves or with their chums. Perhaps it is only when they are with adults—teachers and parents—that they claim to be bored.

6. Are you more or less bored now than when you were in elementary school or middle school? [I doubt that many youth have given this much thought. In my experiences with first graders, none ever seemed bored. When would one begin noticing that students in school are bored?]

7. If you are more bored now than when you were younger, and that is probably the case, why might that be?

8. Do you believe that it is the responsibility of others to "unbore" you?

9. Is it cool to be bored; is it cool to be blasé? Some students might actually admit that boredom is "catching."

10. Could it be that on occasion you say you are bored when in fact you aren't? You might say you are bored because you are unable to perform a task; you don't want to do something; you believe someone will make fun of you if you do something; you can't think of anything else to say; most of your friends say they are. [What if more of them said they were enthused or motivated?]

Modifications and Considerations

In the book *Boredom: The Literary History of a State of Mind,* Spacks (1995) claimed that boredom came about with the upper class in the 18th century when they had too much time on their hands. We might bring up that hypothesis to youth in our discussions.

Monitor

Students could keep data, subjective as it might be, on the times they are bored. They could write daily or weekly anecdotal accounts of their feelings of boredom. Students could also be asked to observe the extent to which others are bored in real-world situations (e.g., church services, concerts, plays, speaking engagements, athletic events). Their task would be to determine how many people were bored and how many were not.

Reference

Spacks, P. M. (1995). *Boredom: The literary history of a state of mind.* Chicago: The University of Chicago Press.

☆ BOREDOM: HOW TO MODIFY IT

Background

In this second piece on boredom, I talk about how to identify it and how to change it, that is, how to be less bored. In this tactic, as well as in the previous one, I am assuming that being bored rather often and for large chunks of time is not a good thing and that all concerned would be better off if there were less boredom.

Who Can Benefit

The primary beneficiaries from this and the previous tactic on boredom would be the pupils who claim to be bored and not motivated. Moreover, all those near the bored individuals—their parents, their teachers, most adult members of the community—would benefit if these attitudes improved. Nearly everyone would agree that it is not a pleasant experience to be around people who act bored and inform others about their boredom.

Procedures

The aims of this tactic are to point out that the following:

- No person is always bored.
- You are, to a great extent, in control of how bored you are.
- You are, to some extent, responsible for boring or not boring others.
- You can actually change the extent to which you are bored and perhaps boring to others.
- You can change behaviors of those who are influenced by your boredom.
- There may be consequences for either saying you are bored or acting bored, and most of them are not good.

Discussion topics:

1. When are you bored?
2. When are you *not* bored?
3. Which of your classmates are bored and when, and how do you know they are bored?
4. Which peers are not bored and when, and how do you know they are not bored?
5. Why is it that when two individuals look at a picture, read a book, listen to someone speak, or see a movie, one might be bored and the other not?
6. If you wanted to, could you decrease the times you are bored? [It is important for students to get the idea that the more knowledgeable they are about a variety of topics, the chances of being bored are reduced. This puts the ball in their court, and many of them will resist accepting responsibility.]
7. What would be the point of being less bored? Would you gain? Would others?

8. Related, are you aware that it is not necessarily the responsibility of others to "unbore" you?

9. If a person is bored most of the time over an extended period of time, do you believe that feeling might lead to another condition such as depression, which, in turn might lead to something even more serious?

10. How can you measure the extent to which you are bored?

11. And what about you, the "borer"? What can you do so that you are not so boring? Have you ever given that much thought?

12. How do your teachers respond to your displays of boredom? [Although students probably have not thought too much about this, by bringing it up they *may* take notice. They need to get the idea that, as they begin to act less bored and perhaps more enthusiastic, their teachers will in turn be more motivated and perhaps become better teachers and the students will be even more turned on to learn, and their teachers will be even more motivated, and on and on.]

13. Are you bored with your parents? [This is a bit of a duplication, but it might be interesting to determine the extent to which youth are bored with their parents. They likely have never entertained the possibility that their parents might be bored with them.]

Modifications and Considerations

As I pointed out, the absolute best way to ensure that one is rarely bored is to become highly knowledgeable about a lot of subjects. There are also some other ways to combat boredom. One is to always have a kit full of activities, wherever one goes, so as to profitably while away the minutes or hours. When some folks go to the airport, for example, to meet arriving friends, they take along a notebook, a laptop computer, a newspaper, a book, or something else to occupy their time while they wait. Another activity that will relieve boredom is to simply watch or listen to people.

According to Edmundson (1997), students in his English classes at the University of Virginia become "unbored" when they evaluate his course. They toil "away like the devil's auditors. They're pitched into high writing gear, even the ones who struggle to squeeze out their journal entries word by word, stoked on a procedure they have by now supremely mastered. They're playing the informed consumer" (p. 39). Edmundson also commented that his students were motivated by the "new." "If it's new—a new need, a new product, a new show, a new style, a new generation—it must be good" (p. 42).

Monitor

Ask students to evaluate each day or each period on a boredom scale, 10 meaning that they were wildly excited about the time and 0 meaning that they were really, really bored. Encourage them to chart these data and study them over time to determine if there were patterns or trends to their feelings of boredom.

Reference

Edmundson, M. (1997, September). On the uses of a liberal education. *Harper's Magazine,* pp. 39–49.

☆ CONTINGENT SOCIALIZATION

Background

Consider this: The main motivation for most high school students to show up at school is to be with their peers! For the great majority of them, the primary reason they come to school, instead of going someplace else, is not the excitement in algebra class, the incredible experiments in biology class, the marvelous set of graphics in American history class, the opportunity to write about what they did last summer in English class, or even the brand new machines in the computer lab. For some of them it is the band, orchestra, or chorus; the sports teams; and the various clubs. But for the great majority of youth, especially those considered at risk, the main reason for rolling out of bed, dolling up in their best jeans and sneakers, and driving to school is their friends. They are highly motivated to see them, to be seen by them, to strut about in their favorite garb, to tell about their recent adventures, and to hear about the exploits of others. So, why not take advantage of that huge "reinforcer" by promoting proper socialization, as well as academic growth? Certainly, Judith Rich Harris (1998) would agree.

Who Can Benefit

The students who would profit from the procedures outlined here are the ones who are late and absent to the extent that their schoolwork suffers.

Procedures

Step 1.

Verify the hypothesis that students are motivated by being around other students. To do this, watch and listen to students on the bus on their way to school, observe them when they first come to school and mill about at their lockers or other places, watch them as they pass from one class to another, pay attention to them during their lunch periods, and observe them during classes when they are not supposed to be socializing. Those data, even if gathered rather casually, would reveal that most youth like to be with their peers.

Step 2.

Study arranged social groups in other schools. Franklin High School in Seattle, for example, has set aside a daily 15-minute period when students can convene and chat in a commons area. Although that is not a contingent situation— that is, the students do not have to earn it—it demonstrates that the idea is powerful.

Step 3.

Explore and consider a variety of locations, times, and other circumstances at school that might be set up as motivational atmospheres.

Step 4.

Explain clearly to the students that, if they behave in a designated way for a certain period of time, they can cash in with a trip to a socialization spot. They might be required to attend school for a certain number of days in a row, complete all their assignments satisfactorily, turn them in on time, behave themselves, or whatever, to earn the time to chat with friends.

Modifications and Considerations

Countless modifications are possible for this tactic. I will mention only a few: the places at which free time is possible; the amount of time allowed per visit; the amount of work or duties required to earn the time; the restrictions on what students can do in these free time areas.

Initially, when observing youth in a variety of social situations, you will probably spot a few students who are not motivated by their peers. In fact, some students may give the impression that they are avoiding others. A number of reasons could account for this, but if it seems that certain youth are not interacting with others because they lack necessary social skills, situations might be set up to teach them (Yager, 1997).

Monitor

Because the main idea behind this approach is to promote attendance, it would be a good idea to acquire and study attendance data prior to and during the involvement of the procedure. Not only would it be important to know, generally, how many students showed up for school each day, but it would be helpful to have specific attendance data on students who are absent a great deal of time.

References

Harris, J. R. (1998). *The nurture assumption: Why children turn out the way they do.* New York: The Free Press.

Yager, J. (1997). *Friendshifts: The power of friendship and how it shapes our lives.* Stamford, CT: Hammacroix Creek Books.

☆ SCHOOLWIDE CHANGES: STUDENTS HELP AT SCHOOL

Background

Many secondary students have bad attitudes toward their teachers, classes, and most everything associated with school. It is hard to say when and how these poor attitudes developed, but they probably begin before middle school and continue through high school (unless students drop out). It is also difficult to pinpoint the reasons for these poor attitudes and lack of motivation; however, many students become disenchanted and alienated with schools because they have not been given any responsibility for the upkeep or governance of the school, and many believe they are not acquiring information that relates directly and immediately to their lives.

Who Can Benefit

This tactic should influence the poor attitudes of many of the students characterized as remedial or at risk, as well as others who appear to be disfranchised by education, schools, and teachers.

Procedures

Listed here are three suggestions for bringing students around so that their attitudes are more positive toward school.

Upkeep and Maintenance

Many pupils have little feeling of ownership or responsibility for their schools. They demonstrate this through verbal disrespect for the school and acts of vandalism. These students believe that schools were built as prisons, or places that contain them and keep them from doing what they want to do. One way to change the attitudes of these students is to involve them in school routines. For example, a high school secretary was asked to watch a boy who had been sent to the office for disciplinary reasons (the vice principal was not there). Because the secretary was busy and could not simply sit with the youth, she enlisted his help with a number of chores. The young man liked the work and asked, a few days after his "sentence" had been served, if he could help some more. Because help was needed, he and others were put into service on a variety of tasks. Consequently, those students were praised for their work, realized they were contributing to the school, and behaved somewhat more respectfully toward their school.

Pupil Governance

Many schools do not elicit the opinions of students on school matters. This is unfortunate, because students' ideas should be requested about a number of activities and policies. Students, like their elders, appreciate being considered when decisions are made on issues that affect them. Although students should probably not be consulted about a number of school matters—the wisdom of the teachers, parents, and school boards should prevail—there are probably fewer of these issues than most educators would believe. Pupils could be given some say in the scheduling of classes; the assignment of teachers to courses; the scheduling of assemblies, parties, and other special occasions; cafeteria menus; bus routes; and even teacher evaluations. They should not have total responsibility in deciding about those important matters, but their opinions should be solicited.

Learning Relevant Skills

Many youngsters find it difficult to listen to lectures and read books about events and circumstances that are not immediately relevant to their lives. Although not every important topic in all classes can be immediately relevant to pupils, many topics are. For example, a seventh-grade earth science class was studying conservation. The teacher had planned a library assignment to cover this topic, but when a number of his students asked if they could do more than just talk and write about it, he redesigned the unit to involve them with their community. The students learned about where and how paper could be collected, what happens to that paper, how paper was made originally, and the effect of recycling paper on workers' jobs in their town. Moreover, students learned on what days the papers would be collected, how they should be tied together, and how many pounds of paper equaled one tree. They asked neighbors to save papers for their paper drive, wrote letters on conservation to the local newspaper, and loaded paper on the trucks.

Modifications and Considerations

One way to better understand students' complaints about schools would be for adults to spend time in schools learning about the students' experiences. One thing that adults would probably want to change about schools, if they spent an entire day sitting in classes, would be the chairs. They are very uncomfortable, and an uncomfortable seat does nothing for a positive attitude.

Edgar (1997) wrote the following comments regarding students as school helpers:

> Perhaps grouped by age, the students, along with a portion of the adults, would take responsibility for maintaining the physical environment. One group might be responsible for the inside of the school building, another for the grounds, another for preparing food, yet another for public art—the possibilities are limitless. Not replacing the workers who have responsibility for these areas but assisting them, the groups would take responsibility for the common good of the community. All members, male and female, rich and poor, those with disabilities and those without, would share this responsibility. Each group would also have some responsibility for the psychological well-being of the community: for conflict resolution, for developing and implementing group workshops on creating a caring community, for developing activities that unite the entire community. Each group would have representation in the governance of the community, in developing a code of conduct, and in enforcing the code of conduct. Finally, each group would be involved in an outreach project to the community outside the school building. (p. 324)

Monitor

It is difficult to measure attitudes, either good or bad, but somewhat easier to monitor the manifestations of those attitudes. Some factors related to good and bad school attitudes are the following: vandalism, absences, fights, and referrals to the principal or other disciplinary figure. A checklist could be developed that included those items and others. It could be completed by teachers, parents, and students.

References

Edgar, E. (1997). School reform, special education, and democracy. *Remedial and Special Education, 18*(6) 323–325.

Krumboltz, J. D., & Krumboltz, H. B. (1972). *Generating enthusiasm for school: Changing children's behavior.* Englewood Cliffs, NJ: Prentice-Hall.

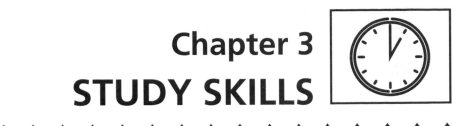

Chapter 3
STUDY SKILLS

♦ ♦ ♦ ♦ ♦ ♦ ♦ ♦ ♦ ♦ ♦ ♦ ♦ ♦ ♦ ♦ ♦ ♦ ♦ ♦

The tactics (actually strategies) summarized in this chapter focus on the primary study skills components: reading, writing, notetaking, test taking, and time management. These techniques differ from those in Chapter 4, Basic Skills, which are designed to actually teach a fundamental skill such as reading, writing, or arithmetic. Study skills techniques are not intended to teach specific academic skills. Instead, they are general skills designed to aid youth to get as much as possible out of each content subject (e.g., biology, history). Therefore, the teacher, in setting aside time to teach either basic skills or study skills, must arrive at a proper balance. The teacher should not devote too much time to instructing reading, writing, and arithmetic at the expense of providing help with content subjects through study skills, and should not schedule too much time on study skills preparation at the expense of actually teaching reading or the other basics. The decision as to how much time to concentrate on either should be made deliberately and with each individual.

There are summaries of 15 techniques in this chapter. The first one, a study skills inventory, is designed to survey the extent to which a youth is aware of the many study skills. There is also information about managing time in that write-up, as there is in the following technique. The next two strategies have to do with reading, and the two following with writing. Next, there are three techniques for assisting with taking notes and two with taking tests. Following is a strategy for memorizing information. The next technique has to do with getting at the true facts, and the one following involves understanding assignments. The final strategy has a combined emphasis on problem solving and vocabulary development.

MANAGING TIME: STUDY SKILLS INVENTORY

Background

One of the most pronounced distinctions between students who do well at school and those who do poorly is their understanding of and ability to apply study skills. All too often students respond to low grades on tests and quizzes with the plaintive cry, "But I did study!" when in reality they merely read or skimmed the material. Although they may have the intent to remember, on which dependable learning is based, they may not have developed the study habits needed to be efficient learners.

This tactic is based on the premise that students who say they are bored by learning are actually frustrated by their own inability to learn, and that finding a good place to study, learning to organize their study time, and becoming aware of the study skills they need to improve can help them overcome some of that frustration and dispel many of their negative feelings about learning.

Who Can Benefit

Content teachers interested in improving their students' ability to learn can help them develop ways to manage their study time more effectively. Students who are aware of their weaknesses in this area, and are willing to learn and apply good study habits, should begin to experience more success in mastering content in the classroom.

Procedures

1. Take a careful look at the subjects you teach and the way you teach them, and determine what study skills would most likely benefit students in your classes. Consider the importance of the following: managing time, reading textbooks, underlining passages, taking notes, outlining, using maps, taking essay tests, and taking objective tests.

2. List the skills you identified and develop a rating scale (see sample Study Skills Inventory by Estes & Vaughn, 1985, in Figure 3.1).

3. Go over every item on the list with the students, providing examples. Make certain that they understand the items and how to rate the extent to which they use them.

4. Ask the students to rate themselves on the items.

5. Fill out a survey form for each of your students.

6. Compare your ratings with theirs.

7. Identify the areas of strengths and weaknesses and the items for which their judgments and yours were alike and different.

8. Discuss those findings with your students.

9. Design a program to teach study skills based on your data and discussions with students.

Implementing Training

The following are suggested activities for instructing one of the more important study skills, managing time.

1. Discuss the main components of good work–study habits:
   - Organizing study time and daily scheduling
   - Establishing a comfortable and familiar place for study

2. Ask students to think of words and phrases they associate with time (e.g., "time is money," "killing time").

3. Generate a discussion on setting priorities with reference to school, work at home, outside work, and leisure activities.

STUDY SKILLS INVENTORY

_____
Student

_____
Date

_____
Course/Period

Directions: Study skills will be important to your success in this course, and this inventory is designed to find out what your strengths and weaknesses may be in these areas. Think carefully about each of the following statements and then answer as honestly as you can. This is NOT a test!!

Circle 1, 2, 3, or 4 next to each statement to indicate whether the statement would be true for you usually, sometimes, seldom, or never.

	Usually	Some-times	Seldom	Never
Managing Time				
1. I spend about 45 minutes each day studying for each of my courses.	1	2	3	4
2. When I study, I can stick with it until I am finished.	1	2	3	4
3. I study where I will not be interrupted.	1	2	3	4
Using a Textbook				
4. I use the table of contents to help me understand how topics are related.	1	2	3	4
5. I use the index in my studying.	1	2	3	4
6. I use the glossary to find meanings of unfamiliar words.	1	2	3	4
Underlining				
7. I underline all important ideas as I read.	1	2	3	4
8. I underline only key words or phrases, not whole sentences.	1	2	3	4
9. I underline details and examples.	1	2	3	4
10. I underline almost everything.	1	2	3	4
Notetaking				
11. When I study, I take notes from my reading.	1	2	3	4
12. When I take notes from my reading, they are clear enough to make sense several weeks later.	1	2	3	4
13. When I take notes from my reading, I put down the page numbers where I got the information.	1	2	3	4
14. When a teacher is lecturing in class, I take clear notes of what is said.	1	2	3	4
15. In my lecture notes, I make sure to write down the main ideas.	1	2	3	4
16. In my lecture notes, I include details and examples that help me clarify ideas.	1	2	3	4

(continues)

Figure 3.1. Sample Study Skills Inventory Form. From *Reading and Learning in the Content Classroom: Diagnostic and Instructional Strategies* (pp. 124–125), by T. H. Estes and J. L. Vaughn, Jr., 1985, Boston: Allyn & Bacon. Copyright 1985 by Allyn & Bacon. Reprinted with permission.

	Usually	Some-times	Seldom	Never
Outlining				
17. I outline the major things I learn when I study.	1	2	3	4
18. In my outlines, I include main ideals in the primary headings.	1	2	3	4
19. In my outlines, I include details as subheadings that clarify the main ideas.	1	2	3	4
Using Maps				
20. I can use the keys and legends when reading maps.	1	2	3	4
21. I can interpret what the maps suggest about historical trends.	1	2	3	4
Taking Essay Tests				
22. When taking essay tests, I read the directions and all the questions before beginning to answer any of the questions.	1	2	3	4
23. When taking essay tests, I think about what I want to write before beginning.	1	2	3	4
24. When taking essay tests, I organize my answer so my ideas will be clear to the instructor.	1	2	3	4
25. I proofread my answers when I am finished and before I turn in my paper.	1	2	3	4
Taking Objective Tests				
26. When answering a multiple choice question, I try to eliminate first the obviously incorrect choices.	1	2	3	4
27. I trust my first guess when unsure of an answer.	1	2	3	4
28. I proofread to make sure no question is left unanswered, even if the answer is a wild guess.	1	2	3	4
29. I read through all the choices before marking an answer, even if the first or second one seems correct.	1	2	3	4
30. I look for clues in other questions that can help in answering questions of which I am unsure.	1	2	3	4

Figure 3.1. *(Continued)*

4. Extend the discussion by asking students to identify benefits that might come from a plan for managing their study time.

5. Instruct students to keep daily records of how they spend their time.

6. Assist them to construct a pie chart that illustrates how they distribute their time.

7. Ask them to comment on the proportion of time they spend studying.

8. Discuss with them how they might reallocate their time so as to spend more time studying.

9. Instruct students to keep records of their study time.

10. Assist students, later, to keep records of their production and its quality—that is, the number of assignments or papers completed and the grades they receive.

11. Point out the relationships between amount of time spent studying, amount of work submitted, and grades.

12. Reassess the quality of students' study time if positive relationships are not noted.

Corresponding activities should be scheduled for other study skills components that may be lacking (e.g., reading from textbooks, notetaking, test taking).

Modifications and Considerations

Students could be required to complete an inventory occasionally to determine whether they are (or think they are) improving. Apart from evaluating their improvement with respect to incorporating study skills, these periodic reviews should serve to remind students of specific skills they should attend to. Learning about study skills should therefore become a set of specific and clearly defined activities.

Students' needs for specific study skills will change as they master those initially targeted for improvement, and as lesson content changes throughout the year. Ask students to help revise the original list from time to time.

Lenz, Ellis, and Scanlon (1996) offered suggestions for teaching youth to generalize study strategies once they have been instructed in one setting. The following are the steps about which they elaborate: (a) Review with the students the progress they have made to date in learning the strategy; (b) discuss generalization as the next phase of strategy learning; (c) discuss when and how students can generalize the strategy; and (d) reconfirm the students' commitment to generalize.

Monitor

Suggestions for monitoring this activity were included in the Procedures, and Modifications and Considerations sections.

References

Estes, T. H., & Vaughn, J. L., Jr. (1985). *Reading and learning in the content classroom: Diagnostic and instructional strategies.* Boston: Allyn & Bacon.

Lenz, B. K., Ellis, E. S., & Scanlon, D. (1996). *Teaching learning strategies to adolescents and adults with learning disabilities.* Austin, TX: PRO-ED.

🕐 MANAGING TIME: BEING PREPARED

Background

Many of us employ a variety of behavioral techniques to manage our own behaviors. We reward ourselves with special items for our accomplishments, make arrangements with ourselves so that we take on necessary but undesirable tasks, withhold things we normally enjoy if we do not behave in certain ways, and assess and revise our methods, depending on how well they work.

When we teach students to self-monitor their behaviors, we are encouraging them to use the same techniques. Initially, we can supplement their self-monitoring programs by providing frequent feedback and rewards. Later, random checks and intermittent rewards should be sufficient to ensure maintenance of the students' programs.

Who Can Benefit

This study was conducted with eight boys, from ages 10 through 12, who had a variety of behavior problems (Layne, Rickard, Jones, & Lyman, 1976). Like many students, they had been exposed to a number of behavior management systems, all of which were controlled by teachers. The technique described here is an ideal tactic for students of that type, for it gives them an opportunity to manage their own actions.

Procedures

1. Identify the behavior or collection of behaviors that will be evaluated (e.g., being prepared for school).

2. Develop a checklist for self-rating components of that topic (see, e.g., Figure 3.2).

3. Establish a criterion for the behaviors and for accurate self-rating. A criterion for the preparation behaviors might be that if all six items are

---

CHECKLIST ITEMS

Name _____ Date _____

	M	T	W	T	F
Has all necessary supplies	☐	☐	☐	☐	☐
Assignments completed	☐	☐	☐	☐	☐
Assignments turned in on time	☐	☐	☐	☐	☐
Papers organized in notebook	☐	☐	☐	☐	☐
Arrives on time	☐	☐	☐	☐	☐
If absent, obtains missed assignments	☐	☐	☐	☐	☐
Total Complete	___	___	___	___	___

X = student rating (mark for each completed task)
+ = teacher verification (mark for each completed task)

Figure 3.2. Checklist for use in managing time: Being prepared for school.

checked, the student will earn a few minutes of free time. To increase the probability that students will rate themselves accurately, they could earn a reward (e.g., time to read a magazine, talk to a friend, or go to the library) if their ratings matched those of the teacher.

Modifications and Considerations

This technique has a variety of applications at home or school. Layne et al. (1976) focused on clean-up activities at a summer camp. It is important to note that students will probably need some type of reward initially to encourage them to carry out the desirable behaviors, and to assure that they accurately record them.

As students progress with this type of management and their needs change, so can the items on their checklists. Eventually, students could even establish their own performance goals.

Flores, Schloss, and Alper (1995) reported on the use of a daily calendar, which increased responsibilities carried out by secondary youth with special needs.

Monitor

Suggestions for monitoring the effects of this technique were provided in the Procedures section.

References

Flores, D. M., Schloss, P. J., & Alper, S. (1995). The use of a daily calendar to increase responsibilities fulfilled by secondary students with special needs. *Remedial and Special Education, 16*(1), 38–43.

Layne, C. C., Rickard, H. C., Jones, M. T., & Lyman, R. D. (1976). Accuracy of self-monitoring on a variable ratio schedule of observer verification. *Behavior Therapy, 7,* 481–488.

READING: MULTIPASS TO INCREASE COMPREHENSION

Background

The Multipass strategy was developed to assist students in secondary schools to deal with increased amounts of content material (Schumaker, Deshler, Alley, Warner, & Denton, 1982). The approach requires students to make three "passes" through the assigned reading material, with a different purpose in mind each time. Because students must perform a number of behaviors in each pass, each one is taught as a unit and in succession.

Who Can Benefit

Schumaker et al.'s (1982) research was conducted with eight adolescents with learning disabilities. Students who are remedial or at risk would also profit from the Multipass technique to handle reading assignments in their science, history, and social studies classes. Many other students would also gain from the Multipass reading strategy.

Procedures

Steps

As mentioned, Multipass is made up of three steps or passes. In the first, students skim through a passage in the text to identify main ideas and note its general organization. This should take only a few minutes. The purpose of the second pass is to gain information and facts from the passage without reading it thoroughly. During the third pass, pupils sort out the information gained from the first two passes. The following is a detailed description of the three passes:

1. *Survey Pass:* Focus on the text features represented by the acronym: TISOPT, which stands for Titles/Subtitles; Introduction; Summary; Organization/Outline of chapter; Pictures (read captions); Table of Contents (how passage fits with others). No more than 30 seconds should be spent on each page for this pass.

2. *Size-Up Pass:* Students should read the captions for all illustrations and raise questions about them. They should then scan the pages for more information about which to ask questions. As students go through the passage, they should paraphrase the information and take notes. The letters IQWH:RASPN can serve as memory cues: Illustrations; Form Questions about illustrations; Words in bold type (ask what they mean); Headings (form questions about them); Read; Ask; Scan; Paraphrase; Note

3. *Sort-Out Pass:* For this final pass, students should answer the questions that are generally at the end of a section or chapter. Students should read the questions and follow these instructions:

   If You Know the Answer—Say it and write it. Make check mark beside that question. Say and write next question.

   If You Don't Know the Answer—Mark it with a square. Look at the subheadings. Decide on the likely section(s) to search for the answer. Say and write the answer.

Instructions

1. Analyze students' current reading habits: Have them read a section in a textbook. Ask them what approach they used to read and learn the material.

2. Describe the new strategy as an alternative to methods they may have been using (e.g., "Here's a way that's been proven to work," "Students can go through material faster and understand more").

3. Give students reasons for learning the new technique (e.g., "You will be a more efficient reader and get better grades").

4. Model the new strategy (e.g., "Here's how we do the Survey Pass").

5. Conduct verbal rehearsal exercises for each sort (e.g., TISOPT).

6. Assign easy passages for students to read as they learn the strategy.

7. Provide positive and corrective feedback to students, according to their performances.

8. Practice on content materials at grade level after students have used the strategy with easier materials.

9. Provide more feedback and reinforcement to them.

Modifications and Considerations

The Multipass Worksheet in Figure 3.3 is a simplified checklist of the three passes. These can be used individually or with groups of students. The teacher may instruct the pupils to use letters such as TISOPT to serve as reminders for certain passes. If the letters are confusing or otherwise not helpful, other letters or symbols could be selected, or that feature of the program could be dropped.

Students are given a number of suggestions and a fair amount of feedback during the various stages of learning the Multipass strategy. It is important that they learn to accept and deal with that information, particularly those comments that may be critical of their current methods of reading and studying from textbooks.

A number of researchers, including Espin and Deno (1993), have demonstrated that a reasonable way to determine how well students read from content-area texts is to have them read selected passages orally and time their performances. In general, if youth read passages from science or social studies textbooks at rates slower than 125 words per minute, they should receive assistance in reading generally, along with assistance in reading study skills.

Monitor

Teachers may want to monitor how well students remember the steps for the various phases (e.g., TISOPT). To obtain these data, teachers can develop a checklist and occasionally assess students' ability. More important, teachers might want to know whether the tactic helped students retain more information from their textbook passages. To do so, teachers can develop a set of questions from passages for which the reading strategy was scheduled and some for passages for which it was not used. Each student's data from passages studied with and without Multipass could be compared to determine whether the technique was helpful.

References

Espin, C. A., & Deno, S. L. (1993). Content-specific and general reading disabilities of secondary-level students: Identification and educational relevance. *The Journal of Special Education, 27*(3), 321–337.

Schumaker, J. B., Deshler, D. D., Alley, G. R., Warner, M. M., & Denton, P. H. (1982). Multipass: A learning strategy for improving reading comprehension. *Learning Disability Quarterly, 5,* 295–304.

MULTIPASS WORKSHEET

Survey Pass

1. Write title. _____

2. What is the main idea in the introduction? (one sentence)

   _____

3. What is the main idea in the summary? (one sentence)

   _____

4. Write main headings.

5. Which pictures, titles, maps, time lines are most important?

6. How does this chapter fit in with the whole book?

Size-Up Pass

1. Write questions.

2. Write subheadings.

3. Write vocabulary words, italicized words, key words.

Sort-Out Pass

Write answers to questions:

Can't answer question number _____.

Scanned for answer on pages _____.

Write answer

Still can't answer? Mark it and move on.

Return to marked question(s).

_____

Figure 3.3. Worksheet for use in the Multipass strategy.

READING: VISUAL IMAGERY AND SELF-QUESTIONING TO IMPROVE COMPREHENSION

Background

Middle and high school students, including those characterized as remedial or at risk, must learn to acquire information from content materials. The instructional strategies model, with its emphasis on learning how to learn, has proven to be particularly valuable for these adolescents.

Two learning strategies that have been advocated to improve reading comprehension are *visual imagery* and *self-questioning*. In a study by Clark, Deshler,

Schumaker, Alley, and Warner (1984), these two approaches were taught to adolescents with learning disabilities to increase their interaction with the content and enhance their reading comprehension.

Who Can Benefit

Clark et al.'s (1984) study was conducted with six adolescents with learning disabilities. These strategies can be adapted to the content and needs of students in intermediate grades and taught to students of average intelligence who may be low achievers or nonmotivated learners. The authors of the research recommended, however, that to benefit most fully from this approach, students should be able to read at the fourth-grade level.

Procedures

Instructional Steps

1. Administer a pretest.

    - Require the students to read a passage, and then tell you as much as they can about it.

    - In addition, ask them a few questions about the passage.

2. Describe the steps of the strategy (either Visual Imagery or Self-Questioning) to the students and explain how either one will help them.

3. Model the strategy and demonstrate all the steps.

4. Instruct the students to verbally rehearse the steps of the strategy. Require 100% accuracy.

5. Require the students to practice using the strategy with materials written at their ability levels.

6. Expand the practice to include grade-level materials when students are comfortable with easier material.

7. Provide positive and corrective feedback to the students.

8. Administer a posttest (a readministration of the pretest).

Visual Imagery Strategy (RIDER)

1. <u>R</u>ead—Read the first sentence.

2. <u>I</u>mage—Make an image or a picture in your mind.

3. <u>D</u>escribe—Describe your image.

    - If you cannot make an image, explain why and go to the next sentence.

    - If you can make an image, decide whether it is an old one (an image in memory from the most recent sentence), an old image that has been modified, or an entirely new image.

    - Once you have an image, describe it.

4. Evaluate—Evaluate your image for its completeness. Make certain that the image includes as much of the sentence's content as possible. If some content is missing, adjust your image and continue. If your image is comprehensive, continue.

5. Repeat—Read the next sentence of the text and repeat Steps 1 through 4.

Self-Questioning Strategy (RAM)

1. Read a paragraph. Ask wh– questions as you read to keep yourself engaged in reading.

2. Answer your questions as you read.

3. Mark your answers with the appropriate symbol for the type of wh– question. (Use symbols for each type of question: a clock face for "when" questions, a circle face for "who" questions, a square for "what" questions, an arrow for "where" questions, a capital Y for "why" questions, and a capital H for "how" questions.)

Modifications and Considerations

Based on the previous instructions for the visual imagery strategy, pupils are encouraged to form an image after each sentence. If the density of material in a passage makes that task too difficult, it may be more appropriate to conceive of images following each paragraph. The opposite instruction may be appropriate for the Self-Questioning strategy. Whereas it was recommended in the previous instructions that pupils develop questions following each paragraph, it may be helpful, depending on the richness of material, to form questions following each sentence.

Although the two strategies are independent of each other, they could be used together. That, of course, would depend on the type of material and on the ability of the pupil.

Whether one strategy or another or a combination of the two is scheduled, students, to gain the most from the approaches, should be taught when to rely on one or the other. Generally, the Visual Imagery approach would be an appropriate selection if, in the material, several objects or scenes were described. The Self-Questioning strategy might be a wise choice if a number of facts or statements were included in the passage.

The poet Ted Hughes (1997) claimed that one of the brain's spontaneous techniques for fixing anything in the conscious memory is to connect it with a visual image. According to him, "the more absurd, exaggerated, grotesque that image is, the more unforgettable is the thing to which we connect it" (p. x). He explained how to memorize a list of words or a poem by offering the following example: "A peaty burn (stream); a brown horse; an avalanche; a roaring lion; a hen-coop; a comb; a fleece; foam; a flute; a lake; home" (p. x). Hughes suggested that for "peaty burn," one simply imagines a dark torrential mountain stream coming down among boulders. The next item, "brown horse" might be connected to the burning stream by imagining the horse swimming in the stream. He went on to explain how images could be made of the other words and how each of them might be connected to previous images. If each image is "photographed" mentally, according to Hughes, "it will not be forgotten easily. And each image will bring on the next which has been connected to it. Even when you are remembering a very long list, the procedure is quite small-scale and automatic because you are never remembering more than one connection at a time and each connection provides you with the next" (p. xi).

Monitor

There are a number of ways to measure the effects of these approaches. One would be to ask students to say or write facts or summaries of stories they had read prior to being instructed to use one of the approaches. Those data might then be charted as number of words, facts, judgments, or whatever per unit of time. Following this baseline, when neither technique was involved, those same data could be gathered while one or both tactics were being instructed. Data from the two phases could then be compared to determine whether the comprehension techniques improved students' performance.

References

Clark, F. L., Deshler, D. D., Schumaker, J. B., Alley, G. R., & Warner, M. M. (1984). Visual imagery and self-questioning: Strategies to improve comprehension of written material. *Journal of Learning Disabilities, 17,* 145–149.

Hughes, T. (1997). *By heart: 101 poems to remember.* London: Faber and Faber.

⏱ WRITING: AN ERROR MONITORING STRATEGY (COPS)

Background

One important goal of education is to instruct students to express their thoughts in writing in a concise, cogent manner. Another goal is to develop independent behaviors. The COPS strategy (Deshler, 1984) was designed to focus on both goals: to assist youngsters to improve their writing and to be independent in the process.

Who Can Benefit

Junior high students of normal intelligence have learned to use this strategy. It has also been used with students with learning disabilities and students who generally have poor study habits. With all of these cases, COPS has proven to be a beneficial tactic when students are required to write sentences.

Procedures

Introduction

1. Explain to students that it is important for them to check their own writing for errors. Encourage them to offer suggestions on how to do this.

2. Introduce the COPS strategy as a simple way to remember specific features when self-checking their written work. Explain the meaning of the acronym COPS:

C: Capitalization (first words, proper nouns, dates, etc.)

O: Overall editing and appearance

P: Punctuation

S: Spelling (handwriting, neatness, margins, complete sentences, etc.)

Implementation

Encourage students to follow these steps as they self-check their writing assignments:

1. Write on every other line (this makes it easier to make corrections).

2. Reread each sentence, considering the COPS strategy.

3. Write the appropriate letter (C, O, P, or S) at the beginning of each sentence in which an error or correction is found.

4. Indicate the location of the error or correction with a check mark.

5. Go back over the assignment and make the necessary corrections.

6. Rewrite the paper, and read it over carefully. Then hand it in.

Modifications and Considerations

One way to modify the COPS tactic is to write the COPS acronym on a note card and tape it to the desks of students who particularly need to employ the steps. Review the COPS method and remind students to use it when writing papers. COPS can also be modified for the appropriate level of instruction (elementary, junior, or senior high). The teacher can go into as much detail as necessary for individual students.

To help students check their spelling, provide them with a "Bad Spellers Dictionary." Students could also exchange their papers with one another to check on spelling and other features of writing.

For this tactic to be truly effective, students must apply the steps consistently. Check students' papers to see that they are relying on the COPS strategy. Reinforce their efforts to do so and point out instances when they should have used certain features.

To assist youngsters to be good, or at least adequate writers, schedule times for them to write. Often, too little time is set aside for writing, and what is scheduled is generally devoted to rules and principles, not to actual writing.

Also, give students assignments to write that are functional, meaningful, and motivating. Too often, assignments for adolescents are patronizing, boring, and meaningless.

Shannon and Polloway (1993) used the COPS strategy successfully with 12-year-old children with learning disabilities. In their study students relied on the COPS strategy in 10 types of writing: love letters, homework assignments, spelling practice, job applications, English papers, written math problems, health questions, history exam questions, friendly letters, and written instructions.

Monitor

To monitor the extent to which students relied on the COPS technique while checking their papers, a checklist could be developed. On it, the four letters could be written vertically, and across the top a succession of days could be printed. With that chart, the teacher, a peer, or pupils themselves could mark the features that were incorporated in their corrections for each session. As a measure of ability, someone could count the number of words written each session and plot those frequencies on a graph.

References

Deshler, D. (1984). COPS tactic presented in a study skills workshop sponsored by Lake Washington School District #414, Kirkland, WA.

Shannon, T. R., & Polloway, E. A. (1993). Promoting error monitoring in middle school students with LD. *Intervention in School and Clinic, 28*(3), 160–164.

LEARNING LOGS: TOOLS FOR COGNITIVE MONITORING

Background

Students can rarely explain why various learning strategies either help them or could help them. Therefore, students need opportunities to explore their own thinking and to evaluate their own progress in using the strategies typically deemed necessary for success in high school or college. This tactic involves students in writing their perceptions about learning to learn.

Who Can Benefit

According to Commander and Smith (1996), "many students lack experiences that teach them to monitor their academic progress, engage in self-regulation of learning, and share their thoughts with their instructor" (p. 446). In other words, numbers of students have a hard time dealing with the information that comes their way. This tactic should help them. Journal writing has been used with diverse populations, including kindergarten students, junior high students, college students, and many others.

Procedures

See Figure 3.4 for a description of the general components of learning logs. Commander and Smith (1996) described 10 types of learning logs. The following are questions for students to consider before writing:

LEARNING LOG ASSIGNMENT OVERVIEW

Description

Your learning log is a written record of your perception of how you are "learning to learn." It is a structured opportunity for you to reflect on your awareness of how you are learning, rather than what you are learning. As you will discover, we all learn in many ways. We learn from listening, doing, thinking about ourselves, and watching others. All of these learning activities can be included in your logs.

Purpose

The purpose of writing your thoughts in a weekly log is to make you more aware of your own cognitive development and to allow you to share your thoughts with your professor. Learning to study is a process. For example, did a teacher ever take you through each step of writing a term paper, giving you grades at the completion of the steps, as well as a grade on the final paper? If so, that teacher was using a process method of teaching writing. In a similar manner, this course will emphasize the separate steps in studying and becoming a successful student. The purposes of LSH 075 are for you (a) to be successful in HIS 113 and (b) to become a long-term successful student at the university.

Grade

Learning log entries will be collected every Tuesday at the *beginning* of the period. Learning logs will not be accepted late. Your entries can be daily or weekly but cannot be written during the class period and then submitted. They should be dated and on notebook paper. You will receive a grade on your journal, but the grade will be based on effort rather than on a notion of correct or incorrect responses. You will be assigned 10 log topics. The maximum score for each log entry is 10 and the minimum is 0.

Format

Your weekly learning log entry should be on one or two sheets of notebook paper. The maximum length for the full 10 points is two pages and the minimum is a full one page. Please be aware that your professor knows the difference between a "serious" one-page length and a "fabricated" page. The objective is for you to learn.

Topics

The topics for the learning log entries will be assigned each Tuesday. The weekly entry must address the assigned topic. Topics will reflect our class discussions and will include your thoughts on time management, notetaking techniques, collaboration, and others.

Models of learning logs

The following are unedited excerpts taken from the learning logs of LSH 075 students. These are provided as models for what the assignment means and not as examples to copy. Your log entries should be written in your own style and reflect your own thoughts. Both positive and negative thoughts can be included. The two excerpts are examples of what is OK and what is not OK.

(continues)

Figure 3.4. Description of the components of learning logs. From "Learning Logs: A Tool for Cognitive Monitoring," by N. E. Commander and B. D. Smith, 1996, *Journal of Adolescent & Adult Literacy, 39*(6), p. 448. Copyright 1996 by *Journal of Adolescent & Adult Literacy.* Reprinted with permission.

Excerpt from log receiving 10 points:

My grade wasn't what I wanted, but I understand that my study habits weren't what they should have been, so I expected it. That doesn't mean I'm going to keep expecting it. I was very hurt and disappointed.

I viewed the way I studied and recently (since Thursday) I've been doing a little better. The bed will not be a study place any more. Even if it is the most private and comfortable place at home. I studied at the dining room table the other night, and I found that I get done quicker and I was more satisfied with what I had learned. It's better for my posture too.

I talked to my mother about my study habits, and she gave me some advice. This weekend I really studied. I think I'm going to do better on the next test. No! I know I'm going to do better. I'm getting advice from my mother, professors, and other students that is helpful. I'm already putting these ideas into action.

Excerpt from log receiving less than 10 points:

Hellllooo boys and girls alike! It's time once again for a nice lovely journal entry. Well this past week was a little rough since I had yet another quiz in history. But I think it's going to turn out ok. The topic for the day is "groups." So I guess I have to give you a little input about my little group in the back.

To be honest w/ you, I really don't know where my opinion lies about the set up. One day we'll be motivated to get terms and facts together and then other days half the group will talk up a storm about some juicy gossip freshly squeezed from the 'ol grapevine. It also seems that the motivation level tends to increase as a quiz or test comes about. Personally, I don't rely or depend on anyone in general, but I would definitely not rely on these folks to help me through a test if my life depended on it. But don't get me wrong, the people are really nice and friendly, but it seems that they are having some studying difficulties.

Figure 3.4. *(Continued)*

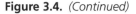

1. *Observation of academic behaviors.* Carefully observe the behavior of other students in your class (e.g., history, English, biology). What are the students of various types doing? Are you surprised by anything? If you were the teacher, would you be pleased with what they are doing, and why?

2. *Reflections on notetaking.* Reflect on your ability to take notes from lectures or discussions in the class and from the textbook for that class. How would you describe your method? Has it improved? How do some other students take notes? Should you try out one of their methods? What do you do with your notes; that is, how do you use them?

3. *Report on seeking help.* Find a good time to ask your teacher for help in a class. Describe what happened. What did you ask? What did you learn? Do other students ask for help in this way? What will you do differently the next time you ask for help?

4. *Test debriefing.* Following a test, ask yourself and write about some of the following: What was your score or grade? Is that what you expected? How did you go about studying for the test? Did that studying (if you did any) help? What will you do differently the next time?

5. *Reflection on behaviors.* For this log, think about what it is that is keeping you from being an A student (or what makes you an A student, if you are). Following are some points you may want to write about: Am I motivated? How do I feel when I do poorly? What would it take in terms of time and effort to raise my score a bit?

6. *Reading strategies.* How do you go about reading and studying from a textbook? More specifically, do you go over the assigned pages a number of times, and if so what do you try to get out of each "pass"? Do you take notes as you read? Do you underline passages in the book? If you do take notes or underline, what do you do after you have done that?

7. *Group interaction.* What do you think of "cooperative learning" arrangements? Do you learn some things better in those groups than if you worked by yourself? What types of students do you like to work with? Please comment on whether later in school or in life you would like to work in cooperative learning groups?

8. *Course suggestions.* Now that we are at the end of the school year, reflect on how things went for you. What were the most significant things you learned? What would you have liked to do more of and less of in the class? Do you think that you did your best in the class?

9. *Adjusting to college.* In a few years you may go to college. How do you think you will get along, generally? Do you think the assignments will be harder, longer, about the same, or what? What do you think will be the toughest thing for you to adjust to when you go? Have you talked to other students who have gone to college, and what do they say about the experience?

10. *Reflections on taking biology (or other course).* Now that you are almost finished with this class, think about the advice you would give others who might take it. What should they be prepared to do? What would you tell them about homework? What is the toughest thing about the class? What can they expect to get out of the class?

Modifications and Considerations

Learning logs may be used to explore other aspects of learning, such as time management, learning style, the use of mnemonics and other memory devices, the use of study skills, and summarizing lessons of the day.

The teacher should set specific guidelines for personal journal writing by suggesting that students avoid writing about subjects that she would be legally required to report to authorities.

How to Monitor

As with other instructional practices, the process of learning the strategy and the extent to which it advanced learning can be evaluated. Obviously, the latter is more important than the former, but unless the strategy is carried out properly there is the chance that it will not affect learning as much as it would have otherwise.

As for evaluating the former, the teacher might enlist the help of another teacher or an advanced student to study the logs of various students on a variety of themes and determine which ones were of the highest quality and which ones needed improvement. As for evaluating the latter, one could acquire before and after measures in some content area, such as social studies or science. If a student's performance in one of those subjects improved from "before logs" to "after logs," one could assume that the progress was due, in part at least, to the experience of writing logs.

Reference

Commander, N. E., & Smith, B. D. (1996). Learning logs: A tool for cognitive monitoring. *Journal of Adolescent & Adult Literacy, 39*(6), 446–453.

NOTETAKING: SEVERAL SUGGESTIONS

Background

Good notetaking skills make important information more accessible to students. Taking notes requires them to consider and evaluate the content of their lessons in ways that merely listening cannot. Furthermore, students who take and review their notes from lectures learn more than those who just listen. It is not enough to simply tell students to take notes. Students must be convinced, first, that there are good reasons to improve their notetaking skills and, next, that they can learn to do so and profit from their notes. This tactic offers suggestions for helping students recognize the need for notetaking, and presents a variety of ways for instructing them to take notes (Bos & Vaughn, 1998).

Who Can Benefit

Secondary students will profit from learning to take notes, since the majority of lesson content in junior high and high school is delivered through lectures and texts. Teachers who take the time to instruct students in useful notetaking practices will provide their students with valuable, generalizable skills that can help them learn more in most learning situations they will encounter.

Procedures

1. Present a brief (10- to 15-minute) lecture on some familiar topic and ask students to take notes.

2. Test them on information from the lecture.

3. Ask them to evaluate their ability to take notes and how their notes helped them on the test.

4. Teach students two formats for notetaking (see Figure 3.5).

5. Provide students with a list of hints for taking notes (see Table 3.1).

SAMPLE TWO-COLUMN SYSTEM

Topic _____

Date _____

_____

Triggers or Key Concepts   Class Notes
_____

SAMPLE THREE-COLUMN SYSTEM

Topic _____

Date _____

_____

Triggers or Key Concepts   Class Notes   Text Notes
_____

Figure 3.5. Two formats for notetaking.

6. Use video- or audiotapes to provide practice in listening and note-taking by

   • Allowing students to replay a tape to watch or listen for main ideas.

   • Playing a short segment of a taped lecture, and having students list the cues and explain their importance.

   • Replaying the segment to let students verify their list of cues.

7. Teach students to review notes for tests by

   • Using key concepts to formulate questions.

   • Finding or developing answers from notes.

8. Elicit discussion about other classes in which notetaking skills would be helpful.

Table 3.1. Hints for Taking Notes

1. Take notes using either a two-or three-column system.
2. Take notes on only one side of the paper.
3. Date and label the topic of the notes.
4. Use a modified outline format, indenting subordinate ideas and numbering ideas when possible.
5. Skip lines to note changes in ideas.
6. Write ideas or key phrases, not complete sentences.
7. Use pictures and diagrams to relate ideas.
8. Use consistent abbreviations (e.g., w/ = with, & = and).
9. Underline or asterisk information the lecturer stresses as important.
10. Write down information the lecturer writes on the board or transparency.
11. Draw a line if you miss an idea you want to include so you can fill it in later.
12. Spell a word the way it sounds or the way you think it looks if you cannot remember how to spell a word.
13. Review the previous sessions' notes immediately before the lecture.
14. Read the information before listening to the lecture, if the lecture is about an assigned reading topic.
15. Go over your notes as soon as possible after a lecture. Fill in the key concept column, and list any questions you still have.
16. Summarize the major points presented during the lecture after going over your notes.
17. Listen actively! Think about what you already know about the topic being presented and how it relates.
18. Review your notes before a test!

Note. From *Strategies for Teaching Students with Learning and Behavior Problems* (4th ed., p. 209), by C. S. Bos and S. Vaughn, 1998, Needham Heights, MA: Allyn & Bacon. Reprinted with permission.

9. Help students develop a simple monitoring procedure to examine the effectiveness of their notetaking in other classes, including

- Length of notes
- Format
- How well they think they have taken notes
- Test scores

Modifications and Considerations

Match the complexity of your lectures to current levels of notetaking and listening instruction by

1. Beginning with short, well-organized lectures

2. Using several visual aids

3. Basing lectures on simple, familiar material

4. Gradually increasing lecture length, difficulty, and novelty of material, and reducing number of visual aids

Table 3.2 provides an overview of the events of instruction involved in teaching good notetaking, and how they help students learn more.

Table 3.2. Notetaking and the Events of Instruction

Instructional Event	Lecturer Might Operationalize This Event in the Following Ways	Which Encourages Notetakers To Do the Following
1. Gaining attention	Physical movement (e.g., move to podium). Arrange lecture notes. Switch on overhead projector. Verbal interaction. "Good morning. Let's begin." Overview the lecture content.	Prepare to listen. Locate place to take notes.
2. Informing learner of objective	Suggest how the information will be useful.	State why the material should be noted. Retrieve critical information.
3. Stimulating recall of prerequisite learning	Review terminology. Summarize main points from previous lecture. Ask questions to determine if students recall key terminology, concepts, principles. Provide a few minutes for students to review notes from an earlier session.	Search for past associations. Review earlier notes.
4. Presenting the stimulus material	Speak at a comfortable pace. Organize the points of the lecture. Pause to allow for questions, clarification.	Alternate between your own words and lecturer's words.
5. Providing "learning guidance"	Use verbal cues such as "Note the following," "This is important to remember," "Record this in your notes." Use chalkboard, overhead transparencies to highlight major points. Raise questions to test comprehension of an idea. Provide an outline.	Discriminate between essential and nonessential information. Use mnemonics.
6. Eliciting performance	During lecture, provide sample questions/ problems similar to those that will be presented on an examination.	Practice performance by overtly or covertly responding to questions/ problems. Highlight notes, material relevant to responses.
7. Providing feedback about performance correctness	Request students to respond to other students' answers. Model responses to questions/responses.	Correct inaccuracies. Attend to essential information.
8. Assessing the performance	Encourage distributed and massed review of lecture content.	Rehearse notes in preparation for examination.
9. Enhancing retention and transfer	Present divergent examples, nonexamples, and problem situations during lectures. Explicitly link information from previous lecturer with current lecture.	Integrate new information into existing notes.

Note. "Notetaking Research: Implications for the Classroom," by C. A. Carrier, 1983, *Journal of Instructional Development, 6,* p. 25. Copyright 1983 by the Association for Educational Communications and Technology. Reprinted with permission.

To assist students to discriminate between good and poor sets of notes, develop a few models of each type. These sets could be evaluated by individuals, small groups, or the class.

Suritsky and Hughes (1991) noted several points that lecturers and listeners should consider in efforts to improve notetaking, some of which have been mentioned. Suggestions for lecturers: pause during lecture; ask questions during lecture; offer objectives before lecture; give cues (e.g., numbers) during lecture; emphasize important information; and encourage integration of material from different sources. Suggestions for listeners: paraphrase material; use abbreviations and symbols; use lecturer's cues; review notes, generally; and review with respect to criterion tests (e.g., multiple-choice exams).

Monitor

As with other techniques in this Study Skills chapter, it is important to measure the extent to which students learn the skill and how, by learning that skill, they are better able to acquire knowledge or information. For this technique, teachers could assess students' ability to take notes by judging the extent to which they wrote main ideas, organized the information, or incorporated other features of proper notetaking. A rating scale or checklist could be developed for this purpose. To determine whether students acquired more information from textbooks or lectures because of improved notetaking skills, arrange a test or two. Write questions for students to answer from the content to be given before and after the notetaking instruction. Pupils' scores on those tests could be charted as number or percentage correct.

References

Bos, C. S., & Vaughn, S. (1998). *Strategies for teaching students with learning and behavior problems.* (4th ed.). Needham Heights, MA: Allyn & Bacon.

Carrier, C. A. (1983). Notetaking research: Implications for the classroom. *Journal of Instructional Development, 6*(3), 19–25.

Suritsky, S. K., & Hughes, C. A. (1991). Benefits of notetaking: Implications for secondary and post-secondary students with learning disabilities. *Learning Disability Quarterly, 14,* 7–18.

NOTETAKING: A SIMPLE FORMAT

Background

Notetaking is a skill that becomes increasingly important as the emphasis shifts from skill building at the elementary school level to the acquisition of content information at the secondary level. The tactic explained here takes a unique approach to notetaking in that a structure is provided for writing notes and comments about them.

Who Can Benefit

The article that stimulated this tactic is a review of notetaking procedures for secondary-age students with learning disabilities (Saski, Swicegood, & Carter,

1988). This tactic should be considered, however, for students who are at risk, remedial, or average who have difficulty taking notes in content-area classes where lecture and textbook notes are required.

Procedures

1. Instruct students to divide a sheet of paper into three columns, or give them paper that has already been divided. The first and widest column should be labeled "Basic Ideas," the middle column "Background Information," and the last column "Questions." Provide a line at the top of the page for the topic (see Notetaking Format in Figure 3.6).

2. Instruct students to use the form as they take notes, and tell them what each space is for:

   • *Topic*—Identify the main idea (e.g., what started World War I; how seeds germinate; steps for administering cardiopulmonary resuscitation).

   • *Basic Ideas*—Write in the facts, figures, dates, names of people, and places. Include the material that will be needed to pass tests and write reports.

   • *Background Information*—Include information that is related to the basic ideas or is of interest to the student.

   • *Questions*—Include comments about information that is unclear and questions that should be asked.

3. Teach students to use the form by guiding them through several lectures. Tell them what to write in the various columns. You may need to write the notes for some students. This could be done on an overhead projector or on their papers.

4. Require students to identify relevant and irrelevant information from lectures or textbook activities.

5. Give students a topic sentence and have them complete notes from the textbook or lecture.

6. Move about the room and check on the students' ability to write notes. Assist those who have problems.

Modifications and Considerations

Following the steps noted here will not ensure independent notetaking. It is necessary to teach students several related skills—subordinating, listening, abbreviating, studying, and test-taking strategies—that they can rely on before and during the time they take notes. Learning to subordinate helps students organize notes. Learning to listen orients them to verbal clues from lectures (e.g., "The first reason . . ." or "The most important point . . ."). Learning to abbreviate helps students write more information. Learning appropriate study and test-taking strategies helps them prepare for tests and to do as well as possible when they take them.

NOTETAKING FORMAT

Topic _____

Basic Ideas	Background Information	Questions
(Include information necessary for tests, reports, etc.)	(Related or interesting information)	(Comments on points about which there should be more information or clarification)

Figure 3.6. Form setup for use in notetaking format.

Students could assist one another with notetaking. One way to promote their willingness to help others would be to have them compare notes and make suggestions for improving each others' notes. Most students should realize that by helping others take notes, they may benefit themselves. Knowing this could provide an opportunity for discussing why good citizenship involves working not only for oneself, but for others as well.

To increase motivation to take notes, announce occasionally that students will be allowed to refer to them during tests. That is, you will give "open-note quizzes."

Fister and Kemp (1995) described a four-fold format to promote better notetaking. For this, fold the paper in half vertically then fold it horizontally, leaving twice as much space in the lower part as in the upper. Students record their name, date, topic, and lesson objective in the upper left box. They record a personal statement related to the teacher's lecture in the upper right box. This statement answers the question. "What personal meaning does this information have for me in my life?" In the lower left box, students number and record the main ideas from the lecture. In the lower right box, they number and record supporting details (e.g., definitions, examples, clarifications) related to the main ideas.

Monitor

To monitor the effects of this technique, the suggestions in the previous tactic could be followed. In addition, pupils could write about what they had read for a few days before receiving instruction on notetaking, and for a few days after they had been offered instruction. Data, in terms of number of words written, concepts detailed, or other features from the two phases, could be graphed and compared.

References

Fister, S. L., & Kemp, K. (1995). *TGIF: But what will I do on Monday?* Longmont, CO: Sopris West.

Saski, J., Swicegood, P., & Carter, J. (1988). Notetaking formats for learning disabled adolescents. *Learning Disability Quarterly, 6*(3), 265–271.

ORGANIZING LECTURES: ADVANCE ORGANIZERS

Background

Students in the intermediate grades and at the secondary level are faced with a different set of problems from those encountered by children in the primary grades. The older students are required to use information processing skills, which they often lack or fail to activate, to deal with content subjects. One way to assist students who are at risk or remedial in meeting the demands of content teachers is to instruct them to listen for and use advance organizers.

Who Can Benefit

Several adolescents, either with or without learning disabilities, were the pupils in the original research (Lenz, Alley, & Schumaker, 1987). Junior and senior high school students in content-area classrooms and many in the intermediate grades could also benefit from the ability to apply advance organizers.

Procedures

1. Plan lessons in which advance organizers are presented verbally, in writing, or with a visual aid, or are elicited through questions throughout the lesson.

2. Introduce the following 12 advance organizer components to students, beginning with this introductory statement: "Advance organizers are a set of behaviors that precede the learning act and generally incorporate one or more of the following components."

   • Inform the learner of the purpose of the advance organizer.

   • Clarify the task's physical parameters in terms of actions to be taken by the teacher.

   • Clarify the task's physical parameters in terms of actions to be taken by the student.

   • Identify the topic of the learning task.

   • Identify subtopics related to the task.

   • Provide background information.

   • State the concepts to be learned.

   • Clarify the concepts to be learned.

   • Motivate students through rationales.

   • Introduce or repeat new words.

   • Provide an organizational framework for the learning task.

   • State the outcomes desired as a result of engaging in the learning activity.

3. Provide students with a worksheet on which the components of advance organizers are listed.

4. Demonstrate the types of information that might be written alongside the components (e.g., identify topic).

5. Instruct students to listen for and take notes on advance organizers presented in class.

6. Tell students that once they are able to consistently identify components of advance organizers, they should attend to those features as they listen to lectures, but they need not rely on the worksheets.

Modifications and Considerations

Critical to the effectiveness of this tactic is the teacher's own use of advance organizers and his or her ability to activate students to attend to them. Lenz et al. (1987) found that teacher behaviors alone were not enough; students must specifically be educated to attend to advance organizers and make use of them, if there are to be positive gains in their performance.

The purpose of this tactic is to teach students one of the all-important attributes for success in school and on the job: how to get information before starting a task. Armed with the ability to listen for and identify key information, students will be better prepared to complete assigned work in a variety of situations. Although it is important for students to be able to recognize and put into use the 12 steps that make up this advance organizer, the true measure is whether or not they acquire more information from lectures and are able to assimilate that knowledge because of learning about the organizers.

Hudson (1996) demonstrated that when learning sets (i.e., interactive review of the previous day's content, statements of lesson objectives and performance expectations, and a discussion of the lesson's importance) were involved, students' performances improved on social studies tests.

Monitor

As with other study skills, teachers may want to evaluate the extent to which students learn the study skill itself and determine the effects that learning may have on their ability to acquire information from lectures or textbooks. For the former, a teacher could develop a checklist on which some features of advance organizers were listed. With that list the teacher, or another, could periodically monitor the extent to which pupils relied on advance organizers.

References

Hudson, P. (1996). Using a learning set to increase the test performance of students with learning disabilities in social studies classes. *Learning Disabilities Research & Practice, 11*(2), 78–85.

Lenz, B. K., Alley, G. R., & Schumaker, J. B. (1987). Activating the inactive learner: Advance organizers in the secondary content classroom. *Learning Disability Quarterly, 10,* 53–67.

⏱ TAKING TESTS: RESPONDING TO VARIOUS QUESTION TYPES

Background

Most schools and many businesses rely heavily on testing to evaluate the potential and current performance levels of students and employees. Difficulty with the test-taking process can be a major stumbling block for some individuals. Specific hints for responding successfully to several types of objective tests are included in this tactic (Menard et al., 1984).

Who Can Benefit

Learning more effective ways to respond to various types of test questions would benefit anyone faced with a testing situation. Students who have been described as at risk and remedial could experience marked improvement in test scores, which might in turn result in improved self-concept and school success.

Procedures

Introduction

List and explain the major characteristics of the following types of test questions:

1. *Questions of Fact*—Generally short, requiring answers consisting of a few words.

   ▶ **Examples:** Who discovered Australia?
   Where did Marie Curie work?

2. *Sentence Completion*—A statement, usually written out, with blanks where important words have been omitted. Students are to provide the missing word(s) that best complete the statement.

   ▶ **Examples:** Lewis and _____ explored the Northwest.
   Molecules are made up of _____.

3. *True/False*—Written in statement form, these questions are often found on teacher-made, textbook, and achievement tests. The student determines whether the statement is completely correct.

   ▶ **Examples:** All soda pop is free of sugar.
   Some oceans contain salt water.

4. *Analogies*—Probably the most difficult; students are given three bits of information and expected to establish a relationship between two of them, and then identify a mate for the remaining item. The outcome should be that both sets resemble one another.

   ▶ **Examples:** Day is to night as light is to _____.
   Lead is to pencil as ink is to _____.

5. *Matching*—A popular form found on many tests. Pupils are to select items from one list that match items on a second list.

▶ **Examples:** 1. dog   a. VCR
         2. ice   b. canine
         3. TV   c. frozen water

Another common format is to write blanks to the left of the numbers in the first column, on which students write the letters of the correct answers from the second column.

6. *Multiple Choice*—Probably the most common test format. A statement is presented along with a number of words, phrases, or symbols from which to choose. The correct choice completes the statement or answers the question.

   ▶ **Example:** A noun is the name of a person, place, thing, or _____.
                ape   rock   idea   verb

7. *Essay*—Generally the most difficult to respond to (or grade). Pupils must come up with answers on their own, ordinarily without cues.

   ▶ **Example:** Explain photosynthesis.

Helpful Hints

Once students demonstrate an understanding of the differences among the most common types of tests, teachers should provide pupils with strategies to employ in each case.

Questions of Fact

1. Inform students that they must be able to perform these operations:

   - Identify the key word: *who, what, when, where, why,* or *how.*
   - Consider the type of word or phrase prompted by each of these terms.

     Who = a name
     What = something or an act
     When = a date or period of time
     Where = a location
     Why = defend some act or decision
     How = explain something

2. Provide questions that include all the asking words. Instruct students to mark their answers as follows:

   - Circle or check the key words.
   - Write answers to the questions.

Sentence Completion. Teach students to recognize and respond to the following cues:

1. Number of blanks = number of words in answer.

2. Look for a missing part of speech in the incomplete statement. (If there is no action word in the statement, then the missing word must be a verb.)

3. A conjunction before the blank indicates type of word to follow. (It should be the same type of word as the one before the conjunction.)

True/False

1. Remind students that they should read directions carefully and study sample items to find out how to mark the answers.

2. Explain that the words *all, every, none, more, exactly, always,* and *never* set absolute conditions. Since things are rarely absolute, statements with these words are often false.

3. Discuss the fact that qualifiers such as *some, sometimes, usually, occasionally, rarely,* or *frequently* are not as definitive as those in the first set, so questions containing these words are more likely to be true.

4. Suggest that the longer the statement, the greater the chance it will be false, since it would be rare for every part to be accurate.

Analogies. Prepare several sets of analogies to use as examples. Point out that a relationship exists between two words in each analogy. Assist students as they

1. Identify these relationships.

2. Study the third (unattached) word and determine how it corresponds with its match.

3. Identify a term to link with the third word.

Matching

1. Remind students to read directions carefully to discover if they are to identify the correct answer by placing a letter in a blank, drawing a line between the two related items, or doing something else.

2. Point out that sometimes there are more items in the second column than in the first; therefore, some items will have no match.

3. Suggest that it is best to match the easier parts first, then attempt to join the harder ones. Checking off items in the second column as they are used will help students avoid using an item more than once.

Students should practice on several tests of this type, mastering first the easy statements that are readily matched, and have the same number of items in each column, then moving on to more complex test questions with more items in the second column than in the first.

Multiple Choice

1. Instruct students to determine from the directions which approach to answering multiple-choice questions they should take:

   • Circle the appropriate choice.

   • Write the number of the correct choice beside the number of the corresponding statement.

2. Instruct pupils to watch for the following types of incorrect answers:

   • Words that sound or look a little like the correct word

   • Choices that may be reasonable but are not the best answer

   • Obviously absurd possibilities

Reading the statement and *all* choices before making a decision should help eliminate the obviously incorrect answers first, thus leaving less information to deal with.

3. Teach students to look carefully to see if the word *a* or *an* precedes the choice word. These words provide clues as to choosing an answer that begins with a vowel or a consonant.

Salend (1995) offered several additional suggestions for creating multiple-choice items: Make sure that the stems and the answer alternatives are grammatically correct. Make response choices shorter than item stems. Relate the stem to only one major point and provide students with only information necessary to answer the question. See that the answer alternatives contain only one correct answer. Present the choices within a vertical format.

Essay

1. Stress the importance of reading directions. On an essay question this is especially important, as there will be no other cues.

2. Instruct students to identify "determiners" (words that tell what to write, how to write it, what style to employ, and how much they should write):

   • *Describe*—Write about some setting, circumstance, or event they are familiar with so that others "get a feel" for the situation.

   • *Outline*—Write about familiar events in outline form (e.g., their three daily meals).

   • *Trace*—Write about, for example, the first 10 events of the day (begin with dressing, eating breakfast).

   • *Paraphrase*—Listen to or read something, then write about it in their own words, retaining the accuracy and order of the original.

   • *Interpret*—Read a statement and explain it in terms of message, moral, metaphor, or allegory.

3. Progress from simple messages and very short stories with obvious morals to more sophisticated passages.

4. Teach these general techniques for writing responses to essay questions:

   • Write an outline.
   • Restate the questions.
   • Respond to all queries.
   • Proofread.

Modifications and Considerations

In teaching about each type of test, example questions should proceed from extremely simple to gradually more complicated.

Allow students to make initial responses orally, followed by written answers. This will provide more opportunities for immediate feedback. Teachers could assist pupils to improve on essay tests if they gave a few as open-book and open-note tests. This approach reinforces students' efforts to read more thoroughly and take better notes.

A good follow-up to determine how well students actually understand the differences between the various types of questions they have studied would be to ask them to compose their own questions.

Monitor

The expected outcome from this tactic is that, having been taught a number of test-taking strategies, pupils will do better on actual testing. Thus, it is important for them to have this information and to be able to readily access it. One way to determine this ability would be to quiz the pupils on the important points for taking certain types of tests prior to testing. To obtain those data, a checklist could be developed.

References

Menard, C., Mickelson, G., Orumchian, J., Cassidy, R., Koehl, E., & McCaffrey, A. (1984). *Study strategies for secondary students: Goal setting, time management, test taking* (pp. 42–64). Kirkland, WA: Lake Washington School District No. 414.

Salend, S. J. (1995). Modifying tests for diverse learners. *Intervention in School and Clinic, 31*(2), 84–90.

TAKING TESTS: DEBRIEFING

Background

Students who are at risk, who seldom do well on tests, may find the test-taking process so unrewarding that the last thing they would want to do is to review the test, analyzing their mistakes and approaches for taking it. Whereas some successful students commonly review their performances on tests, thus learning from their mistakes or poor test-taking strategies, students who are at risk seldom profit from their errors, or learning opportunities. If youngsters who are remedial and at risk can be convinced that it is in their best interest to do well on tests, that it is up to them to improve their abilities, and that techniques are available for increasing their scores on tests (apart from knowing more about the content), they will begin to experience more success on tests, and perhaps more success in school.

Who Can Benefit

The approach explained here was designed for secondary-age youngsters with mild disabilities (Lovitt, 1983). These steps for debriefing students following a test should, however, be suitable for secondary-age youngsters of many types, including those identified as at risk or remedial.

Procedures

1. Develop a checklist of skills and behaviors students need in order to succeed in testing situations. The following are a number of items to consider:

    - Determine if students put their names and date on the test.

    - Point out students' scores on the test; tell them how many answers were correct and incorrect, and how many were left out.

    - Analyze students' performance by type of question (e.g., essay, true/false, multiple choice, matching).

    - Evaluate students' handwriting: Was it legible?

    - Determine whether students carefully read all the directions.

    - Ask them if they read the entire test, especially directions, before responding to any of the items.

    - Discover if, by reading all the items before responding, they found answers for a few items.

    - Ask if students paced themselves while working in order to respond to all the items.

    - Find out if they responded to the easy questions first.

    - Ask if they checked their work when finished.

    - Ask if they requested help during the test for items or directions they did not understand.

    - Ask if they know where the items on the test came from (i.e., lecture, text, video).

    - Ask them to describe how they studied for the test and how much time they devoted to this.

2. Determine what students should concentrate on for the next test by reviewing with them the points in the list they failed to observe.

3. Give students a copy of the checklist to use as they prepare for the next test.

4. Emphasize to students that if they pay attention in class, listen to lectures, read the textbook assignments, study their notes, and consider the steps proposed here for taking tests, they will do better on tests and make better grades.

5. Provide time during class for students to prepare for tests and to evaluate tests that are returned.

6. Conduct private interviews with students who require individual assistance on test taking, at which time general problems and concerns may also be brought up. Encourage students to comment on the points of this approach that are, for them, particularly difficult or helpful.

Modifications and Considerations

A more general test-taking strategy, SCORER, has been proposed by Carman and Adams (1972). Following are the six points of that approach:

S = Schedule your time for responding to all the test items.
C = Clue words, be certain to identify and react to them.
O = Omit difficult questions and do the easy ones first.
R = Read test items and directions carefully.
E = Estimate your answers to see if they are "in the ballpark."
R = Review your work after responding to as many items as possible.

Meltzer et al. (1995) offered several suggestions for teachers to help students prepare for tests: (a) Provide explicit study guides that describe exactly what students are expected to know for the test; (b) give examples of previous tests; (c) give students a mock test, demonstrating various levels of information they will need to answer the different types of questions; and (d) tell students how to prepare for each type of test question (e.g., true/false).

Monitor

Keep track of the students' scores on tests during the time when you work with them on the debriefing approach. After all, the point of this procedure is to raise test scores. As scores go up, point out the reasons for the increases to the students. Inform them that the improvement is not related to chance. If, however, their scores do not improve, determine why not, and make suitable adjustments. If the test scores are reported as percentages, a chart could be developed on which the scores were entered.

References

Carman, R. A., & Adams, W. R., Jr. (1972). *Study skills: A student's guide for survival.* New York: Wiley.

Lovitt, T. C. (1983). *Debriefing performance on tests.* Unpublished manuscript; University of Washington, Seattle.

Meltzer, L. J., Roditi, B. N., Haynes, D. P., Biddle, K. R., Paster, M., & Taber, S. E. (1995). *Strategies for success.* Austin, TX: PRO-ED.

 MEMORIZING INFORMATION: MNEMONICS

Background

The ability to learn multiple attributes is an important factor in the mastery of concepts. Research on the use of keywords and pegwords to teach associations between facts—such as vocabulary words and definitions, or mineral names and hardness levels—has shown mnemonic strategy instruction to be effective. The techniques described here would be helpful for remembering related facts in a variety of areas (e.g., geography—multiple features of states and countries; biology—multiple functions of organs and systems).

Scruggs, Mastropieri, Levin, and Gaffney (1985) examined four methods for teaching multiple attributes of a concept: direct instruction, mnemonic instruction, reduced-list direct instruction, and free study.

Who Can Benefit

Fifty-six junior high school students with learning disabilities participated in this study (Scruggs et al., 1985). Their improvements in learning and retention indicated that mnemonic procedures can be more effective for students than any of the other three instructional approaches arranged in their research.

Procedures

Basic Concepts

1. Develop an understanding of the basic terms and concepts of mnemonic instruction, notably *keywords* and *pegwords*.

   Keywords: Incorporate the "3 Rs" of associative mnemonic techniques: recoding, relating, and retrieving.

   Recoding—An unfamiliar term is transformed into a concrete, familiar word that sounds like a part of the new word to be learned and can be easily pictured.

   ▶ **Example:** new term—*viaduct*
   keyword—*duck*

   Relating—A keyword is linked to a desired response via an interactive picture.

   ▶ **Example:** *viaduct = bridge;*
   interactive picture: *duck* crossing *bridge.*

   Retrieving—Learner is led systematically from the stimulus to the response.

   ▶ **Example:** *viaduct* (stimulus) → duck
   (keyword) → duck crossing bridge
   (interactive picture) → *bridge* (correct response).

   Pegwords: Numbers 1 through 10 are recoded as familiar rhyming words (e.g., 1 = *bun,* 2 = *shoe,* 3 = *tree,* 4 = *floor,* etc.).

   The combination of keywords and pegwords results in a mnemonically interactive picture to be used by students to learn the attributes of a concept.

   ▶ **Example:**

   Concept: The mineral *wolframite* has a hardness level of 4 and is used for making lightbulbs.

   Keyword: *wolf*

   Pegword: *floor*

   Interactive picture: A wolf sitting on a floor in front of lights (see Figure 3.7).

Additional attributes can be represented by expanding the pictorial representations, adding color (if a relationship can be drawn), and establishing more acoustical links. Of the three, pictorial representations are usually the most effective.

2. Determine which concepts contain multiple attributes that students will need to learn. Identify those attributes and decide how to represent them mnemonically.

3. Prepare the following materials prior to instruction: A set of interactive illustrations drawn on 8½ × 11-inch paper. Each illustration should include some or all of the following, depending on the number and nature of the attributes to be mastered:

    a. The name of the fact to be learned and its keyword
    b. Numerical information and its pegword
    c. A color that would enhance association
    d. A representation of the use or importance of the fact

Instruction

1. Inform students that they are to learn information about a topic (in this example, minerals), and there will be a quiz over this information at the end of the period.

Figure 3.7. Mnemonic strategy for remembering wolframite. From "Facilitating the Acquisition of Science Facts in Learning Disabled Students," by T. E. Scruggs, M. A. Mastropieri, J. R. Levin, and J. S. Gaffney, 1985, *American Educational Research Journal, 22*(4), p. 580. Copyright 1985 by the American Educational Research Association. Reprinted with permission.

Memorizing Information: Mnemonics ♦ 109

2. Explain to them that they will be using a new technique that will help them remember what they are taught.

3. Teach students the rhyming pegwords for numbers 1 through 10 (if numbers are among the attributes to be learned).

4. Teach the keywords as follows:

   a. Show students a picture of the keyword and the new word to be learned.

   b. Say, "The keyword for (*word to be learned*) is (*word the picture represents*)."

   ▶ **Example:** "The keyword for *bauxite* is *box*."

5. Present the interactive illustrations for each concept to be learned and explain the relationships between the cues and facts as succinctly as possible. Be consistent in wording.

   ▶ **Example:** (Refer to the Figure 3.7 illustration for the mineral *wolframite*.)

   a. Say, "*Wolframite* is *4* on the hardness scale, *black* in color, and is used for making *light bulbs*."

   b. Explain that the word cue for *wolframite* is wolf, and 4 is *floor*.

   c. Point out that the wolf in the picture is *black*, because that is the color of the mineral *wolframite*, and that the *light bulbs* are a reminder of the mineral's use.

6. Discuss the retrieval process. Give examples of how students should use the mnemonic cues to respond to specific questions.

   ▶ **Example:** If asked, "What is the hardness level of wolframite?" students should:

   a. Think first of the keyword (*wolf*).

   b. Go back (mentally) to what is happening to the wolf in the picture.

   c. Find the pegword (*floor*) and answer "4."

   d. Use the same process to answer questions about color and use (or whatever attributes students are learning for a particular topic).

7. Teach the remaining concepts in a like manner, but omit the pegword instruction.

Modifications and Considerations

Direct instruction is often recommended for students who are remedial and at risk, but results of the Scruggs et al. (1985) study indicated that it was considerably less effective than the mnemonic strategy. Of all the methods attempted, free study was least effective, probably due to the poor organizational skills of most students with learning disabilities.

It may be necessary to involve students in the development of materials, because this can become a time-consuming and expensive aspect of this type of instruction. In most cases commercially produced illustrations tend to be more recognizable than student-drawn pictures, so it might be advisable to make photocopies of pictures from magazines and newspapers or to trace over illustrations in books. This could become a class project, or could be offered to individuals as an extra credit option. If artistically talented students are in the class, they could submit designs for the mnemonic picture clues.

Seaman (1996) described 10 memory tools: repeating, copying, taking little bites, grouping, using mini practices, learning something new (i.e., locating details about what you are trying to memorize), visualizing, remembering key words, using first letters, and counting (i.e., determining how many words there are in a list to remember).

Monitor

One approach for evaluating the effects of mnemonics would be to select several sets of words for which youth were to learn definitions, then alternate teaching them using the mnemonic technique and another approach; that is, use an alternate technique for the first set, the mnemonic approach for the second, and continue to rotate the techniques. Administer a test following practice or training on each set of words. Check each student's paper for the various sessions, chart those data, and compare scores across conditions.

References

Scruggs, T. E., Mastropieri, M. A., Levin, T. R., & Gaffney, J. S. (1985). Facilitating the acquisition of science facts in learning disabled students. *American Educational Research Journal, 22*(4), 575–586.

Seaman, J. (1996). *Teaching kids to learn: An integrated study skills curriculum for grades 5–7.* Longmont, CO: Sopris West.

⏱ SWIMMING THROUGH THE BABBLE

Background

The following two paraphrased messages, both reported by Turner (1998), set the purpose for this tactic. The first is attributed to H. L. Mencken:

> We take pride in the fact that we are thinking animals, and like to believe that our thoughts are free, but the truth is that nine-tenths of them are rigidly conditioned by the babbling that goes on around us from birth, and that the business of considering this babbling objectively, separating the truth in it from the false, is an intellectual feat of such stupendous difficulty few men are able to achieve it.

The second message was allegedly delivered by Harold Macmillan, a prime minister of England, who quoted one of his professors as he addressed a group of students beginning their studies at Oxford:

Gentlemen, you are about to embark upon a course of studies which will occupy you for two years. Together they form a noble adventure. But nothing that you will learn in your studies will be of the slightest possible use to you in years to come save only this: that if you work hard and intelligently you should be able to detect when a man is talking rot, and that, in my view, is the main, if not the sole, purpose of education.

Who Will Benefit

The ideas advanced here should be useful for everyone, but they will be especially valuable to naive or unsophisticated individuals who accept most of what they hear, read, and see at face value. These thoughts are from a speech by Lovitt (1998) to high school students.

Procedures

Get a handle on the type and quantity of drivel that bombards us. Some individuals like to offer advice, truths, and other proclamations. For example, a fellow student drops some of these jewels: "Did you know that you only need 14 credits to graduate, not the 16 that our counselor has been telling us?" "Anyone can get into Stanford if they have a 2.8 grade point average, and know the right people." "Most anyone can get a scholarship to Whitman College, even if their grade point average is fairly low." "If you are on the volleyball team, you will probably get a full scholarship to one of the state schools." "It doesn't make much sense to study French or any other language; you will never use them." And a gabby father drops a few pearls: "They can't arrest someone your age for sending threatening letters." "What's the point in educating individuals with mental retardation or learning disabilities? They will never contribute to society." "There is no danger of contracting AIDS if you stay with one partner." "Smoking cigarettes is not addictive; I can quit any time I want." "It doesn't really matter what you eat. Doctors are forever changing their minds on what's good and what's bad." Those are only a few choice bits spewed by a friend and a father. Think of all the other individuals who lambaste you with messages.

Other sources of gibberish include these:

- Television (satellite owners can receive over 100 channels)
- Newspapers (they all have advice and information columns)
- Books (some are fact, some fiction, and others are "faction")
- Movies (many purport to be factual but take great liberties with the truth)
- Internet (anyone can send anything they want over the waves)
- Radio (we are living in the day and age of talk or babble radio)

How can we strain the babble? How do we check it out? Fortunately, there are ways to begin separating gibberish from truth. Those ways, of course, depend upon the form or type of prattle that comes forth:

- Does the comment fit with your experience? If it is outlandish and bizarre, chances are the remark was false.

- Is the person or source credible?

- Has the piece of information been confirmed by someone else?

- Have you read or heard the opinion of an expert?

- Do you merely wish or will that the information coming to you is true?

Modifications and Considerations

One extremely important consideration of this tactic is that the quest to cut through the blather never ends. More and more of it comes our way, from more and more sources, at greater and greater speeds.

Although it is a good idea to challenge everything you read, hear, or even see, it is not advisable to be so skeptical of everything that you lose all faith in certain individuals or sources of information. Justified faith is okay.

The flip side to all this is that, just as we need to filter and screen the babble that comes to us, we need to cut down on the extent that we "babbilize." When asked an opinion on something you do not know much about, it is okay to simply say, "Beats me."

Monitor

It would be informative to keep a log of the babble that comes your way and to note where it came from. One could also categorize the drivel somehow, such as stuff that pertained to health, to school, to development, to economy. The amount will no doubt be amazing.

References

Lovitt, T. C. (1998, May 21). *Success or personal accomplishment.* Presentation to the Inglemoor High School Honor Society, Bothell, WA.

Turner, D. (1998, March 28). First, look beyond energetic ignorance to find quiet truth. *The Seattle Times,* p. A10.

UNDERSTANDING ASSIGNMENTS

Background

The motivation for this tactic comes from a class I taught recently at the University of Washington, Seattle. There were only 11 students in the class, but many of them did not understand some of the assignments. Admittedly, I gave the students several assignments throughout the quarter, a few of which were rather complex, but most of them were written out for the students and all of them were discussed in class, several of them more than once.

The major point of this tactic is that the teacher and the students should work together to increase the probability that more students will understand more of the assignments. The assumption is that if the assignments are better understood, pupils will be better able to carry them out and will get more out of the class.

Who Can Benefit

This tactic differs from most in this book in that it is designed for both the students and their teacher. Both parties are responsible for seeing that everyone understands the assignments.

Procedures

On Figure 3.8, the 10 assignments I gave the class are noted across the top. Following is a brief explanation of those tasks:

- *Weekly critique*–Students were to write a 250- to 500-word critique of the readings assigned for the week. Readings were from either the textbook (Lovitt, 1995) or articles I had given them.

- *Weekly readings*—Students were expected to discuss the assigned readings in class.

- *Weekly tactics*—Students were to submit a tactic on the week's theme (e.g., reading, mathematics, expressive writing).

- *Tactic format*—They were expected to write up the tactics in the approved format (i.e., background, who can benefit, procedures, how to monitor, modifications and considerations, reference).

- *Quarter project topic*—Students were asked to select a topic (e.g., classroom management, social skills training, phonemic awareness) and write up six tactics on that subject.

- *Quarter project format*—They were to include an introduction and conclusion with the write-ups of the six tactics.

- *Quarter presentation*—Students were asked to inform the class about their quarter project, and describe one or two tactics from either that set or from one of the weekly assignments they had submitted.

- *Select student tactics*—Students were encouraged to select a few tactics, during the final session, that other students had written or presented. They gave me a list of those to copy; I ran them off and returned them.

- *Reading timing*—Students wrote for 10 minutes, during the last class session, about what they learned about reading in this class.

- *Other timing*—Students wrote for 10 minutes about what they learned about another topic we discussed in class (e.g., expressive writing, spelling, mathematics).

Modifications and Considerations

Several things could be done to make assignments more understandable to more students:

UNDERSTANDING ASSIGNMENTS CHART

Pupils		Weekly Critique	Read-ings	Weekly Tactics	Tactic Format	Quarter Topic	Quarter Format	Quarter Presen-tation	Select Student Tactics	Read-ing Timing	Other Timing	Total
						Assignments						
Karen		+	+	+	+	+	+	+	+	−	−	8
Tresje		+	−	+	+	+	+	+	+	+	+	9
Stan		+	−	+	−	−	−	−	+	−	−	3
Brenda		−	−	−	−	−	−	−	−	−	−	0
Sonia		−	−	−	−	−	−	−	+	−	−	1
Greg		−	−	−	−	−	−	−	−	−	−	0
Greta		+	−	+	+	+	+	−	+	+	+	8
Chris		+	−	+	+	+	+	+	+	+	+	9
Jenifer		+	−	+	+	+	+	+	+	+	+	9
Jeane		+	−	+	−	−	−	−	−	−	−	2
Faye		−	−	−	+	−	−	−	+	−	−	2
		7	1	7	5	5	5	4	8	4	4	

Summary

- Range of scores: 0 (Brenda and Greg) to 9 (Tresje, Chris, and Jenifer)
- Mean = 5.1
- Class overall average = 46% (51 ÷ 110)

Figure 5.8. Sample Understanding Assignments Chart.

- Limit the number of assignments, especially for some pupils.
- Go over the assignments more often. Give them both orally and in writing.
- Be more specific with instructions to carry out the assignments.
- Request students to ask questions and make comments about the assignments.
- Request students to repeat the instructions to the teacher, orally or in writing.
- Ask students to explain the instructions to classmates who arrive late or missed a session or two.
- Offer quick and concise feedback to students as to whether they understood or complied with the instructions.
- Set up extra sessions for students who do not understand assignments.
- Encourage students to e-mail you with queries and comments about the assignments.

Monitor

At the end of the quarter, I marked either a + or a − for each of the 10 assignments for each of the 11 students. As indicated in the figure, the class did quite poorly. Only three students were given a 9, two students had a 0, and one student had only a 1. The average for the class was 5.1.

Reference

Lovitt, T. C. (1995). *Tactics for teaching.* Upper Saddle River, NJ: Merrill/Prentice-Hall.

Lovitt, T. C. (1998, Winter quarter). *Techniques for instructing basic skills to elementary age students.* (Graduate class). University of Washington, Seattle.

PROBLEM–SOLUTION–EFFECT ANALYSIS, TIMELINE, AND VOCABULARY INSTRUCTION

Background

The idea promoted here is that, to assist some youth to learn important details and concepts in subjects such as history or biology, a number of related techniques must be used.

Who Can Benefit

Kinder and Bursuck (1993) carried out research with students with learning disabilities in a middle school. A composite technique such as this would probably assist many other youth, including those not characterized as learning disabled, at risk, or remedial.

Procedures

The following are the components of the intervention and brief descriptions of each:

- *Problem–solution–effect training*—Initially model and later require students to read problem–solution–effect passages and answer four questions: What was the problem? Why was it a problem? What was the solution? What was the effect of the solution?

- *Vocabulary instruction*—Ask students to skim a section they had previously read and record the boldfaced words in a notebook. Next, require them to read the paragraphs in which the words appeared, look up the words if necessary in a dictionary, and write out definitions for each using their own words.

- *Timelines*—Request youth to skim a previously read section until they find the first date, record it and proceed to other listed dates in the section and record them as well in a vertical list. Ask students to write a corresponding incident or person's name beside each date on the vertical timeline.

- *Reciprocal teaching*—Give students instruction in the four components of this process: asking questions, summarizing, clarifying, and predicting.

Organize small groups of youth and encourage them to take turns as teachers and to carry out the four components.

Modifications and Considerations

Kinder and Bursuck (1993) indicated that students generally did not like the problem–solution–effect analysis aspect of the intervention as well as they did the other components. According to the researchers, most of the youth were less adept with this treatment component than with the others, and believed that if they had received more assistance with it they would have viewed it more highly.

Another point to consider with this intervention, which also pertains to the instruction of other learning strategies, is that teachers should assist youth to generalize the approach to types of lessons and subject areas different from the one in which it was initially taught. Although not an easy chore, teachers should point out the types of situations to which the new strategy would lend itself and ones to which it would not apply. Teachers then should set up opportunities for the strategy to be transferred, instruct youth to self-manage the instructional components, and arrange rewards for carrying out the strategic notions in different circumstances.

How to Monitor

Kinder and Bursuck (1993) developed a test that contained four types of questions: timeline, short answer, definitions, and multiple choice. They administered this test before and after instruction and compared students' gain scores. Whether the test contains short answer or multiple-choice items, it is a good idea to test the types of learning that were stressed, in this case learning vocabulary, developing timelines, and analyzing problem–solution–effect.

Reference

Kinder, D., & Bursuck, W. (1993). History strategy instruction: Problem–solution–effect analysis, timeline, and vocabulary instruction. *Exceptional Children, 59*(4), 324–335.

Chapter 4
BASIC SKILLS

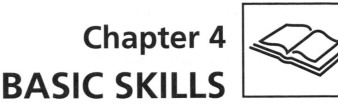

◆ ◆ ◆ ◆ ◆ ◆ ◆ ◆ ◆ ◆ ◆ ◆ ◆ ◆ ◆ ◆ ◆ ◆ ◆ ◆

As I mentioned in the preceding chapter, although study skills and basic skills are interrelated, there is a significant difference. The tactics in this chapter are intended to teach a fundamental, or basic, skill: reading, writing, spelling, or mathematics. The tactics—actually strategies—in Chapter 3, Study Skills, are designed to assist youth to make the most of their basic skills, and in the process gain from instruction in various content areas (e.g., biology, history, geography).

With respect to many youth with learning disabilities and others said to be at risk or remedial, there has been a perennial debate about the focus of their instruction. Some educators argue that they should be given an adjusted curriculum, one that is about the same as the one offered other students but somehow easier. Other experts recommend that, because the basic skills abilities of these youth are lacking, they should receive large doses of study skills. A third set of educators maintains that it is never too late to learn, and that time should be spent teaching the basic skills.

In my view, this is a fruitless argument, like so many others in education. We should, instead, strike some balance between adjusting the difficulty of the offerings and providing study skills and basic skills instruction. As for the latter, I am convinced that if certain youth were given sound and consistent basic skills instruction, they would improve and be more motivated to stay in school.

In this chapter I offer nine tactics. Three of them deal with reading, two with math, three with expressive writing, and one with spelling.

READING: A GENERAL ASSESSMENT

Background

There are three reading tactics in this chapter. The first one details ways to assess how well youth can read and do many of the things necessary to read, the second tactic promotes the extent that youth read, and the third tactic deals with comprehending or understanding material that has been read. For this set of tactics, I have taken the position that, whereas it may be difficult to teach some older students to read to the extent that reading will benefit them, it is never too late for them to learn. In my view, there is no point in giving up on reading instruction after the fourth or fifth grade, as is now often the case.

Who Can Benefit

The students to benefit from this tactic will be those who have struggled with reading and have perhaps given up on learning to read or whose teachers have given up on them. More specifically, this tactic and the two that follow would serve those youth who can read at about the second- or third-grade level. They probably know the names of letters and the most common sounds of those letters. Chances are they know about consonants and vowels and that they take on various sounds depending upon their place in words. When pressed, I imagine they will reluctantly agree that reading is important, if not critical to their futures, but they probably dread being asked to read. Also, they likely know that others read better than they do.

Procedures

Before administering this reading assessment and prior to engaging the other two reading tactics, the first thing to do with youth of the type I have identified is to convince them that they can become better readers. It is important during this pep talk to tell them that you, the instructor, can give them solid and simple ideas and suggestions for improving their reading. In addition, you must level with them, informing them that they must work with these ideas; there is no magic bullet. They must put in time and effort in order to improve.

Following are some reading components that you should assess:

1. *Phonemic awareness*—Although you might assume that youth know the names and sounds of letters and know about rhyming, blending, and segmenting, it would be a good idea to do a modest assessment of those skills to make sure. This could be done by developing practice sheets on which a number of the elements (e.g., letters) are printed and asking the youth to respond (i.e., name) to them for 1 minute, then tallying and charting the number of correct and incorrect responses. For more information on how to do this, see *Basic Skill Builders Handbook* (Beck, Conrad, & Anderson, 1995).

2. *Phonics instruction*—For phonics assessment, you might develop practice sheets that focus on common phonics elements and administer them in the way described earlier. Following are a few of those common elements: CVC words (e.g., *rat, pet, win*), consonant blends and digraphs (e.g., *st, pr, bl*), CVCe words (e.g., *cope, cute, bide*), and vowel digraphs (e.g., *heal, meek, moan*). Although students with reading difficulty probably have been through several phonics lessons from kindergarten on, it is possible that they have only a smattering of knowledge about these important "word attack" skills and probably have confused certain rules, principles, and so forth.

3. *Structural analysis*—For structural analysis assessments, you could develop practice sheets that feature common elements of structure. The sheets could be administered and evaluated just like the ones described for the preceding two sections. Following are a few important structural elements: *er, ing, ed, un, est, be, re, de con, ment, ful, dis, less, pro,* and *ly.*

4. *Regular words*—To assess reading of regular words, you could pull out words from materials of the level at which the youth can read rather comfortably and develop practice sheets. Some words from a popular second-grade book are these: *time, last, spent, went, had,* and *run.*

5. *Irregular words*—Similarly, you might develop practice sheets to assess the student's ability to pronounce irregular words at their instructional level. Some of those from a second-grade reader are these: *fort, though, one, off,* and *circle.*

6. *Vocabulary instruction*—To assess vocabulary knowledge, you might take words from books or other materials a student is able to read and ask him or her to define them. From a second-grade reader, these words might be presented: *pioneer, hazard, possession, independent,* and *slavery.*

7. *Oral reading*—To assess oral reading, you might use material from an informal reading inventory, one in which samples have been taken from books of various levels. Or, you could ask the youth to read a few passages from other materials that are at or slightly above his or her reading level (e.g., school magazines, sections from a sports page). Ask the youth to read orally for 1 minute from those sources and note the words that were aided or mispronounced. Following the reading, tally and chart the number of words read correctly and incorrectly.

8. *Comprehension*—Following a few of the passages the youth read orally, you might (a) ask him or her to tell as much as possible about the passage or (b) ask a few questions about the material. As for data, you could count the number of facts given or the number of correct and incorrect answers.

Modifications and Considerations

This tactic could be varied in a number of ways. For example, although the components mentioned here are perhaps the most basic, there are others that could be assessed. Also, whereas I recommended a precision teaching type format for the assessments, others could be used. Likewise, although I suggested that rate data be kept and charted to indicate the pupil's ability on the various assessments, other means could be chosen.

Obviously, when gaps, deficits, or problems are detected by these assessments, you should design and carry out ways to deal with them.

Monitor

All the assessments described here could be considered a pretest. Based on the data from these assessments, you should instruct the student(s) as needed. Then, after a period of time, readminister the assessments, especially those that pertain to components that were taught.

Reference

Beck, R., Conrad, D., & Anderson, P. (1995). *Basic skill builders handbook.* Longmont, CO: Sopris West.

READING: DO A LOT OF IT

Background

The notion advanced in this tactic is that individuals must read a great deal if they are to learn to read and get anything out of what they read. They must practice. According to Anderson, Wilson, and Field (1986), the top fifth graders in their research each read over 4.5 million words per year. That includes all kinds of reading. If a person read only books of the type fifth graders commonly read (averaging 14,500 words per book), one would have to read 310 books a year, almost one book a day!

Who Can Benefit

Like the preceding tactic, this one is also designed for youth who have certain fundamental reading skills, but are not proficient and have been exposed to numerous remedial sessions. The ideas advanced here would be suitable for students in intermediate or secondary grades, and for many adults, especially those considering postsecondary education.

Procedures

The following suggestions are intended to help and encourage youth to read more and to get more out of what they read.

Interview Them

- Find out what in life interests the youth. What do they like to do, to watch, to see, and so on? How do they spend their time? That information will be useful in arranging materials and topics for them to read.

- Ask the youth about their reading habits: what they read and how much. Initially, ask for this information in an open-ended way, then probe more specifically. Many youth of the type we are concerned with have no reading habits.

- Learn about their attitudes toward reading. It is important to know how they feel about reading. Regrettably, some youth believe that reading is something they should be able to do only in emergencies.

Evaluate Them

- Take a few oral reading samples. Ask students to read orally from a few passages, which could be familiar to them. As suggested in the preceding tactic, keep rate data on words read correctly and incorrectly.

- Ask them about what they read. Following their reading of the passages, ask them to tell you about what they read. Ask if they have read about that topic before. Determine whether they can incorporate newly read material with passages read previously.

- Ask about possible reasons to read. Ask students to name a few things they might gain from reading. Why do they think others, those who already read well, would want to read even more? What do they get out of reading? Are they aware that some individuals have personal libraries? Why would they do this?

- Ask about their sources for reading. Do they read books, magazines, pamphlets, signs, menus, bus schedules, instructional manuals? What sources do they know about, even if they do not use them?

Suggestions for Them

- Focus on a few topics. Assist students to identify a few topics that are of great interest to them. Point out that, if they continue reading on those themes, they will expand their knowledge of the topic and probably become even more interested in it.

- Branch out into other sources. If they read only books, encourage them to read magazines, topics on the Internet, and other materials, especially ones that focus on their interests.

- Carry reading material with them at all times. Taking along something to read is especially important if there is a chance they will have to wait for something or someone (e.g., doctor's office, airport).

- Talk to others about what you read. Most folks are motivated to read if they know others are reading the same thing. They enjoy chatting with others about a common book or article. Help students locate and set up these situations.

- Talk to yourself about what you read. Tell students to review mentally the stories they have read or current readings. Encourage them to find a piece of writing that is so interesting that they cannot wait to read more.

- Find a special place and time to read. Many people have special places to read, whether it is in a comfortable chair at home with a cup of tea, in bed, or someplace else.

- Write notes about what you read. Keep a notebook and write down confusing sentences or unknown words. Write about the most interesting parts.

- Find persons to help them. Suggest that the students consider who can help them to interpret something, explain something else, define a word, or help locate a book. Help them line up some possible helpers.

Modifications and Considerations

Someone will need to work regularly with students of the type featured here. Constant encouragement is especially important at the beginning of their effort to read more.

Monitor

Have students keep a log of what they read, how many pages they read, and how much time they spend reading. Periodically, I have recorded what and how much

I read. Over one 17-week period, I read 11 books, mainly contemporary novels. On average, there were 350 words per page and I read a total of 3,268 pages. That would total 1,143,800 words, or 9,611 words per day. If I kept that up for a year, that would come to about 3,508,000 words per year. If I included the number of words I read from newspapers, magazines, the Internet, and other sources, I imagine I would read about as much as a competent fifth grader.

Reference

Anderson, R. C., Wilson, P. T., & Fielding, L. G. (1986). *Growth in reading and how children spend their time outside of school* (Tech. Rep. No. 389). Champaign: University of Illinois at Urbana-Champaign.

READING: COMPREHENDING AND REMEMBERING

Background

Remedial readers at the secondary level are often caught in a cycle of failure: being assigned to a special reading program that does not work, being assigned to another program that does not work, and so on. Instead of considering reading as something they can do, they view it as something to be avoided.

Who Can Benefit

This tactic, like the previous two, is aimed to help readers who have negative experiences with reading generally, and who view reading as a process of getting the words right rather than an act of making sense of the material. The suggestions in this tactic are intended to assist youth to better comprehend the material they read.

Procedures

The following seven approaches for improving comprehension have been backed by considerable data.

1. *Story Grammars*—Narrative stories often follow a pattern, such as the following: setting, beginning, reaction, attempt, outcome, and ending. Inform students about that organization, and encourage them to look for it as they read and try to remember the flow of narrative stories. (For a detailed description of this procedure and the others noted here, see Lovitt, 1995; Pressley, Johnson, Symons, McGoldrick, & Kurita, 1989.)

2. *Text Structures*—Expository passages often follow certain patterns: cause and effect, temporal sequence, problem and solution, description, and enumeration. As with the story grammars, inform students that

many expository passages adhere to one or more of those structures, and encourage them to look for the structures as they read that type of material.

3. *Semantic Webs*—Webbing is a process of organizing and constructing a visual display of information categories, showing the contents of each category as well as how each is related to other categories. Webbing is an effective way to present materials and concepts, and to help students understand what they have read.

4. *Free Description*—For this method students retell what they have read. This procedure is especially worthwhile in that students are not given prompts from which to indicate their comprehension. With this method their comprehension is passage dependent. Another advantage of using this approach is that youth may gain with respect to language development.

5. *Asking Questions*—Students ask questions about what they have read. Like the previous technique, the students' comprehension is passage dependent. This technique encourages pupils to be active in assessing and developing their comprehension skills.

6. *Paragraph Restatements*—For this technique the pupils read a paragraph, then restate it; read another paragraph, then restate it; and so forth. After several paragraphs have been read, they summarize the whole passage. This method is especially useful with narrative passages.

7. *Mental Imagery*—In this method students conjure up a "picture" to represent the passage or story that was read. Mental imagery has a definite relationship to cognition and language, and the ability to use imagery in an effort to comprehend written discourse is central to differentiating good from poor readers.

Modifications and Considerations

The following are three general notions to keep in mind in efforts to increase students' comprehension:

1. Focus on a few topics. Assist students to identify two or three topics about which they are very interested and want to learn more. Encourage them to read in those areas and to begin compiling more pieces of information about them. Convince them to become "experts" in those chosen fields.

2. Read and recall short pieces. Daily, or at least often, encourage students to read a dozen or so summaries of articles in newspapers. Ask them to recall as much about as many of them as they can.

3. Incorporate reading study skills. Encourage students to rely on some of the tactics dealing with reading that are outlined in Chapter 3, Study Skills, such as the Multipass approach, the visual imagery method, and the mnemonics technique.

Monitor

The following are three methods to assess students' reading comprehension, all of which can be set up as pretest and posttest: pupils say facts about what was read; they respond to questions prepared by the teacher; and they supply missing words in a cloze method.

References

Lovitt, T. C. (1995). *Tactics for teaching* (2nd ed.), Upper Saddle River, NJ: Merrill/Prentice-Hall.

Pressley, M., Johnson, C. J., Symons, S., McGoldrick, J. A., & Kurita, J. A. (1989). Strategies that improve children's memory and comprehension of text. *The Elementary School Journal, 90*(1), 3–32.

MATH: FOR HEAVEN'S SAKE, LEARN TO ADD!

Background

Fundamental to all math is the ability to add, subtract, multiply, and divide. Before individuals can manage a checkbook, plan a budget, understand interest (compound or otherwise), or estimate how much a sack of groceries will cost (before getting to the checkout line), they must have a handle on the basic computations.

This tactic differs from most others in the book in that it identifies a set of suggestions and resources. I believe that, if all or many of the ideas endorsed here were acted on, the abilities of many youth to deal with mathematics, especially the functional type, would be greatly aided.

Who Can Benefit

The students for whom this tactic, and the other two in this set, are directed can add and subtract fairly well but are less able to multiply and divide. Furthermore, we assume that they are not reliable with their calculations in any of the processes and are not at all fluent. This tactic is intended to help those youth compute in the four processes.

Procedures

1. Carry out a thorough assessment to determine how well the students compute various problems in the four processes. Include problems of several types. See suggestions in the math section of *Teaching Students with Learning Problems* (Mercer & Mercer, 1998) for ideas on developing and administering an informal math assessment.

2. Develop practice sheets based on the assessment that focus on the students' difficulties. For information on constructing and administering practice sheets, see *Basic Skill Builders* (Beck, Conrad, & Anderson, 1995). See the mathematics section in *Tactics for Teaching* (Lovitt, 1995) for information on aims and standards.

3. Arrange techniques for developing computation abilities. See, for example, the mathematics section in *Tactics for Teaching* (Lovitt, 1995) and the suggested techniques in *Designing Effective Mathematics Instruction: A Direct Instruction Approach* (Stein, Silbert, & Carnine, 1997).

4. Encourage students to use calculators as early as possible. See support for their use and suggestions for using them in Mercer and Mercer (1998).

5. Assist students to estimate. For suggestions on teaching students to form approximate answers and to check the reasonableness of calculations, see *Effective Instruction for Students with Learning Difficulties* (Cegelka & Berdine, 1995).

Modifications and Considerations

Practice with Numbers

When waiting for someone, rehearse the "count-bys" (e.g., the 2s, 5s, 10s). When you see a street address (e.g., 14323 118th Ave.), add the numbers, regroup them, and memorize the important numbers.

Practice Estimating

When walking to the bus stop, driving to the mall, eating dinner, or doing something else, estimate how long it will take to do it. Practice estimating weights and distances as well.

Practice with a Calculator

Just for fun, make up problems and calculate the answers. Experiment with all the computer's capabilities.

Monitor

From time to time assign pupils practice sheets that represent the problem types being taught. Calculate their correct and incorrect rates, chart them, and relate them to a standard and to their previous scores.

References

Beck, R., Conrad, D., & Anderson, P. (1995). *Basic skill builders: Helping students become fluent in basic skills.* Longmont, CO: Sopris West.

Cegelka, P. T., & Berdine, W. H. (1995). *Effective instruction for students with learning difficulties.* Boston, MA: Allyn & Bacon.

Lovitt, T. C. (1995). *Tactics for teaching.* Upper Saddle River, NJ: Merrill/Prentice-Hall.

Mercer, C. D., & Mercer, A. R. (1998). *Teaching students with learning problems* (5th ed.). Upper Saddle River, NJ: Merrill/Prentice-Hall.

Stein, M., Silbert, J., & Carnine, D. (1997). *Designing effective mathematics instruction: A direct instruction approach* (3rd ed.). Upper Saddle River, NJ: Merrill/Prentice-Hall.

MATH: WHEN TO USE IT

Background

After students can add, subtract, multiply, and divide with some dependability and fluency, it is time they learn how to use those skills. It is important to be able to do ordinary, day-to-day math problems.

Who Can Benefit

This tactic should be useful for all students, but especially for those who are remedial and at risk.

Procedures

1. Review with students how they use math in their daily lives. This could be considered a crash course or a review of *math awareness*. Many students who are remedial or at risk are unaware of the dozens of times they are confronted by math daily. At first, you might simply ask them to note the places they see numbers (e.g., on street signs, pages of books, calendars, statistics in newspapers). Next, have the students present their observations to the class. Then, based on the observations and discussions, students could develop problems and solve them.

2. Ask the youth to solve *story problems* from real-world situations that have redundant information. For these, they will have to read (or listen to) the problems carefully, identify and eliminate the unnecessary information, decide what process(es) to use to solve the problems, and then solve them. Following is a relatively simple example: If you have $2.50 and spend $1.25 and someone gives you 10 sheets of paper and takes one of them away, how much money do you now have?

3. Ask students to keep track of events or circumstances that have to do with time, distance, and weight. Request them to share their observations with the class. Then compose problems based on the observations and solve them.

4. Request students to keep track of examples in their lives having to do with money and making change. As with the other assignments, encourage them to describe these instances to the class, design problems based on them, and solve them.

5. Provide students with aids for solving story problems that appear in textbooks or come from actual situations. The following example of one such strategy was developed by Montague and Bos (1986):

   • *Read* the problem aloud. The student asks you to pronounce or define unknown words.

   • *Paraphrase* the problem aloud. State important information, giving close attention to the numbers in the problem. To provide focus on the outcome of the problem, self-questions should be posed (e.g., "What is asked?" or "What am I looking for?").

- *Visualize.* Graphically display the information. Draw a representation or picture of the problem.

- *State* the problem. This includes completing statements such as "I have . . ." or "I want to find . . ." Underline important information in the problem.

- *Hypothesize.* Complete statements such as "If I . . . then . . . ." "How many steps will I need to use to find the answer?" Write the operation signs, such as addition and subtraction signs.

- *Estimate.* "My answer should be around. . . ." The skills of rounding and estimating are practiced in this step.

- *Calculate.* Show the calculation and answer. Self-check features such as the current form of the answer, the correct place for decimal points, and the correct place for percent or dollar signs.

- *Self-check.* Refer to the problem and check every step to determine accuracy of operation selected and correctness of response and solution. Check computations. Use a self-questioning technique.

Modifications and Considerations

Another strategy for solving word problems is RIDGES (Snyder, 1987):

Read the problem for understanding. The student should be aware that rereading may be necessary to grasp the details of the problem.

I know statement. Student lists all the information in the problem.

Draw a picture. The student should include all the information from Step 2 in a drawing, but it need not be elaborate. This step is particularly beneficial for students who have difficulty relating to abstract meaning.

Goal statement declared in writing. The student writes, "I want to know _____." This statement may give the student a clue for the next step.

Equation development. The student writes an equation that allows him or her to solve the problem.

Solve the equation. The student "plugs in" the necessary information to reach the goal and solve the problem.

Interesting and important math activities can be developed from the business or other sections of most newspapers. The front page of the Business Day section of the *New York Times* on May 26, 1998, showed several tables that could form the basis of a useful session; one had to do with the occupancy of hotel rooms and the other about Coca-Cola consumption throughout the world.

Monitor

You may want to evaluate students' abilities to learn the strategy taught and determine the effects of learning it on their ability to solve word problems.

For the former, occasionally ask students to recite the steps of the strategy and explain what they mean. For the latter, set up a two-phase experiment. During Phase 1 assign word problems prior to instructing the strategy, and during Phase 2 teach the technique. You can compare data from the two phases.

References

Montague, M., & Bos, C. S. (1986). The effect of cognitive strategy training on verbal math problem solving performance of learning disabled adolescents. *Journal of Learning Disabilities, 19*(1), 26–33.

The New York Times, (1998, May 26) Business Day section, p. 1.

Snyder, K. (1987). RIDGES: A problem-solving math strategy. *Academic Therapy, 23,* 261–263.

WRITING: WHEN AND WHY FOLKS DO IT

Background

According to information in *The Bottom Line: Basic Skills in the Workplace* (U.S. Department of Education & U.S. Department of Labor, 1988), a large metropolitan bank discovered that a major reason for low productivity among the secretarial and clerical staff was that 70% of dictated correspondence had to be redone at least once because of spelling and grammatical errors.

When potential employers were asked which writing skills they believed to be the most important for employees (Algozzine, O'Shea, Stoddard, & Crews, 1988), the following were noted in order of their importance: writing accurate messages, writing requests, noting assignments, completing forms, writing formal letters, completing checks and stubs, and completing money orders. In another survey of employers to identify their writing demands, Emerson and Jenkins (1988) came up with four types of writing: filling out applications, writing incident reports, writing daily and weekly logs, and taking employment tests.

Who Can Benefit

The primary beneficiaries of tactics that promote functional writing skills are individuals who expect to survive in the world after school. The secondary recipients are employers who despair over the lack of functional skills shown by those applying for jobs. To indicate the seriousness of this matter, the New York Telephone Company, as reported in the *Bottom Line* publication, claimed that only 16% of applicants passed the examinations for jobs ranging from telephone operator to service representative.

Procedures

A fundamental idea behind the suggestions in this tactic is that learning to write is not unlike learning to read, playing the piano, or shooting free throws: there is a right and a wrong way to do it, individuals must be told which is which, and they must practice doing it correctly. Included here are suggestions for becoming more proficient in the first four types of writing noted in the Algozzine et al. (1988) survey.

Writing Accurate Messages

One activity to promote this skill would be to practice giving messages over the phone and taking messages for someone else. Another activity to advance accurate message writing would be to give students one or more of the following assignments (all of which should deal with real activities and actual circumstances):

- Write to someone about what you did today.
- Write to your teacher about your plans for the week.
- Write to a restaurant or another place that you attended recently and tell whether you were satisfied with its services.

Writing Requests

To practice writing requests, students could write to

- Businesses requesting information about certain products
- Teachers asking about future assignments
- Mail-order houses requesting catalogs
- Potential employers seeking outlines of their hiring process
- Vocational or higher education institutions asking for course outlines and schedules
- Branches of the military requesting information on types of training schools

Noting Assignments

Students could be shown a number of ways to keep track of assignments:

- Write them in three-ring notebooks that have considerable information about several classes
- Write them in a special notepad that is just for assignments
- Write them in a sort of diary that contains various information, including that about assignments
- Write them in a special folder on the computer

Once those ways and others have been introduced, the students could be asked to select one or some combination that they would use consistently for keeping track of assignments.

Completing Forms

Select application forms that are representative of others, run off multiple copies, and require pupils to fill one out. Provide help on completing items that are difficult for certain pupils. Once students can fill in items accurately on that form, give them a different form. Although certain of their learnings would transfer to that second form, others might not. Point out the differences in the forms. Students should work with the second form until they can fill it in accurately in a reasonable time, and then be given a third, and so forth. They should then be able to generalize more and more information across types.

Modifications and Considerations

In 1998 I heard about another type of writing that may come into play in the world of work. This information came over National Public Radio, probably from the "All Things Considered" program. At any rate, a businessman described an approach to interviewing job applicants that was quite unique. He said that he told interviewees, following their interview, to write a summary of the meeting. The man said he pointed to a room in which there was a computer, a typewriter, a pad, and a pen, and asked the applicant to go in and write about the interview for 30 minutes or so. This employer was interested in not only how well the person could write but how accurately he or she could summarize the interview. If the interviewer and employer was not pleased with the written summary, he crumpled it up, threw it away, and asked his secretary to call the person and say that the application process was over.

Monitor

To monitor students' message writing improvement, give students several messages to write over a period of days. Acquire data on the number that were accurately written and the number that were indecipherable. For writing requests, give students a specific assignment and a definite time to carry it out. For noting assignments, give students three or four brief assignments to write down. For filling out forms, ask them to fill out one they have never seen. All four assessments could be administered prior to and following instruction. Difference data from one administration to the other would reveal the effects of any treatment.

References

Algozzine, B., O'Shea, D. J., Stoddard, K., & Crews, W. B. (1988). Reading and writing competencies of adolescents with learning disabilities. *Journal of Learning Disabilities, 21,* 154–160.

Emerson, J. C., & Jenkins, J. R. (1988). *Deriving job skills from the workplace: Employer survey results.* Unpublished manuscript, Experimental Education Unit, University of Washington.

National Public Radio. (1998, May 26). Program on interviewing candidates for positions.

U.S. Department of Education and U.S. Department of Labor. (1988). *The bottom line: Basic skills in the workplace.* Washington, DC: Authors.

WRITING: A STRATEGY TO IMPROVE COMPREHENSION OF EXPOSITORY STRUCTURE

Background

The purpose of this research is to provide a rationale for the reading and writing connection. From a review of research, McLaughlin (1987) drew five conclusions: (1) paragraphs with explicit main ideas aid comprehension; (2) main ideas located at the beginnings of paragraphs promote understanding; (3) sensitivity to text structure can be taught; (4) the more opportunities children have to structure their own thoughts and writing, the better prepared they will be to interpret the structures of others; and (5) varied writing experiences will lead to a heightened awareness of the author's message and the framework used to convey it.

Who Can Benefit

This tactic would be appropriate for students as young as second graders. It is a particularly important technique for students in Grades 4, 5, and 6 as they begin reading expository narration. It would be helpful for older students as well.

Procedures

Three steps are involved in the technique: preparation and completion of an interview grid, preparation of an outline, and creation of paragraphs.

Interview Grid

Students begin by determining a topic (e.g., pets, holiday traditions, forts). They are then instructed to create three questions relevant to the topic and to list them in the left-hand column (see Figure 4.1). Students next look for answers to the questions. Initially, interviews should be about familiar topics (e.g., family

---

Topic: Forts in the U.S.A.
Student's name: Keith (4th grade)

	Source: *The American Republic*	Source: *New Standard Encyclopedia*
Question 1:		
A. What were some famous forts in America?	1. There was Fort McHenry where Francis Scott Key wrote the "Star Spangled Banner," and 2. Fort Sumter that started the Civil War.	3. Fort Donelson: Grant's Civil war victory here led to his promotion to general. 4. Fort Bridger: way station on Oregon Trail.
Question 2:		
B. Why were forts built?	1. Protection from Indians on the frontier.	2. To protect seaports from other countries.
Question 3:		
C. What kind of forts were there?	1. Star forts have regular designs with many sharp angles.	2. A bastion has works called bastions which go out from the main fort.

Figure 4.1. A completed interview grid. From "QuIP: A Writing Strategy to Improve Comprehension of Expository Structure," by E. M. McLaughlin, 1987 (March) *The Reading Teacher, 40,* 652. Reprinted with permission of Elaine M. McLaughlin and the International Reading Association.

or friends). Later, topics that are not as familiar could be chosen so that sources such as reference books are required to supply answers.

Outline

The completed grid provides a transition to the creation of an outline (see Figure 4.2). The three questions become the subheadings, and the responses become supporting details.

Paragraphs

After developing the outline, students are ready to shape the material into paragraphs. Each heading becomes a main idea followed by supporting information. After all the paragraphs are written, a concluding sentence that restates the major theme should be added.

Modifications and Considerations

Once students have written a few paragraphs and have a rather cohesive story, they should, of course, edit and revise their work. As one part of this process, and in an effort to blend their paragraphs into a unified whole, students should be instructed to use such connectives as *whereas, however, moreover,* and *on the other hand.*

According to McLaughlin (1987), this technique is particularly suitable with the compare and contrast expository format, which is said to be among the more difficult text structures for students to comprehend.

Also, according to McLaughlin, this technique not only will assist students to write, but will help them come to internalize the structures they encounter when reading. The result will be better comprehension of text.

According to Gelernter (1998), thanks to e-mail and fax machines, writing is more popular again. He went on to say that "the Internet could be a fine teaching tool—a way to share good, scarce writing teachers. One teacher could manage a whole district of students if they were all connected electronically" (p. 55). Although I agree in principle, I believe it would be impossible for one teacher,

---

U.S. military in the 1800s
I. Forts in the USA
  A. Famous forts in America
    1. Fort McHenry
    2. Fort Sumter
    3. Fort Donelson
    4. Fort Bridger
  B. Reasons for forts
    1. Protection from Indians
    2. Seaport defense
  C. Kinds of forts
    1. Star fort
    2. Bastion

Figure 4.2. Outline developed from the interview grid. From "QuIP: A Writing Strategy to Improve Comprehension of Expository Structure," by E. M. McLaughlin, 1987 (March), *The Reading Teacher, 40,* 652. Reprinted with permission of Elaine M. McLaughlin and the International Reading Association.

even with e-mail, to monitor the writing of students in an entire district. Realistically, however, one person could handle a dozen or so students.

Monitor

Data should be obtained on the extent to which students write paragraphs containing main ideas and supportive information. Data should also be gathered on their ability to integrate paragraphs into a smooth and reasonably logical story. Moreover, data should be kept on the overall effect of their stories. To acquire all that information, a checksheet could be constructed that enables evaluators to note the components of the text that were indicated in the student's writing. Evaluators should also simply make general comments regarding the student's writing, such as whether or not it makes sense, is convincing, and is interesting.

References

Gelernter, D. (1998, May 25). Should schools be wired to the Internet? No. Learn first, surf later. *Time, 151*(20), 55.

McLaughlin, E. M. (1987). QuIP: A writing strategy to improve comprehension of expository structure. *The Reading Teacher, 40,* 650–654.

WRITING WITH COMPUTERS: USING SCAFFOLDING DIALOGUES, AND STRATEGY INSTRUCTION

Background

The idea supporting this project (Bahr, Nelson, & Van Meter, 1996) is that successful tactics and strategies designed for paper-and-pencil writing may also be beneficial to students writing with computers.

Who Can Benefit

There were nine students with learning disabilities, ranging from fourth to eighth graders, in Bahr et al.'s (1996) research. Most if not all of the procedures would be applicable for a wider range of students.

Procedures

Two sets of techniques were used in combination to assist these youngsters to write: scaffolding dialogues and strategy instruction. In addition, students were given keyboard training. Following is a brief description of each:

Scaffolding Dialogues

Teachers asked questions and offered comments and cues to help students organize and focus their writing. Following are two example questions: "What are the two questions to ask as you write stories?" "Is your story clear and is it interesting?"

Strategy Instruction

Strategy instruction represents the internalized structures that scaffolding is designed to teach. Prompts were designed to remind students to include the five major story grammar elements in their writing: *setting* (including main characters, time, and place), *problem* (the events that stir the need for action), *action* (sometimes preceded by a clear statement of the main character's plan for dealing with the problem), *outcome* (sometimes includes a description of how the main character felt about the outcome), and *ending* (tells about the resolution of the problem that was raised).

Keyboarding Instruction

Students practiced the individualized computer-based tutorial typing program *Type To Learn* (Hermann, 1991) for 15 minutes per session. Following is a statement by Dwyer (1994) regarding keyboarding instruction:

> Children, even very young ones, did not find the keyboard a barrier to fluid use of the computer. In fact, with as little as 15 minutes of keyboarding practice daily for six weeks, 2nd and 3rd graders commonly typed 20–30 words per minute with 95 percent accuracy. By comparison, children at that age typically write 9 to 11 words per minute by hand. (p. 5)

Following are steps and suggestions for the writing program:

- Schedule at least 30 minutes each day to write.

- Provide instruction on three stages of writing: planning, writing, and revising.

- Schedule scaffolding dialogues.

- Give students a prompted scrolled writing file: List two or three ideas for a story. Choose one of your ideas and type a working title. Why did you choose this topic? Who or what is the main character or characters? Where does the story take place? When does the story take place? What happens to the main character or characters? What does the main character or characters do? Why does the main character or characters do that? How does the main character or characters feel? How will your story end?

- Require them to respond to each query.

Modifications and Considerations

Another approach to instructing writing that was outlined by Bahr et al. (1996) is to use the graphics-based planning tool *Once Upon a Time* (Urban, Rushing, & Star, 1990). This program encourages students to create graphic scenes prior to writing, then asks them to generate text to accompany the pictures.

Monitor

Bahr et al. (1996) kept several indices of writing, some of which, if simplified, could be used by classroom teachers. For a measure of linguistic complexity, the software program *Systematic Analysis of Language Transcripts* (Miller & Chapman, 1986) could be used. Pupils' narrative maturity scores (Stein & Glenn, 1982) could also be obtained. This system requires judgment about whether the story is merely a set of isolated descriptions, or whether it is (with progressing maturity) an action sequence, a reactive sequence, an abbreviated episode, a complete episode, a complex episode, multiple episodes, or interactive episodes.

References

Bahr, C. M., Nelson, N. W., & Van Meter, A. M. (1996). The effects of text-based and graphics-based software tools on planning and organizing of stories. *Journal of Learning Disabilities, 29,* 355–370.

Dwyer, D. (1994). Apple classrooms of tomorrow: What we've learned. *Educational Leadership, 51*(7), 1–10.

Hermann, M. (1991). *Type to learn* [computer program]. Pleasantville, NY: Sunburst Communications.

Miller, J. F., & Chapman, R. (1986). *Systematic analysis of language transcripts* [computer program]. Madison, WI: Language Analysis Laboratory, Waisman Center on Mental Retardation and Human Development.

Stein, N. L., & Glenn, C. G. (1982). Children's concept of time: The development of a story schema. In W. Freeman (Ed.), *The developmental psychology of time* (pp. 255–282). New York: Academic Press.

Urban, D., Rushing, L., & Star, J. (1990). *Once upon a time* [computer program]. New Haven, CT: Compu-Teach Corporation.

SPELLING: SEVEN PROVEN METHODS

Background

Memorizing weekly spelling words is a task that is easy for some and difficult for others, but nevertheless is required of most elementary and many secondary students. Research studies (Graham & Miller, 1979) have shown that several of the commonly scheduled techniques for studying spelling words (e.g., writing the words in the air, writing the words multiple times, studying the hard spots in words, allowing students to determine their own study methods) are not efficient and do not promote success in spelling. To master spelling, students must be given research-based strategies for studying words. This tactic includes seven such techniques.

Who Can Benefit

Pupils who have difficulty memorizing spelling words would benefit most from these techniques. However, the methods would be beneficial to any student or adult in memorizing the spelling of an unfamiliar word.

Procedures

Fitzgerald Method

1. Look at the word carefully.
2. Say the word.
3. Visualize the word with eyes closed.
4. Cover the word and then write it.
5. Check the spelling.
6. Repeat Steps 1 through 5 if the word is misspelled.

Horn Method 1

1. Look at the word and say it to yourself.
2. Close your eyes and visualize the word.
3. Check to see if you were right.
4. Cover the word and write it.
5. Check to see if you were right. (If not, begin at Step 1.)
6. Repeat Steps 4 and 5 two more times.

Horn Method 2

1. Pronounce each word carefully.
2. Look carefully at each part of the word as you pronounce it.
3. Say the letters in sequence.
4. Attempt to recall how the word looks, then spell the word.
5. Check this attempt to recall.
6. Write the word.
7. Check this spelling attempt.
8. Repeat the above steps if necessary.

Visual–Vocal Method

1. Say the word.
2. Spell the word orally.
3. Say the word again.
4. Spell the word from memory four times correctly.

Gilstrap Method

1. Look at the word and say it softly. If it has more than one part, say it again, part by part, looking at each part as you say it.

2. Look at the letters and say each one. If the word has more than one part, say the letters part by part.

3. Write the word without looking at the book.

Fernald Method Modified

1. Make a model of the word with a crayon, grease pencil, or felt-tip marker; say the word as you write it.

2. Check the accuracy of the model.

3. Trace over the model with your index finger, saying the word at the same time.

4. Repeat Step 3 five times.

5. Copy the word three times correctly.

6. Copy the word three times from memory correctly.

Cover-and-Write Method

1. Look at the word. Say it.
2. Write the word two times.
3. Cover the word and write it one time.
4. Check your work.
5. Write the word two times.
6. Cover the word and write it one time.
7. Check your work.
8. Write the word three times.
9. Cover your work and write it one time.
10. Check your work.

Modifications and Considerations

To be successful with these techniques, students must be able to follow written, step-by-step directions. The teacher should most likely model the techniques several times, and closely monitor students as they learn the procedures step by step.

The teacher might make small copies of a particular technique to tape to the students' desks for quick reference. A wall chart would also be helpful.

Mercer and Mercer (1998) provide a number of suggestions for assessing and teaching spelling. They also describe a number of spelling games.

Monitor

Because no one technique has been proven the most effective for all individuals, Graham and Miller (1979) suggested that the teacher present each technique individually for several weeks, and then teach the next one. The teacher should record all spelling test scores and note which technique was used for each list of words. Once all techniques had been attempted, each student could decide with the teacher which technique was the most successful. The student can adopt that particular technique as his or her own study aid.

References

Graham, S., & Miller, L. (1979). Spelling research and practice: A unified approach. *Focus on Exceptional Children, 12,* 1–16.

Mercer, C. D., & Mercer, A. R. (1998). *Teaching students with learning problems* (5th ed.). Upper Saddle River, NJ: Merrill/Prentice-Hall.

Chapter 5
HOMEWORK

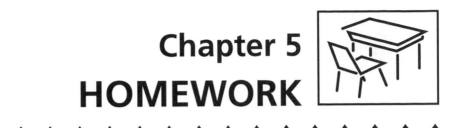

Professionals debate in what grade homework should be given, how much should be given at one time, and how often it should be assigned. Some educators maintain that no homework should be assigned at all. They contend that children work hard enough as it is and need time at home to either play or interact with their family. Scores of parents would breathe sighs of relief if children had no homework because that routine has led to ongoing and major homefront battles.

In my view homework should be given only for one of three reasons: (1) for practice—some skills can be acquired only with a lot of practice, like playing scales on the piano; (2) for extension—at times it is necessary to go beyond what was taught in class, such as learning about other African countries when only Egypt was studied at school; and (3) for makeup—if the student missed out on important work, he or she should make it up.

Before assigning homework, consider a few questions: Is it really important? Does the youngster know how to do it? Will he or she have help with it at home? Will I check it over when it is returned?

The seven tactics in this chapter are intended to help teachers to in turn help youth (and their parents) understand and carry out homework assignments. They include suggested rationales and justifications for homework and recommended approaches for teachers, students, and parents for carrying it out.

HOMEWORK: RATIONALES, SURVEYS, AND BEST PRACTICES

Background

With respect to homework, this tactic is rather general. Ideas are offered for presenting rationales for assigning homework, for surveying students about their homework habits, and for arranging homework situations.

Who Can Benefit

Most students would profit from these fundamental notions, but those who are somewhat disorganized and not motivated to do their homework (or even schoolwork) would be especially helped.

Procedures

Many of the ideas and suggestions in this tactic are from *Teaching Kids to Learn* (Seaman, 1996). Most of the topics mentioned could be bases for discussions. Later, students could be asked to write about the topics. (See the tactic on Learning Logs in Chapter 3, Study Skills.)

Rationales

It is important for teachers to justify in their own minds and in those of students exactly why they are giving homework. Of course, you could simply tell the students your justifications. Another approach would be to ask the students to tell you why they think teachers assign homework and what the value it may be for them. Record their responses on the board and, as I noted earlier, have them discuss and possibly write about them. The following are a few reasons you might try to elicit from students. Not only should general reasons be evoked from them, but they should give examples as well.

1. Homework gives students opportunities to practice skills that cannot be adequately developed at school. Examples: playing the trumpet, shooting free throws, memorizing poetry or lines in a play.

2. Homework provides more time to learn new information. Examples: students could learn about one type of cancer at school but about many others at home using the Internet, books from their local library, or other sources.

3. Doing homework helps students get used to acquiring information in places other than school. Examples: students need to develop the attitude that they can learn at home, in libraries, from community organizations, from their church, and so on.

4. Homework will be part of learning in future grades and in college. For example, students will be expected to do a great deal of homework if they attend a college or university or are accepted into certain military training programs.

5. Many jobs require homework of some kind. For example, teachers take work home, as do lawyers, accountants, and architects. More and more people are working out of their homes.

6. When students miss a class or two, they need to make up the work at home. Examples: band members practicing for a concert; students on excused vacations; students who are sick.

Survey

The following are questions to ask students about their current homework habits. This survey could be given at the beginning of a term.

- How long do you usually spend doing homework each night?
- Where do you do your homework?
- How do you remember what your homework is when you arrive at home?

- How do you decide what assignment to do first?
- If you get "stuck" with something, how do you get help?
- How do you get homework back to school without losing it?
- When do you turn in your homework?
- What happens once your homework has been turned in?
- What gains have you seen from doing homework?
- What suggestions do you have regarding homework assignments?

Best Practices

As with thoughts in the previous sections, the following ideas might be introduced for discussion. Later, students could write on one or more of them.

- Work at the same time every day. Why might this be a good idea?

- Work at the same place every day. What do the students think about this?

- Choose a quiet spot away from distractions. (It is likely that some students will not agree with this.)

- Write out a list of assignments. Where and how do they do this?

- Do the most difficult and longest assignments first. Do they believe this is a good idea?

- Take short breaks. When would they take them and for how long?

- Place work in a folder to return to school. Do students have some type of folder or notebook?

Modifications and Considerations

I will comment on two of the above suggestions. I do not believe that beginning with the most difficult and longest homework assignment is always the best way to approach work. Sometimes I begin with the easiest and shortest assignment or chore, simply to get something going. Taking breaks is a good idea, but I have found that it is sometimes best to take only a few breaks at the beginning when I am fresh, and longer and more frequent breaks when I begin to tire. Decisions on both those matters need to be individually determined, however.

Monitor

To monitor homework, tally the number of assignments given and the number completed, and with what degree of satisfaction. Data could also be kept on suggestions and comments from students regarding homework. You could give them the items in the survey, noted earlier, as a pretest and a posttest.

Reference

Seaman, J. (1996). *Teaching kids to learn.* Longmont, CO: Sopris West.

HOMEWORK AND SELF-MONITORING

Background

To move through a curriculum at an acceptable pace, students often must do some work at home, and they must set aside time to work on it. Also, most students require assistance to complete their assignments successfully. One way to provide that is in the form of checklists to follow as they tackle their assignments. By referring to items on such lists, students can be better organized and their parents can be more helpful to them.

Who Can Benefit

Clary (1986) carried out research with students with disabilities at the middle and high school levels. Students of about any type or age, however, could benefit from following these guidelines for homework assignments.

Procedures

1. Distribute a checklist similar to the example in Figure 5.1 to students and review the steps with them.

2. Answer any questions students might have about the checklist.

3. Encourage students to take the list home and review it with their parents. This will give them another chance to familiarize themselves with the items, while involving their parents.

4. Using the checklist as a guide, parents will be better able to assist their youngsters with homework assignments.

5. Request students to rely on their checklist regularly, and address any additional questions that arise after they have used it for a few days.

6. Ask students to discuss, with other students, how the checklist has helped them.

Modifications and Considerations

Checklists may be used for many types of homework (e.g., calculating problems, carrying out research, writing reports). Teachers should construct them depending on the types of students, the subjects, and other considerations. Pupils' opinions should be sought and taken into account when developing and modifying the lists.

Because the checklist is to be used primarily at home, students will soon discover how important it is to get all the information they need to complete an assignment before they leave school. Knowing this should increase their attention to directions in class and encourage them to ask questions about what they do not understand. To ensure that students know how to do their homework before taking it home, teachers should require them to work on a few problems or sentences at school. They should then review their work and provide assistance or examples to those who need it.

CHECKLIST FOR MONITORING STUDY

Before Study

☐ 1. Have I organized the necessary time, space, and materials for study?

☐ 2. Do I know exactly what the assignment involves? If I am unsure about anything, have I asked the teacher?

☐ 3. Have I previewed the assignment?

☐ 4. Do I need to ask the teacher to give me more background on the subject?

☐ 5. Have I checked the words for which I do not know the meanings?

(List with page numbers.) _____

_____

☐ 6. Have I thought of questions that could be answered from what I read?

☐ 7. Have I checked with the teacher on the kind of organization that is expected? (Check the appropriate types.)

    ☐ underline
    ☐ list
    ☐ take notes
    ☐ outline
    ☐ retell
    ☐ write a summary
    ☐ write practice exam questions (comparison/contrast, draw conclusions, explain procedures)

☐ 8. Have I attempted the following when I don't understand? (Choose one or more.)

    ☐ reread
    ☐ jump ahead
    ☐ use an outside reference (glossary, dictionary, map)
    ☐ ask someone
    ☐ write down questions to ask the teacher

After Study

☐ 1. Have I reviewed the question?

☐ 2. Have I listed questions to ask the teacher?

☐ 3. Is my material organized properly? (See number 7 on previous list.)

☐ 4. Have I rehearsed the information in an appropriate way? (Check those that apply.)

    ☐ reading the next assignment
    ☐ solving problems
    ☐ doing laboratory assignments
    ☐ writing a paper
    ☐ taking a test

Figure 5.1. Checklist for use in self-monitoring. Adapted from "Help for the Homework Hassle," by L. M. Clary, 1986, *Academic Therapy, 22,* pp. 58, 59. Copyright 1986 by PRO-ED, Inc. Adapted with permission.

Several excellent suggestions for managing homework are offered in an article by Frith (1991). They have to do with technological considerations, enhancing self-concept, peer-related approaches, and other topics.

Monitor

To monitor the extent to which homework is completed, turned in, and satisfactorily carried out is a rather simple process. Records should be kept of these instances. Beyond those matters, teachers should reflect on *why* the homework is assigned in the first place, and then design appropriate means to evaluate it. If the point of homework assignments is to offer pupils more opportunities to practice vocabulary definitions, mathematics problems, or historical facts, then tests should be constructed to determine if homework has effects on those abilities.

References

Clary, L. M. (1986). Help for the homework hassle. *Academic Therapy, 22,* 57–60.

Frith, G. (1991). Facilitating homework through effective support systems. *Teaching Exceptional Children, 24*(1), 48–49.

HOMEWORK AND ATTAINING GOALS

Background

This tactic assists students to set goals, a skill that must be practiced. After pupils have had experience in setting goals and attaining them at school, they should be encouraged to set aims with respect to their homework assignments and their personal goals as well. When students learn to monitor their own progress, teachers can expect to shift more of their energies from nagging about completing assignments to arranging sophisticated and stimulating environments.

Who Can Benefit

Although Nielson (1983) targeted adolescents, self-management skills are important for everyone because they are the means whereby long-term goals are attained. This tactic is designed specifically for students who are lax about turning in homework assignments, who lack the ability to set goals, and who have poorly developed self-management skills.

Procedures

1. Assist students to set performance goals that are slightly beyond their present levels. Tell them what their present levels are; explain to them what constitutes a reasonable goal; and provide examples of goals with upper and lower limits. Explain to students that their goals must be easy to keep track of so that credit for progress can be easily documented.

2. Assist pupils to develop their own reward systems. They could reward themselves for reaching their goals, for approximating them, or for reaching them a number of days in a row. Penalties could also be arranged for not accomplishing something, but generally the denial of a reward alone is sufficient. *Note:* Make sure the reinforcement is generous at the beginning of the program by arranging for daily rewards. Later, the rewards could be faded out.

3. Design contracts with students that detail assignments to be completed, schedules to be met, and rewards to be given (see example in Figure 5.2).

4. Assist pupils, initially, to set attainable goals, yet ones that require effort. Once they understand how to set reachable goals and have arrived at a few, allow them to set their own, continuing to make

STUDENT CONTRACT FOR HOMEWORK

Name _____

Date _____

Assignments to Be Turned In:

_____

_____

_____

_____

_____

_____

_____

By:

_____

_____

_____

Rewards:

_____

_____

_____

_____

_____

Figure 5.2. Sample student contract for homework.

sure they are attainable, easy to measure, and specified for a short period of time.

5. Require students to submit progress reports that explain the extent to which they achieved their goals. Show them how to keep track of their progress by charting it daily.

6. Help students rewrite their contracts periodically. The first few should be written to cover only a day or two.

Modifications and Considerations

This tactic has potential benefits beyond its initial purpose, that of increasing the extent to which students turn in their homework. Pupils could also develop important self-management skills that would serve them well in many areas for years to come: saving money, breaking unwanted habits, using time wisely, improving relationships with others, and so forth. (Chapter 14 deals specifically with self-management.)

Moreover, students could learn generally about goal setting. They could learn to set goals that are attainable and experience the satisfaction derived from reaching them. It could be that some students, prior to experiences such as these, had never set goals for themselves, much less attained them. The self-concepts of those students would be greatly bolstered if they had success in those endeavors.

As another potential gain from this tactic, once students have successfully written and carried out a few contracts dealing with homework, they could be instructed to set up other agreements at school, at home, and on the job.

Monitor

There was some mention of monitoring in the Procedures section. To recap, students should begin monitoring their short-term homework assignments. This could be done with a simple chart on which they plot the number of assignments given each period (e.g., week) and the number completed and submitted on time. Later, students should be encouraged to identify long-term goals (e.g., writing term papers) and to keep data throughout an extended period on how they worked toward the goal.

Reference

Nielson, L. (1983). Teaching adolescents self-management. *The Clearing House, 57,* 76–80.

HOMEWORK TARGET AND HOMEWORK TEAMS

Background

Two techniques are described here for involving peers in carrying out homework assignments (Fister & Kemp, 1995). *Homework Target* is a procedure that involves pairs of students working together, and *Homework Teams* is a structure in which teams of three students are assigned specific responsibilities for completing homework.

Who Can Benefit

These tactics are most suitable for youngsters who need help with their homework, and for those who need practice working with others.

Procedures

Homework Target

1. Divide the class into two teams. Pair up students in each team as homework partners. Tell them they will work together to complete their homework target. Give each pair a copy of a target (see example in Figure 5.3).

2. Instruct students how to use the chart. When homework is assigned, give the partners one point if they both write information about the assignment in their notebooks. Give the partners one point if they both complete the assignment, and one point if both turn in their assignments on time. Each point is entered as a tally mark in the corresponding day of the chart.

3. Ask partners to total their points and record them at the end of the week on the score line. The week number or date can be written in the target bullseye. At the end of the month, add the totals of all partners

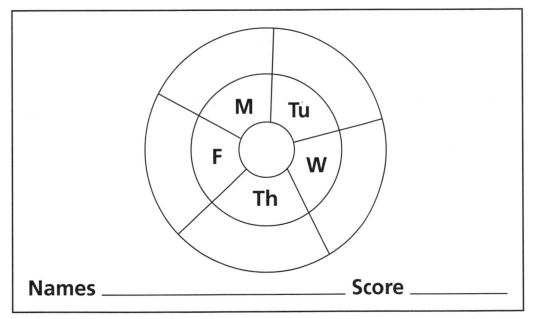

Figure 5.3. Hit the Homework Target. Adapted from *TGIF: But what will I do on Monday?* (p. 117), by S. L. Fister and K. A. Kemp, 1995, Longmont, CO: Sopris West. Copyright 1995 by Sopris West. Adapted with permission. (Some design ideas were adapted by Fister and Kemp from *Assignment notebooks,* by K. Pidek, 1991, Hoffman Estates, IL: Success by Design.)

on each team for the team score. The team with the highest score for the month is recognized.

4. Team members and partners can be rearranged at the beginning of the next month.

Homework Teams

1. Organize students into teams of three. Assign these roles: scorekeeper, manager, and coach.

2. Train students in the responsibilities of their role (Fister & Kemp, 1995, p. 117):

   • *Scorekeeper*—collect all homework assignments; correct each assignment; give each assignment a score; give all materials to the manager

   • *Manager*—correct each assignment again; score each assignment again; fill out daily Team Scorecard; write score on Team Poster

   • *Coach*—Set team goals; pass out peer tutoring folders if needed; review at least one team strategy for meeting the homework goal; pass out rewards in the form of "tickets"; pass out new homework sheets

   Explain that those tasks should be carried out each day that homework is assigned. Inform them that all students should know the roles and responsibilities of the other two.

3. Use a daily team scorecard and a team poster to monitor and record the students' progress. Students should note all the homework sheets returned on the daily team scorecard (see example in Figure 5.4). Post the team's daily scores as the total or as an average on the team poster (Jensen et al., 1993).

4. Provide reinforcement to both individuals and teams based on performance.

Daily Team Scorecard

Team Name: Killer Bees   Date: 10/23/93

Homework Returned	80% or Above Correct	90% or Above Correct	100% Correct
Scott yes no	yes no	yes no	yes no
Joe yes no	yes no	yes no	yes no
Chris yes no	yes no	yes no	yes no
All returned? Team Ticket: ✓ Yes ___ No	(# of "yes"s circled = # of tickets)		All 100% Team Ticket: ___ Yes ✓ No
Individual Tickets: 7	Team Tickets: 0 ① 2 (circle one)		Total Tickets: 8

Figure 5.4. Daily Team Scorecard. From *Homework Teams: Homework Management Strategies for the Classroom* (p. 17), by W. Jensen et al., 1993, Longmont, CO: Sopris West. Copyright 1993 by Sopris West. Reprinted with permission.

Other suggestions for setting up cooperative groups are offered in Chapter 11, Peer-Mediated Instruction.

Modifications and Considerations

Several variations with respect to the assignment are possible: give the same assignment to all students, give different assignments, and give different parts of the same assignment. Likewise, variations are possible with the students' roles. Instead of the three suggested in the Homework Teams approach, other roles could be assigned, such as researcher, writer, editor, and reactor. The number of children in each group also could vary.

Monitor

Count the number of assignments given, and of those the ones completed. Measure, over time, the quality of the assignments turned in. Monitor the extent the members carry out their assigned roles.

References

Fister, S. L., & Kemp, K. A. (1995). *TGIF: But what will I do on Monday?* Longmont, CO: Sopris West.

Jensen, W., Olympia, D., Andrews, D., Bowen, J., Valum, L., & Hepworth-Neville, M. (1993). *Homework teams: Homework management strategies for the classroom.* Longmont, CO: Sopris West.

Pidek, K. (1991). *Assignment notebooks.* Hoffman Estates, IL: Success by Design.

HOMEWORK FOLDERS AND TRACKING CHARTS

Background

The procedures outlined here, and the accompanying forms, are designed for students, teachers, and parents (Fister & Kemp, 1995). They are based on the notion that at times it is necessary for students to do schoolwork at home. Assistance, in the form of charts, is often necessary to help students complete the work.

Who Can Benefit

The forms described here would help students do their homework and turn it in. Moreover, their teachers would profit by learning which students were handing in work, and the students' parents would gain by knowing the extent their youngsters submitted their work.

Procedures

Homework Folders

1. Provide students with folders and send them home each day.

2. Include work in the folders that has been completed in class along with assignments that need to be worked on.

3. Attach a log sheet inside the folder to track the status of assignments (see example in Figure 5.5).

4. Keep parents informed regarding assignments completed and not completed, along with due dates of the assignments.

5. Award points for parent initials, work submitted, and returning the folder each day.

Homework Tracking Charts

1. Keep a class homework tracking chart to monitor and assist in evaluating students' homework performance (see example in Figure 5.6).

2. List the names of the students in the left column and make a mark each time an assignment is turned in.

3. For homework, note daily the status of each student in the class on the Homework Tracking Chart.

Modifications and Considerations

As mentioned earlier, the procedures outlined here will keep parents informed about their youngsters' progress. It is also important to keep them informed about available resources to help their children. One such resource is the National Parent Information Network (NPIN), which is available on the Internet (www.npin.org) and through a toll-free telephone number (800/583-4235). Established by the Educational Resources Information Service, the network draws on the largest education database in the world. The service draws information from more than 850,000 records of journal articles, teaching guides, books, and other sources. Their material is made available by 16 clearinghouses on separate education topics, some of which are the following: adult education; community colleges; disabilities and gifted education; law-related education; consumer education; higher education; information and technology; and reading, English, and communication (Thomas, 1998).

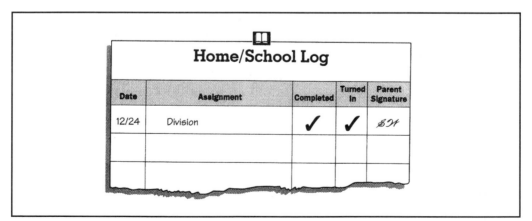

Figure 5.5. Home/School Folders. From *TGIF: But what will I do on Monday?* (p. 116), by S. L. Fister and K. A. Kemp, 1995, Longmont, CO: Sopris West. Copyright 1995 by Sopris West. Reprinted with permission.

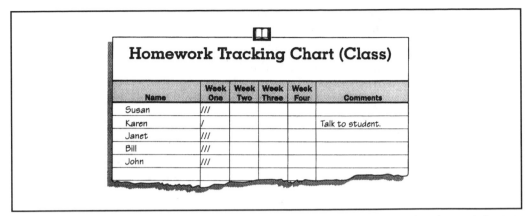

Figure 5.6. Homework Tracking Chart. From *TGIF: But what will I do on Monday?* (p. 116), by S. L. Fister and K. A. Kemp, 1995, Longmont, CO: Sopris West. Copyright 1995 by Sopris West. Reprinted with permission.

A number of excellent resources are noted as links from the NPIN Web site, such as these few: 4My-TEEN (a teen drivers monitoring service); Adolescence Directory On-Line (topics include conflict and violence, mental health issues, health risks); and EDLAW, Inc. (current text of the Individuals with Disabilities Education Act, analysis and commentary on recent court decisions).

Monitor

The simplest type of data to keep for these forms would be the number or percent of homework assignments turned in. Data could be kept for each student and for the class generally. Student and parent opinions could be obtained regarding the process.

References

Fister, S. L., & Kemp, K. A. (1995). *TGIF: But what will I do on Monday.* Longmont, CO: Sopris West.

Thomas, J. (1998, November 4). Where parents (at home) can go for expert advice on child rearing. *The New York Times,* p. A22.

 **PARENTS HELPING YOUTH WITH HOMEWORK**

Background

Lack of homework completion has been reported as a factor contributing significantly to poor academic performance and school failure of youth at risk. Reviews of homework practices suggest the following with respect to students at risk: (a) homework assignments should have a reasonable chance of being completed; (b) homework should be carefully monitored by teachers and parents; and (c) parents should be involved in various aspects and stages of homework assignments (Callahan, Rademacher, & Hildreth, 1998).

Who Can Benefit

As with the other tactics in this chapter, youth who stand to profit most from this procedure are those who have difficulty carrying out their assignments and turning them in on time, as well as difficulty with schoolwork in general. The tactic should also benefit the parents of those children.

Procedures

The Assignment

1. Assign problems or exercises that can be reasonably dealt with and completed. In Callahan et al.'s study (1998), teachers assigned 25 arithmetic problems representing four different math skills, including word problems.

2. Ask students to begin the assignment at school before taking it home. Ensure that they understand the assignment and are able to carry it out.

Parent Training

1. Convince parents that some homework is necessary. This may take some doing for certain parents.

2. Give them suggestions for assisting youth with homework: setting a time, finding a place to work, offering assistance and providing rewards, and checking the final product.

Student Training

1. Provide rationale for students that homework is necessary. This may present a challenge with some pupils.

2. Explain the type of problem or homework that is being assigned and set goals.

3. Suggest reasonable rewards for successful and consistent completion of assignments.

Modifications and Considerations

Armstrong and McPherson (1991) offered suggestions for enlisting the help of parents with their students' social skills (see Figure 5.7). They also provided ideas for communicating about activities in various classes (see Figure 5.8).

Hoover and Patton (1995) included a chapter "Home-Based Study Skills Programs" in their study skills book. They offered several worthwhile suggestions for assisting students in the 11 study skills components of their program.

Monitor

The simplest way to monitor this tactic is to count the number of homework assignments given and the number adequately turned in on time. Beyond that,

---

SAMPLE SOCIAL SKILLS HOMEWORK FORM

Name _____ Date Assigned _____ Date Completed _____

Grader _____ Date Graded _____ Grade _____

Instructions: Your social skills homework is an assignment that follows the lesson that has been taught in class. You need to practice the social skill five times with people other than the special education teacher that taught the skill or peers other than the ones in your class. Write or have someone write for you: 1. a description of what happened, when it happened, and where it happened in each practice example; 2. what you said and did; 3. what the other person said and did.

Behavioral Definition _____

_____

	What Happened?	What You Said and Did	What the Other Person Said and Did
1			
2			
3			
4			
5			

Signature of Cooperating Parent, Teacher, or Peer _____

Figure 5.7. Sample social skills homework form. From "Homework as a Critical Component in Social Skills Instruction," by S. W. Armstrong and A. McPherson, 1991, *Teaching Exceptional Children, 24*(1), p. 46. Copyright 1991 by Council for Exceptional Children. Reprinted with permission.

parents and students could be interviewed about the process to find out what they liked and did not like about the scheme. A more sophisticated evaluation of the tactic would be to measure and determine the effects of turning in homework assignments on the students' general skill level.

References

Armstrong, S. W., & McPherson, A. (1991). Homework as a critical component in social skills instruction. *Teaching Exceptional Children, 24*(1), 45–47.

SAMPLE PAGE FROM COMMUNICATIONS NOTEBOOK

	M	T	W	T	F	M	T	W	T	F
Teacher: Thomas										
Raises hand without talking										
Keeps a neat desk										
Reports teasing to teacher										
Uses "please" and "thank you"										
Teacher: Harper										
Raises hand without talking										
Keeps a neat desk										
Reports teasing to teacher										
Uses "please" and "thank you"										
Teacher: McPherson										
Raises hand without talking										
Keeps a neat desk										
Reports teasing to teacher										
Uses "please" and "thank you"										
Teacher: Lee										
Raises hand without talking										
Keeps a neat desk										
Reports teasing to teacher										
Uses "please" and "thank you"										
Teacher: Armstrong										
Raises hand without talking										
Keeps a neat desk										
Reports teasing to teacher										
Uses "please" and "thank you"										
Teacher: Smith										
Raises hand without talking										
Keeps a neat desk										
Reports teasing to teacher										
Uses "please" and "thank you"										
Brings supplies and homework										

Figure 5.8. Sample page from communications notebook. From "Homework as a Critical Component in Social Skills Instruction," by S. W. Armstrong and A. McPherson, 1991, *Teaching Exceptional Children, 24*(1), p. 46. Copyright 1991 by Council for Exceptional Children. Reprinted with permission.

Callahan, J., Rademacher, J. A., & Hildreth, B. L. (1998). The effect of parent participation in strategies to improve the homework performance of students who are at risk. *Remedial and Special Education, 19*(3), 131–141.

Hoover, J. J., & Patton, J. R. (1995). *Teaching students with learning problems to use study skills.* Austin, TX: PRO-ED.

HOMEWORK HELP FROM THE WEB

Background

A tremendous amount of material on the Internet will help youngsters as they do their homework. New sites that are indirectly or directly geared toward youth and homework are being developed all the time. A Web site that I have used and believe will be available for some time is Homework Central, which is discussed more later.

If youth are to profit from material on the Internet, they should have at least rudimentary keyboarding skills and should know something about operating computers. They should, in addition, have some fundamental instruction in search engines—what they are, which ones are best for various needs, and other related matters. Also, it is important for youth to understand the mechanics and metaphors of "Hypertext" in order to get the most from their Internet experiences.

Who Can Benefit

All children, young and old, stand to gain from the Internet. Youngsters who have access to computers and the Internet at school and home will stand to profit the most, however. Fortunately, many public libraries have computers with Internet connections available for their patrons. At my local library, which has four such machines, folks sign up to use them for 60 minutes at a time.

Procedures

Following is a brief description of the Homework Central Web site (http://www.homeworkcentral.com). The user has the option of selecting one of three levels: elementary, secondary, or college. What follows here is the path I took after opening the secondary level.

- I was first shown the branches of study, of which there are 20. They pertain to all the subjects emphasized in secondary schools (e.g., science, geography, world history, U.S. history, math, English, literature, languages) and more topics (e.g., law, museums, religion, current events, philosophy).

- Next, I clicked on History of the United States. From that screen I was given eight choices (e.g., Native American history, history by time period, research tools).

- I clicked on research tools and was given three choices: Lecture notes from colleges, United States history search engines, and United States history meta indexes.

- I clicked on meta indexes and was rewarded with an amazing array of possibilities under three headings: historical studies (64 entries), archival resources (39 entries), and general history resources (25 entries).

- I then clicked on the Irish Famine in the historical studies category and was able to read several articles from the Cork *Examiner* about the famine in Ireland. They were fascinating, especially the one on "The Landlords of Fermanagh" (Fermanagh is a county in what is now Northern Ireland).

All in all it was an exciting journey. Although the examples outlined here were in history, the material in the other areas was just as well organized and informative.

There are a number of other features in the Homework Central site, one of which is "Ask the Experts." Several general topics are listed (e.g., history, business, science, art) and students can tap into these and ask questions. For the one on the Holocaust, students can type in their questions to a survivor of that terrible event.

Another feature of this site is the listing of the "Top 8 Research Sites." They change from time to time. Three titles that were listed one time when I tapped in were "Professor Stephen Hawking's Homepage," "Biophysical chronology," and "What makes a good short story?" The Web site designations were given for all those titles.

Modifications and Considerations

Most school districts have Web sites. Indeed, many elementary or secondary schools in those districts have their own Web sites, as do some teachers. Information from those sites can be helpful to children and youth as they do their homework. One of the best school sites I have seen is the one developed by the Kent School District, located south of Seattle (http://www.kent.wednet.educ: 80/toolbox/index). It was a finalist for the prestigious Global Information Infrastructure Award in 1998. From the Teachers' Toolbox, the second screen on their site, dozens of entries are noted by symbol and label. Some of them are Student Information, News Sources, Internet & Curriculum, and Technical Information. From the Internet & Curriculum page, one can access entries in various Subject Areas (e.g., reading, mathematics, social studies) and the Planning/Research Section (e.g., Kent Student Learning Objectives, The Impact of Technology on Learning). In addition to those topics, a number of libraries and references are noted, one of which is the King County Library. By clicking on it, one can obtain information on several entries, including Summer Reading, Community Libraries, and Inter-Library Loan. Students can access the Library of Congress from the Library section. There, students can find hundreds of facts about Congress, access important documents, find out how bills are written and acted on, and gather information on dozens of other features about the federal government.

One last word on this: Simply because something is sent out over cyberspace does not make it a fact. There is a lot of drivel out there.

Monitor

An easy way to evaluate the Internet usage would be simply to tally the number of times it had been accessed. Beyond that, one could keep track of a student's path or paths through the sites (as I did earlier). Another straightforward evaluation of Internet usage would be to interview pupils. Ask what they thought about it, what they gained from it, and what problems they might have had navigating through it. The most sophisticated and meaningful evaluation of the Internet would be to gather information on its effects—that is, whether it helped pupils write better papers, calculate more advanced problems, or learn more French vocabulary.

Chapter 6
ADAPTING MATERIALS

♦ ♦ ♦ ♦ ♦ ♦ ♦ ♦ ♦ ♦ ♦ ♦ ♦ ♦ ♦ ♦ ♦ ♦ ♦

The primary intent of this chapter, although by implication, is that if certain youth are to gain from the regular curriculum, specific accommodations must be made. Toward that end, I discuss the wide range and types of accommodations that may be set up to assist youth. Data regarding many of these adjustments indicate that if they are properly arranged great numbers of students are able to grasp the gist of the typical curriculum. Those students might not, even with those modifications, be able to master all the nuances and subtleties of the subjects, but they will be able to pick up the basics. With the adjustments explained here, and when used correctly, there will not be a need to schedule a condensed version of the typical curriculum or one that is wholly different from that provided the majority of students.

Many of the adjustments explained here blend with certain study skills. Study guides and graphic organizers, for example, are related to the reading study skills explained in Chapter 3.

There are eight tactics in this chapter. The first one is general, its purpose being to demonstrate the range of circumstances in schools that can be changed in efforts to help students learn. Tactics two and three explain how to design and use study guides. The next two techniques show how graphics or visual displays can be developed and implemented. The next tactic describes a method for teaching vocabulary, and the last two approaches are combinations of events that can be arranged to help students.

⌐⊙⊙ CLASSROOM ACCOMMODATIONS AND ADAPTATIONS

Background

In this tactic, I identify a variety of events or circumstances that teachers can modify or adapt in their efforts to accommodate the needs of certain youth, and hence better educate them. These suggestions cover a much wider range of situations than do the other tactics in this chapter.

Who Can Benefit

Youth of several types will be assisted by the accommodations noted here. Many of those students have been characterized with learning disabilities, or as remedial, at risk, not motivated, or downright lazy.

Procedures

The following is one of various ways to categorize the adaptations. Several of the specific techniques noted are expanded on considerably in other sections of the book.

- Architectural or layout of the classroom—seat pupils in places that are most helpful; place them in locations with minimal distractions; lay out the pupils' corner of the room in some preferred way (e.g., favorite poster or color scheme); adjust transportation or parking arrangements.

- Presenting materials or assignments—modify the schedule; break up tasks into workable steps; gain pupils' attention before giving assignments or directions; provide students with copies of reading material with main ideas underlined or highlighted; provide students with a summary of the day's lecture or reading; consider using a tape recorder; provide succinct rationales for engaging in the assignments. (See Chapter 3, Study Skills.)

- Responding to questions or assignments—place a chart that lists steps for carrying out the assignment near the pupils; provide a model for the final product near the students; allow them to respond in their favorite or best way (e.g., computer); involve students actively during the lesson (e.g., require them to respond periodically); teach suitable study skills (e.g., notetaking, test taking). (See Chapter 3, Study Skills.)

- Organizational aids—develop a daily or weekly journal; arrange for regular parent contacts (see Chapter 16, Parents); set up contingency contracts; train specific self-management skills (e.g., being on time to class, bringing proper materials to class, asking questions periodically); place students on a weekly, or perhaps daily, schedule of reporting progress; review assignments, lectures, or other activities following certain class periods. (See Chapter 14, Self-Management, and Chapter 5, Homework.)

- Providing different or more support—assign peers to assist the students (see Chapter 8, Social Skills); arrange for a parent to assist the students; encourage the pupils to ask others for assistance.

- Evaluation—allow the students to take tests in private or at different times; allow the students to negotiate the way in which they will be evaluated (use the type of evaluation that is the closest to real work circumstances, commonly referred to as "authentic assessment").

Modifications and Considerations

When teachers speak of making adjustments for certain youth, they invariably bring up the following two: reducing the assignment and giving more time. Although one can understand why those suggestions come up, neither should be given much consideration when making adjustments for students. As for the first, if an assignment has been carefully thought out, then all of its features, problems, or activities should be learned by all students. If, for example, a teacher gave her class a list of 20 vocabulary words to learn but asked the special student to learn only 10 of them, that pupil was denied the opportunity to learn half the lesson. As for the second adaptation, basically the same criticism holds. If, for example, the class was given 30 minutes to finish an assignment and the special student was allowed 60 minutes, the latter pupil missed out on what the others were doing for the 30 minutes after they finished the first assignment.

Wood (1998) offered a vast range of situations that can be adapted for youth, and West, Idol, and Cannon (1989) presented a plan for determining the extent to which accommodations should be made for students. See Figure 6.1.

ADAPTING CURRICULUM AND INSTRUCTION FOR STUDENTS WITH SPECIAL NEEDS: A LEVELS OF INTENSITY OF INTERVENTION DECISION-MAKING FRAMEWORK

Level 1. What can be learned in the general program of instruction to the same performance standard as required of normally achieving students?

Level 2. What can be learned with normally achieving peers, but with adjustments in performance standards (e.g., task mastery or grading criteria), according to the student's needs as determined through curriculum-based and portfolio assessment?

Level 3. What can be learned with adaptations in instructional procedures, activities, materials, techniques, or tasks, provided with consultative support to the general classroom teacher?

Level 4. What can be learned with adaptations in instructional procedures, activities, materials, techniques, or tasks, provided jointly by general classroom and support staff?

Level 5. What can be learned with adaptations in the *content* of the general classroom curriculum to be taught jointly by general classroom and support staff?

Level 6. What curriculum and/or instruction must be adapted substantially and taught primarily by support staff?

Level 7. What are those few situations in which the general classroom curriculum is inappropriate? What is the alternate curriculum or instructional program, taught primarily by support staff, that is appropriate for the instructional needs of the student?

Figure 6.1. Levels of adapting. From *Collaboration in the Schools: Communicating, Interacting, and Problem Solving—Instructor's Manual* (p. 86), by J. F. West, L. Idol , and G. Cannon, 1989, Austin, TX: PRO-ED. Copyright 1989 by PRO-ED, Inc. Reprinted by permission.

Monitor

The teacher should keep before and during data on the effects of any of these adaptations. Those effects could be in the form of showing up for class more often, participating in class activities, turning in assignments on time, learning certain facts or definitions, and so on.

References

West, J. F., Idol, L., & Cannon, G. (1989). *Collaboration in the schools: Communicating, interacting, and problem solving—Instructor's manual.* Austin, TX: PRO-ED.

Wood, J. (1998). *Adapting instruction for mainstreamed and at-risk students* (3rd ed.). Upper Saddle River, NJ: Merrill/Prentice-Hall.

LEARNING FROM TEXTBOOKS: STUDY GUIDES

Background

Study guides take a variety of forms, many of which can be useful when adapting textbook passages for students depicted as remedial or at risk. Researchers have pointed out that some textbook passages are so poorly organized that comprehension becomes difficult for many students. Providing organized supplementary material as described in this tactic can to some extent alleviate that problem.

Who Can Benefit

Study guides designed in a framed outline format have been proven effective in research with adolescents with and without learning disabilities (Lovitt & Horton, 1987). With that format, facts and concepts are arranged in a sequence so there is a logical and coherent narration. This greatly helps students grasp the main ideas of a passage.

Procedures

Constructing Study Guides

1. Scan the entire textbook and mark the chapters that will and will not be covered.

2. Note the sequence in which the chapters will be assigned.

3. Read every part of the first chapter, including the introduction, summary, figure captions, study questions, graphics (i.e., tables, figures, charts), and other material carefully.

4. Pay particular attention to the featured words and phrases (i.e., headings, italicized words, boxed text, or material that is highlighted in other ways) and to information in summary or review sections.

5. Read the passage again and underline all important ideas and concepts. Err on the side of underlining too much. Cross out material you do not intend to cover.

6. Divide the chapter into logical sections of about 1,000 to 1,500 words each, depending on how detailed the material is and how much is important.

7. Write down the main ideas.

8. Sequence the main ideas (this may vary from the order in which the ideas appear in the text). Type this sequence on a sheet and review it. Check to see that the ideas and their arrangement are coherent.

9. Write brief sentences containing the main ideas. Arrange them so that a story unfolds. Develop a narration that brings it all together so that one idea leads to another. In writing the narration, use a simple structure while maintaining the style of the text.

10. Leave out a few words in each sentence: nouns in some, verbs in others, and other parts of speech in still others. Vary the number of words omitted depending on the ability of the students. If writing is a slow process for some students, leave out only a word or two. On the other hand, if writing speed or skill is not a concern, omit several words.

11. Prepare two copies of the sequenced study guides for you. On one, all the words are provided; on the other, a few words are missing. Prepare one study guide for the students, on which some words are not included.

12. Allow 2- to 3-inch margins on either side. See Figure 6.2 for a sample study guide. The words that are left out on the study guide are italicized in Figure 6.2.

Presenting Study Guides

1. Require pupils to read the text passage before using the study guides.

2. Designate a pupil to pass out the study guides after students have read the material. There are a number of ways to select this person:

   - Ask the same student to hand out study guides each day.

   - Ask for a volunteer to pass them out.

   - Have students take turns handling this task as they generally do other classroom chores.

   - Require students to earn the privilege of passing them out by achieving a certain standard of performance.

3. Begin the lecture. Place the transparency that has missing words on the overhead projector. Show only the first sentence, and ask students to take out their copies of the outline and a pencil.

4. Explain to the students that they should listen to the lecture and, as the topics on the outline are discussed and the missing words are filled in on your transparency, they should fill in the blanks on their copies.

STUDY GUIDE

Student _____ Teacher _____

Date _____ Period _____

TOPICS *Compounds* (pages 139, 144–146)

Mixtures (page 147)

1. A compound is made up of 2 or more different elements. The *molecules* in a compound have 2 or more different kinds of *atoms.*
2. For example: Water is a *compound.* Its molecules have 2 hydrogen *atoms* and 1 *oxygen* atom.
3. Although compounds are different from each other, they have some similar *properties* and can be classified according to these *properties.*
4. Two major kinds of compounds are *acids* and *bases.* Another kind of compound is *salt.*
5. All *acids* have hydrogen atoms joined to 1 or more other kinds of atoms. Acids taste *sour.*
6. All *bases* contain atoms of some kind of metal. Each *base* contains 1 atom of oxygen joined to 1 atom of hydrogen; this is called a *hydroxyl* group. Bases taste *bitter.*
7. *Indicators* such as litmus paper change *color* in the presence of an acid or *base.* They tell us whether something is an *acid* or base.
8. When an acid and a base react, they *change* chemically and form 2 new *compounds,* a salt and water.
9. Salt is formed when an *acid* reacts with a metal oxide. It does not taste bitter or sour—it tastes *salty!*
10. A metal oxide is a *compound* formed when oxygen and a metal combine. *Rust* is a metal oxide, formed of oxygen and iron atoms.
11. Mixtures are different from *compounds.* In mixtures, different kinds of matter are joined together in one place. They do not form a new *compound.*
12. *Solutions* are one kind of mixture. Solutions are mixtures that appear to be the *same* throughout.
13. Solutions can be liquid, gas, solid, or a combination of these. One kind of solid solution is an *alloy.* Alloys are usually made up of one or more *metals.*

Figure 6.2. Example of a study guide.

5. Keep the lesson active and moving. Vary the style of presentation and sustain student involvement by doing the following:

- Stop from time to time and ask questions, rather than merely reading the sentences and filling in the missing words.

- Explain and clarify the concepts with examples.

- Review phrases when necessary, and reiterate certain facts or concepts.

- Supply linking ideas when the transition from one thought to another is not clear.

- Ask pupils, occasionally, to supply the word or phrase that should be written in the blank(s).

- Elicit both individual and unison responses.

6. Roam about the room during the lecture to be sure that all the youngsters are filling in the blanks. (A student could operate the overhead projector while you move about.)

7. When finished, review all the sentences, and perhaps give additional examples.

8. Write notes on your outline, and encourage pupils to do the same on their sheets.

9. Remind students to store their outlines in a folder or some type of notebook where they can be quickly retrieved.

10. Inform them that in the very near future they will be given an important test over the material just covered.

Modifications and Considerations

The following are a few additional ways to incorporate framed outlines into the teaching routine.

1. *Pair (or Peer) Teaching*—One student (as the teacher) uses the filled-in version of the outline while the other student (as the pupil) fills in the blanks. The student teacher may read the material while the pupil fills in the blanks. Or, the two students may take turns asking each other for answers.

2. *Homework*—Students may take the sheets home and ask a parent or other family member to drill them on the ideas, or students can simply practice with the materials themselves.

3. *Review*—If students keep their sheets in an organized and sequenced manner, they can review them for 6-week, semester, and end-of-year quizzes and tests.

4. *Odd Moments*—When there is not enough time to begin a new activity but order must be maintained and time used productively, ask questions from the study guides. This could be developed into an ongoing game by dividing the class into teams. A running score could be kept, and a winner announced at the end of a period of time.

Keep in mind when developing the narrative from main ideas in the chapter that the major concern is for students to get the gist of the subject. Consider whether, if you had read only the sequenced main ideas and not the entire chapter, you would have enough information to get the central idea.

To move from a teacher-directed to a student-directed activity, print page numbers beside the sentences in the study guide to show students where to look in the text to find the missing words. Then, require students to fill in the blanks on their own.

To reinforce correct spelling, print a few difficult but essential vocabulary words on the bottom of the study guides. Students can refer to them as they fill in the blanks.

Horton, Lovitt, and Christensen (1991) studied the effects of differential levels of study guides with students of secondary age. They determined that multilevel guides, ones that contained different levels of referential cues, were the most effective.

Monitor

A number of possibilities are available for monitoring the influence of study guides on pupils' performance. In a study by Lovitt, Rudsit, Jenkins, Pious, and Benedetti (1986), the researchers scheduled chapter tests developed by publishers. Tests of that type were administered following chapters for which study guides were available and following others for which they were not used. The sequence of the chapters alternated from those with study guides to those without study guides. From those data, the researchers learned that the guides were helpful for all types of students.

References

Horton, S. V., Lovitt, T. C., & Christensen, C. C. (1991). Matching three classifications of secondary students to differential levels of study guides. *Journal of Learning Disabilities, 24*(9), 518–529.

Lovitt, T. C., & Horton, S. (1987). How to develop study guides. *Journal of Reading, Writing and Learning Disabilities, 3,* 213–221.

Lovitt, T., Rudsit, J., Jenkins, J., Pious, C., & Benedetti, D. (1986). Adapting science materials for regular and learning disabled seventh graders. *Remedial and Special Education, 1,* 31–39.

USING A HYPERTEXT STUDY GUIDE TO TEACH UNITS OF SOCIAL STUDIES

Background

This tactic is based on research that investigated the effects of a computer-based study guide using hypertext (Horton, Boone, & Lovitt, 1990). Hypertext is a generic term for high-level software that allows users to interact with information in a nonlinear fashion.

Who Can Benefit

Students in Horton et al.'s (1990) study were in a high school Washington state history class. The hypertext format would be suitable for youngsters of all types and many age levels in practically any subject. Most students are familiar with the hypertext concept, having spent considerable time on the Internet, which is based on that notion. In addition, several secondary schools offer special classes in hypertext construction, and students are expected to generate hypertext projects in other classes (e.g., English, U.S. history).

Procedures

The following is a description of Horton et al.'s (1990) procedure.

1. A few reading passages were selected from a text. Those passages averaged 575 words in length, and required about five screens of text each.

2. Two multiple-choice questions were created for each screen of text. These also appeared on the computer screen (see Figure 6.3). The pupil was given instructions to click on the letter of the correct answer. If the response was correct, the phrase "That was correct" was shown and a second multiple-choice question appeared.

3. If the response was not correct, the phrase "That was not correct" was presented and the student was directed to click on a bar at the top of the page, which produced a Level One cue. For that, the original screen of text was shown with a question at the top and a direction at the bottom to click on the line(s) where the answer is found (see Figure 6.4).

4. If the student was not successful with that cue, a Level Two cue was provided (see Figure 6.5). For this, the cues were identical to Level One, with the additional assistance of fading a portion of text that did not contain the answer, thus reducing extraneous information. The student was again directed to locate the answer.

5. If the pupil still did not select the correct line(s), a Level Three cue was provided. For this, a cue was added to the previous aids by highlighting

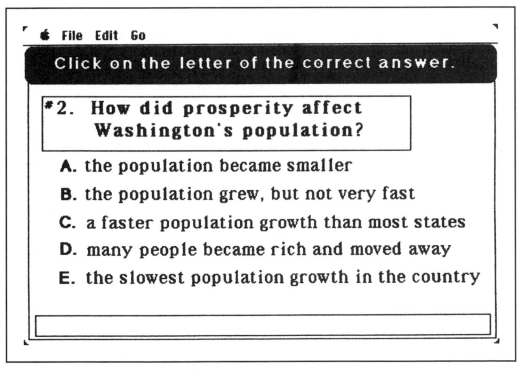

Figure 6.3. A multiple-choice question associated with a screen of text. From "Teaching Social Studies to Learning Disabled High School Students: Effects of a Hypertext Study Guide," by S. V. Horton, R. A. Boone, and T. C. Lovitt, 1990, *British Journal of Educational Technology, 21*(2), p. 122. Copyright 1990 by the *British Journal of Educational Technology.* Reprinted with permission.

```
  ⬛ File  Edit  Go
```

How did prosperity affect Washington's population?

In the middle of the 20th Century, industrial growth and personal prosperity went hand-in-hand. Average family incomes climbed steadily during this period. The median income in Washington increased from $3,523 a year in 1950 to $10,407 in 1970--nearly three times as high. This meant that people had more money to spend. They were able to produce and sell more goods.

Growing businesses meant more jobs. These jobs attracted more people to the state. Washington's population continued to grow faster than that of most states, and the larger population created an even bigger local market for goods. The economy was booming, and unemployment decreased, reaching a low of 3.5% in 1968.

Click on the line(s) where the answer is found.

Figure 6.4. A Level One instructional cue containing the question at top and a direction at bottom. From "Teaching Social Studies to Learning Disabled High School Students: Effects of a Hypertext Study Guide," by S. V. Horton, R. A. Boone, and T. C. Lovitt, 1990, *British Journal of Educational Technology, 21*(2), p. 123. Copyright 1990 by the *British Journal of Educational Technology.* Reprinted with permission.

the line(s) of text containing the answers and directing the student to click there.

Modifications and Considerations

Dozens of changes could be made to the program detailed here. Certain words, phrases, or sentences could be highlighted on the screen, and the student directed to access them to gain additional information: definitions of words, pictures of objects, references of additional material. The incorporation of those additional "layers" in the program would qualify it as a hypertext format. A consideration with this project is the frequency with which data are to be gathered. In addition to giving posttests to each screen, pretests and posttests could be administered over each screen or for an entire passage or unit, and a composite test that covered material from several passages could be given. Also, the mode of the test could be changed from multiple choice to essay or some other format.

In a more recent study, Boone and Higgins (1992) corroborated the fact that hypermedia applications are effective means to teach content material to youth.

Monitor

Suggestions for monitoring this tactic were given in preceding sections. Yet another way to evaluate the effects of this program would be to encourage stu-

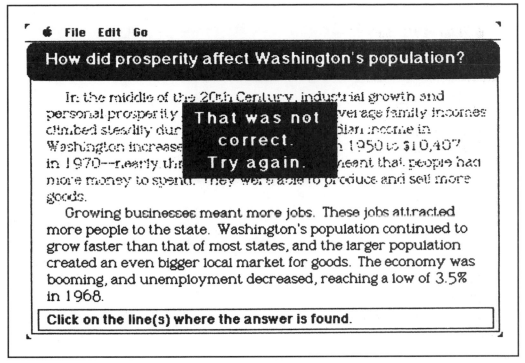

Figure 6.5. A Level Two instructional cue showing a portion of text faded. From "Teaching Social Studies to Learning Disabled High School Students: Effects of a Hypertext Study Guide," by S. V. Horton, R. A. Boone, and T. C. Lovitt, 1990, *British Journal of Educational Technology, 21*(2), p. 124. Copyright 1990 by the *British Journal of Educational Technology*. Reprinted with permission.

dents to write narratives on the computer about what they learned from each page, passage, or larger unit.

References

Boone, R., & Higgins, K. (1992). Hypermedia applications for content-area study guides. *Reading and Writing Quarterly: Overcoming Learning Difficulties, 8,* 379–393.

Horton, S. V., Boone, R. A., & Lovitt, T. C. (1990). Teaching social studies to learning disabled high school students: Effects of a hypertext study guide. *British Journal of Educational Technology, 21*(2), 118–131.

LEARNING FROM TEXTBOOKS: GRAPHIC ORGANIZERS

Background

Most regular content-area classes accommodate heterogeneous clusters of students characterized as remedial, at risk, learning disabled, and behaviorally disordered. Considering the range of abilities inherent in such settings, classroom teachers have justifiable concerns about providing for individual needs.

With this tactic, teachers will learn to construct and implement graphic organizers (GOs) to teach content to all of these students in the same setting at the same time. Two types of GOs, hierarchical and compare–contrast, are presented, and three techniques for implementing GOs are suggested.

Who Can Benefit

Middle and high school students with learning disabilities, and others in remedial and regular education were included in the studies on which this tactic is based (Bergerud, Lovitt, & Horton, 1988; Horton & Lovitt, 1989). Students in each group demonstrated gains in the acquisition of information when GOs were employed to teach science, social studies, and health. A major benefit to students and teachers alike is that GOs can be implemented without changing classroom location, textbooks, grouping arrangements, or existing sequences of instruction.

Procedures

Constructing Graphic Organizers

1. Determine which textbook chapters will be taught and arrange them in sequence.

2. Divide chapters into 1,500- to 2,000-word instructional units.

3. Outline the main ideas in the passage.

4. Choose a format:

   a. *Hierarchical*—Most text information converts easily to this format (arranged by major and minor categories), which can be approached either top–down (deductive) or bottom–up (inductive). (Figure 6.6 shows a modification of the hierarchical format.)

   b. *Compare–contrast*—This format is best for materials arranged by similarities or differences (see example in Figure 6.7).

5. Develop teacher and student versions of the GO:

   a. Prepare the teacher version first.
   b. Keep it to a single page.
   c. Select and number specific items to be completed by students.
   d. Remove some information from the student's copy.

Implementing Graphic Organizers

1. Decide when to use the GOs:

   a. Before reading a passage (advance organizer)
   b. During instruction (intermediate organizer)
   c. After reading (post organizer)

2. Choose the type of activity for the lesson:

   a. In class
   b. Large or small group
   c. Homework

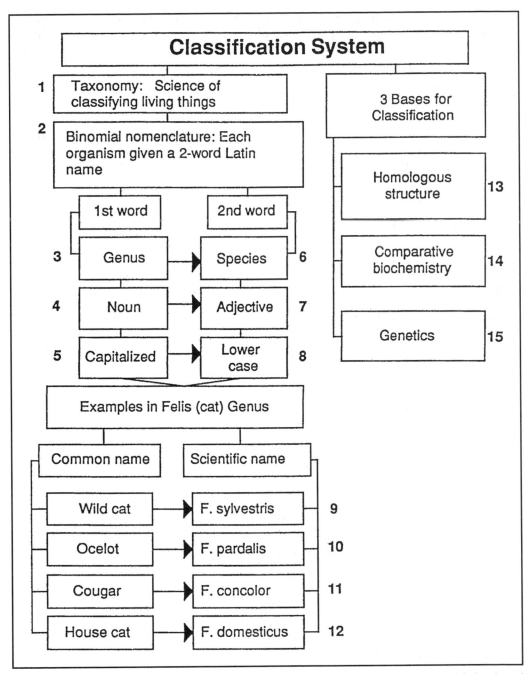

Figure 6.6. Example of a graphic organizer using a hierarchical format. From material developed from a grant from U.S. Government, Department of Education, to T. C. Lovitt and S. V. Horton, 1985–1988.

3. Determine which method of implementation to use:

    a. Teacher directed

    b. Student directed with text references

    c. Student directed with clues

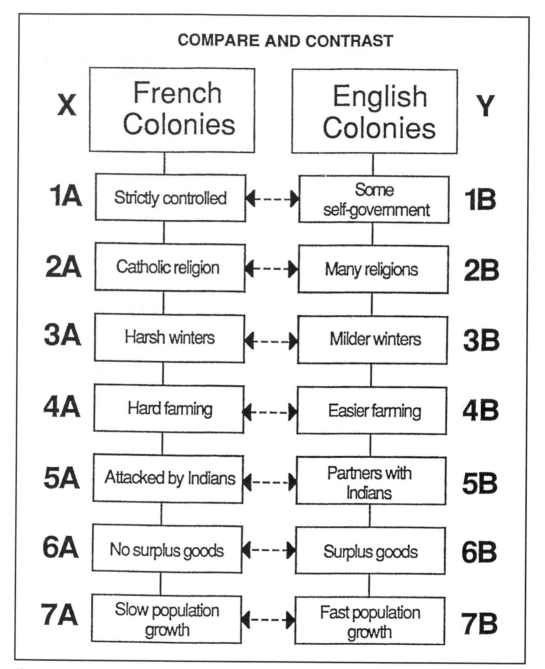

Figure 6.7. Example of a graphic organizer using a compare–contrast format. From material developed from a grant from U.S. Government, Department of Education, to T. C. Lovitt and S. V. Horton, 1985–1988.

Teacher Directed

1. Ask students to mark the pages in their textbook that are involved in the GO.

2. Instruct students to read and reread the passage for 15 minutes.

3. Tell students to close their books. Give each pupil a copy of the student version of the GO.

4. Place a transparency of the teacher's version on the overhead projector, and point out the relationships between items shown on the diagram.

5. Help students fill in the answers on their copies:
   a. Cover an answer on the transparency.
   b. Call on a student to provide the answer orally.
   c. Uncover the answer.
   d. Request students to write the answer on their copies.
   e. Repeat until all answers have been filled in.

6. Allow 3 minutes for students to study their completed GOs.

7. Pick up student copies and give a test.

Student Directed with Text References

1. Repeat Steps 1 through 4 of teacher-directed GOs.

2. Attach a cover sheet that shows the page and paragraph number for locating each answer.

3. Direct pupils to use that information to complete their diagrams.

4. Circulate among the pupils to keep them on task and to provide assistance as necessary.

5. Review the filled-in GOs by placing a transparency of the teacher's version on an overhead. Ask students to correct their copies.

6. Allow 3 minutes for students to study their completed GOs.

7. Collect the completed GOs and give a test.

Student Directed with Clues

1. Arrange the answers to the numbered boxes on the GO in random order on a cover sheet. Include directions for completing the GO.

2. Attach the cover sheet to the student's version.

3. Follow the steps, except number 5, described in the "Student Directed with Text References" section above. Instead of number 5, have students complete the diagram by studying the relationships between categories, referring to a list of clues, and checking the reading passage in the textbook.

Modifications and Considerations

Research with youngsters with mild disabilities indicates that information acquired through GOs transfers more readily to both testing formats (graphic-to-graphic and graphic-to-prose) than that presented in a prose style.

When selecting chapters to present with graphic organizers, you may wish to choose those that are poorly organized or have caused problems for students in the past. Dividing those chapters into shorter reading passages lessens the chance that students will be overwhelmed by too much information, and makes it easier for teachers to analyze the material.

Generally, GOs are most effective under the following conditions: when used as post organizers; when based on specific reading passages rather than overall content; and when presented to students of secondary and college age.

According to many content-area teachers who have continued employing GOs after studies were completed, their reason for doing so is that GOs are effective with large heterogeneous groups.

There is a section on graphic aids in Hoover and Patton's (1995) study skills book. They provide suggestions on three critical elements of graphic aids: understanding their purposes, developing one's own graphics, and attending to the relevant elements of those aids.

Monitor

To determine the effects of this technique, use a fill-in-the-blanks or a cloze procedure. In other words, require students to fill in some of the information on graphic organizers when they are given only the geometric shapes and a few clue words. Students could be required to fill in this information on forms that *were not* presented to them as graphic organizers and on forms that were scheduled as organizers. To maintain data, award a point for each blank completed properly. (There were 14 opportunities, for example, to supply information for the boxes underneath "French" and "English" in Figure 6.7.) Data from both conditions—with and without graphic organizer instruction—could be compared.

References

Bergerud, D., Lovitt, T. C., & Horton, S. V. (1988). The effectiveness of textbook adaptations in life science for high school students with learning disabilities. *Journal of Learning Disabilities, 21,* 70–76.

Hoover, J. J., & Patton, J. R. (1995). *Teaching students with learning problems to use study skills.* Austin, TX: PRO-ED.

Horton, S. V., & Lovitt, T. C. (1989). Construction and implementation of graphic organizers for academically handicapped and regular secondary students. *Academic Therapy, 24,* 625–640.

LEARNING FROM TEXTBOOKS: VISUAL-SPATIAL APPROACH

Background

In the visual-spatial (V-S) approach to teaching, an association is made between key words and certain shapes, which are then linked together to form a visual representation of the relationship among main ideas in a written passage. This format works best with materials that fit one of two classic styles of organization: (1) presenting a main idea supported by subordinate ideas or (2) showing interrelationships among main ideas. As explained here, the Direct Instruction method of teaching is used to instruct the concepts and relationships in the V-S approach.

Who Can Benefit

In a study by Lovitt, Stein, and Rudsit (1985), the V-S technique was employed with seventh graders with learning disabilities in a resource room. Although the subject matter in these studies was science, V-S formats can be applied to most content areas. Using visual cues to aid retention of facts should be especially beneficial to students who have difficulty processing written information.

Procedures

Creating a Visual-Spatial Display

1. Read the chapter carefully, looking for arrangements such as those mentioned in the Background section above. Also note pictures and ideas that could serve to enhance the V-S approach.

2. Highlight the main points in the chapter. Indicate related and subordinate features as well.

3. Arrange and group these key facts and related items on a page arranged like an organizational chart (see Figures 6.8 and 6.9).

   a. Start with main ideas, branching out and adding others that pertain to primary and subordinate ideas.

   b. Use different shapes to indicate degrees of importance and relationships and to trigger students' memory.

Initial Teaching Presentation

1. Provide each student with a copy of the completed visual-spatial chart, and display an identical copy on the overhead projector.

2. Direct students to look at the first piece of information, for example, 3 in Figure 6.9.

3. Read aloud the words in that space, "Water is made of molecules."

4. Instruct students to repeat the fact or phrase you just read. (Cue: "Say it.")

5. Provide related information and further explanations as appropriate.

6. Follow up by telling students to remember the phrase, its position on the chart, and the shape that encloses it.

7. Drill students over the other phrases and words using this same approach.

Expanded Teaching Presentation

1. Place a transparency of the incomplete visual-spatial chart on an overhead projector.

2. Give each student a copy of the blank chart.

3. Tell students to look at the first blank shape.

4. Instruct them to listen to the words that go in the blank.

5. Read the words to them.

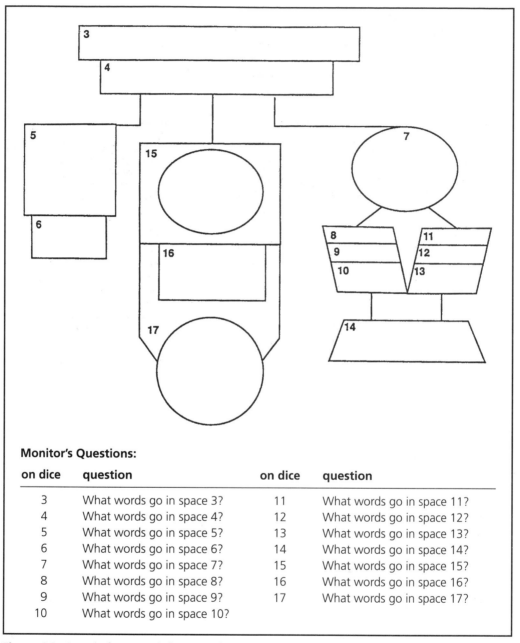

Monitor's Questions:

on dice	question	on dice	question
3	What words go in space 3?	11	What words go in space 11?
4	What words go in space 4?	12	What words go in space 12?
5	What words go in space 5?	13	What words go in space 13?
6	What words go in space 6?	14	What words go in space 14?
7	What words go in space 7?	15	What words go in space 15?
8	What words go in space 8?	16	What words go in space 16?
9	What words go in space 9?	17	What words go in space 17?
10	What words go in space 10?		

Figure 6.8. Sample framework for a visual-spatial display. From material developed from a contract from U.S. Government, Department of Education, to R. Dixon, 1983–1984.

6. Require students to repeat what you have just said.

7. Repeat the process with all facts needed to fill in the chart.

8. Ask students to look at the first blank space again.

9. Request them to say the words that should go in the blank.

10. Repeat this procedure for all the facts.

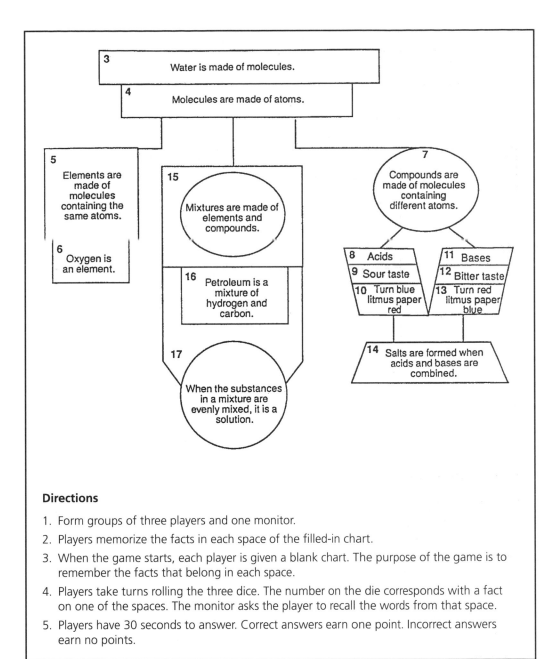

3 Water is made of molecules.

4 Molecules are made of atoms.

5 Elements are made of molecules containing the same atoms.

6 Oxygen is an element.

15 Mixtures are made of elements and compounds.

16 Petroleum is a mixture of hydrogen and carbon.

17 When the substances in a mixture are evenly mixed, it is a solution.

7 Compounds are made of molecules containing different atoms.

8 Acids
9 Sour taste
10 Turn blue litmus paper red

11 Bases
12 Bitter taste
13 Turn red litmus paper blue

14 Salts are formed when acids and bases are combined.

Directions

1. Form groups of three players and one monitor.
2. Players memorize the facts in each space of the filled-in chart.
3. When the game starts, each player is given a blank chart. The purpose of the game is to remember the facts that belong in each space.
4. Players take turns rolling the three dice. The number on the die corresponds with a fact on one of the spaces. The monitor asks the player to recall the words from that space.
5. Players have 30 seconds to answer. Correct answers earn one point. Incorrect answers earn no points.

Figure 6.9. Example of a completed visual-spatial display. From material developed from a contract from U.S. Government, Department of Education, to R. Dixon, 1983–1984.

V-S Game

1. Begin playing the V-S Game when students have demonstrated familiarity with all items.
2. Form teams. Either the teacher or the students may choose the team members.

3. Appoint the highest performing student in each group as the monitor for that team.

4. Explain that the teams are to take turns throwing three dice, one team member at a time.

5. Give each team monitor a script of the questions and a list of all the pupils on his or her team.

6. Instruct monitors to ask a student the question that corresponds to his or her roll of the dice (e.g., if a student rolls a 3, ask him or her to supply information for space 3).

7. Direct the monitor to mark a 1 next to the name of each pupil who gives a correct answer. For incorrect answers, the monitor will read the correct answer and ask the student who erred to repeat it.

8. Alternate this question-and-answer procedure between the teams until all the questions have been answered.

9. Award prizes to teams, individuals, or both.

Modifications and Considerations

Once pupils have learned to play the V-S Game, the teacher should allow them to manage the game themselves, and step in only if necessary to ensure that it runs smoothly. It would be a good idea to establish a few basic management rules before turning things over to the students.

The V-S procedure could be expanded by having students develop their own V-S charts for later chapters, and including other subjects in the process. Examples of other sets of facts or features that could be represented visually would be (a) a diagram of the atom, showing electrons, protons, and neutrons; (b) a chart explaining the metric system; (c) maps, including rivers, cities, mountain ranges; (d) derivations of words; (e) a schematic of the automobile's electric system; and (f) the families of instruments in the orchestra (Engleman, Davis, & Davis, 1986).

Monitor

The V-S approach could be evaluated in a rather traditional way, using teacher-developed tests or tests prepared by the textbook publishers, only some of which are accompanied by the V-S Game.

References

Engleman, S., Davis, K., & Davis, G. (1986). *Your world of facts I: A memory development program.* Tigard, OR: CC Publications.

Lovitt, T. C., Stein, M., & Rudsit, J. (1985). *The use of visual spatial displays to teach science facts to learning disabled middle school students.* Unpublished manuscript, Experimental Education Unit, University of Washington, Seattle.

⊡ LEARNING VOCABULARY: PRECISION TEACHING VOCABULARY SHEETS

Background

Students must learn the important words of a subject to fully understand it. The following are some physical science words that seventh graders are expected to know: *observation, experiment, probing, investigate, environment, chemistry, solution, amplify, voltage, molecule, compound, nuclear,* and *dissolve.* The approach for teaching vocabulary described here is based on features of Precision Teaching (PT): setting performance aims, charting performances, making instructional decisions from those data, and practicing on those materials until aims are reached.

Who Can Benefit

Mastery of the specialized vocabulary of most content-area classes can be especially difficult for students whose reading ability is below average. In a study by Lovitt, Rudsit, Jenkins, Pious, and Benedetti (1985), pupils from several seventh-grade science classes were instructed using PT sheets. Those students were instructed in groups of six: two high-performing, two average-performing, and two low-performing students.

Procedures

Constructing Vocabulary Sheets

1. Identify the key words in a chapter or passage in one of the following ways:

   a. Select the italicized words or those the publisher has otherwise highlighted.

   b. Copy the words the publisher identified in a vocabulary section (often located at the end of the chapter).

   c. Select the essential words from the introduction or summary section of the chapter.

   d. Select those words identified in the book's glossary.

   e. Choose key words from the index.

   f. Require a few pupils to read the chapter, and note words they cannot pronounce or those for which they do not know the meaning.

2. Write simple definitions for the words that were identified, following these guidelines:

   a. Include words familiar to the students.

   b. Keep definitions short (4 to 10 words) with no unnecessary words.

3. Print the words and definitions at the top of the vocabulary sheet. Below these words, print the vocabulary words over and over on the grid so that each term appears three or four times (see Figure 6.10, Answer Side of PT sheet).

4. Print only the vocabulary words (no definitions) at the top of the other side of the sheet (see Figure 6.11, Question Side of PT sheet). Below these, write only the definitions over and over on the grid so that they correspond with the words on the other side of the sheet.

Completing the Precision Teaching Package

1. Give each student a manila folder. Attach an acetate sheet to one of the inside flaps; on the inside of the other flap, tape a graph (see illustration of Precision Teaching folder in Figure 6.12).

2. Personalize the folders. Ask students to write their names on the folders. Students could decorate their folders according to a theme of their choice.

3. Establish a management system for storing and handing out folders. Choose methods that are straightforward and fit with your management style.

4. Purchase erasable marking pens for the students.

Teaching with PT Vocabulary Sheets

1. Pass out folders and pens.

2. Give the following directions:[1]

   a. Turn the folder lengthwise so that the hinge of the acetate sheet is in the middle and opens nearest to you.

   b. Place the practice sheets under the acetate with the "blank" definitions facing you.

   c. With the special pen, fill in the blanks on your sheets using the proper vocabulary words as fast as you can.

   d. Start with the item farthest to the left on the top row, move one at a time across that row, then to the item on the left on the next row. Do not skip around.

   e. Write as neatly and as rapidly as you can.

   f. If necessary, refer to the list of words at the top of the page to check your spelling.

   g. If necessary, flip the sheet over and look at the definitions if you cannot remember the meaning of a word.

3. Allow students to work for 1 minute.

---

[1]Give Instructions f and g only if necessary.

ANSWER SIDE

buoyance = upward push on an object placed in a liquid

displacement = way to determine the volume of an odd-shaped piece of matter

SI = international system of units (Metric System)

standard = fixed quantity used in measuring

hypothesis = proposed answer to a question or tentative solution to a problem

observing = taking notice and gathering data; using senses to find out things

inference = conclusion based on observation

scientific method = orderly way to solve problems: observing, measuring, explaining, and testing

SI (SI)	observing (ob)	standard (stan)	displacement (dis)	displacement (dis)
hypothesis (hyp)	buoyancy (buo)	inference (in)	hypothesis (hyp)	scientific method (s.m.)
displacement (dis)	observing (ob)	scientific method (s.m.)	inference (in)	displacement (dis)
inference (in)	scientific method (s.m.)	SI (SI)	observing (ob)	hypothesis (hyp)
standard (stan)	buoyancy (buo)	standard (stan)	observing (ob)	buoyancy (buo)

Figure 6.10. Example of answer side of Precision Teaching vocabulary sheet.

QUESTION SIDE

buoyance (buo)
displacement (dis)
SI (SI)
standard (stan)

a hypothesis (hyp)
observing (ob)
an inference (in)
scientific method (s.m.)

Student ______
Date ______
Teacher ______
Period ______

______ is an international system of units (Metric System).	______ is taking notice and gathering data; using senses to find out things.	A fixed quantity used in measuring is ______.	______ is a way to determine the volume of an odd-shaped piece of matter.	______ is an international system of units (Metric System).
______ is a proposed answer to a question or tentative solution to a problem.	The upward push on an object placed in a liquid is called ______.	A conclusion based on observation is called ______.	______ is a proposed answer to a question or tentative solution to a problem.	______ is a way to solve problems: observing, measuring, explaining, and testing.
______ is a way to determine the volume of an odd-shaped piece of matter.	A fixed quantity used in measuring is ______.	______ is a way to solve problems: observing, measuring, explaining, and testing.	A conclusion based on observation is called ______.	______ is a way to determine the volume of an odd-shaped piece of matter.
A conclusion based on observation is called ______.	______ is a way to solve problems: observing, measuring, explaining, and testing.	______ is an international system of units (Metric System).	______ is taking notice and gathering data; using senses to find out things.	______ is a proposed answer to a question or tentative solution to a problem.
A fixed quantity used in measuring is ______.	The upward push on an object placed in a liquid is called ______.	A fixed quantity used in measuring is ______.	______ is taking notice and gathering data; using senses to find out things.	The upward push on an object placed in a liquid is called ______.

Figure 6.11. Example of question side of Precision Teaching vocabulary sheet.

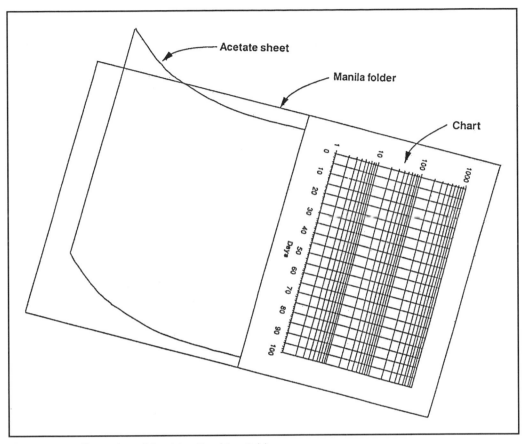

Figure 6.12. Illustration of Precision Teaching Folder.

4. Instruct students to check and count their answers, when finished, in the following manner:

   a. Flip the practice sheets over and compare your responses with the answers on the sheet.

   b. Circle incorrect answers and write in the correct word.

   c. Count the number of correct and incorrect answers.

5. Describe the components of a graph (inside the folder) to students and explain how to chart their data:

   a. Vertical lines = *Day Lines* (Sunday is represented by heavy lines, with each succeeding line representing successive days of the week.)

   b. Horizontal lines = *Rate Lines* (Explain what the 1s, 10s, and 100s, and the lines in between them indicate.)

   c. Place data from the first timing on the first day's line of the first week, and so on.

   Note: Four timings, one after another, 3 times a week, is recommended.

6. Ask students to evaluate their scores by comparing their best score with a classroom goal.

7. Collect folders and pens, quietly and quickly. File the folders so they can be accounted for and distributed easily the next session. Count pens to see that all have been returned.

Modifications and Considerations

PT vocabulary sheets can be altered in several ways. For instance, the number of words could vary from the example, or abbreviations might be used in place of whole words for definitions. The advantage to using abbreviations is that students can cover more ground during the 1-minute timings. A word of caution, however: Test students periodically to make sure they remember what words the abbreviations stand for.

As with other types of adaptations—study guides or graphics—vocabulary sheets can be used for peer tutoring, pair teaching, homework, or review sheets.

McDade and Olander (1990) carried out studies with flash cards to teach vocabulary referred to as SAFMEDS (SA = say; F = facts; one M = minute; E = each; D = day; then S = shuffle). Results showed that the procedure was quite effective in teaching vocabulary.

Monitor

Suggestions for monitoring appear in numbers 4 and 5 of "Teaching with PT Vocabulary Sheets." The classroom goal mentioned in number 6 may be based on the performance of one of the best students in the class. The suggested rate is about 20 correct answers per minute.

References

Lovitt, T., Rudsit, J., Jenkins, J., Pious, C., & Benedetti, D. (1985). Two methods of adapting science materials for learning disabled and regular seventh graders. *Learning Disability Quarterly, 8,* 275–285.

McDade, C. E., & Olander, C. P. (1990). SAFMEDS design: A comparison of three protocols. *Journal of Precision Teaching, 7*(2), 69–71.

THE UNIT ORGANIZER ROUTINE

Background

The *Unit Organizer Routine* (Lenz, Bulgren, Shumaker, Deshler, & Boudah, 1995) is one of nine components in *The Content Enhancement Series.* Two others in the series are *The Course Organizer Routine,* broader than the Unit Routine, and *The Chapter Survey Routine,* more specific than the Unit Routine. According to Lenz et al., a unit is a "chunk" of content that is selected to organize information into lessons and ends in some type of closure (i.e., a test). The Unit Routine is used to help introduce and build a block of material so that students can

- Understand how that unit can be part of bigger ideas or sequences of units.

- Experience a method for organizing knowledge.

- Define the relationships associated with knowledge.

- Clarify what has been taught with what must be learned.

- Monitor progress and accomplishments in learning.

- Recognize what has been learned through self-questioning.

Who Can Benefit

The Unit Routine and other routines in *The Content Enhancement Series* are designed to help students in content areas such as social studies and science. The Unit Routine and related routines are especially helpful for students who have limited backgrounds in those subjects, or are disorganized in their attempts to gather information from those subjects.

Procedures

The following are general points to consider when arranging the Unit Routine:

- Introduce the routine explicitly.
- Use the routine regularly.
- Adapt the routine to meet the unique needs of students.
- Vary the use of the routine occasionally.
- Integrate the routine over time with other routines in the series.
- Actively involve the students with the routine.

The following are specific suggestions for using the Unit Routine:

- Present a visual device, the Unit Organizer, to students to introduce each unit.

- Follow a set of embedded Linking Steps within an instructional sequence, the Can-Do Review Sequence, during the interactive presentation of the Unit Organizer.

The 10 sections of the Unit Organizer
(1 through 8 are on Figure 6.13 and 9 and 10 are on Figure 6.14)

1. *Current Unit*—Title of the new unit.

2. *Last Unit/Experience*—Name of the last unit that was covered.

3. *Next Unit/Experience*—Name of the unit that will follow.

4. *Bigger Picture*—Name of the idea or theme that holds several units together.

5. *Unit Map*—Includes two types of information. Unit Paraphrase is written in the oval at the top of the section and the Content Map is a graphic depiction of how the unit content is organized.

6. *Unit Relationships*—The names of the relationships that might be important to look for as unit information is processed.

7. *Unit Self-Test Questions*—Questions that students should be able to answer when the unit is complete.

8. *Unit Schedule*—Summarizes the schedule of required tasks, activities, or assignments.

9. *Expanded Unit Map*—Reverse side of the map is used to expand the Unit Map by adding subtopics and key vocabulary.

10. *New Unit Self-Test Questions*—Questions the teacher and students identify as they explore the unit.

The Five Linking Steps

1. *Create a Context*—Help students see how information in the current unit is connected to previous and future learning.

2. *Recognize Content Structures*—Assist students to see how information in the unit can be structured to aid comprehension.

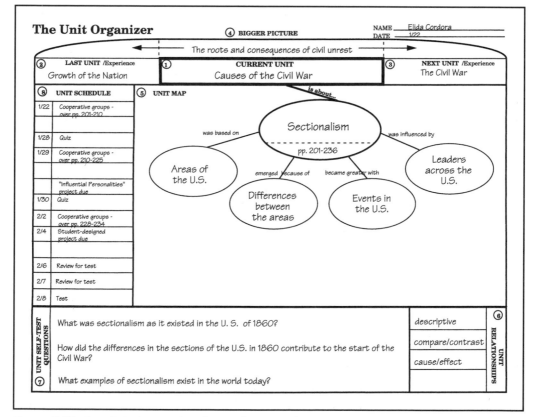

Figure 6.13. Sample Unit Organizer, front side. From *The Unit Organizer Routine,* by B. K. Lenz, J. A. Bulgren, J. B. Schumaker, D. D. Deshler, and D. A. Boudah, 1995, Lawrence, KS: Edge Enterprises. Copyright 1995 by Edge Enterprises. Reprinted with permission.

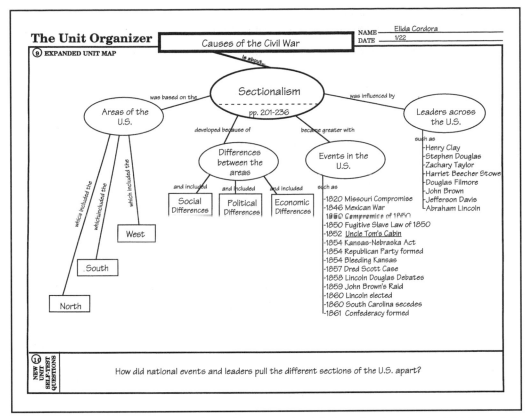

Figure 6.14. Sample Unit Organizer, back side. From *The Unit Organizer Routine,* by B. K. Lenz, J. A. Bulgren, J. B. Schumaker, D. D. Deshler, and D. A. Boudah, 1995, Lawrence, KS: Edge Enterprises. Copyright 1995 by Edge Enterprises. Reprinted with permission.

3. *Acknowledge Unit Relationships*—Ask students, after they see how information can be structured, to identify relationships that might be important to understand the information.

4. *Frame Unit Questions*—Lead students to generate and discuss the types of questions that might be posed about important relationships in the unit.

5. *Tie Content to Tasks*—Create Unit Schedule to assist students to see how tasks are related to help answer test questions and understand relationships shown in the Unit Map.

Modifications and Considerations

The Linking Steps are listed here in an order that several teachers have found to be effective. Other orders can be arranged, however. The way the Unit Organizer is presented can also be varied. Blank organizer forms can be distributed to students, and the class or groups of students can construct the material. Another option is for the teacher to use a blank organizer on the overhead projector and work with the class to construct portions of it, then require students to complete the rest on their own.

Monitor

One way to evaluate the effects of this routine would be to assay the extent to which students responded correctly to the questions posed and incorporated in the routine. Another, broader way to evaluate the effects of the routine would be to have the students write freely about what they learned in the current unit and how that tied in with material from previous units.

Reference

Lenz, B. K., Bulgren, J. A., Schumaker, J. B., Deshler, D. D., & Boudah, D. A. (1995). *The unit organizer routine.* Lawrence, KS: Edge Enterprises.

STUDENTWORKS: A MULTIMEDIA METHOD

Background

StudentWorks (Sladden, 1998) provides students with an engaging computer learning environment for organizing, storing, and retrieving information in purposeful ways. According to Sladden, the power behind *StudentWorks* is that it assists students to build mental templates that create a filing and organizational system that they can draw on their entire lives. Extending the use and power of computers is a basic and crucial skill for children growing up in this Information Age. The *StudentWorks* templates motivate students to acquire information and vocabulary in context, rather than through isolated and often unrelated activities.

Who Can Benefit

A wide range of age levels and types of students can profit from this program.

Procedures

Seven distinct but interconnected files comprise the *StudentWorks* program:

1. *Index Card NoteTaker*—NoteTaker provides index card layouts for notetaking. With this file the student can create up to eight categories and use unlimited keywords for labeling information. It helps pupils to learn about indexing and identifying main ideas. New words may be transferred to the WordBank file, along with contextual notes and research tags.

2. *Bibliography Maker*—This file is suitable for any reference style and is updated for the Internet. This template provides a layout noting source information ready to post into the NoteTaker file.

3. *Write a Report*—Notes in this file may be sorted into customized categories or converted into an outline format, ready to export to a word processor as an initial draft.

4. *WordBank*—Students may enter new vocabulary, personal definitions, pictures, and sounds into this file, the contents of which transfer automatically from NoteTaker. This file works in conjunction with any on-line dictionary or the customized dictionary of *StudentWorks*. It aids in teaching connotation by asking students to choose the best synonym for a context, and illustrates word structure through a word derivation feature. The file features an on-screen cloze rehearsal exercise, printed lists, and card games. (See Figure 6.15.)

5. *Custom Dictionaries*—The dictionaries may be customized to match content area (e.g., U.S. history) and the students' level of understanding. Dictionaries of Latin roots, common homonyms, and a sample set of basic social studies vocabulary words are automatically included in a student's WordBank on matching word entry.

6. *Word Work Games*—Spelling words identified while notetaking or entering words into the WordBank may be rehearsed on screen as cloze exercises or printed as lists.

7. *Graphic Organizers*—Paragraph structure screens motivate students to recognize and use compare–contrast, cause–effect, simple listing, and time–order patterns. Drop-down lists aid retrieval of signal words.

All files provide hard copies of flash cards, index cards, and reference lists.

Modifications and Considerations

A consideration of this program would be to ensure that students know a fair amount about computers generally and about navigating through this program specifically. Those students who have reasonable keyboarding skills would profit the most from such a program. As for modifications, one could focus on certain aspects of the program and leave other options open or available for a later time. For example, the teacher might see fit to work with a youngster, or a group of students, with vocabulary definitions.

Monitor

One way to measure the effects of this program would be to schedule unit or chapter tests, that is, to give a series of tests over large chunks of material. The student could use the *StudentWorks* program for some and use a different program for others. Pupils' scores on those tests could be compared. A more focused evaluation would be to determine how well the program helped students learn definitions to vocabulary, since learning vocabulary is one of the key units of this package.

Reference

Sladden, E. (1998). *StudentWorks*. New York: The Learning Studio.

WORD LIST AS OF MARCH 1, 1999

Word	Definition	Sentence
befall Part of Speech: verb Synonym: come Antonym: go My Definition: happen	To happen to one	And may no accidents **befall** our children.
flowed Part of Speech: verb Synonym: rushed Antonym: dallied My Definition: comes	To move or run smoothly.	The Iroquois believed that the "sweet water" **flowed** from the maples because the trees wanted to help them.
sympathy Part of Speech: noun Synonym: pity Antonym: cruelty My Definition: care	Concern for someone in misfortune.	A player who got injured received little **sympathy** from his teammates because they thought it was a disgrace to get hurt.
famine Part of Speech: noun Synonym: shortage Antonym: abundance My Definition: no food or water	A drastic, wide-reaching food shortage.	A good game might please the spirits who favored it so much that they would drive away **famine** and disease.
impatient Part of Speech: adjective Synonym: eager Antonym: reticent My Definition: can't wait	Intensely desirous or interested.	The maple candy was given to the **impatient** children.
ceremony Part of Speech: noun Synonym: service Antonym: abundance My Definition: a play	A special act or set of acts to be done on special occasions such as weddings or funerals.	The **ceremony** lasted far into the night.
raise Part of Speech: verb Synonym: lift Antonym: lower My Definition: lift up	To move to a higher position; elevate.	There is a special way to walk with snowshoes. The children learn to turn in their toes and **raise** each foot higher than usual with each step.

Figure 6.15. Word list for *StudentWorks*. From *StudentWorks,* by E. Sladden, 1998, New York: The Learning Studio. Copyright 1998 by the Learning Studio. Reprinted with permission.

Chapter 7
TESTING AND GRADING

♦ ♦

Testing and grading youth is one of the most bothersome issues that educators face, particularly the testing and grading of youth in English as a Second Language or Title 1 programs, or youth with disabilities. Testing and grading are related: The teacher gives a few tests, then adds up or averages the scores and assigns a grade. However, when it comes to giving a particular type of test and granting certain types of grades, many teachers are not confident as to why they "do what they do." Many of their evaluation choices may be based on expedience or tradition.

So why test? There are a couple of good reasons. One would be to determine how well a student was doing something or how well a teacher was instructing. When it comes to testing, it should be both direct and frequent—direct because there should be concordance between what is taught and what is tested, and frequent because it is necessary to know when and if progress is being made. As for grading, I assume that the primary reason is to grant the level of merit that has been earned, be that a high or a low grade. Ideally, testing and grading should be used to motivate the performer to do better next time.

In this chapter I offer several approaches for testing and grading youth, especially those classified as disabled. I have also included write-ups that pertain to a few troublesome evaluation issues with respect to youth with disabilities. In addition to the tactics in this chapter, two test-taking techniques were explained in Chapter 3, Study Skills.

ADAPTING CLASSROOM TESTS

Background

According to Wood (1998), tests can be adapted during their preparation, as they are administered, or by providing alternative test sites.

Who Can Benefit

Most youth, especially youth with disabilities, would be assisted in their test taking if some of the ideas offered here were implemented.

Procedures

Adaptations During Test Construction

Test Directions

1. Keep directions short and simple; avoid unnecessary words.

2. Type directions or print them neatly.

3. Place directions at the beginning of each separate test section.

4. List directions vertically, when more than one is given.

5. List only one direction in each sentence.

6. Underline the word *Directions* to focus the student's attention. Possibly color code the directions.

7. Read some of the directions orally.

8. Roam around the room as the test is being administered to see if youth are reading and following the directions.

Adapting Test Items

9. For multiple-choice tests, avoid fillers (e.g., "either–or," "all of the above").

10. Allow students to circle the correct answers rather than placing answers on a separate sheet.

11. Place all matching items and choice selections on the same page.

12. Use small groups of matching questions. Avoid long matching lists.

13. Have only one correct answer for each item.

14. Keep all matching items brief.

15. Avoid starting true–false questions negatively.

16. Avoid statements that are trivial or do not assess student knowledge.

17. Place the words *true* and *false* at the end of the sentence, for that type of test item.

18. Provide large blanks for students with poor handwriting for completion items.

19. Provide word banks for completion items.

20. Underline clue words.

Test Design

21. Use test items that reflect techniques you used in teaching.

22. Prepare a study guide that matches the design of the test.

23. Prepare the test in short sections that you can administer individually if necessary.

24. Arrange tests so that questions that count the most come first.

25. Use canary yellow paper with black print for the test.

26. Write the point value for each section on the test.

27. Number all pages of the test.

Adaptations During Test Administration

1. Avoid long talks before giving the test.

2 Allow students to tape-record responses to essay questions or to the entire test.

3 Provide an example of the expected correct response.

4. Remind students to check tests for unanswered questions.

5. Provide breaks during lengthy tests.

6. Do not threaten dire consequences for failure.

Alternative Test Sites

1. In the special education or resource room

2. At home, with supervision

3. In the library

Modifications and Considerations

It is important to match up the test with the previous instruction. This is a major criticism of some tests. In my view, there is no point in instructing one thing and testing another. It is important also, in selecting a format for the test, to choose one that is to the pupils' liking, one they are familiar with, one they can work with, and one that matches with the task they have been taught. As for the latter, if students are being taught to drive nails with a hammer, it would be better to assess their mastery of that skill as they drove nails rather than to give a written multiple-choice test. The former type of assessment is referred to as an authentic assessment.

Monitor

It would be helpful to evaluate whatever type of testing accommodation was arranged. Before and after arrangements would be revealing.

Reference

Wood, J. W. (1998). *Adapting instruction for mainstreamed and at-risk students.* (3rd ed.). Upper Saddle River, NJ: Merrill/Prentice-Hall.

SEVERAL WAYS TO GRADE STUDENTS WITH DISABILITIES

Background

Valdes, Williamson, and Wagner (1990) reported that 60% of high school students with disabilities had grade point averages of 2.24 or lower, and that 64% of mainstreamed secondary students with disabilities were graded on the same standards as their general education peers. Of those students in special education classes, 74% of them were graded on standards different from those used in general education.

Who Can Benefit

As with other write-ups in this chapter, the students who stand to gain the most from the suggestions offered here are those with special problems or needs.

Procedures

Lazzari (1992) offered 10 ways to evaluate students. She defined and gave an example of each approach (see Table 7.1). I will simply make a comment or two on each, being especially mindful of their use with students with disabilities.

1. *Traditional grading*—An advantage of this method is that it is the same way in which other students are graded. This system may be unfair to some students with disabilities, however. They may not be able to achieve at the same level as other students.

2. *Pass/fail system*—This approach has two possible advantages: (1) students may feel less pressure to compete and perhaps less anxiety, and (2) the teacher does not have to compare a student's work with that of others. It also has two possible disadvantages: (1) students may do less work when freed of traditional grade pressure, and (2) teachers may find it difficult to define minimum standards. According to Polloway et al. (1994), this option was used in 25% of the cases they sampled.

3. *IEP grading*—Teachers should resist any temptation to minimize short-term expectations by writing shorter and easier objectives to help students achieve better grades. It is important when this method of evaluation is used to be certain the IEP objectives are ones worth achieving.

4. *Mastery-level or criterion systems*—If the material is divided into subcomponents, the components should be as equal as possible. It is necessary to convince students that each part is important and essential to make up the whole.

5. *Multiple grading*—The weighting of the components (e.g., attitude, effort, accomplishment) could be adjusted from time to time. According

Table 7.1. Alternative Approaches to Student Evaluation

Approach	Definition	Example
1. Traditional grading	Letter grades or percentages are assigned.	Students earning 94% or greater of the total points available will earn an A.
2. Pass/fail system	Broad-based criteria are established for passing or failing.	Students who complete all assignments and pass all tests will receive a passing grade for the course.
3. IEP grading	Competency levels on student's IEP are translated into the school district's performance standards.	If students have an IEP that requires a 90% accuracy level and the range of 86–93 equals a letter grade of B on the local scale, the students receive a B if they attain target accuracy level.
4. Mastery-level or criterion grading	Content is divided into subcomponents. Students earn credit when their mastery of a certain skill reaches an acceptable level.	Students who can name 38 of the 50 state capitals will receive a passing grade on that unit of the social studies curriculum.
5. Multiple grading	The student is assessed and graded in several areas, such as ability, effort, and achievement.	Students will receive 30 points for completing the project on time, 35 points for including all of the assigned sections, and 35 points for using at least four different resources.
6. Shared grading	Two or more teachers determine a student's grade.	The regular education teacher will determine 60% of the student's grade and the resource room teacher will determine 40%.
7. Point system	Points are assigned to activities or assignments that add up to the term grade.	The student's science grade will be based on a total of 300 points: 100 from weekly quizzes, 100 from lab work in class, 50 from homework, and 50 from class participation.
8. Student self-comparison	Students evaluate themselves on an individual basis.	Students who judge that they have completed the assignment on time, included the necessary sections, and worked independently assign themselves a passing grade for this assignment.
9. Contracting	The student and teacher agree on specific activities required for a certain grade.	Students who come to class regularly, volunteer information at least once during each class, and turn in all required work will receive a C.
10. Portfolio evaluation	A cumulative portfolio is maintained of each student's work, demonstrating achievement in key skill areas from Kindergarten to Grade 12.	Cumulative samples of handwriting show progress from rudimentary manuscript to legible cursive style from Grades 1 to 4.

Note. From "Alternative Grading Procedures," by A. M. Lazzari, in *Adapting Instruction for Mainstreamed and At-Risk Students* (pp. 350–351), by J. W. Wood, 1992, Upper Saddle River, NJ: Merrill/Prentice-Hall, Copyright 1992 by A. M. Lazzari. Reprinted with permission.

to Polloway et al. (1994), a sizable number of districts sampled used this grading option.

6. *Shared grading*—The two or three teachers who determine the grade for a student should get together from time to time to discuss matters of balance and equity. In those schools that advocate co-teaching, this would be an option to consider. Polloway et al. (1994) reported that only 12% of the cases sampled used this method.

7. *Point system*—A possible advantage of this approach might be that many students in special education are familiar with token economies and point systems.

8. *Student self-comparison*—It may be important to involve students in other aspects of self-determination before they are allowed to grade themselves. Ultimately, however, this would be one of the goals of a self-management program.

9. *Contracting*—As with point systems, a possible advantage of this approach is that many pupils in special education have had experiences with contingency contracts.

10. *Portfolio evaluation*—Portfolios are excellent ways to evaluate and grade. It is necessary to decide exactly what will go into them and occasionally clean them out.

Modifications and Considerations

Another type of grading that has gained some favor is the "rubric" method. When it is used the anticipated performance is described in several ways. For the top grade, pupils must carry out all the events in that description, but for a lesser grade, they may comply with fewer requirements.

Monitor

Something to keep in mind when selecting a way in which to grade or test is the match between the method of evaluation, whatever is being taught, and the purpose or objectives of the instruction. Those three features of teaching are not always lined up as perfectly as they should be. Sometimes there is one set of objectives, another thing is taught, and yet another thing is evaluated.

References

Lazzari, A. M. (1992). Alternative Grading Procedures. In J. W. Wood, *Adapting instruction for mainstreamed and at-risk students* (2nd ed.) (pp. 350–351). Upper Saddle River, NJ: Merrill/Prentice-Hall.

Polloway, E. A., Epstein, M. H., Bursuck, W. D., Roderique, T. W., McConeghy, J. L., & Jayanthi, M. (1994). Classroom grading: A national survey of policies. *Remedial and Special Education, 15* 162–170.

Valdes, K. A., Williamson, C. L., & Wagner, M. M. (1990). *The national longitudinal transition study of special education students* (Vol. 1). Menlo Park, CA: SRI International.

SEVERAL MORE WAYS TO GRADE STUDENTS WITH DISABILITIES

Background

Whereas the suggestions for grading in the preceding tactic are more traditional, the ones briefly explained here are not as widely used and are perhaps a bit more imaginative.

Who Can Benefit

Youth characterized as at risk or remedial and others with special needs could be motivated to improve their performances by these techniques.

Procedures

The following suggestions are from Fister and Kemp (1995).

1. *Combination grading*—This approach involves the use of different performance measures, such as demonstrations, interviews, projects, exhibits, oral tests, and other approaches. All of the student's scores are taken into account to arrive at a grade.

2. *Coded grading*—Coded grading utilizes three levels within each of the standard letter grades (e.g., A1, A2, A3, B1, B2, B3). The numbers assigned to each letter grade represent the following:

   1 = use of above grade-level material
   2 = use of on grade-level material
   3 = use of below grade-level material

3. *Asterisk grading*—An asterisk indicates that certain accommodations were made in order to meet the student's needs. The specific accommodations could be indicated by marking them on a checklist (e.g., "Test was read to the student").

4. *A/B/C/Not yet*—This approach is based on a mastery learning premise that all students will succeed. If a student does not demonstrate minimal competency performance or above, then a "Not Yet" is given and reteaching is provided.

5. *Double grading*—The student is given two grades, such as A/C or C/C. The top grade represents the student's learning over the instructional time period, compared to his or her beginning performance. The bottom grade represents the student's performance compared to the entire class' performance.

6. *Challenge grading*—Different point values are assigned for test questions (or other performance measures, such as demonstrations, interviews, projects, exhibits) based on their level of difficulty. The student is given the option of answering or performing the following:

- A group of 10 easier level questions or tasks valued at 10 points each (total 100 points).

- A group of 5 slightly more difficult questions or tasks valued at 20 points each (total 100).

- A group of 4 more difficult questions or tasks valued at 25 points each (total 100).

Modifications and Considerations

It is important to keep in mind that most individuals are pleased when they are given a high grade (with whatever form of grading is used) and when they believe they earned it. It can be counterproductive to simply grant high marks to someone who did not earn them and when that person knows full well that he or she did not earn the marks.

Monitor

It is not easy to evaluate grading procedures. Although the simplest way might be to ask for individuals' opinions regarding the method on which they had been graded, the results would not necessarily be useful. Another, more complex, way would be to determine whether any grading method had the effect or impact on individuals that it was supposed to have, such as to motivate youth to do more and better, to encourage youth to stay in school, or to encourage youth to ask more questions about what they were being taught. Educators need to spend more time thinking about just why grades are assigned in the first place.

Reference

Fister, S. L., & Kemp, K. A. (1995). *TGIF: But what will I do on Monday?* Longmont, CO: Sopris West.

INCREASING INTEREST IN SCHOOLS: ALLOWING STUDENTS TO PARTICIPATE IN GRADING

Background

This procedure can ensure uniformity of grading when implemented throughout the elementary, middle, and high school levels (Zoboroski, 1981). When these ideas are practiced, teachers have more time to work individually with students, and students become more independent and involved in their learning because they have access to lesson plans they helped to develop. Furthermore, the immediate feedback and clearly stated goals, which are a part of this procedure, can also help students achieve their goals.

Who Can Benefit

This tactic is suitable for many students who are at risk and remedial and others who appear to be overwhelmed or disfranchised by the grading process. This approach is particularly appropriate for students who require more precise feedback more often with respect to their assignments and grades.

Procedures

Part A: Structuring for Planning and Grading

1. Design a weekly lesson plan based on the academic status for each student involved in the program (see example in Figure 7.1).

   * Separate assignments by subject matter.

   * Place the title of the textbook or workbook, pages to be completed, and related objectives in the appropriate spaces (by subjects).

2. Check assignments immediately after they are completed.

3. Provide corrective feedback in the form of written comments on the work and with individual student conferences.

4. Record the number correct over the number possible below the specific assignment on the lesson plan.

5. Calculate and record daily percentages in the space below that.

6. Figure weekly averages by adding the percentages obtained on each assignment and dividing by the number of total grades for the week. Record the weekly average in the appropriate box.

Part B: Involving Students

Involve students in the grading process by having them check their own work and calculate their daily and weekly percentages.

1. Explain to students that, by taking on additional responsibilities for their work, they will learn to become more independent.

2. Hand out copies of individual lesson plans.

3. Discuss the format of the weekly lesson plan. Probe for their understanding of the plan by asking questions such as the following:

   * In what order will you complete each day's assignments? How is this shown on the weekly lesson plan?

   * How will you know which book to use and what pages to complete for each subject?

   * What have you done so far in any of the subjects?

4. Ask students to raise their hands when they have completed an assignment so you can check it and provide immediate feedback.

5. Explain to pupils that you will write their scores on each assignment showing the number correct over the number possible (e.g., 9/10), and review how to figure percentages.

6. Show students where to enter these scores on the weekly lesson plan, explain how to figure a weekly average, and indicate where to enter this figure.

WEEKLY LESSON PLAN

_____ Middle School

Resource Room

Name _____ Date _____

Subject	Monday	Tuesday	Wednesday	Thursday	Friday
Reading Oral/Silent Comprehension					
Weekly Average					
English					
Weekly Average					
Language Arts					
Weekly Average					
Vocabulary					
Weekly Average					
Spelling					
Weekly Average					
Phonics					
Weekly Average					
Skill Series					
Weekly Average					
Math					
Weekly Average					
Homework					
Science					
History					
English					
Math/Other					
Weekly Average					
Independent Work					
Weekly Average					

Figure 7.1. Example of a weekly lesson plan for allowing student participation in grading process. From "Planning and Grading LD Students," by J. Zoboroski, 1981, *Academic Therapy, 16,* pp. 466–467. Copyright 1981 by PRO-ED, Inc. Reprinted with permission.

7. Set aside a time at the end of each week or at the beginning of the following week during which students average their weekly grades and hand in their completed lesson plan sheets.

Modifications and Considerations

Carpenter (1985) recommended involving students in grading. According to him, they should assist in determining the objectives and in setting up contracts having to do with attaining those objectives.

Seattle middle school and high school students were asked to evaluate their teachers by completing a two-page form (Nelson, 1997). Not surprisingly, many of their teachers were outraged. Universities require that professors be routinely evaluated by their students. A few of them are outraged as well.

Monitor

Copies of all lesson plans and scores should be kept on file to document student performances. The information on these forms will be helpful in parent conferences, staffings, and other situations that require discussions of and decisions about educational progress and future planning for students.

As an incentive for students to improve in a specific area, chart (or have them chart) information that would illustrate their performance—for example, daily scores, percentage of assignments completed, or number of lesson plans turned in. This could be done on an individual basis, or could become a class project if competition is effective with your students. (See numbers 4, 5, and 6 of Part A and numbers 5, 6, and 7 of Part B.)

References

Carpenter, D. (1985). Grading handicapped pupils: Review and position statement. *Remedial and Special Education, 6*(4), 54–59.

Nelson, R. T. (1997). Seattle students have chance to grade teachers. *The Seattle Times,* Section B, p. 1.

Zoboroski, J. (1981). Planning for and grading LD students. *Academic Therapy, 16,* 463–471.

⏛ SOME VEXING ISSUES

Background

In this piece I discuss concerns regarding minimum competency tests, aptitude and achievement tests, and the awarding of diplomas, as these issues affect students, especially those with problems and disabilities. These important topics have troubled educators, parents, and students for decades.

Who Can Benefit

Presumably, if more careful thought and deliberation went into the topics discussed here, students of all types would be assisted, especially those who present special problems or have different needs.

Procedures

Following are four major topics having to do with evaluation and grading. I identify a few issues related to each. I also comment on and make suggestions for involving accommodations.

Minimum Competency Tests

Some states and districts grant diplomas to students when, and only when, they pass a minimum competency test. The primary reason for linking minimum competency tests to graduation is that schools do not want to put their stamp of approval on students who cannot read, write, or do much of anything else. According to Bodner, Clark, and Mellard (1987), 21 of 50 states reported requiring students to pass a test of this type to graduate. Those researchers also reported that a number of states offered certain accommodations to youth with disabilities as they took these tests. For example, in the year 2006, Washington State students will be required to earn a *State Certificate of Mastery,* which requires them to meet standards in reading, writing, communication, and mathematics. The determination of proficiency in those subjects will be based on performance on state-level assessments. This certificate is one of three requirements for graduation. Students will also have to meet state board of education requirements and any additional local district requirements. Along with plans for the certificate, safeguards are being developed to protect the rights and interests of students in special education, students with Section 504 plans, English as a Second Language and bilingual students, and migrant students.

Achievement Tests

Most states mandate achievement tests to track the numbers of students who are achieving at, above, and below grade level. In Washington State, for example, several types of achievement tests are given to youngsters at certain benchmark grades. Students in 3rd and 8th grades have been tested with the *Iowa Tests of Basic Skills, Form M* (Hoover, Hieronymus, Frisbie, & Dunbar, 1996), and students in the 11th grade have been tested with the *Iowa Tests of Educational Development, Form M* (Feldt, Forsyth, Ansley, & Alnot, 1996). The scores from those tests, especially the ones given the 3rd graders, are widely circulated, often published in newspapers, by district and school. Students in the 4th, 7th, and 10th grades have also been tested on the *Washington Assessment of Student Learning* (WASL) (1998), which has subtests in reading, mathematics, writing, and listening.

There is always debate as to which students, if any, should be excused from taking these tests. Considerations are given to youth taking the WASL, for example. Because the tests are not timed, students may have as much time as they need to complete their work. Moreover, rather elaborate guidelines for accommodations have been published. In the introduction to those guidelines is the caution that accommodations should not be used for pupils the first time they take the test. The guidelines are as follows:

1. For students receiving special education services, the IEP team should determine and document how they will be assessed and the nature of their accommodations.

2. For Section 504 students and ESL/bilingual and migrant students, a planning team should determine the appropriate accommodations.

3. For students with multiple needs, planning teams should take all the needs into account when recommending accommodations.

4. Parents should be involved in matters of assessment.

5. Planning teams should review their accommodation decisions from time to time.

Several "allowable" accommodations are listed for all students, including those with special needs. They have to do with scheduling and timing (e.g., providing more testing time, allowing frequent breaks, adjusting materials to attention span); setting (e.g., assessing students in a familiar school environment that maximizes their performance); aids or assistance (e.g., allowing math manipulatives as indicated, except calculators permitted only as specifically dictated in test directions); and format (e.g., allowing Braille or large-print editions of the assessment).

Scholastic Aptitude Test (SAT) (College Board, 1994)

Scores on the SAT and similar tests are used to determine, in part, whether a student is admitted to a 2- or 4-year college. The Educational Testing Service (ETS) has recommended several types of accommodations for special children and youth. Prior to arranging any of them, however, ETS wants certainty that the recipients are "special." Toward that end they have published an elaborate set of instructions and policies for determining types of disabilities, namely learning disabilities and attention deficit disorder. Some accommodations pertain to computer-based testing: extended testing time, additional breaks, detectable background and foreground colors, test reader, sign language interpreter, Kensington Trackball mouse, HeadMaster Plus mouse, intellikeys keyboard, and ZOOMTEXT. Other accommodations pertain to paper-and-pencil testing: extended testing time, additional breaks, writer to record answers, reader to dictate test questions, and sign language interpreter. They also suggest alternate test formats: Braille, enlarged print, large-print answer sheet, audiocassette with large-print figure supplement, and audiocassette with Braille figure supplement. ETS also asks that each recommended accommodation be accompanied by a rationale. [Those interested in accommodations or adjustments should contact the Services for Handicapped Students, P.O. Box 6226, Princeton, NJ 08541-6226.]

Diplomas

States have developed a variety of diplomas. Generally, one of three types may be awarded to youth with disabilities. *Regular diplomas* are awarded to students who take standard types of courses (e.g., math, English, science, social studies), or who exhibit competence in experiences listed on their IEPs, or who follow some combination of those two plans. In recent years, numbers of students with disabilities "defer" their diploma by not taking it after 4 years of high school or when they are 18 years old; instead, they remain in school a few more years, up to age 21, and then take their diploma. A regular diploma is also given in some locales to youth if they passed a literacy test or minimum competency test, or met other local or state regulations. *Special diplomas* or *modified diplomas* are sometimes awarded to students in special education who may not have earned the necessary units or passed the essential test, but who satisfactorily met other requirements, possibly those listed on their IEPs. *Certificates of attendance* are occasionally awarded to students who have not earned units or completed IEP requirements but who complied with some other obligation as prescribed by a local board.

Modifications and Considerations

Once schools have carefully considered and announced what it takes to earn a diploma, certificate of mastery or attendance, or other official affidavit, I believe they should stick with their plan; they should not quickly or casually abandon or even modify it. I hasten to inject, however, that there will always be some students who, try as they may, are unable to attain or even make progress toward the goal. It would not be appropriate to keep holding out the prize from those who are making efforts to succeed. To deny these students diplomas or something else until they pass the test could be demoralizing and cause many to become discouraged and drop out of school. Therefore, it is necessary to accommodate them in some way, such as establishing standards that they could master or modifying aspects of their situations so that they could be kept on line to receive the document. Most educators need to be informed as to the variety of possible accommodations. (See the lead write-up in Chapter 6, Adapting Materials.)

Regarding the latter type of accommodation, I like the idea advanced by ETS staff of providing a rationale for any modification or adaptation. That would cause professionals to think seriously about what they were trying to accomplish with the student. In presenting any rationale, the teacher should cite research (formal or otherwise) to support its value, and should include in the plan some method for evaluating the effects of this accommodation.

If educators are to assume that some good comes to youngsters from taking achievement tests, I would recommend that every child who is able to take the tests should, but those who would be troubled or totally baffled by them should not. Modifying achievement tests bears some serious thought, however. If they are to be given in the one prescribed way, as most test makers say they should be, then modifications would invalidate the data. But if the purpose is to give as many children as possible the "opportunity" to take these tests, then why not make the necessary adjustments? The question I have about giving achievement tests, and many other formal tests, is whether they are really helpful, and worth the time and effort that goes into giving, scoring, and reporting about them. Although the results of these tests often give districts or schools bragging or moaning rights, they are of little help for individual children.

Another point related to achievement tests and their reporting is that the pressure on schools to have students do well on them and to look good in the eyes of the local citizens and state officials is great. Unfortunately, because of this intense pressure, there have been instances of cheating and falsifying scores. As a result, educators need to rethink the purpose of the tests and their use.

Monitor

The caution in the Washington State assessment (the WASL) that accommodations should not be made for pupils the first time they take the test implies that students might be given the same test again, when accommodations were arranged. Such an arrangement offers a marvelous opportunity to evaluate the effects of various accommodations. If that procedure was used with a number of students and an assortment of accommodations, a school district would have a repository of documented adjustments, which could be put into effect by other "accommodators" with confidence. Over time, other educators could add to this bank.

References

Bodner, J. R., Clark, G. M., & Mellard, D. F. (1987). *State graduation policies and program practices related to high school special education programs.* Lawrence: University of Kansas, Department of Special Education. (ERIC Document Reproduction Service No. ED 294 347)

College Board. (1994). *Scholastic Assessment Test.* Princeton, NJ: Author.

Feldt, L. S., Forsyth, R. A., Ansley, T. N., & Alnot, S. D. (1996). *Iowa Tests of Educational Development, Form M.* Itasca, IL: Riverside.

Hoover, H. D., Hieronymus, H. N., Frisbie, D. A., & Dunbar, S. B. (1996). *Iowa Tests of Basic Skills, Form M.* Itasca, IL: Riverside.

Washington Assessment of Student Learning. (1998). Olympia: State of Washington, Superintendent of Public Instruction.

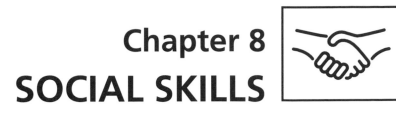

Chapter 8
SOCIAL SKILLS

◆ ◆ ◆ ◆ ◆ ◆ ◆ ◆ ◆ ◆ ◆ ◆ ◆ ◆ ◆ ◆ ◆ ◆ ◆ ◆

Many students who are at risk or have disabilities are lacking in certain social skills. However, these youth certainly are not the only ones in need of social enhancement. Many students are without basic social graces, such as saying "please," "thank you," and "you're welcome." Others have difficulty being assertive, accepting criticism, making requests, or communicating effectively. And still others have difficulty getting along with other people and controlling their anger.

Educators disagree as to whether social skills should be taught directly. Opponents argue that it is the teacher's job to instruct the academics and the parents' job to instruct children in social skills. Proponents feel that, because scads of youngsters come to school without skills necessary to get along with teachers, their peers, or even themselves, teachers need to help them. Another, more tactical debate has to do with where and when these social skills should be taught. Some educators advocate that these skills be instructed proactively in the classroom and at regularly scheduled times, whereas others believe that these skills should be taught when "natural" opportunities arise at school, on the playground, on the bus, and at home.

There are 13 tactics in this chapter. The first two set a foundation for the development of social skills; the next four offer ideas for generally "getting along with others"; the next six deal with specific social skills; and the final one is a computer-assisted social skills program.

AN OVERVIEW OF SOCIAL SKILLS TRAINING

Background

The ideas presented in this tactic are more general than those in the tactics that follow. After reading and studying this account, along with the preceding introduction, one should have a fairly good handle on the business of social skills training: what it is, why it is important, and how to go about doing it. This tactic is taken from *Social Skills* (Walker, 1996), one of six video presentations in *The Tough Kid Video Series*. The five other titles in that series are Behavior Management: Positive Approaches, Behavior Management: Reductive Techniques, Instructional Strategies, Study Skills, and School-wide Techniques.

Walker (1996) stated that when children enter school, they are required to make social skills adjustments of three types:

- *Teacher related*—Students need to develop an effective working relationship with teachers. This is more complex and necessary at the secondary level because youth are in contact with a half dozen different teachers each day.

- *Peer related*—Students need to develop an effective working relationship with others, or at least learn to work "in parallel" with their peers. At the secondary level, youth are in close contact with over 100 different students each day.

- *Self-related*—Students need to learn to manage their moods and to cope with difficult situations. At the secondary level, youth are confronted with more complex and serious problems than in grade school.

Who Can Benefit

Unfortunately, many secondary-level students are unprepared to take instruction from adults, to relate to peers, and to take on responsibilities themselves. The suggestions in this write-up are intended to help them.

Procedures

The following are a few key social tasks that students can work on: managing anger, asserting oneself, asking for assistance, resolving conflict, making friends, accepting criticism, dealing with teasing and provocation, and expressing emotions appropriately. When it comes to teaching those and other specific social skills, there are two primary approaches:

- *Skills-based approach*—uses direct instruction techniques to teach several social skills. The assumption is that when students learn the skills, the generic strategies that link them will be acquired.

- *Strategy-based approach*—focuses on cognitive problem solving and teaches a set of broad strategies for dealing with difficult social situations. The assumption is that as students carry out these strategies, they will eventually acquire the skills needed to make them work.

Walker (1996) recommended that teachers use a combination of the two approaches. See Table 8.1 for a list of common adaptive skills than enhance or impair relationships with teachers or peers.

The following are several "rules" Walker (1996) suggested for teaching social skills:

1. *Teach social skills as academic content.* Use the same instructional procedures used to teach reading or U.S. history (e.g., justification, presentation, illustration, review).

2. *Provide feedback and incentives.* Programs should have sufficient opportunities to respond and obtain feedback, and ample incentive systems in natural settings to support mastery.

3. *Assess students' type of deficit.* There are two types: The "can't do" type are skill deficits, and the "won't do" type are performance deficits.

Table 8.1. Common Adaptive Skills that Enhance or Impair Relationships with Teachers and Peers

---

Teacher-Related Social Adjustments

Adaptive Behaviors	*Maladaptive Behaviors*
• Comply promptly	• Steal
• Follow classroom rules	• Defy or provoke teacher
• Control anger	• Throw tantrums
• Make assistance needs known	• Disturb others
• Produce acceptable work	• Damage property
• Work independently	• Cheat
• Adapt to different instructional situations	• Swear/make lewd gestures
• Respond to teacher corrections	• Be aggressive
• Listen carefully	• Ignore teacher

Long-Term Outcomes

• Teacher acceptance	• Teacher rejection
• Success in school	• Referral for specialized placement
	• Failure in school
	• Low performance expectation

Peer-Related Social Adjustments

Adaptive Behaviors	*Maladaptive Behaviors*
• Be cooperative	• Disrupt the group
• Be supportive	• Be snobbish
• Defend self in arguments	• Be aggressive
• Remain calm	• Start fights
• Achieve	• Lose temper
• Be a leader	• Brag
• Be independent	• Seek help constantly
• Be complimentary	• Be a low achiever
• Make friends	• Get in trouble with teacher

Long-Term Outcomes

• Peer acceptance	• Social rejection/neglect
• Positive relationships	• Low self-esteem
• Peer friendships	• Weak social involvement
	• Few friends

Note. From *Social Skills* (from *The Tough Kid Video Series*), by H. Walker, 1996, Longmont, CO: Sopris West. Copyright 1996 by Sopris West. Reprinted with permission.

4. *Assess the validity of social skills.* Ensure that students value the skills being taught and will use them. Social skills valued by peers include the ability to dispense and receive praise.

5. *Involve parents.* Parents can offer suggestions on which skills to teach, along with providing support and opportunities for practice of the skills at home.

6. *Explain the social skills program before instruction.* Students should know the general rationale for the program, and specifically what is expected of them.

7. *Teach directly.* Teach the various skills head on; do not beat around the bush. Examples should be given of how the skill could be adapted to other situations.

8. *Provide supervised practice.* Once a social skill is conceptualized, students should have opportunities to practice it in the classroom and elsewhere at school. The teacher should provide coaching and cueing during this phase.

9. *Consider social context.* Make certain that students are aware that social consequences change from time to time and from one situation to another.

10. *Assess integration to natural settings.* This is the critical test of training programs. Students must know how and when to use the newly acquired social skills.

11. *Use social skills training with behavior reduction techniques.* Certain behaviors should be reduced or eliminated if students are to attain some degree of social competence.

Modifications and Considerations

The following are suggested discussion topics for teachers interested in setting up social skills training programs:

- Talk about why the acquisition of proper social skills is as important as learning various academic skills.

- Discuss how you will fit the social skills training into your classroom routine.

- Discuss approaches you might use to generalize the use of appropriate social skills to different environments.

Monitor

The proof of the success of any social skills training program is the extent that students can easily call on the skills learned and apply them to situations in their daily lives. Those instances of transfer or generalization should be monitored.

Reference

Walker, H. (1996). *Social skills* (from *The tough kid video series*). Longmont, CO: Sopris West.

 **SOCIAL SKILLS TRAINING: WHICH ONES TO WORK ON AND WHERE TO DO IT?**

Background

The idea underlying this tactic is that social skills should be taught to certain youth, and that instruction should take place, to the extent possible, in natural settings.

Who Can Benefit

This tactic would be most helpful to teachers who have a desire to modify certain social behaviors of their students, and who want to accomplish this within the contexts of the school. Certainly, the students should benefit in the process.

Procedures

1. The first assignment for teachers intending to instruct social skills is to identify the social behaviors that youngsters in their classes need. That determination should come from an assessment of the students' social capabilities in a range of school settings, and over time. The number and type of social skills that teachers identify and intend to work on should depend on how much help they have to deal with them, and how much time and effort they intend to allow for those matters. Teachers should be realistic in identifying the target social behaviors for they have other important skills and behaviors to mold. A teacher might decide to deal with the social skills that are needed by the most children in the class, or that would do the most immediate good, or that would be the easiest to take on. There could be other bases for the selection of target social skills.

2. The second assignment for teachers setting out to instruct social skills would be to list the times throughout the day that the identified behaviors are most likely to occur. (See Table 8.2 for some social skills and times during the school day when they are most likely to be needed.)

3. A number of teaching strategies are available for developing the various skills. I will briefly explain five; using examples of behaviors from Table 8.2.

   - *Coaching*—Using the behavior "ask questions," instruct youngsters in the several steps of this behavior, ask them to perform the steps, and give them feedback on their efforts to do so.

   - *Modeling*—Using the behavior "look and act interested," show pupils how to do this and stress the importance of doing so. The teacher might show students how to look interested and then how to look uninterested or bored (as if they need help with this).

   - *Reinforcement*—Praise or give points or other previously determined reinforcers to youngsters when they display any of the identified behaviors. Conversely, mildly reprimand youngsters who do not comply with specified objectives (e.g., "overlooking goofs").

- *Cognitive behavior modification*—Pupils should be instructed, whenever possible, to self-manage their social interactions. They should set objectives, keep charts on which they plot frequencies of the behaviors, and possibly select their own interventions to help reach the aims.

- *Cooperative Intervention*—Identify pairs of youngsters on the basis of their abilities and other important variables. Set up situations so that the students are dependent on one another, and to gain a reinforcement both must accomplish certain objectives. (See the tactics on cooperative learning in Chapter 11, Peer-Mediated Instruction.)

Modifications and Considerations

When it comes to selecting specific social skills for instruction, teachers might consult one of the many commercially available social skills programs. There are, however, three concerns about relying on those programs: (1) the social skills targeted in any one commercial program may not be the ones that are needed by the youth in a given class; (2) these programs may seduce teachers into instructing "by the book," that is, starting at the beginning of the workbook (or other presentation format) and proceeding through the program; and (3) teachers may be tempted to schedule set periods to instruct social skills, just as they do science and social studies.

Monitor

Data on the success of a program of this type would be readily available from the youngsters who were encouraged to self-record. They would know the extent of their improvement on certain behaviors. Otherwise, the teacher might develop a checklist that included students' names and their social behaviors needing improvement. The list could be marked before and during social skills instruction.

Reference

Lovitt, T. C. (1987). Social skills training: Which ones and where to do it? *Reading, Writing, and Learning Disabilities, 3,* 213–221.

GETTING ALONG WITH OTHERS: SOLVING INTERPERSONAL PROBLEMS

Background

The Teaching, Learning, and Caring (TLC) curriculum is an interpersonal problem-solving skills training program (Vaughn, 1987) developed to teach specific social problem-solving strategies to adolescents with behavioral disorders. Following are some of the topics the TLC curriculum addresses: being impulsive, identifying and responding to the affective state of another, generating a range

Table 8.2. Social Skills

Activity	Please and thank you	Look/act interested	Ask questions	Compliments	Generally positive	Ask for help	Offer assistance	Provide support	Take turns	Cooperate	Accept criticism	Apologize	Accept apology	Overlook goofs
Bus ride		X	X	X	X				X			X	X	
Opening exercises		X	X	X	X				X					X
Reading		X	X	X	X	X	X		X	X	X			
Lunch	X		X	X	X	X	X							X
Recess	X			X	X	X	X		X			X	X	X
Music		X	X	X	X	X	X	X	X	X	X			X
Dance		X	X	X	X	X	X	X	X	X	X			X
Drama		X	X	X	X	X	X	X	X	X	X			X
Sports			X	X		X	X	X	X	X	X	X		X

Note. From "Social Skills Training: Which Ones and Where To Do It?" by T. C. Lovitt, 1987, *Reading, Writing, and Learning Disabilities, 3,* p. 216. Copyright 1987 by Taylor and Francis Publishers. Reprinted with permission.

of responses to problem situations, evaluating consequences of behaviors before acting, communicating wants and needs, and responding to the desires of others.

Eight components make up the TLC curriculum: goal identification, cue sensitivity, empathy, alternative thinking, consequential thinking, communication mode, skills implementation, and integration. This tactic outlines procedures for teaching the first five of those listed components.

Who Can Benefit

The TLC curriculum was designed for adolescents with severe emotional problems and learning disabilities. It was developed and field-tested for a 2-year period in a school where some students were in a self-contained special classroom and others were in a regular classroom. The 18 students who participated in Vaughn's study were between the ages of 14 and 18. The tactic, as paraphrased here, was geared toward students characterized as at risk or remedial, or with learning disabilities. Because the ability to listen and respond appropriately in typical day-to-day conversations is a prerequisite to adequate social competence, students who have not developed these skills are most likely to benefit from this tactic.

Procedures

Goal Identification

Purpose. Teach students to identify problems; discern what they and others want when a problem situation arises; establish both long- and short-range goals; and differentiate goals from needs.

1. Ask students to list academic subjects in which they would like to improve.

2. Help them select one thing that they could do immediately to improve their performance in the subjects they have listed.

3. Request students to offer their proposals to the class for constructive feedback.

4. Instruct pupils to keep personal written journals of their progress. This will help them share information about it in weekly class discussions.

5. Continue with the class meetings, but extend the goal-setting period from weekly to monthly intervals, and then to longer periods in the future.

   ▶ Example: *Monthly*—Read four books in October.

           Long Range—Pass all classes with at least a C average for a semester.

6. Encourage students to incorporate personal goals into their plans after they have had some success with academic goal planning.

Cue Sensitivity

Purpose. Help students understand both verbal and nonverbal messages consistently.

1. Provide students with the following examples of nonverbal communication:

   Smile = Approval
   Furrowed eyebrows = Confusion
   Touch = Intimacy
   Stepping backward = Person must leave

2. Cut out pictures from magazines and ask students to identify possible nonverbal messages that people in them could be giving. Direct students to consider dress and body language as well as facial expression. Watch television programs (especially soap operas) without sound. Practice identifying body language and facial expressions.

3. Ask students to summarize a few real-life situations in terms of verbal and nonverbal cues.

   ▶ Example: "I knew Bill didn't understand what I was saying to him when he furrowed his eyebrows, so I tried to explain it a different way. The smile on his face when I finished told me that this time he understood."

4. Present several role-play situations for students to observe and note verbal cues.

5. Arrange for students to observe each other to identify and evaluate the cues they are sending to others.

Empathy

Purpose. Teach students to recognize their own feelings and the feelings of others.

1. Teach students the meanings and applications of words that indicate feelings, such as *frustrated, disgusted, jealous, perturbed, disappointed, delighted, concerned, furious, outraged,* and *embarrassed.*

2. Ask students to take turns describing emotional situations and how they would feel if placed in those situations.

   ▶ Examples: They are witness to a hit and run incident.

   They see someone shoplifting at a department store.

   They are asked to say a few words at the funeral of a friend.

   One of their parents does something to embarrass them in the presence of a few of their friends.

   Someone says something very negative about one of their friends.

   A peer teases a girl who rides the school bus.

3. Discuss the possible consequences of various responses to the situations described above.

Alternative Thinking

Purpose. Provide a strategy for generating solutions to a problem, rather than acting impulsively.

1. Make a "problem box" and place it somewhere accessible to students.

2. Ask students to write a note about a problem they have or have had with others (peers, neighbors, parents, or teachers) and place the note, without their name on it, in the box.

3. Take a few notes from the box every day for several days, and encourage students to discuss possible solutions to the problems mentioned.

Consequential Thinking

Purpose. Help students develop the ability to anticipate the possible consequences of a behavior before engaging in it.

1. Write the following questions on the board:

"What might happen next if I do . . . (the intended behavior)?"

"What will happen in the long run if I do . . . ?"

2. Compile a list of examples from the lesson on alternative thinking to be discussed in the context of these two questions.

3. Ask students to provide examples from personal experiences of times when they "thought ahead" and times when they did not but wished they had.

4. Conduct a class discussion about the consequences of thinking ahead and not thinking ahead in a variety of situations (see Table 8.3 for TLC Skill Checklist).

Modifications and Considerations

Teachers may wish to use all or part of this tactic depending on their students' skills. For example, all students in a group may seem to understand verbal and nonverbal cues and be able to recognize feelings, yet have difficulty setting goals. The teacher could skip Cue Sensitivity and Empathy to spend more time on Goal Identification.

This tactic could be expanded by analyzing interpersonal social situations in terms of more than one component. Students also might analyze the behaviors of their "most admired person" in terms of the various components.

Obiakor (1994) wrote about making right choices from a multiethnic point of view. He identified a number of success-oriented ingredients, such as, "When in doubt, learn the facts."

Table 8.3. Teaching, Learning, and Caring (TLC) Skill Checklist

Communication Mode

1. Repeating the content of another's message
2. Identifying the main idea of the content of another's message
3. Identifying the stated feelings in another's message
4. Identifying the underlying feelings in another's message
5. Identifying the main idea of the content of one's message
6. Identifying the underlying feeling in one's message
7. Using self-disclosure appropriately
8. Using open and closed questions appropriately
9. Listening to the problems of another with discounting
10. Listening to the problems of another and to hypothetical situations that influence behavior

Empathy

1. Identifying words that convey emotions (e.g., jealous, hurt, angry, hostile, shy, afraid, furious)
2. Matching past situations and the feelings associated with the situations
3. Discussing the importance of identifying emotional states as the first step in responding appropriately to them
4. Identifying how you would feel in hypothetical situations
5. Identifying the feelings of others in pictures, films, and hypothetical situations

Goal Identification

1. Defining own goal(s) when in a problem situation
2. Defining the goal(s) of another when in a problem situation
3. Identifying immediate and long-term goals
4. Sharing identified goals with the student group and accepting feedback
5. Listing the steps to reaching identified goals
6. Charting progress toward reaching goals
7. Identifying and describing the needs and goals of others

Cue Sensitivity

1. Identifying environmental cues in pictures and responding by asking questions and summarizing content and feelings
2. Identifying environmental cues in real situations that influence behavior
3. Identifying the personal cues people use and what they mean in role-plays and films
4. Identifying the personal cues used by others in real situations
5. Identifying own cues when interacting with others and what they mean
6. Identifying several cues you want to include in your repertoire
7. Identifying cues of others, your typical response to them, and possible alternative responses

Alternative Thinking

1. Identifying likely alternatives to solving hypothetical problems
2. Identifying likely alternatives to solving real problems
3. Identifying nonaggressive alternatives to solving hypothetical problems
4. Identifying nonaggressive alternatives to solving real problems

(continues)

Table 8.3. *(continued)*

Skills Implementation

1. Identifying the best procedure for implementing the selected alternative
2. Identifying a person who implements the alternative well and describing what they do
3. Describing the step-by-step process for implementing the selected alternative
4. Role-playing, practicing, and rehearsing the selected alternative
5. Using feedback from self and others to make changes in the procedures
6. Implementing selected alternative
7. Evaluating the outcome and the procedure

Consequential Thinking

1. Predicting the likely consequences of a series of events that do not involve them
2. Predicting the likely consequences of hypothetical stories and role-play situations
3. Predicting the likely consequences of interpersonal interactions of others
4. Identifying short-run and long-run solutions to solving hypothetical problems
5. Identifying problems in the long run when implementing short-run solutions to hypothetical situations
6. Identifying the consequences of selected behaviors in interpersonal situations involving others
7. Identifying the consequences of selected behaviors in interpersonal situations involving self
8. Implementing a "stop and think" approach to solving interpersonal difficulties

Integration

1. Observing models (counselors, teachers, and peers) integrate the problem-solving process in solving hypothetical problems
2. Observing models (counselors, teachers, and peers) integrate the problem-solving process in solving real problems
3. Integrating the problem-solving process in solving group problems
4. Integrating the problem-solving process in solving hypothetical problems
5. Integrating the problem-solving process in solving real problems

Note. From "TLC—Teaching, Learning, and Caring: Teaching Interpersonal Problem-Solving Skills to Behaviorally Disordered Adolescents," by S. Vaughn, 1987, *The Pointer, 31*(2), p. 28. Reprinted with permission of the Helen Dwight Reid Educational Foundation. Published by Heldref Publications, 1319 Eighteenth St., N.W., Washington, DC 20036-1802. Copyright 1987.

Monitor

This project, like others intended to assist students to get along with peers, could be evaluated by arranging a sociometric instrument. Youth could be asked, before and after training, to identify a best friend or a person with whom they would like to work, or in other ways rate their peers.

Students might keep a detailed notebook that includes subheadings for each category and notes from the class discussions. Recording their approaches to problem situations and the outcomes would provide ongoing documentation of their growth in this area. For example, they could record the number of times a day they acted with empathy, thought of alternative solutions, or thought about the consequences of an action.

References

Obiakor, F. E. (1994). *Learning and teaching with a smile: The eight-step multicultural approach.* Dubuque, IA: Kendall/Hunt.

Vaughn, S. (1987). TLC—Teaching, learning, and caring: Teaching interpersonal problem-solving skills to behaviorally disordered adolescents. *The Pointer, 31*(2), 25–30.

GETTING ALONG WITH OTHERS: A FOUR-STEP PROCESS

Background

Individuals who lack opportunities to learn social behaviors in their natural environments may end up with social skill deficits that negatively affect their interactions. Teaching social skills incidentally within either natural environments or deliberately created social situations has proven to be an effective process. In the tactic explained here, practice in getting along with others is gained through role playing. Students are taught a few simple steps for analyzing a problem, planning ways to solve it, and evaluating the outcome.

Who Can Benefit

This tactic was developed from a comprehensive social skills training package that was originally written for elementary-age children (Jackson, Jackson, & Monroe, 1983). It has been modified, however, and used successfully with other populations. The examples explained here are suitable for students at the secondary level who have not developed adequate skills for getting along with others in difficult situations. Students with limited experience in interpersonal relations should benefit most from learning to interact successfully with others.

Procedures

1. Tell students that the subject for the day is "solving problems related to getting along with others."

2. Write the following target behaviors on the board:

   - Listening carefully
   - Treating others respectfully
   - Joining in with others
   - Maintaining a good attitude
   - Taking responsibility for self
   - Staying calm and relaxed
   - Solving problems

3. List the following situations where problems can occur:

   - Neighborhood
   - Home (parents, siblings, other relatives)
   - School (peers, teachers, administrators)

4. Ask students to provide examples of people getting along and not getting along in each of the above situations to be sure they understand these concepts. (Advice columns such as that written by Ann Landers in newspapers or magazines are rich resources for such an activity.)

5. Explain the following four-step process for solving problems to students:

   a. Take a deep breath in an attempt to create a calm body and a good attitude.

   b. Identify the problem.

   c. Think of at least three possible solutions to the problem.

   d. Select the best one and try it.

6. Model an example of this four-step process (see suggested role plays in Table 8.4). For example, to show students how to stay calm and relaxed when there is a problem involving parents, model the following steps:

   • *Take a deep breath*—Remind students that this is to develop a calm body and a good attitude.

   • *Identify the problem*—Your mom promised to give you a ride to the skating rink, but then tells you that she forgot and made plans to have your hair cut.

   • *Think of three solutions*—These could be to (a) yell at your mom, run to your room, and refuse to come out; (b) keep the appointment to have your hair cut without objecting, but then give your mom the silent treatment for the rest of the night; or (c) remind your mom of her promise, and ask her if your haircut could be rescheduled.

   • *Select the best solution and try it*—Tell students that the best choice for this situation is the last one.

7. Read several other examples from Table 8.4 and guide a student discussion of possible solutions following the four-step solution process. Point out that the target behaviors offer clues to solutions.

8. Provide students with examples to role-play with their partners. Encourage pupils to come up with their own solutions for the sample problems.

9. Organize a class discussion of ideas and outcomes.

Modifications and Considerations

The subject of getting along with others is broad enough to allow teachers to modify procedures by choosing examples that are appropriate to the specific needs of their students. Teachers may also wish to expand on certain behaviors that might fall under each category of Table 8.4 to better prepare students for the exercises in this tactic.

To add variety to the approach, the problem-solving activities could be handled as a written exercise. Students could choose examples from the list, write out three solutions for each one, then rank them in order of appropriateness to the situation.

Table 8.4. Role Plays

Situations/ Target Behaviors	School Problems (Teacher/Peers)	Neighborhood Problems	Sibling Problems	Parent Problems
Listen carefully	During reading the teacher calls on you to read out loud, but you don't know where to start.	You're taking care of the neighbors' cat, and you can't remember where they said the key would be.	Your sister asks you to do her a favor and says she'll bring you a treat for doing it. You forgot what she asked you to do.	You are at a friend's, and you aren't sure what time your mom said to be home.
Treat others nicely	A kid that everyone calls "nerd" asks you to help her with her math during free time.	A neighbor kid you don't like trips and falls down. One of the lenses in his glasses breaks out and rolls away.	Your sister comes in your room when you are outside and plays with your toys.	You're eating dinner with your family, and you don't like what was cooked.
Join in with others	At lunch a group of kids are talking about skiing: You'd like to talk to them, but you don't know anything about skiing.	You feel really bored and are riding your bike. You see a group of kids playing basketball. You've never met these kids.	Your mom is taking you and your sister to the movies. They are talking about seeing a movie that is not what you'd choose.	Your aunt is visiting, and she and your family are deciding where to go sightseeing.
Keep a good attitude	You get a C on your report card, but you think you deserved a better grade.	You are playing ball with a friend, and another kid comes up and takes the ball away from you.	Your little brother hits you, and just as you hit him back, your dad walks in and gets mad at you.	Your dad is watching TV, and it's almost time for your favorite show.
Take responsibility for self	A group of kids are fighting at recess. The teacher is standing close, but you're not sure she will see them.	You and your neighbor are at a movie, and you want some popcorn, but you don't have any money. You still owe this kid money.	Your brother and you are at the store getting some things for your mom. You also want some candy, but there isn't enough money.	You run the vacuum cleaner over a hairpin because you don't think it will matter. Then it makes a loud, awful noise.
Stay calm and relaxed	You are on the playground; three kids gang up on you and start calling you a nickname you hate and threatening to hit you.	You are playing softball in front of your house. You hit the ball, and it goes through a neighbor's window. She is very mad.	You have been waiting all day to get home and have a special snack that you bought yesterday. Your sister ate it.	Your mom promised to take you roller-skating, but then tells you she forgot and made plans to get your hair cut.
Solve problems	You spent your whole allowance over the weekend. On Monday you need some money to buy something at a bake sale at school.	A friend invites you to a movie. You agree, but you forgot you already promised to go over to another friend's house.	You're playing a game with your brother, and he keeps moving your "man," taking your turn, etc.	Mom tells you to clean your room before school, and then she leaves. You remember that you have to be at school early today.

According to an article in the *New York Times* (Gilbert, 1997), a series of studies have found that people with a broad array of social ties are significantly less likely to catch colds than those with sparse social networks. If we extrapolate from that study, although that is always dangerous, one could say that the lack of friends makes one sick.

Monitor

For this approach, data on its effects could be obtained in the role-playing situations. Students could act out any of the themes suggested in Table 8.4 or others, while an observer uses a checklist to tally the extent that the individuals engaged in certain listed behaviors.

References

Gilbert, S. (1997, June 15). Social ties reduce risk of a cold. *New York Times,* p. B10.

Jackson, N. F., Jackson, D. A., & Monroe, C. (1983). *Getting along with others: Teaching social effectiveness to children.* Champaign, IL: Research Press.

GETTING ALONG WITH OTHERS: STRUCTURED LEARNING WITH SELF-MONITORING

Background

With an increased emphasis on vocational training and community placement of youth characterized as at risk or with mild disabilities, knowledge and practice of appropriate social skills are becoming more and more important for this population. One of the main reasons for failure in job placements is a lack of interpersonal and social skills. Often, the effects of social skills training in schools are limited only to that setting. Kiburz, Miller, & Morrow, (1984) sought to ensure that skills taught in a structured situation would transfer to circumstances outside of that setting and continue after training had ended. They implemented a four-phase intervention consisting of modeling, role playing, performance feedback, and self-monitoring with and without reinforcement. The purpose of the first three phases of the intervention was to teach the social skills directly, whereas the intent of the self-monitoring phase was to promote generalization and maintenance of the learned behaviors.

Who Can Benefit

An 18-year-old with mild retardation and behavior disorders, a resident of a mental health and developmental center, was the focus of training for the cited study. The intervention would be appropriate for observing behaviors in an environment in which there were both structured and nonstructured settings. This technique would be best suited for youth who had rather severe, chronic behavior problems.

Procedures

1. Set aside 30 minutes each day for training, which should consist of four components: modeling, role-playing, performance feedback, and self-monitoring (with and without reinforcement).

2. Select the behaviors to be taught by having several teachers report which ones they believed the students needed to improve most (e.g., initiating conversation, greetings, saying thank you and please, or more serious ones).

3. Simulate a situation for the students in which one of the targeted skills can be performed, and ask the students to perform it.

4. Require students to describe the steps taken to perform the behavior. From the description and observation of the behavior, the teacher should determine a criterion for the functioning level of the skill that is based on the students' ability and need for improvement.

5. Decide what additional steps should be added to the target behavior to make it socially acceptable.

6. Continue training until the students master 100% of the steps of the target behavior.

Modeling

1. Form a small group of students and include the targeted individuals.

2. Break the skill down into component parts and model each one for the students.

3. Model the target behavior with several examples of its application in several settings for the students.

Role Playing

1. Start a group discussion on what the students saw and heard during the modeling experience and how the behaviors relate to their lives.

2. Ask the students to role-play or practice the skills taught in the modeling situations. In addition, ask them to role-play true-to-life situations.

3. Encourage students to coach and support those who are role-playing the parts.

Performance Feedback

1. Elicit performance feedback (i.e., praise, compliments, approval, constructive criticism) from the group members following the role playing.

2. Give support as well as constructive suggestions to students so as to improve their performance of the target behaviors.

Self-Monitoring

1. Model self-monitoring for the students. Explain to them that self-monitoring is the systematic monitoring and recording of one's performance of a target behavior.

2. Allow students to role-play the self-monitoring behavior and provide feedback on their performance.

3. Give students a self-monitoring form, and ask them to take it with them at the beginning of each day and record, by circling a number, each time the targeted skill was performed correctly.

4. Ask the students to use the form outside of the classroom (i.e., in the cafeteria, study hall, gym, outside school grounds).

5. Instruct students to return the form on the following day, and give them praise or some other reward for returning the form promptly.

Self-Monitoring with Reinforcement

1. Continue the self-monitoring, but give points to students for the number of times they performed the target behavior correctly.

2. Allow students to exchange the points for privileges or other rewards.

Modifications and Considerations

In Kiburz et al.'s (1984) study, generalization and maintenance of the learned social skills were most effective under the self-monitoring plus reinforcement phase. The authors reported, however, that the target behavior did improve after only the training.

Before initiating training, teachers might rehearse the modeling and instruction of the target behaviors. Performance criteria should be set up before-hand, based on the students' ability and time limits. An example of a criterion for initiating a conversation is the student saying, "It's a nice day" or "What did you do over the weekend?" 10 seconds after an "opportunity." In that example, opportunity is defined as being within 3 feet of the other person with no other persons between the student and the other person. The other person must not be engaged in conversation. The student must make eye contact, use a moderate tone of voice, make content-appropriate statements, and make the initiation statement only once.

Monitor

The effects of this rather extensive approach could be evaluated qualitatively; that is, a number of individuals, familiar with the youth being assisted, could be interviewed before and during the treatment period. The youth's parents, friends, or siblings could be asked to comment on specific and more general social behaviors of the individual and to judge whether or not they had noted improvement.

Data regarding this set of techniques could also be obtained in a role-playing situation. A teacher or other observer could, by using a checklist, mark the times that designated incidents occurred, and write out descriptions of other happenings as well.

Sabornie (1991) offered a number of ways to measure social skills of youth in general education classes that are worth considering.

References

Kiburz, C. S., Miller, S. R., & Morrow, L. W. (1984). Structured learning using self-monitoring to promote maintenance and generalization of social skills across settings for a behaviorally disordered adolescent. *Behavioral Disorders, 10*(1), 47–55.

Sabornie, E. J. (1991). Measuring and teaching social skills in the mainstream. In G. Stoner, M. R. Shinn, & H. M. Walker (Eds.), *Interventions for achievement and behavior problems.* (pp. 161–177). Silver Spring, MD: The National Association of School Psychologists.

GETTING ALONG WITH OTHERS: ARRANGING PSYCHOSOCIAL ACTIVITIES

Background

The addition of psychosocial activities to the curriculum of underachieving adolescents can help improve scholastic learning by providing a more interesting class environment, creating more opportunities for personal development, and allowing the acquisition of new interpersonal skills. The inability to get along with others manifests itself in disruptive classroom behavior, making it nearly impossible for others to learn or get any work done.

The most common problem of misbehaving youth is a lack of autonomous and responsible behaviors. In an effort to enhance student social relations and in turn improve the general classroom learning environment, Mills (1987) implemented the group activities described in this tactic. The goals of the sessions were to teach students to listen to one another, respect others and their opinions, and become aware of the emotions of their peers.

Who Can Benefit

Nine seventh-grade students with either learning disabilities or behavior disorders participated in the study (Mills, 1987). Their ages ranged from 12 to 14 years. This tactic would be most suitable for adolescents who have difficulty relating to others. It is important for teenagers to develop these skills, because it can make a significant difference in their future employability and general well-being.

Procedures

Implement one of the following group activities for 90 minutes a day for 3 weeks, then proceed to the next.

Relaxation Sessions

These sessions are created to reduce fidgety and tense behaviors in students.

1. Center discussions around personal development, such as functions of the body during sleep (i.e., rapid eye movement, sleep cycles, muscle relaxation, respiration).

2. Instruct students to lie on the floor with their eyes closed and lights out after the daily discussion.

3. Ask students to begin by tightening the muscles in their feet and then releasing the tension.

4. Work up through the entire body as students progressively tighten and relax their muscles.

5. Continue until all muscles are relaxed and students feel the release of tension and anxiety from their bodies.

Magic Circle Activities

These activities are implemented to decrease the incidence of teasing, criticizing, and laughing at one another among students. This is achieved through the nonjudgmental, accepting atmosphere of the *Magic Circle.*

1. Form a circle, and engage the class in a group discussion.

2. Select the topics for discussion ahead of time. Encourage students to help select the topics, which could relate to school, relationships, families, or about anything else.

3. Encourage all students to take part in the discussions. Ordinarily, a student would be selected to begin the activity with a sentence that others would add to.

4. Stop the activity if the behaviors become disruptive.

5. Point out disruptive behaviors to the offenders and remind them of the rules of the *Magic Circle:* to be accepting and nonjudgmental of others.

6. Require the person who ridicules or annoys another to explain how that person must feel.

7. Give students who interrupt the opportunity to speak when they are not interrupting. Often, students interrupt just to receive attention and do not really have anything to contribute.

Smith and Milani (1989) extended the *Magic Circle* procedures to the world of work. They maintained that, as intimacy increased through these activities, the need for costly restrictions arising from distrust decreased dramatically.

Art Sessions

The goal of the art sessions is to assist students to gain a better understanding of themselves through self-expression and to work cooperatively with others.

1. Ask students to draw a picture of themselves and to share the picture with the group. This promotes self-awareness and expression.

2. Discuss with students how the picture might reflect their classroom conduct and how that conduct affects others.

3. Allow students to doodle while they state their feelings; this is another technique aimed at increasing self-awareness and expression.

4. Encourage students to work together on a large mural to instill cooperation, planning, and organizational skills.

Future-Planning Groups

These sessions are aimed at encouraging students to think about their futures, while keeping in mind their limited education and experiences.

1. Center discussions around the students' plans and future aspirations.

2. Help students to understand the limits of their options, at their current educational level.

3. Illustrate how important education is to the attainment of loftier goals and jobs.

4. Discuss other topics with respect to the future: marriage, family, type of home, travel, city in which to live.

Decision-Making Groups

The goal of these groups is to aid students to make proper decisions and, in the process, to be more responsible and independent.

1. Choose an issue about which a decision must be made, for example, a class project.

2. Prompt a number of possible options.

3. Determine the feasibility of each option, in terms of availability of materials and the interest of the other students.

Miscellaneous Activities

The following are two suggestions for setting up classroom management routines.

1. Develop a point system whereby students who gained the most points for good conduct at the end of the week were able to skip one class period and go instead to, for example, the library, music room, or computer lab.

2. Write all the students' names on the board in columns, and place a check next to those who spoke out of turn or otherwise misbehaved. This will enable students to become more aware of the frequency of their disruptions.

Modifications and Considerations

The use of psychosocial activities in the classroom effectively reduced disruptive behaviors in Mills's (1987) study. Other results were noted: Students were better able to disclose more of their feelings. Girls spoke and participated in activities more than before, and felt more comfortable in their interactions with boys. There was also an increase in school attendance during the class activities, and students developed a more positive attitude toward school.

Students in the study reported enjoying the relaxation technique the most. The *Magic Circle* routine gave them the most difficulty at first, but they believed that it had the greatest impact on their understanding of how others felt and how similar their problems were to their peers.

Teachers should take care in setting up any of these practices to see that students do not rely on them too much. Although these techniques should be arranged as required, teachers should be reinforced more by the generalized results of the training than by the process of carrying out the techniques. Moreover, trainers should make every effort to transfer as much control for carrying out the procedures to the students as possible.

Monitor

The effects of these activities could be evaluated specifically and generally. For the former, you could pinpoint only one critical behavior that might be influenced by training (e.g., being disruptive, interacting with others, contributing to discussions). Over time, frequencies of those behaviors (for individuals or groups) could be acquired and graphed.

To ascertain the effects of these techniques more generally, you might interview a few of the youth's relatives and acquaintances. You could ask them a few questions from time to time as the training was being conducted (e.g., "How does he get along with others?"). Their responses could be summarized and studied to determine whether progress was being noted in real-life settings.

References

Mills, M. C. (1987). An intervention program for adolescents with behavior problems. *Adolescence, 22*(85), 91–96.

Smith, B. R., & Milani, M. M. (1989). *Beyond the magic circle: The role of intimacy in business.* Charlestown, NH: Fainshaw Press.

LEARNING TO COMPROMISE: THE ART OF NEGOTIATION

Background

The tactic outlined here is for teaching teenagers the art of negotiation as an alternative to inappropriate, harmful, or disruptive behaviors. ASSET (Hazel, Schumaker, Sherman, & Sheldon-Wildgen, 1981), the program from which this tactic is derived, provides professionals with a comprehensive array of social skills training techniques. Whereas a variety of media make up the ASSET program, the procedures outlined here rely primarily on direct instruction and role playing to help students learn and practice the basic steps for successful negotiation.

Who Can Benefit

Although all students can benefit from opportunities to improve their negotiation skills, this type of training has special significance for secondary students who have failed to learn these skills.

Procedures

1. Explain to the students that they will be learning to come to an agreement with another person. Tell them that this is the skill of negotiation.

2. Discuss the importance of negotiating and give examples of amicable negotiations throughout the world, in the community, and in the school (e.g., Northern Ireland, the Middle East).

3. Hand out a negotiation checklist (see example in Figure 8.1) to the students and go over the fourteen points that are listed.

4. Role-play the situation of a parent and a teenager who is asking for a larger allowance. Below is a suggested sequence to follow:

   S: I would like a raise in my allowance from $7.50 to $10.00 a week.

   P: I wish we could, but we're a bit tight on money just now.

   S: How about a raise to $9.00?

   P: No, that's still out of our budget. Perhaps we can talk about it in a few months.

   S: What if I take on a couple more household chores?

   P: What did you have in mind?

   S: I could do the dinner dishes and take out the trash.

   P: Okay, I'll agree to $9.00 a week if you will do those things regularly and without being told.

   S: Okay.

5. Discuss what happened during the scene, identifying negotiating skills that were and were not used.

6. Explain the rationales of negotiation. Ask why it was important to use good negotiation skills in the allowance scene. Make clear the following points:

   - If you negotiate you will probably get what you want more often, but you will probably have to give up something or do more of something else.

   - Related to the above, negotiation often leads to compromise, but both parties come out of it reasonably happy.

   - Being able to compromise and negotiate often leads to immediate, as well as long-term, benefits.

   - Negotiation can get you through difficult situations without loss of respect or friendship.

7. Give examples of situations that could require negotiation:

   - You want to stay out later than the curfew your parents have set.

   - You want to drive the family car, but your parents say that you are not responsible enough to drive.

   - You and a friend want to see a movie, but cannot agree on which one to see.

   - You want some extra time to complete an assignment at school.

NEGOTIATION CHECKLIST

Student's Name _____ Date _____

Criterion Tests

1	2	3	4	Did the student:
___	___	___	___	1. Face the person during the conversation?
___	___	___	___	2. Maintain eye contact with the person?
___	___	___	___	3. Keep a neutral facial expression?
___	___	___	___	4. Use a normal tone of voice—positive and nonaccusing?
___	___	___	___	5. Maintain an erect posture?
___	___	___	___	6. Ask to talk to the other person?
___	___	___	___	7. State what he or she wanted?
___	___	___	___	8. Give a reason for the request?
___	___	___	___	9. Wait for a response?
___	___	___	___	10. If the response was positive, thank the person? If the response was negative, ask the person if he or she could think of anything the student could do to get what was wanted?
___	___	___	___	11. Listen to the other person's response?
___	___	___	___	12. If satisfied with the solution, agree and thank the person? If not satisfied, propose a compromise?
___	___	___	___	13. If the other person agreed with the compromise, thank him or her? If the other person did not agree, ask for another solution and continue negotiating?
___	___	___	___	14. Pay attention to the other person while he or she was talking by giving head nods and saying "mm-hmm" and "yeah"?

Figure 8.1. Negotiation Checklist for use in learning to negotiate. From *ASSET: A Social Skills Program for Adolescents* (p. 112), by J. S. Hazel, J. B. Schumaker, J. A. Sherman, and J. Sheldon-Wildgen, 1981, Champaign, IL: Research Press. Copyright 1981 by the authors. Reprinted with permission.

- Your boss has given you more work than you believe you can do in the allotted time.

8. Ask students to think of additional examples.

9. Instruct students to choose partners and have the pairs role-play various negotiations, following the steps in the checklist. You might make suggestions depending on how well the negotiations proceed.

10. Evaluate the situations with the negotiation checklist. Fill in one for each participant.

11. Lead a class discussion about the dramatizations, emphasizing alternative solutions that could have been offered.

Modifications and Considerations

Figure 8.2 is an example of a Home Note form that could be helpful in efforts to involve family members who might encourage the development of negotiating skills at home. Students could be asked to return the notes with comments from adult caregivers regarding evidence that training has generalized into the home setting.

Videotaped scenes of adolescents involved in situations requiring negotiation skills could be used to help students see the need for these skills. Moreover,

---

HOME NOTE

Dear _____:

The group discussed and practiced negotiation this week.

_____ has agreed to practice this skill with you three times this week. We would appreciate it if you would record what the practice situation was and how well the skill was performed. Figure 8.1 is a Negotiation Checklist which shows the steps for correctly carrying out this skill. Please check your teenager's performance against these steps. For each of the three practice situations give a check mark for a correct performance only if the teenager made no more than two mistakes during the practice. Please sign the form after the practices, and encourage your teenager to return it. Thanks for your help.

Situation	**Performed Correctly?**	**Steps Omitted**
1.		
2.		
3.		

Signed _____ Date _____

Figure 8.2. Home Note form to involve family members. From *ASSET: A Social Skills Program for Adolescents,* by J. S. Hazel, J. B. Schumaker, J. A. Sherman, and J. Sheldon-Wildgen, 1981, Champaign, IL: Research Press. Copyright 1981 by the authors. Reprinted with permission.

those tapes could focus on particular behaviors that are or are not effective in various situations, and could stimulate discussion and further exploration of solutions. (For examples of nonlistening, a behavior that often inhibits negotiation or even simple communication, ask students to watch some of the news shows on TV, some of which are being labeled as "yell TV.")

Throughout training, emphasize that being able to negotiate results in compromise, not one-sided victory. Students should be made to understand that a negotiable position is required when establishing objectives for the intended negotiations.

Rivera and Smith (1997) offered steps for enhancing and maintaining motivation to solve interpersonal problems, including the willingness to negotiate. Among those steps is to determine whether there is any reason the individual might have for wanting the interpersonal problems not to occur or for them to continue.

Monitor

As noted, one way to monitor this approach would be with videocassettes made of various groups of students engaged in role-playing situations. Those cassettes could be used for training individuals or to evaluate the effects of a program. For the latter, a group could be filmed interacting on some topic prior to and following training. The video could then be shown to judges, unfamiliar with either the students or the training, who could comment on the differences noted, if any.

References

Hazel, J. S., Schumaker, J. B., Sherman, J. A., & Sheldon-Wildgen, J. (1981). *ASSET: A social skills program for adolescents.* Champaign, IL: Research Press.

Rivera, J. P., & Smith, D. D. (1997). *Teaching students with learning and behavior problems* (3rd ed.), Needham Heights, MA: Allyn & Bacon.

 # MAINTAINING YOUR POSITION: DENYING INAPPROPRIATE REQUESTS

Background

This tactic is based on a program that provides social skills instruction in four general areas: basic social interaction skills, conversing with others, being positive and making friends, and being assertive (Cheney, Morgan, & Young, 1984). The tactic explained here is concerned with denying requests, one specific skill within that program.

Who Can Benefit

Often, adolescents give in to inappropriate requests from peers, requests they would rather refuse. However, because they are uncomfortable with the situation or simply cannot say "no," they give in. Adolescents, particularly those who are at risk, can benefit from learning to deny unreasonable requests in a manner that is convincing yet polite.

Procedures

1. Inform students that they will learn a technique for denying requests that they believe are inappropriate.

2. List the following social interaction skills on the board. Review them with students, and ask if there are any questions.

   • Getting the person's attention and maintaining eye contact
   • Speaking with appropriate voice and volume control
   • Maintaining a proper distance
   • Waiting until the other person pauses before speaking

3. Teach students to decide when it is appropriate to deny requests, giving thought first to their relationship with the person making the request, and second to the consequences of denying the request. Teachers and students might come up with a variety of examples to discuss, such as those listed in number 6.

4. Teach a variety of denial and rejection statements appropriate to the situation under consideration. The following are some possibilities:

   • "I'd like to, but I'm busy at that time."
   • "No, thank you."
   • "I'm sorry, but I am unable to."
   • "Let me think about it."
   • "I would prefer not to . . ."
   • "I'm not allowed to . . ."
   • "No, please excuse me."

5. Teach the art of polite rejection by modeling examples of some of these responses to unreasonable requests.

6. Ask students to form pairs to practice role-playing the denying of requests in the following hypothetical situations:

   • You have gone to a party and someone offers you something to eat that you really do not want.

   • Your mom asks you to go to the store for her, but you are expecting a phone call.

   • A friend wants to borrow $10 from you, but you do not like to loan money.

   • A classmate asks to copy your homework assignment. You have worked on it for quite a while, and you do not want to give it to him or her.

   • An acquaintance asks if you would like to try a new drug.

   • Your teacher has just asked you to take part in the school play. You have a part-time job and do not have time.

   • Some friends ask you to skip school with them.

7. Summarize with the class what they learned in the role-play exercises through class discussions. Respond to their questions.

8. Give each student several monitoring forms (see example in Figure 8.3). Ask them to complete these after they deny requests. Later, some of this information could form the basis for class discussions.

Modifications and Considerations

Students should be encouraged to describe situations of their own for the role-playing exercises. Make note of these topics for future class discussions.

DENYING INAPPROPRIATE REQUESTS

Trial # _____   Date _____

Briefly describe the situation: _____

_____

_____

Preskills

Did the person who was practicing Denying Inappropriate Requests (Check items that apply):

☐ 1. Get the other person's attention and maintain eye contact?

☐ 2. Speak with appropriate voice and volume controls?

☐ 3. Maintain an appropriate distance?

☐ 4. Wait until the other person paused before speaking?

Denial and Rejection Statements

Which statements were used? Were they effective? (Check items that apply and comment in the space provided.)

Comments

☐ 1. "I'd like to, but I'm busy at that time."

☐ 2. "No, thank you."

☐ 3. "I'm sorry, but I am unable to . . ."

☐ 4. "Let me think about it."

☐ 5. "I would prefer not to . . ."

☐ 6. "I'm not allowed to . . ."

☐ 7. "No, please excuse me."

☐ 8. Other (Please write in.)

Figure 8.3. Form for use in denying inappropriate requests. Adapted from *Assertiveness Skills for Adolescents,* by D. Cheney, D. P. Morgan, and K. R. Young, 1984, Logan: Department of Special Education, Utah State University. Adapted with permission.

With the prevalence of threats to the well-being of adolescents, including the use of drugs, alcohol, and sexual abuse, students should be taught to err on the side of being "old-fashioned" and conservative. Parents and teachers should make it clear to youth that the consequences for that type of attitude will be understanding and reassurance. Training to deny inappropriate requests is an ongoing process; it is not like mastering a few addition facts. It should be the responsibility of every teacher and should be engaged in within the contexts of all situations at the secondary level. Teachers should keep in mind that role playing is only one way to get the message across.

Monitor

Suggestions for monitoring this technique were sprinkled throughout the write-up. For one, teachers could use the role-playing situations to gather data. Teachers could, in fact, set up two phases to evaluate the impact of their training. Throughout a phase before instruction, they could gather data from the checklist as students role-played a few situations. Similar data could be acquired on a few occasions after the treatment had been scheduled. The teacher and participants should then study those data to see if there were changes.

Reference

Cheney, D., Morgan, D. P., & Young, K. R. (1984). *Assertiveness skills for adolescents.* Logan: Department of Special Education, Utah State University.

ASSERTIVENESS TRAINING PROGRAM FOR ADOLESCENTS

Background

This tactic is based on Bandura's (1986) social cognitive theory. According to Wise, Bundy, Bundy, and Wise (1991), social skills are abilities necessary for effective interpersonal functioning. They defined assertiveness as the expression of one's rights and opinions with respect for the rights of others.

Who Can Benefit

The students in this research (Wise et al., 1991) were sixth graders in social studies classes in a middle school. A program of this type would be especially beneficial for youth who need help to be either more or less assertive.

Procedures

1. The curriculum focuses exclusively on peer interactions, emphasizing the concept of responsible assertion, which implies an equal regard for the rights of self and others.

2. The students receive six semi-weekly 40-minute lessons covering the learning objectives.

3. Presentation of the concepts of assertion, nonassertion, and aggression include information about underlying ideology, verbal content, and non-verbal components (i.e., gestures, posture, facial expression, and voice).

4. Students are taught to anticipate likely social, physical, and emotional consequences of assertive responses and their alternatives, and to choose reasonable behaviors associated with positive feelings.

5. Guidelines are provided for responsible uses of assertion, including when not to be assertive, how to use persistent assertion and workable compromise, and how to foster assertive behavior in others.

6. A game-show atmosphere is maintained in scripting and directed role-play activities through the use of oversized posters, individual performances, and audience applause.

7. Scripts pertaining to adolescent interactions are used to encourage participation. Students read the scripts, and class members use posters to identify the rights featured in the various situations.

8. Identification of verbal and nonverbal components of assertive, aggressive, and nonassertive behavior is facilitated through puppet interviews. Three puppets "visit" the class and interact with students and instructors as they present various attitudes and nonverbal behaviors connected with their styles (i.e., assertion, aggression, or nonassertion).

9. A videotape can be made in which students (not those in the classes) portray some typical adolescent interactions as they demonstrate assertion, nonassertion, and aggression. Students then discuss these presentations.

Modifications and Considerations

Possible modifications of Wise et al.'s (1991) curriculum include the length of the treatment, the focus of the objectives, the components of the treatment, and the means for delivering instruction. Although Wise et al. used puppets to illustrate various positions, actors also could be used.

Monitor

Following each lesson, Wise et al. (1991) gave a short written test covering the day's objectives. Although it is a good idea to obtain data on the objectives of the program, it is more important to gather data with respect to students' actions in the real world, that is, the extent that they generalize use of the skills in actual social settings.

References

Bandura, A. (1986). *Social foundations of thought and action: A social cognitive theory.* Englewood Cliffs, NJ: Prentice-Hall.

Wise, J. L., Bundy, J. A., Bundy, E. A., & Wise, L. A. (1991). Social skills training for young adolescents. *Adolescence, 26*(101), 233–241.

ACCEPTING CRITICISM: LISTENING AND RESPONDING

Background

The steps outlined in this tactic are a combined and modified version of methods advocated by Black and Downs (1992) and Hazel, Schumaker, Sherman, and Sheldon-Wildgen (1981) in their programs for assisting students who are disruptive. Accepting criticism is a skill of great importance, because it is a part of life in both the structured academic settings of school and the more independent areas of home and work.

Who Can Benefit

Because individuals with demonstrated social skills deficits are likely to receive more than the average amount of negative feedback, it is crucial that they learn to accept and act positively on that criticism. If they react negatively to suggestions and other comments, that often increases the frequency of criticism they receive.

Procedures

The following suggestions for reacting to criticism are not listed in an order to be followed, and some are more important than others.

1. Face the person who is delivering the criticism, and make eye contact with him or her.

2. Maintain a neutral expression, and speak with a normal tone of voice.

3. Stand up straight and near the critic.

4. Listen attentively to the critic so you will know exactly what he or she is saying. Do not interrupt.

5. Nod occasionally, or let the critic know in other ways that you are listening.

6. Ask the person to clarify anything you do not understand. Say something like, "I don't quite understand what you mean or what you think I did wrong," or "I'm not sure why you're so upset; please fill me in."

7. Apologize if you agree with the criticism, or say that you understand why the critic is upset. If it is not obvious what you should do or not do on future, similar occasions, ask for suggestions.

8. It may be that you understand why the person is upset, but believe he or she has somehow misinterpreted what happened. In such a case, ask the person to listen to your version of what took place.

9. As you try to defend your position, keep in mind the status of the person who gave you the criticism. If the critic is an authority figure, you may want to back off after calmly and succinctly presenting your case,

once. That, of course, would depend on the nature of the criticism, the intensity of the criticism, how justified it may have been, how frequently this person has criticized you in the past, and a number of other factors.

10. After the first wave of criticism has been delivered, and depending on how you feel and the critic's acceptance of your reaction, you may want to excuse yourself and say that you will think about the person's comments and get back to him or her in a day or so.

Modifications and Considerations

It might be effective to approach this topic by asking students to role-play a number of different, but typical situations in which they may need to deal with criticism. Begin with situations that might occur at school, and later ask students to suggest other scenarios. Discussions about why certain approaches worked (or did not) might generate additional options that could help students. Alternatively, you might ask students what they actually did the last few times they were criticized for something, and to recall the consequences of those reactions.

Monitor

You might want to gather data on the extent that pupils dealt with criticism in role-playing situations and in actual encounters. For the former, a checklist could be designed to acquire data as students acted out a variety of scenarios as critics and recipients of the criticism.

To determine whether role-playing episodes had any impact on real life, students could keep records of the times they were criticized, noting the critics, the criticisms, and their reactions.

References

Black, D. D., & Downs, J. C. (1992). *Administrative intervention: A school administrator's guide to working with aggressive and disruptive students.* (2nd ed.). Longmont, CO: Sopris West.

Hazel, J. S., Schumaker, J. B., Sherman, J. A., & Sheldon-Wildgen, J. (1981). *ASSET: A social skills program for adolescents.* Champaign, IL: Research Press.

 # MAKING REQUESTS: APPROPRIATE AND EFFECTIVE QUESTIONING TECHNIQUES

Background

Knowing how to make requests appropriately can be critical for successful interactions in classroom situations, at work, at home, or elsewhere. The method described here was adapted from the work of Black and Downs (1992) at Father Flanagan's Boys' Town, in Nebraska.

Who Can Benefit

Requests make up a large part of daily conversations. In school, teachers and students spend a good part of their time making requests of one another (e.g., "Please hand in your papers now," "May I be excused?"). People usually begin phone calls with a request to speak to a certain person, often followed by a request for information. Many jobs require the ability to make appropriate requests, such as "How may I help you?" Because requests are such an integral part of everyday lives, and youth who are at risk and remedial are generally weak with respect to communication skills, those youth, especially, should profit from this technique.

Procedures

1. Offer a rationale to students for learning to make requests. Include in the rationale discussion of

   - Benefits to students that will result from employing the skill
   - Negative consequences that will occur if they do not
   - Concern for the effect their actions have on others

2. Explain to students that they will now be expected to use this social skill in these instances:

   - Before they use something that belongs to someone else
   - When they approach someone to ask for help

3. Explain and model the following steps for making requests:

   - Wait until the person is not busy to make your request.
   - Maintain eye contact with that individual.
   - Stand close to that person and remain still.
   - Keep a pleasant facial expression.
   - Say "please" when making your request.
   - Say "thank you" after the individual reacts to your request.

4. Point out that not all requests will be granted, and outline ways to deal with denials through negotiations and compromises such as the following:

   - Maintain eye contact and close proximity; do not fidget and move around.

   - Verbally acknowledge denial, maintaining a quiet voice and pleasant facial expression.

   - Ask, if you do not understand, why your request was denied.

   - Wait to discuss it at a later time with the individual if you disagree or still do not understand the reason for the denial.

   - Ask to talk privately to the individual again about the matter, and at a time convenient to him or her.

   - Make a statement of empathy or concern to the person about his or her decision.

- State your disagreement or misunderstanding.
- Offer your rationale for disagreeing with the person.
- Thank the individual for listening.

Modifications and Considerations

This is only one of a number of social skills included in the Boys' Town program. Others include accepting criticism and consequences, greeting others, getting the teacher's attention, disagreeing appropriately, and following directions. Suggestions for teaching students to compromise are included in this tactic as a way to deal with the denial of requests, another tactic in this series.

Monitor

One approach to consider for evaluating the impact of this treatment would be for students involved in the training to self-record the times they made requests. They could begin taking these notes a week or so before training begins and continue for some time during and after the program. In addition to obtaining data on the number of requests, information could be acquired as to the results of the requests and about the episodes generally. Data regarding the frequency of the requests could be charted and evaluated.

Data regarding the training itself could be obtained by setting up role-playing situations. Those interactions could be videotaped and evaluated later with the assistance of checklists.

Reference

Black, D. D., & Downs, J. C. (1992). *Administrative intervention: A school administrator's guide to working with aggressive and disruptive students* (2nd ed.). Longmont, CO: Sopris West.

COMMUNICATING EFFECTIVELY: TALKING TO TEACHERS ABOUT PROBLEMS

Background

Students who get the best grades at school are generally not afraid to approach teachers. Students who are less successful do not seek out their teachers when they have problems. Perhaps they are afraid that teachers will embarrass or yell at them, or that they will not know what to say and teachers will think they are stupid. Students can benefit from learning to interact with those in authority by applying the technique introduced here at school, home, and work.

Who Can Benefit

Most students will benefit from explicit instructions on communicating with authority figures. Students who are at risk especially need this skill. If they can communicate their willingness to deal with problems, they may be able to work out plans with their teachers to overcome them.

Procedures

The following steps are from a program developed by Stoker (1980):

1. Ask students to think of a problem or concern they have in one of their classes. It might be one of the following: They do not understand the assignment; they want to change their seat; they believe they deserve a higher grade; or they have missed a few assignments or classes and want to see about making up the work. (It might be necessary to inform some students about issues that do matter, that is, to assist them to know when they have a problem.)

2. Discuss ways in which students can deal with the problem. They could let it slide, give excuses, or offer a possible solution. (It may be necessary to convince some students that if they have identified a problem, it is often to their advantage to solve it.)

3. Show students the difference between owning a problem and blaming it on others. The first is positive, the second negative. Compare "I statements" to "Blaming statements": "I don't understand . . . the assignment is too hard for me" versus "Your assignments and grades are unfair." Inform students that the former statements are more apt to get positive results than the latter.

4. Inform students that they must convince the teacher that they are willing to work with him or her on the problem. To indicate this attitude, they might ask, "What do you think I could do about this?"

5. Model for students how to set up a discussion with a teacher: "Mr. Jones, I'd like to talk with you about _____. When would be a good time for me to come by?" Explain to the students that they must agree on a time that is acceptable to both parties, and they must make a note of it and show up at the right place at the right time.

6. Discuss with the students how they could offer their ideas in an acceptable manner. "I've thought about it. Maybe I could . . . or maybe it would help if I . . ."

7. Explain to students that they need to listen as the teacher offers suggestions.

8. Tell the students that they must be responsible to end the discussion by agreeing to an acceptable solution. They should write it down and put it into practice.

9. Assign students to partners, particularly individuals they do not know, and have them take turns role-playing the aforementioned steps.

10. Ask students, following the role playing, to write a paragraph about their experiences, explaining what it was like for them to play the teacher, how closely they followed the proper steps, where they got stuck, and what they learned.

11. Instruct students to fill in the following form at the end of an instructional period:

When will you approach a teacher with a problem using what you learned today?

SET IT UP: Write below the problem you have and a date when you'll talk to the teacher about it.

_____

_____

_____

Turn this page in to your teacher today. The teacher will check back with you on _____.

Modifications and Considerations

After students have communicated a concern to one of their teachers, they could discuss the interaction: What did the student say? What did the teacher say? How did the conversation come out?

When students have become reasonably successful with this interaction approach at school, they should be encouraged to apply it to situations at work and at home.

Jenson, Rhode, and Reavis (1994) offered a number of suggestions for tracking students and their activities. Such devices serve to enhance teacher and student interactions.

Monitor

Data from the role-playing situations could be acquired with the help of a checklist. Interaction data could also be acquired by an observer, who would mark each statement of the person who initiated the request and those of the other individual. Furthermore, those data would be coded to indicate the "tone" or type of remark, either positive or negative, acceptable or unacceptable, or some other way. By analyzing those data, you may learn that when the frequency of these interactions increases (between two people), the chances for a favorable result are increased.

References

Jenson, W. R., Rhode, G., & Reavis, H. K. (1994). *The tough kid tool box.* Longmont, CO: Sopris West.

Stoker, J. (1980). *Grab H.O.L.D.: Help overcome learner dropouts. Classroom guidance manual.* San Jose, CA: Resource Publications.

A COMPUTER-ASSISTED SOCIAL SKILLS INTERVENTION

Background

The goals of this study were to examine the effects of a computer-supported intervention (Margalit, 1995). The intent was to investigate not only teachers' ratings of the students' social skills and classroom behaviors in terms of disruptive and aggressive acts, but also students' self-reports of feelings of loneliness, and peer-rated social acceptance levels.

Who Can Benefit

Children with an intellectual disability have been found to demonstrate social difficulties and to be considered deficient in social skills and social knowledge. Moreover, they have been described as reporting high levels of loneliness, social distress, and general dissatisfaction with their social lives. Students in Margalit's (1995) study were boys and girls from 11 to 15 years of age who were characterized as "intellectually disabled."

Procedures

The following are major components of the intervention and a brief description of each:

- Teachers who delivered the training were instructed to use the social skills software, *I Found a Solution* (Margalit, 1990), and the accompanying noncomputerized intervention procedures. Emphasis was placed on encouraging the transfer of the social understandings gained from the program to classroom and home environments.

- The computer program consisted of 24 interpersonal conflict scenarios, which were presented on the screen. One of them was "Ronnie arrived at school feeling restless and bored. He doesn't know what to do. What would you suggest for him to do?" Students selected one of the proposed alternative solutions. Three adventure games were also presented on the computer. They reflected difficult social events in various environments: school, work, family life, and leisure activities. The contents of these scenarios were based on descriptions of interpersonal difficulties reported by youngsters and adults.

- Training of the students was conducted over a 3-month period, with 1-hour sessions twice weekly in groups of four or five children. Each child worked on a computer for 20 to 25 minutes. Teacher-guided individual work, small group discussions focusing on evaluating children's real and optional behaviors during actual social conflicts, examining homework tasks, and role playing of different social roles were performed for an additional 25 minutes.

- After viewing the scenarios, the teachers occasionally set up role-playing sessions to expand on the theme or topic of the day.

- Students sometimes were given homework that pertained to the computer exercises. They might be asked, for example, to watch for incidents of the theme that was presented.

Modifications and Considerations

Results of this study indicated that children in the intervention group demonstrated better social skills and less disruptive behavior, and were more accepted by peers. Results failed to demonstrate, however, that the students were less lonely, as measured by a scale. The authors conjectured that, once a person takes on a particular social role, such as being lonely, it is very difficult to change that. They posited that, to facilitate the entry into a network of friendships, one may need to seek out environments saturated with opportunities and support for social interrelations. Asher, Parkhurst, Hymel, and Williams (1990) carried out considerable research in identifying ways in which to develop friends.

Monitor

Data from three sources were obtained in the referenced study:

1. *Student ratings*—A questionnaire was given that consisted of 16 primary items (e.g., "I feel alone at school") and 8 filler items ("I like school").

2. *Teacher ratings*—Two scales were administered. One was a measure of aggression that consisted of 10 items, each rated by teachers on a severity index. The other was a social skills measure. For this, the teacher filled in information on three skills: cooperation, assertion, and self-control.

3. *Peer ratings*—Children were asked on a 5-point Likert scale to rate each of their classmates as to the extent they liked to be with them and to work with them.

References

Asher, S. R., Parkhurst, J. T., Hymel, S., & Williams, G. A. (1990). Peer rejection and loneliness in childhood. In S. R. Asher & J. D. Coie (Eds.), *Peer rejection in childhood* (pp. 253–273). Cambridge: University Press.

Margalit, M. (1990). *Effective technology integration for disabled children: The family perspective.* New York: Springer-Verlag.

Margalit, M. (1995). Effects of social skills training for students with an intellectual disability. *International Journal of Disability, Development and Education, 42*(1), 75–85.

Chapter 9
PARTICIPATION

In Chapter 1, I dealt with participation in the broadest sense—that is, showing up for school. The tactics in this chapter are concerned with participation in the context of learning and instruction, once a student does show up. Participation in this sense means getting involved in what is being taught, that is, asking and answering questions, cooperating with others, and offering suggestions. Teachers want students to participate to show that they are paying attention and understanding what is going on. If students do not say or write something, teachers do not know what is going on in their minds. Teachers need to know what students are doing or thinking in order to praise them, straighten them out, and advise them.

Teachers would likely agree that some students participate too much, many not enough, and a few just the right amount. Teachers would probably also concede that students who are at risk or remedial, or who have learning disabilities are often the ones who do not participate enough, and when they do it is often in inappropriate ways. The main purpose of this chapter is to offer techniques for encouraging more youth to participate in their academic affairs more often and at higher levels. A related purpose is to provide ways to determine the quantity and quality of the students' interactions. Another goal is to offer suggestions for determining whether a student's increased participation is related to enhanced learning.

The eight tactics in this chapter are all intended to expand some form of participation. They have to do with asking and answering questions and generally getting involved in class discussions.

ASKING QUESTIONS: TICKET OUT THE DOOR

Background

The idea of this tactic is to ask students to participate in class by writing questions. By doing so, students stand to gain in two ways: in participation and in writing. Many of the students who are at risk or remedial are lacking on both fronts. For this tactic, students respond as individuals at any time during the class period. Another idea to support this tactic is that, when students write and submit their questions and you react to them after class, at your leisure, you can give more time and thought to them than you could when oral questions are asked in class.

Who Can Benefit

Most students would profit from this technique, especially those who are reluctant to ask questions. This technique might be especially effective for students who have questions they do not want to ask in front of their peers, for fear that others will make fun of them and think they are "stupid."

Procedures

Discuss with the students the importance of asking questions. Tell them that one of the best ways to learn about anything is to ask questions, to reflect on the responses to those questions, to take notes on the responses if they are fairly complex, and to ask additional questions that stem from studying responses to the first set. (That process assumes that individuals who answer the questions know what they are talking about and give accurate and clear answers.)

1. Ask the students to mark off a series of squares on an 8½ × 11 inch sheet of paper. Ask them to draw a vertical line down the center of the paper, and draw four horizontal lines to make 4 equal sized boxes in each column (see sample in Figure 9.1). They write "student questions" above the boxes on the left and "teacher answers" above the boxes on the right.

2. Inform the students that each day before they leave class, they must write two questions (the designated number could be more or less) that pertained to that day's session. This is their "Ticket Out the Door."

3. Discuss the matter of writing questions with the students and model several questions for them. (You may choose to set up a few guided practice sessions in which the class participates in coming up with questions about a unit of work.)

4. Require the students to turn in their sheets with the required number of questions before they leave the class. Glance at each student's sheet to see that he or she has asked reasonably pertinent questions.

5. Following the class, study the students' questions and write responses to each of them on the right side of the sheet. Also, note the questions that were asked by several students.

6. Return the sheets to the students at the next session and ask them to go over their questions and your answers. (Allow a few minutes for this.) If they are still confused, and your answers do not clarify their queries, they should write questions seeking clarification for the next day.

7. Review with the class the questions that were asked by several of the students.

Modifications and Considerations

You could ask students to write comments rather than questions for their "Ticket Out the Door." For example, require them to write about the following: their favorite section or part of the day's lesson; the part that was the most confusing; or the part about which they would like more information. Alternatively,

Student Questions	Teacher Answers
1.	
2.	
3.	
4.	

Figure 9.1. Examples of Ticket Out the Door question sheet.

ask students to summarize the day's work, or write about what the next class session will be about (assuming they have glanced ahead in their textbook or syllabus), or write about what they are supposed to do prior to the next session.

By writing these comments each day, the students would have a sort of diary of what was going on in class, and what they got out of it. Likewise, by reading the pupils' responses over time, you would have a good idea as to how they were thinking and getting along in the class.

Monitor

Gather data on the effects of this tactic by keeping track of the students' scores on tests taken prior to putting the procedure into effect, and then while it was in operation. If no or minimal effects were observed, either change the tests or modify the requirements of the "ticket" procedure.

Reference

Personal communication with Larry Maheady, May 24, 1997, Applied Behavior Analysis conference, Chicago.

ASKING QUESTIONS: FIVE TECHNIQUES

Background

According to Kitagawa (1982), about 80% of classroom exchanges are initiated by teachers. The common pattern for these exchanges is for the teacher to ask a question, a student to reply, and the teacher to evaluate it. In the procedure explained here, the teacher is a question creator: one who sets up procedures whereby pupils generate the questions.

Who Can Benefit

Many students who are at risk and remedial, or those with learning disabilities should profit from this tactic. It would be helpful also for pupils who need practice in framing questions or communicating generally.

Procedures

The following five techniques can be used to assist students to ask questions. The examples are based on a literature class in which the students have read a number of American novels, and most recently have been assigned Willa Cather's *Lucy Gayheart.*

1. Provide a brief sketch of the novel before asking the students to read it. Encourage them to ask questions about what the author might write about in the book.

2. After they have read the novel, encourage students to ask questions that were not sufficiently answered or ones about which they would like more detail. As examples, students might ask for additional information about Lucy's mother, her sister (Pauline), or Sebastian's trips abroad.

3. Direct students to ask themselves and others about what information or experiences they had prior to reading the novel that helped them relate to it. Following are some examples: Nebraska, life in the 1900s, Chicago, the music business, train travel.

4. Request students to ask questions and stimulate discussions about what the author might write about next if she wrote a sequel to the present story. Some possibilities are these: what happened to Gordon, the town of Haverford, or to Fairy Blair?

5. Ask *who, when,* and *why* questions following certain passages. Ask pupils, following a portion of the story, if that portion pertained more to one of those questions than to the others. One example passage would be Sebastian's drowning in Italy.

Modifications and Considerations

Using one of these five techniques, encourage pupils to question each other's questions. Using this approach, you can continue to guide discussions and evaluate the content and relevance of the various contributions.

Following are a few other ideas for stimulating question asking, beyond those offered in this tactic. Write a few questions about a passage on slips of paper, and give them to certain pupils (perhaps to those who have difficulty coming up with questions), or have a drawing to determine which students receive the slips, or require certain students who have difficulty forming questions to earn the question slips. For any of these situations, ask the pupils those questions and, when they answer correctly, acknowledge and otherwise reinforce their contributions. Yet another approach would be to set up a cooperative situation whereby you group together youngsters after they have read a passage. In groups, they would write out questions that they later ask of other groups. A group contingency plan could also be arranged. For this, students in groups would be required to ask questions, one at a time. After all have posed their queries, they would all receive some reward.

Algozzine and Ysseldyke (1995) offered several tactics to encourage student participation. They referred to one as the "thumbs up–thumbs down approach." For this, periodically ask students to indicate if they are following and understanding the ongoing lesson by showing an "up" or "down" thumb.

Monitor

It would be informative to keep data on pupils' contributions when the ordinary type of classroom routine was in effect, and continue keeping data on their contributions when one of these procedures was arranged. Beyond these measures it would be important to know the extent the pupils' questions influenced their academic performance, in this example, the thoroughness with which they understood the story.

References

Kitagawa, M. M. (1982). Improving discussions or how to get the students to ask the questions. *The Reading Teacher, 36*(1), 42–45.

Algozzine, B., & Ysseldyke, J. (1995). *Strategies and tactics for effective instruction.* Longmont, CO: Sopris West.

 # ANSWERING QUESTIONS: REPHRASING QUESTIONS

Background

When students are asked questions, sometimes they ask for the question to be repeated, mutter something to themselves, or drop their notebook onto the floor as a diversionary tactic. At other times they do not respond at all. A contributing factor to these weak or lack of responses is the failure to understand what was asked. This technique helps students answer questions by requiring them to repeat it before answering it (Webb & Baird, 1980).

Who Can Benefit

This tactic is suitable for many students who have been classified as at risk or remedial. Many of them do not attend to teachers' instructional programs, and rarely contribute to class discussions.

Procedures

1. State the question simply. Do not elaborate or rephrase the question at this point; that might further confuse students. It will help to have clearly thought out the questions prior to asking them to ensure that you say exactly what you want to say the first time.

2. Instruct students to ask themselves the question in their own words, whether or not they are called on. This nonverbal exercise will help them understand the question.

3. Call on a student to respond. Require the student to precede his or her answer with a rephrased form of the question.

4. Ask the pupil to restate the question even if he or she cannot answer it. This is an excellent form of feedback to help determine if the question was effectively communicated. If not, rephrase the question yourself.

5. Repeat Step 3. If a particularly good response is given, you may wish to have another student rephrase it. If students expect this type of routine, they will be more attentive to the answer.

Modifications and Considerations

Always ask a question first, and then call on a student. If you call on a student before a question is asked, other students may not listen to it because they know that someone else has to answer it.

This tactic should benefit "askers" as well as "answerers," in that teachers and pupils should learn the importance of asking clear and unambiguous questions that increase the chances of correct answers. The importance of asking good questions could be pointed out in reverse by asking long, drawn-out questions or ones that are confusing in other ways. Students would learn quickly how difficult it is to paraphrase them, much less answer them. (For questions of this type, the class could listen to the questions asked by reporters at presidential press conferences.)

Monitor

Prepare two sets of questions, both on topics that are interesting or have been studied by the students. One set of questions would be clear and concise, whereas the other set would be vague and rambling. Mix up the questions and ask them of the students. The students have three tasks: Note whether the question was "clear " or "unclear," rephrase it, and answer it. A checklist could be developed to acquire those data, which would provide some evidence as to the effects of question type and whether or not it was rephrased.

Reference

Webb, C. D., & Baird, H. J. (1980). Three strategies for motivating pupils. *The Clearing House, 54,* 27–29.

ASKING QUESTIONS AND EXPLAINING ANSWERS

Background

According to constructivist theories, understanding and memory of material are enhanced when individuals actively construct knowledge and integrate it with previous knowledge. Complex knowledge construction is indicated in a number of ways, including explanations, inferences, justifications, hypotheses, and speculations.

Who Can Benefit

Children in King's (1994) study, which is described here, were fourth and fifth graders in a science class. The approach is general enough that it would be useful for older students in most content areas.

Procedures

1. To determine prior knowledge of the unit topic, systems of the body, each student constructed a knowledge map of systems and parts of the body. Those maps served as a way to assess the accuracy and complexity of students' constructed knowledge. Such maps are graphic representations of information, and consist of nodes that represent concepts, parts, or attributes and links to represent relationships among the nodes.

2. Students then received training and practice in how to formulate explanations in one of two questioning strategies (lesson-based questioning or experience-based questioning) or an unguided questioning approach.

3. They were provided with strategy prompt cards that corresponded to their condition. The cards were used by students during the practice and subsequent lesson-discussion sessions to prompt their discussion. Cards for the three conditions are shown in Figure 9.2. (Note that for the two guided questioning conditions, the three comprehension questions and four of the connection questions are the same. The last three connection questions differ.)

4. Students in all three groups received *Explanation Training*. For this, teachers first explained to students the differences between describing something and explaining it. They used examples of descriptions and explanations from students' previous lessons on the circulatory system. Teachers then demonstrated how to develop an explanation using concepts and processes from that same lesson. They emphasized the importance of telling *how* and *why,* using the students' own words, and connecting the idea being explained to something already known.

5. Students in the two trained questioning groups received *Questioning Training* separately. For this, teachers taught students to differentiate

Comprehension questions
  Describe . . . in your own words.
  What does . . . mean?
  Why is . . . important?

Connection questions
  Explain why . . .
  Explain how . . .
  How are . . . and . . . similar?
  What is the difference between . . . and . . .?
  How does . . . affect . . .?
  What are the strengths and weaknesses of . . .?
  What causes . . .?

Prompt card given to students in the lesson-based questioning condition

Comprehension questions
  Describe . . . in your own words.
  What does . . . mean?
  Why is . . . important?

Connection questions
  Explain why . . .
  Explain how . . .
  How are . . . and . . . similar?
  What is the difference between . . . and . . .?
  How could . . . be used to . . .?
  What would happen if . . .?
  How does . . . tie in with . . . that we learned before?

Prompt card given to students in the experience-based questioning condition

DIRECTIONS:

Discuss the lesson with each other.

Ask each other questions.
Answer each other's questions by giving explanations.

Prompt card given to students in the unguided questioning condition

Figure 9.2. Strategy prompt cards. From "Guiding Knowledge Construction in the Classroom: Effects of Teaching Children How To Question and How To Explain," by A. King, 1994, *American Educational Research Journal, 31*(2), 338–368. Copyright 1994 by *American Educational Research Journal.*

between *memory* questions and *thinking* questions. They provided examples of each type. Teachers gave examples of converting memory questions to thinking questions. Students were encouraged to do this. Thinking questions were further classified into *comprehension questions* and *connecting questions*. Comprehension questions were those that checked how well the students understand a lesson. Connecting questions were those that linked two ideas from a lesson together. Several examples were provided. Students were told to use the question stems on their prompt cards to practice generating examples of comprehension and connecting questions.

6. Students in all groups were told that asking and answering questions would help them to understand and remember the material presented in the lessons.

7. Students moved into dyads to practice asking each other questions on the lesson they had on the circulatory system. Partners used their newly acquired skills of explanation to answer the questions posed by their partners.

8. Students completed the written posttest and constructed knowledge maps representing the lesson content.

9. A new lesson was assigned using the same procedures with the students. The idea of this was to determine whether the students would transfer their newly acquired skills. They were not given prompt cards for this session.

10. Following each lesson, students rated how well they understood the materials, as well as their use of specific aspects of the explaining and questioning procedures.

Modifications and Considerations

This technique might be seen as an advanced way in which to deal with participation. Whereas other tactics in this chapter deal with the basics of participation and offer rather straightforward ways to do it, this technique offers more sophisticated approaches to interacting. King's (1994) data indicated that both kinds of questions induced complex knowledge construction, but questions designed to access prior knowledge and experience were more effective in enhancing learning.

Monitor

In King's (1994) study, cognitive and metacognitive measures of performance were administered. As for the *cognitive* measure, tests were developed for each unit that contained 10 items in multiple-choice format that assessed students' literal comprehension of points emphasized in the lesson and 5 questions in open-ended written format that assessed their ability to make inferences, provide explanations, integrate concepts, or go beyond what was presented in the lesson. As for the *metacognitive* measure, children developed knowledge maps for each lesson and for the unit as a whole.

Reference

King, A. (1994). Guiding knowledge construction in the classroom: Effects of teaching children how to question and how to explain. *American Educational Research Journal, 31*(2), 338–368.

 # PARTICIPATING IN DISCUSSIONS: SELF-MONITORING

Background

Although most students benefit more from classroom experience if they participate through asking questions, giving opinions, and sharing ideas, the number of techniques for stimulating classroom participation is limited. This tactic seeks to introduce the concept of self-monitoring as a way to increase classroom participation among students.

Who Can Benefit

A study involving college students was the basis for this tactic (Delprato, 1977). Because the instruction of high school students often follows a lecture–discussion format like that for college students, the procedures and benefits of the techniques described here should apply to high school students as well.

Too often, students characterized as remedial or at risk, or those with mild learning disabilities, who are mainstreamed into regular classes are hesitant to ask questions or express opinions. This tactic could serve as a method for helping them become more involved in classroom interactions.

Procedures

The following steps are designed for an entire class or a cluster of students in a class:

1. Select one student to serve as an observer. Inform this student of the participatory behaviors he or she should watch for (i.e., asking questions and giving answers). Provide the observer with a form to gather these data. On the form write each student's name down the left side of the paper, and the days of the school week across the top, in five spaces, with each further divided into two sections, one to indicate questions and the other for answers.

2. Instruct the observer to make a check for each of those behaviors he or she observes for each pupil. (It may be necessary to have a discussion with the observer as to what constitutes a question and an answer.) Gather those data for a few days, and consider them as baseline measures.

3. Discuss with the students the importance of their participation in class discussions. Inform them that when they ask or answer questions, they

indicate they are staying in touch, and those interactions inform you about the level of their understanding.

4. You may need to set up a couple of modeling situations in which you ask questions and provide answers, and then have a session or two in which you guide them to ask questions and answer them.

5. Inform students that they will be asked to keep data on the times they ask and answer questions. Tell them that these data will show their levels of participation.

6. Give each student a form on which to record his or her own data. On it, list the five school days and divide each day's space for students to record the number of questions asked and the number of answers offered. Ask students to make a tally in the appropriate slot for each interaction.

7. Advise the student observer to continue recording the two types of participatory behaviors for each student.

8. Ask the students at the end of a week to tally the number of questions and answers and possibly chart them on a graph.

9. Ask the observer to do the same for the entire class.

10. Set up a few class discussions regarding students' interactions and how they might have influenced the atmosphere of the class.

Modifications and Considerations

Some students could be encouraged to set aims. They could indicate on their personal chart the number of questions or answers they would like to offer per day or week. Teachers could help them set and achieve those goals. For that matter, the class as a whole could set goals.

As some students reach aims with questions and answers, they could be encouraged to record other types of interactions during lecture and discussion sessions. Some of those might be follow-up comments, remarks that integrate pieces of information, alternative solutions or options, or information from sources other than the lecture or text.

If teachers want their students to be more engaged in discussions, they should allow them plenty of opportunities to do so and should reinforce them when they do. Some teachers will need to cut back on the amount of time they simply talk.

Fister and Kemp (1995) offered a number of suggestions for encouraging student participation, one of which is to provide them with dot-to-dot figures. Using these, pupils make a mark from one point to another for each question, answer, or other type of exchange.

Monitor

Suggestions for monitoring the effects of this procedure were offered in Steps 5 through 9 of the Procedures section.

References

Delprato, D. J. (1977). Increasing classroom participation with self-monitoring. *The Journal of Educational Research, 70*(4), 225–227.

Fister, S. L., & Kemp, K. A. (1995). *TGIF: Making it work on Monday.* Longmont, CO: Sopris West.

 # PARTICIPATING IN DISCUSSIONS: LOOKING ALIVE

Background

Successful students learn to attend to the teacher and behave appropriately. Furthermore, their body language generally indicates that they are tuned in and motivated. Less successful students do not attend, often misbehave, and, as indicated by their verbal behaviors and body language, do not tune in. Many of these students, however, can be taught to recognize various social and body gestures, to know the meanings or implications of those expressions and movements, and to incorporate them into their interactions with teachers and others. By looking like they are participating, these students may prompt more interactions with teachers, and hence become regular participants.

Who Can Benefit

Given explicit explanations, students at any age can learn strategies for appearing "alive." This strategy is particularly suitable for remedial students who may be insensitive to body language (Ellis, 1989).

Procedures

1. Introduce the SLANT strategy to students as a way to at least appear to be paying attention.

2. Explain to them that this strategy works (has effects on others) because an individual's body language sends out strong messages.

3. Ask students to consider this question: "What body language are you using and what is it saying to the teacher?"

4. Write the letters of the SLANT strategy on the board, and ask students to go over them with you.

   S = Sit up. (Sit up straight in the chair, with your feet in front of you.)

   L = Lean forward.

   A = Act like you're interested. (Have materials ready and write notes.)

   N = Nod your head. (When you agree or understand something, show it.)

   T = Track the teacher with your eyes. (Teachers will see that you are following along.)

5. Involve the students in the process by asking them to explain why the steps might be effective.

6. Instruct students to memorize the steps for the strategy and to practice it in the class in which it is being taught until it becomes natural. Then, ask students to use SLANT in other classes and report back to you on how it worked out (i.e., How did you get along with it? How did others react?).

7. Encourage students to look for examples of this type of body language from other students, their teachers, and in situations outside of the school.

Modifications and Considerations

To get some ideas about using SLANT and its effects, students could watch students in another class who were modeling the strategy. They could get other ideas on looking interested by interviewing successful students, and asking them what they do to maintain focus in a class and to appear attentive and interested.

If pupils use this strategy, they might be called on by the teacher. (That teacher might get the idea that they are truly interested.) To prepare for that, students should learn another strategy for interacting with teachers, such as the following: (a) Paraphrase what the teacher said, (b) ask questions, and (c) say what you think is important.

In addition to the strategy advanced here to encourage involvement and participation, students could be asked to offer other ideas and techniques. Moreover, they could be asked to embellish on the following ideas for attending and not daydreaming:

1. Jot down distracting thoughts and put them aside.

2. Write down at least one word that pertains to the topic every 30 seconds.

3. Write the numbers 1 to 10 on a blank sheet and write in an item from the lecture for each number.

4. Write questions about the lecture.

5. Draw pictures or symbols to reflect the ideas of the lecturer.

Sprick and Howard (1995) offered a number of suggestions for increasing student participation. One approach was to give students advance notice of the questions that will be asked, make certain that they know the answers, and call on them.

Monitor

A videotape might be developed to help students identify the subtleties of body language. The tape could be of a class in which some listeners used body language to indicate they were interested and motivated. Other participants could, with their body language, show that they were bored with the lecture (lots of students would audition for those roles). Viewers of the tape would point out the various forms of body language and note, when possible, the effects of that language on the speaker.

References

Ellis, E. (1989). A metacognitive intervention for increasing class participation. *Learning Disabilities Focus, 5*(1), 36–46.

Sprick, R. S., & Howard, L. M. (1995). *The teacher's encyclopedia of behavior management.* Longmont, CO: Sopris West.

 # PARTICIPATING IN DISCUSSIONS: POINTS FOR INTERACTING

Background

It is important for students to participate in class discussions. Teachers want them to respond to questions voluntarily and when called on, and to contribute relevant information to class discussions. Furthermore, teachers would like for all pupils to contribute, not only a few. When students participate, teachers are informed as to who is listening and how well students understand the information and are able to assimilate it.

Who Can Benefit

The procedures explained here should be considered for many students who are at risk or remedial, or others who are reluctant to participate voluntarily in class discussions (Smith, Schumaker, Schaffer, & Sherman, 1982).

Procedures

1. Explain to the students why it is important to participate in class discussions.

2. Review the rules before each discussion: raise hand to speak, speak only when called on, offer relevant comments, put down hand when others are speaking, listen to others while they are speaking.

3. Pass out a list of questions to each student at the beginning of each discussion period that relates to the material being discussed. (This would be done for only the first few discussions until the students "got the hang of it.")

4. Give examples of relevant and irrelevant contributions.

5. Designate a student to record the relevant and irrelevant contributions and disruptions of the pupils during the discussions. Prepare a form on which the student can gather these data.

6. Give a point for each relevant remark and take away one for each disruption. (Handle the irrelevant remarks with care and caution. With those that are near to the mark, explain how they might be adjusted to fit more closely with the day's topic.)

7. Give compliments to youngsters for particularly good contributions. Point out why they are especially worthy.

8. Paraphrase some contributions to help clarify them. Then you might ask the student who delivered it to present it again.

9. Explain to the students that they will be given a weekly participation grade and it will make up a portion of their quarterly grades. (Tell them what that portion will be, for example, 25%.)

10. Inform them that they will receive, for example, a C if they end up with 0 points, C+ for 5 points, B− for 7, and so forth.

11. Post the weekly participation grade averages on the bulletin board. As a class, discuss that change (if there is any) from one week to the next.

Modifications and Considerations

Maintain a rapid pace for offering contributions. Set the stage for the discussions, keep the students' comments in line with the topic, guide them back on track if they stray, and encourage pupils to make their comments as succinct as possible.

Inform students of various types of contributions: providing examples from the text, offering samples from other reading or personal experience, comparing two points of view, relating two or more contributions of others, and questioning the logic or reasoning of some comments. Provide several examples of these types. The students might watch videos of talk shows or other audience participation shows and note relevant and irrelevant remarks, and stupid comments and questions.

Fister and Kemp (1995) offered seven suggestions for encouraging student participation. One of them is the "Wild Card Spinner," in which students earn the privilege of spinning a needle by participating a certain number of times. They can win prizes, such as amounts of free time, school supplies, or other reinforcers, depending on where the needle stops.

Monitor

To monitor improvement, develop a group chart with "Number Contributed" printed on the vertical axis and "Successive Days" on the horizontal axis. Also, individual charts could be made that reflected the number of points per day for each student.

References

Fister, S. L., & Kemp, K. A. (1995). *TGIF: But what will I do on Monday?* Longmont, CO: Sopris West.

Smith, B. M. S., Schumaker, J. B., Schaffer, J., & Sherman, J. A. (1982). Increasing participation and improving the quality of discussions in seventh-grade social studies classes. *Journal of Applied Behavior Analysis, 15,* 97–110.

PARTICIPATING IN DISCUSSIONS: USING RESPONSE CARDS

Background

Gardner, Heward, and Grossi (1994) lamented that research in inner-city classrooms indicated that students spent less than 1% of the day responding in each of these ways: reading aloud, answering questions, asking questions, and reciting. Their reviews of research informed them that students in city schools were allowed fewer opportunities to respond than their suburban counterparts.

Who Can Benefit

Gardner et al.'s students were fifth graders in an inner-city classroom studying science. The Response Card technique has wider applicability, however.

Procedures

1. The teacher used an overhead projector to present new science information. The scripted lessons specified the content to be presented, questions to be asked, and the correct answers to those questions.

2. After presenting each new fact or concept to the students, the teacher covered the information on the overhead projector and asked them a question about it.

3. Lessons on meteorology, climates, plants, and the solar system were developed. Each session ran for 45 to 55 minutes.

4. The teacher provided the students with response cards, which were white laminated particle board (22.9 cm × 30.5 cm), on which to write their responses. Students were also given dry-erase markers to write their responses.

5. Following a question the teacher gave the students a few minutes to write their answers. She then asked them to hold up their boards with their answers.

6. She visually scanned their responses and provided praise or corrective feedback.

   - If they were all correct, she said something like, "Good class, water vapor in the atmosphere is a *gas.*"

   - If some responses were incorrect, the teacher might say, "I see that many of you wrote *gas* as the answer. That is correct, water vapor in the air is in the form of a *gas.*"

   - If none of the students had the correct answer, the teacher could say, "I don't see any correct answers. The correct answer is *gas.* Water vapor in the atmosphere is a *gas.*"

7. During the final 5 or so minutes of the class, the teacher asked a series of review questions over the facts and concepts from that day's lesson.

These were items that had troubled most of the students during the main lesson. Response cards were again used.

8: Brief "next-day quizzes" were given at the beginning of each session. Items on those tests were from the previous day's lesson.

Modifications and Considerations

The average presentation rate during the response card sessions was one question per minute. On the average, students responded to teacher questions 22 times per session. That was 14 times their response rate during usual, hand-raising conditions. The students' accuracy was 93% during the response card sessions.

Most of the students said they liked this form of responding better than the usual way. Whereas some students are disappointed when they raise their hands and are not called on, the responses of all students are recognized when response cards are used.

Monitor

Data of the following types were gathered by Gardner et al. (1994): teacher presentation rate, number of student responses, accuracy of student responses, next-day quiz scores, and biweekly review test scores.

Reference

Gardner, R., III, Heward, W. L., & Grossi, T. A. (1994). Effects of response cards on student participation and academic achievement: A systematic replication with inner-city students during whole-class science instruction. *Journal of Applied Behavior Analysis, 27,* 63–71.

Chapter 10
GOALS

♦ ♦ ♦ ♦ ♦ ♦ ♦ ♦ ♦ ♦ ♦ ♦ ♦ ♦ ♦ ♦ ♦ ♦

I t is a good idea to have some goals, to have an idea as to what you want to do and when you want to do it. Teachers should have goals for each of their classes. More specifically, they should have a goal or two for certain individuals in their classes, especially for those with disabilities who have Individualized Education Plans (IEPs).

Knowing how to set goals requires the following:

- Coming up with aims that are important and attainable

- Describing the goals in writing so that they stay with the developer

- Describing them to the extent the writer and possibly others know what they are and would know when they were reached

- Having some way to measure or monitor the extent they are being attained

Once the goal is reached, the person should have some sort of celebration. The six tactics in this chapter are intended to help teachers to assist their students in setting and achieving goals, and in monitoring the attainment of those goals. The write-ups include a general set of ideas for teachers, self-management and goal setting, setting contracts related to goals, setting priorities, the IEP process, and goals and the world of work. Additional tactics related to goals appear in the Study Skills, Homework, and Self-Management chapters of this book.

GOAL SETTING STRATEGIES AND TACTICS FOR TEACHERS

Background

Included in this write-up are strategies and tactics that teachers might consider as they assist students to set goals and to work toward them. Strategies are general ideas for developing behaviors or skills, whereas tactics are specific approaches that relate to those strategies. Learning about self-management as a way to set and achieve goals would be a strategy, and learning about the components of self-management (e.g., defining objectives, counting, recording) would be tactics.

Who Can Benefit

Teachers who rely on these approaches for developing goals would benefit in that they would have worked through many of the steps necessary to teach goal setting to students. The students also would profit, as would their parents.

Procedures

Included here are four strategies and accompanying tactics from Algozzine and Ysseldyke's (1995) text having to do with goals.

1. Establish appropriate goals and objectives.

   • Specify the observable behaviors students will exhibit. Give them plenty of examples, and require them to come up with several others.

   • Specify standards for success in measurable ways. Discuss with students the standards of the class, as well as the state and district standards.

2. Place goals and objectives in priority.

   • Consider what is needed and essential. It is important to teach initially the behaviors that will do the most good, ones that will effect the greatest change.

   • Consider what the student is ready to learn. It may be, for example, that some goals should be skipped and others included in the program, depending on the student's readiness.

3. Communicate goals, objectives, and standards.

   • Develop and use goal notebooks. Each student should have a notebook listing his or her goals and progress, and you should have a master notebook detailing the goals and progress for all students.

   • Write goals on the board. The primary class goals should be visible to all students all the time. Some of the individual goals might be posted privately on students' desks.

4. Check students' understanding of goals.

   • Have students restate goals. It would be a good idea to do this every once in a while. By requiring students to state their goals, you will have to use student-type language.

   • Have students check one another's understanding of their goals. This could lead to some interesting discussions among students.

Modifications and Considerations

In working with students on setting goals, it is important that you spend time justifying why certain goals have been set, that is, why they are important. Although it is tough to convince some students of the importance of certain goals, unless they "buy into" the fact that they are important, they probably will not spend much time working toward them. When students reach a goal, especially one that was important, and they should all be important, it would be nice to commemorate that.

Monitor

Keep track of the goals attained by all students. Be aware of how many students achieve their goals and when they do so. Individual students should, of course, keep a record of their goals and when they reach them.

Reference

Algozzine, B., & Ysseldyke, J. (1995). *Strategies and tactics for effective instruction.* Longmont, CO: Sopris West.

SETTING OBJECTIVES: SELF-MANAGEMENT

Background

Often, adolescents see only the short-term picture rather than a long-term view. Teachers are trained to break down long-term goals or expectations into daily objectives. Students can also be taught to set goals and plan strategies for themselves to meet their goals.

Who Can Benefit

Students whose lives and classwork appear to be scattered or without purpose are prime candidates for this intervention.

Procedures

Phillips (1991) recommended the following steps:

1. Ask students to begin thinking about changes they would like to make at home and at school. Offer some starting points: making new friends, improving school attendance, achieving higher grades.

2. Inform students that they should set two clear objectives for the school year. Write three questions on the board that students should be able to answer as they write each objective.

   • Does it state clearly what I'll be able to do when I reach my goal?
   • Does it include a time deadline?
   • Is there some way I can judge whether I've reached my goal?

3. Request students to determine whether each of the following objectives is clear or unclear.

   "I want to make five new friends by January."
   "I want to have a better life than my parents."
   "I want to be happy."
   "I aim to make money."

4. Ask students to complete these items:

- List behaviors of a successful student.
- List three behaviors that would help you to be more successful.
- Write an objective for the most important of the three behaviors.
- Finish this statement: "Let me show you how I can _____."
- List the behaviors involved in reaching the objective.
- Write in a time to have a progress check.

Modifications and Considerations

This technique would be appropriate with individuals, small groups, or an entire class. In preparing to work with students on goal setting, keep in mind their past experiences and successes in setting aims. Discuss with them the fact that it is generally better to begin with small objectives that are attainable in a few weeks than to pick larger ones that may take months to reach.

This lesson would be most appropriate at the beginning of a year or quarter, or perhaps at the return from a school break.

Monitor

Each objective should be measured to determine whether progress is being made toward it. If a student's objective was to turn in 100% of his or her assignments in U.S. history and biology throughout a semester, or to begin doing that 6 weeks into the term, the student should chart each day the number of assignments given and, of those, how many were turned in.

Reference

Phillips, M. (1991). *The peer counseling training course: Classroom guidance manual.* San Jose, CA: Resource Publications.

ARRANGING CONTRACTS TO ACHIEVE GOALS

Background

Students characterized as remedial or at risk and students with learning disabilities often lack the academic skills and study habits valued by teachers and required for success in school. As a result, those students receive poor grades and scant praise, and consequently become unmotivated and demoralized. In a response to this problem, Tollefson, Tracy, Johnsen, and Chatman (1986) implemented a training program to teach self-management behaviors that included skills in goal setting and planning.

The method used to monitor these self-regulated behaviors was a weekly contract made up of several interrelated features: (a) setting realistic (attainable) academic goals; (b) developing a plan to reach these goals (the contract); (c) implementing, monitoring, and evaluating progress; and (d) accepting responsibility for success and failure in attaining goals. The latter relates to effort attribution, the perception individuals have of the role that effort plays in achievement. To succeed in this task, all four components are essential.

Who Can Benefit

Tollefson et al. (1986) used this technique with junior high students with learning disabilities in a resource room. These practices could be set up for other types and ages of students in a variety of settings. To ensure success, the student and teacher must be committed, and must carry out their part of the contract. The student must attempt to accomplish that which is set out, and the teacher must give the student consistent feedback on his or her efforts.

Procedures

1. Record the number of assignments (the precontract) the students are asked to complete. These data will serve as a baseline.

2. Encourage the students to select a subject or behavior in which they want to improve. Combine information from the student with your own ideas about problem areas in establishing a weekly contract (see example of a weekly contract in Figure 10.1).

3. Explain a contract to the students, noting that it is a promise to fulfill a certain requirement or task. Emphasize that students are obligated to fulfill the task they selected, and when they do, they will receive a reward.

4. Develop a study plan to meet the goal. Specify activities, the time and place the work should be done, and individuals the students can ask for help when needed.

5. Direct students to monitor their daily work by placing a plus or minus sign to indicate whether the plan was followed that day. If the plan was not carried out, students should write a reason why it was not.

6. Instruct students to record their level of satisfaction (*very satisfied, satisfied, not satisfied*) on the form at the end of a week.

7. Explain to students that their level of satisfaction is attributed to their success in establishing a realistic goal and completing the contract. If students have failed, inform them that their failure is due, in large part, to the quality and amount of effort put forth, and not to luck or ability.

8. Review the completed contract once a week, and introduce the one for the next week, which is to be filled out prior to each new week.

Modifications and Considerations

Tollefson et al.'s (1986) research was successful, probably because the weekly reviews between teacher and students provided the feedback necessary to help students attribute their successes and failures to their personal efforts rather than to external factors such as luck. A second reason to account for the success of the project was that the goals set by the students were attainable.

WEEKLY CONTRACT

Subject _____   Student Name _____

Period _____   Teacher Name _____

from _____   to _____

Goal Statement _____

_____

COMPLETION DATES: Task 1 _____

                         Task 2 _____

                                 (fill in as needed)

Study Plan:	Activities	Work Time	Place	Helper
Monday				
Tuesday				
Wednesday				
Thursday				
Friday				

Comments: _____

_____

                       Goal _____

Accomplished	Not Accomplished	Reasons

_____

_____

Level of Satisfaction: Very Satisfied _____

                            Satisfied _____

                            Not Satisfied _____

Reward

Teacher Signature _____

Student Signature _____

Figure 10.1. Weekly contract for use in achieving goals.

Related to attribution and the attainment of goals, it was interesting to note that, in the research, the students' self-esteem remained high, perhaps because they were in control of their performances.

When it comes to writing performance contracts, a number of modifications are possible. The contract could be changed to be simpler or more sophisticated. Contracts could be drawn up in several of a student's classes. The number and type of individuals involved in setting up and carrying out the contract could be varied from the student and teacher situations described here. For example, contracts could be written that involve friends, administrators, or parents. The component of time could be varied as well, moving from weekly to longer term contracts.

A "reinforcer survey" is included in Idol and West's (1993) book (p. 93). Student data from this would be helpful in arranging contracts. The first three items on the survey are these: The things I like to do after school are _____. If I had ten dollars I'd _____. My favorite TV program is _____.

Monitor

Maintain data on the number of goals set and attained per week (or other period of time). Beyond those measures, data could be acquired on the quality of students' performance, their attitude toward the subject, and their grades.

References

Idol, L., & West, J. F. (1993). *Effective instruction of difficult-to-teach students: An inservice and preservice professional development program for classroom, remedial, and special education teachers*. Austin, TX: PRO-ED.

Tollefson, N., Tracy, D. S., Johnsen, E. P., & Chatman, J. (1986). Teaching learning disabled students goal-implementation skills. *Psychology in the Schools, 23,* 194–204.

SETTING PRIORITIES

Background

This activity is based on the Q-sort technique, which involves sorting a set of cards into piles to form a normal distribution (Cummings, Chamberlain, & Kelly, 1979). The sorting process serves to actively involve students as they evaluate the relative importance of each item, in this case, goals.

Who Can Benefit

Students who are at risk or remedial, those with learning disabilities, and others should profit from this technique. They would be given experiences in evaluating and prioritizing goals in three general areas: interpersonal, intrapersonal, and material.

Procedures

Listed here are preparations to make prior to involving students in this technique and steps required for carrying it out.

Preparations

1. Create one set of cards, on which the goals on the Goal Classifications List (Table 10.1) are printed (one per card) for each student.

Table 10.1. Goal Classification List

Interpersonal (Relationships with Others)	Intrapersonal (Personal Concerns)	Material (Concrete Possessions)
Be a good friend	Be close to God	Have enough money to help
Have close friend(s)	Go to heaven	others
Spend time with friends	Help people learn about God	Work to make money
Be close to my family	Do exciting things	Have enough money to buy
Help my family	Have a lot of change in my	what I want
Do things with my family	life	Have a job I enjoy
Marry someone I love	Try everything I want to	Advance in my job
Be happily married for a	Be an attractive person	Be good at my job
long time	Be well liked by others for	Travel to foreign places
Marry someone I know well	what I am	Travel in the U.S.
Have children	Respect myself	Meet people in other
Spend time with children	Feel free to be different from	countries
Be a good example for my	others	Have a recent model vehicle
children	Be able to think on my own	Have good equipment on
Have leadership qualities	Make a living on my own	my vehicle (car, pickup,
Be thought of as a leader	Learn as much as I can	van, etc.)
Be a leader in many areas	Get the best education I can	Own my own home
of my life	Do well in school	Have a nice place to live
Do volunteer work	Work to improve my	Keep my home in good
Work with community	weaknessess	condition
organizations	Develop my strengths and	Collect possessions (things)
Do things for others in the	talents	of interest
community	Know myself better	Have many possessions
Understand others better	Eat the right foods for health	(things)
Talk easily with others	Exercise for good health	Take care of my possessions
Be a good listener	Be healthy all my life	(things)
Be active in sports	Be more patient with myself	Have a lot of clothes
Understand sports	and others	Wear fashionable clothes
Promote sports	Accept things I cannot change	Have comfortable clothes
Live with someone	Be willing to wait for good	Attend shows and other
Remain single	things	events
Be free without ties to	Look natural	Eat at expensive restaurants
anyone		Have a large library

Note. Adapted from "The Q-sort Approach to Helping Adolescents with Goal Setting," by M. N. Cummings, V. M. Chamberlain, & J. M. Kelly, 1979, *Illinois Teacher of Home Economics, 23,* p. 48. Adapted by permission.

2. Construct a folder that opens flat for each student.

- Attach an envelope containing the goal cards to the bottom left inside of the folder.

- Above the envelope, print the following instructions: "In the envelope below you will find 75 cards. A goal is written on each one. On the other page there are seven pockets. The top pocket is for goals you care the most about. The bottom pocket is for those you care the least about. The other pockets are for in-between goals. Read each goal and decide how important it is to you. Put the three goals you care most about in pocket number 1 at the top. Put the three goals you care least about in pocket number 7 at the bottom. In pockets 2 through 6 place the other goal cards from the most to the least important to you. Place only the number of goal cards that are supposed to be in each pocket."

3. Tape seven pockets, vertically arranged, on the right side of the folder (see Figure 10.2).

- Label the top pocket "Goals I Care Most About."
- Label the bottom pocket "Goals I Care Least About."
- Specify the number of cards to be sorted into each pocket.

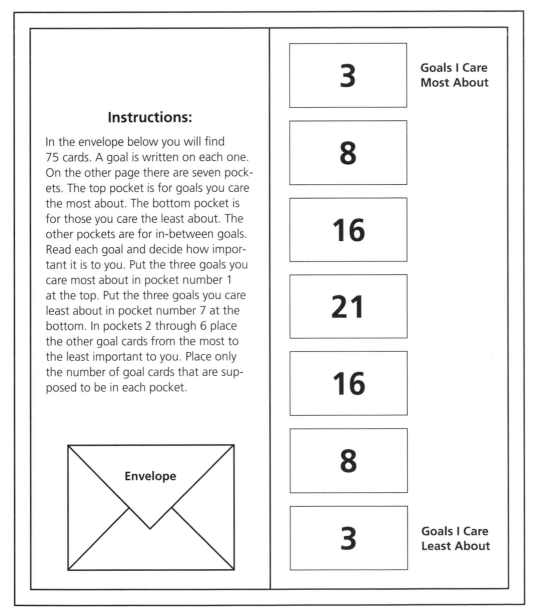

Figure 10.2. Folder for setting priorities.

Steps

1. Discuss goal setting as a way to enhance the quality of one's life and to plan for the future.

2. Inform students that this activity will help them choose their goals.

3. Provide each student with a folder.

4. Instruct students to read the instructions and begin the sort. Ask if they understand the instructions or if they have any questions.

5. Ask students to make a record of their goal distribution on a separate sheet of paper.

6. Ask them how they got along with this activity: What was easy, difficult, confusing?

7. Initiate class discussion about different ways to work toward achieving high-priority goals.

8. Help students begin developing individual plans for achieving their goals.

Modifications and Considerations

Although Cummings et al. (1979) selected 75 goals, students or teachers could choose different ones. Furthermore, the goals in this research were from three categories and fit into seven sections (from least to most meaningful). Fewer or more categories could be used, and fewer or more dimensions (pockets) could be selected.

Monitor

Once students have identified a few important goals to be achieved in a short or long period of time, encourage them to monitor the extent to which they are attaining them. If, for example, one of Sarah's goals was to have a library of 500 classics, she could list the books she intended to purchase, then check them off as they were added to her collection.

References

Cummings, M. N., Chamberlain, V. M., & Kelly, J. M. (1979). The Q-sort approach to helping adolescents with goal setting. *Illinois Teacher, 23,* 46–49.

 # RELATING GOALS AND IEPS

Background

The heart and soul of a student's IEP is the section on goals. All other features of the document pertain to those aims. Not only are teachers and others obligated to set important goals for students with disabilities, they are directed to do so with the advice and counsel of the students themselves and their parents. One could argue that the IEP provides the ultimate opportunity to set goals and to teach students about goal setting, and to give them ways in which to measure the attainment of those goals.

Who Can Benefit

Consideration of the remarks and suggestions in this tactic will certainly benefit youth with disabilities. Not only that, if teachers attended to the remarks and recommendations presented here, their jobs would be easier and more efficient, and they would be more productive.

Procedures

Based on research with dozens of high school students and their IEPs (Lovitt, Cushing, & Stump, 1994), I will note five of the more glaring faults discovered:

1. Many schools include too many goals and objectives in students' IEPs. The teachers cannot remember what they are and neither can the pupils or their parents.

2. Too often "educationese" is used in writing IEP goals. That language is confusing to all concerned, teachers, parents, and definitely the pupils.

3. The IEPs of several students had identical goals; they were not individualized.

4. When students were asked to explain the IEP process, only a few could do so.

5. Most damning was that when students were asked about their goals, very few knew what any of them were.

Some of the following recommendations parallel the negative aspects just noted. In designing IEP goals, teachers should attend to both sets of comments.

1. Meet with students to discuss the overall purpose of IEPs, and how they should take part in developing them. (Although that recommendation is actually written into the process, it generally does not happen.)

2. Identify IEP goals that reflect the entire time a student has left in school, rather than writing yearly goals. Unless this is done, there is apt to be considerable repetition from one year to the next, and it is difficult to see a student's progress over time.

3. Write goals and objectives clearly; use language that is clear and understandable. (To check whether you have done this, ask students to read them and tell you what they mean.)

4. Make every effort to ensure that students understand how their objectives are evaluated. Use methods of evaluation that are simple, straightforward, and authentic.

5. See to it that students know the requirements for graduating and obtaining a diploma. Their IEP goals should be tied into that scheme of things.

Modifications and Considerations

Students should be quizzed once in a while over their IEP goals. If an authorized person came into a student's class and asked a student what his or her IEP goals were, the student should be able to say them, explain how they were being evaluated, and tell how much progress he or she had made toward them.

Monitor

Students should be encouraged and taught to monitor their own IEP goals. They should have notebooks, charts, or other means to monitor each of their goals.

Reference

Lovitt, T .C., Cushing, S. S., & Stump, C. S. (1994). High school students rate their IEPs: Low opinions and lack of ownership. *Intervention in School and Clinic, 30*(1), 34–37.

ATTAINING GOALS: TIPS FROM THE WORLD OF WORK

Background

The following suggestions for time management, tied with the realization of goals, were written by Pauline George, a management training specialist (cited in "Plan Ahead: Mind Your Ps"). According to her, the issue is not one of managing time, because time is a constant, but rather of managing ourselves. Therefore, tough choices have to be made. We need to keep in mind that "If we do this, then we can't do that."

Who Can Benefit

Most teachers and students can benefit from techniques for getting the most out of time. Students who are at risk and remedial stand to profit the most, because they are often disorganized and, as a result, nonproductive.

Procedures

Following are George's (1989) eight Ps for success:

1. *Purpose*—Make priorities and objectives specific, measurable, realistic, and scheduled. Write them down and review them. If an objective from

one week is no longer important, push it down the list or remove it completely.

2. *Patterns*—Your habits are your key to management. Analyze your days to discover your habits. Ask others to tell you how you waste your time. They can see things you cannot.

3. *Plans*—Many people stop after they plan; they do not schedule an activity. Make a to-do list every day. Those things that are scheduled have a better chance of being carried out.

4. *Parasites*—These are pernicious time-wasters such as watching television, answering and talking on the phone (this is especially important in this day and age of telemarketing), waiting for buses and appointments, being interrupted, and engaging in idle chitchat. Try to eliminate these or devise ways to profit from them.

5. *Paperwork*—Analyze and try to handle each piece of paper only once (that includes your mail). Do not set it aside without taking appropriate action. If that means throwing it away, throw it away.

6. *Partners*—Be a good listener; it saves lots of time and prevents many problems. Show people you respect their time. Know whom to go to for what type of assistance.

7. *Procrastination*—Admit it when you are procrastinating. Stop rationalizing and you will be more likely to act. Identify your stalling techniques and eliminate them. Do unpleasant things before pleasurable ones.

8. *Personal*—Be good to yourself. Get enough rest, eat properly, and exercise regularly. Doing that will increase your energy, decrease tension and stress, and allow you to focus better on the identified tasks. Have a life beyond your job.

Modifications and Considerations

Although the eight points noted here were designed for individuals in business, they also apply to students and teachers. It may be informative to students to learn that it is important for individuals of all ages and types to get a handle on their use of time. Point out that all people have the same amount of time, and that some people do "have their acts together." Get over the trendy habit of telling others how busy you are. They are not interested! When a person consistently complains about how busy he or she is, I get the idea that the person either cannot decide what is important, is unable to manage time, or simply likes to whine.

Monitor

Most of the eight points identified by George could be evaluated separately. Take, for example, Parasites. Students could be encouraged to keep track of the minutes spent each day watching television, gossiping on their cell phone, or whatever else keeps them from attaining their goals. Those data could be charted. It would also be revealing if students plotted the number of minutes they devoted to obtaining their number one goal on the same chart. They might see a relationship.

Reference

Plan ahead: Mind your Ps. (1989, May 7). *The Seattle Times*, p. K8.

Chapter 11
PEER-MEDIATED INSTRUCTION

♦ ♦ ♦ ♦ ♦ ♦ ♦ ♦ ♦ ♦ ♦ ♦ ♦ ♦ ♦ ♦ ♦ ♦ ♦

Ideas are offered in this chapter for setting up peer tutoring and cooperative learning situations. Those approaches are referred to collectively as peer-mediated instruction. Several reasons have been advanced for arranging these ensembles. One is that when they are established more students will have more opportunities to respond, and as a result their learning will be enhanced. Considerable data are available to support that argument. Another reason for scheduling these groupings is that when individuals serve as teachers, they themselves learn. There is some data and abundant folklore to argue that point. Yet another motivation for setting up cooperative learning groups is that students will learn to work with one another, and perhaps even cooperate in the process. The data on that point are rather sketchy.

Teachers should have one of those purposes, or others, in mind when scheduling one of the peer-mediated situations. Moreover, they should be alert to the needs of all students—high, middle, and low performers—when appointing them to one of those structures. All students should gain from their membership in any of the communal groups.

Eleven peer-mediated configurations are described in this chapter. They are arranged in somewhat of an order of complexity, with reciprocal teaching explained first. That approach is followed by a write-up of a basic peer tutoring program. Next, I describe a classwide tutoring structure that combines elements of peer tutoring and cooperative learning. The next five techniques are the most popular forms and are of medium complexity, whereas the final three models are the most elaborate.

 ## RECIPROCAL TEACHING: AN ENTRY TO COOPERATIVE LEARNING

Background

The concept of reciprocal teaching was developed by Palincsar and Brown (1988). The technique was designed to help students better comprehend what they have read by following a four-step procedure: generating questions, summarizing, predicting, and clarifying. The ultimate goal of reciprocal teaching is for students to apply the technique to content-area subjects as a means to study and learn that material.

Who Can Benefit

This tactic would be beneficial for remedial as well as other students who are able to apply the four-step process. The technique would be beneficial to intermediate and secondary students as they read from content-area textbooks. A number of researchers have demonstrated the positive effects of reciprocal teaching (e.g., Herrmann, 1988).

Procedures

During the first few reciprocal teaching sessions, model all the steps to help students become familiar with them. Then have students take turns being the teacher, while you act as a member of the group and assist the student teachers if they have difficulty with particular steps.

To begin the process, each member of the group silently reads a short passage or paragraph. When finished reading, each student silently generates answers to the four-step procedure in preparation for being the teacher. Once every member of the group completes the reading, you select one student to act as teacher. The student teacher works through the four steps orally and calls on other students when applicable.

1. *Question*—The student teacher generates a question about the main idea of the paragraph. He or she might say, "The first step is a main idea question. A good main idea question about this paragraph is. . . ." Once the question is posed, the student teacher calls on others for the answer.

2. *Summarize*—The student teacher summarizes the passage in a brief sentence or two. The summary should include the main idea as well as any important details. He or she might say, "The next step is to summarize the paragraph. This paragraph is about. . . ."

3. *Clarify*—The student teacher asks if there are any words in the paragraph that are unfamiliar to anyone. He or she may give a definition for the word or may ask another student to define it. If no one is familiar with the word, they may consult a dictionary.

4. *Predict*—The student teacher predicts what the next paragraph will be about. The prediction should be based on the information in the current passage and on previously read paragraphs in the text. He or she might say, "Because the third to last paragraph described the types of crops in a region, and the next to last paragraph mentioned how they were harvested, I predict that the next paragraph will be about the yields of those crops."

Students silently read the next paragraph or passage, and you select the next student to act as teacher.

Modifications and Considerations

Group size is an important consideration for this technique. The smaller the group, the more turns each student will have and the less chance of any student becoming bored. The technique could be modified for a larger group by having different students act as the teacher for each individual step.

Be careful not to interfere unless absolutely necessary. Jump into the lesson only when a student is unable to complete a step or completes it incorrectly. Even then, act only as a facilitator in helping students generate correct answers or questions.

The steps can be modified and presented in any order. You might choose to put the clarifying step first. The ultimate goal is for students to internalize the steps so that they can use them when studying content-area material.

Monitor

This technique could be monitored by giving students a paragraph to read silently, removing the paragraph after they have read it, then giving them a worksheet of questions pertaining to the text. Or, ask the students to tell or write freely about what they have read. Either approach could be arranged as the Reciprocal Teaching treatment was alternated. It could be used for a few passages, then not scheduled for a few, then rescheduled, and so on. You could count and chart the number of words said or written, the number of facts, or other features during both conditions and compare them.

References

Herrmann, B. A. (1988). Two approaches for helping poor readers become more strategic. *The Reading Teacher, 42,* 24–28.

Palincsar, A. M., & Brown, A. (1988). Teaching and practicing thinking skills to promote comprehension in the context of group problem solving. *Remedial and Special Education, 9*(1), 53–59.

 # PEER TUTORING: GUIDELINES FOR SETTING UP PROGRAMS

Background

Peer and cross-age tutoring has a long history as an effective method for educating students. The benefits for the tutee include individualized instruction and extra practice. Tutors may benefit academically, socially, and personally. Research has indicated that peer tutoring programs are the most cost-effective, and they produce the greatest gains in learning, when compared with other interventions such as decreasing class size or lengthening the school day.

Who Can Benefit

This tactic is based on a review of research that supported tutoring at both the elementary and secondary levels (Jenkins & Jenkins, 1985). Tutoring is designed to assist students with a variety of academic skills, and can be effective in most content areas. The increased amounts of time on task inherent in this approach are particularly valuable for low-achieving students. Students who serve as tutors not only acquire a better understanding of subject matter, but also develop useful management skills in the process.

Procedures

1. Secure support for establishing a peer tutoring program from school administrators, staff, and parents.

2. Select tutors. Suggest to higher achieving students that they might become tutors. An application form should be completed by students who express an interest. Signed permission letters should be obtained from parents of tutors who have been selected. (See examples of a Peer Tutor Application in Figure 11.1 and a permission letter in Figure 11.2.)

3. Select tutees. Identify the students who might benefit from tutoring. Students could also request assistance for themselves.

4. Recruit a good note-taker from the class to take notes on lectures and reading assignments. Provide tutors with a copy of these notes. Training may be provided for note-takers.

PEER TUTOR APPLICATION

Applicant _____ Present Grade Level _____

Mailing Address _____

_____

_____

What subject areas do you consider to be your strongest? Would you be comfortable tutoring someone in these areas? (Please rank order the subjects below with number 1 being the highest priority for you.)

_____ Art   _____ Language Arts

_____ Business Education   _____ Math

_____ Home Economics   _____ Reading

_____ Industrial Education   _____ Science

                                     _____ Social Studies

In 100 words or less, please tell us:

1. Why you would like to be a peer tutor.

2. The qualities you feel you have that would make you a good peer tutor.

Figure 11.1. Sample Peer Tutor Application for use in setting up peer tutoring program.

PERMISSION LETTER

Dear Parents:

Your son or daughter is applying for a position as a Peer Tutor. Peer Tutors are a select group of students who will be trained to provide specific kinds of assistance to students with special learning needs.

I hope you will support your son's or daughter's application.

Sincerely,

_____   _____
(Parent Signature)   (Date)

Figure 11.2. Sample permission letter for peer tutors.

5. Train tutors. This training should be extensive, covering communication skills, analysis, instructional methods and strategies, and study skills.

6. Match tutors and tutees. The more experienced tutors could be placed with those students having the greatest difficulty. Depending on the specific requirements of the tutees, tutors may be able to assist groups of two or three.

7. Specify goals and steps of tutoring for individual students.

8. Supervise tutors and tutees. Circulate about the classroom to be sure that tutoring sessions are proceeding appropriately. Assist students as questions arise.

9. Maintain tutors' involvement and interest. There are suggestions for doing this in the Modifications and Considerations section.

10. Tutees should keep records of their assignments and test scores while they are being tutored.

11. Tutors should monitor these records to see how their assistance helped the tutees' progress. Teachers, in turn, should supervise all record keeping and set up a bulletin board on which students may post their scores.

Modifications and Considerations

Tutors can be honored in a number of ways. Reinforcers could take the form of a school display with tutors' photos, an awards assembly, a page of the yearbook, or a reception. Positive feedback from tutees and teachers can also help maintain tutors' interest.

One of the most important attitudes tutors need to develop in their relationships with tutees is flexibility. No matter how specific the task, or how well structured the procedures, situations will arise that have not been covered in training sessions. Students must be able to adjust their approaches as necessary, and be willing to ask for and accept assistance if they cannot.

Archer, Gleason, Englert, and Isaacson (1995) offered additional suggestions for setting up peer tutoring situations. They included examples of formats for peer tutoring in reading (i.e., for passage words and passage reading).

Monitor

Because this is an organizational tactic, one designed to establish a program, it would be appropriate to keep data on the steps and the process for getting the program under way. Records should be kept of the numbers involved: tutors, tutees, and teachers. Information should also be obtained on the time required for start-up, for daily involvement, and for administrative matters.

To acquire data on the impressions of affected individuals, a series of interviews could be scheduled. Teachers, tutors, tutees, and perhaps parents of tutors and tutees could be interviewed to determine how they felt about the program, what changes they would suggest, and whether they believed the program should be continued.

Beyond those data, information should be acquired on the primary goal of the tutoring program—the improvement of tutees in certain subjects. Data should also be kept on the tutors, to determine whether they, as a result of teaching, acquired important skills.

References

Archer, A. L., Gleason, M. M., Englert, C. S., & Isaacson, S. (1995). Meeting individual instructional needs. In P. T. Cegelka & W. H. Berdine (Eds.), *Effective instruction for students with learning disabilities* (pp. 195–225). Needham Heights, MA: Allyn & Bacon.

Jenkins, J. J., & Jenkins, L. M. (1985). Peer tutoring in elementary and secondary programs. *Focus on Exceptional Children, 17*(6), 1–12.

 # PEER TUTORING: A CLASSWIDE PROGRAM IN SOCIAL STUDIES

Background

Many students, particularly those with learning disabilities or said to be at risk, need opportunities to practice the facts, ideas, and concepts that are dealt with in secondary content-area classes such as social studies. To increase those opportunities, peer tutoring has been recommended. In this particular peer tutoring program, students with learning problems work with peers who are average performers. This is in keeping with the notion of inclusion. Also, students are often motivated to learn if they are allowed to work with other students, and there is a "payoff" for group as well as individual production.

Who Can Benefit

In Maheady, Sacca, and Harper's (1989) study, a regular classroom teacher used classwide peer tutoring (CWPT) with three classes of 10th graders. A number of students with learning disabilities were included in those classes. Allsopp (1997) reported that a CWPT program was successful in aiding middle school students in algebra. The students in his study were characterized as at risk.

Procedures

The following are procedures for implementing the CWPT Program (Maheady et al., 1989).

1. Divide the class into two teams. Ask students to draw a red or a blue colored square from a box; then form a Red Team and a Blue Team.

2. Randomly pair students within each team to form tutoring dyads.

3. Set up a few sessions to train all the students on how to tutor. Those steps are detailed in number 6 below.

4. Arrange 30-minute tutoring sessions in which one member of the pair serves as the tutor and the other as the tutee for the first 15 minutes. Schedule two sessions per week.

5. Dictate the items on a 30-item study guide to the tutee.

6. Require the tutee to write and say the answers to the questions. For a correct answer, say "That's right" or "Correct" and provide 3 points for the response. For an incorrect answer, say "That's wrong" and tell the tutee the correct answer. Then require the tutee to write the correct response three times. Award 2 points for correcting the answer.

7. Reverse roles at the end of the 15-minute period or when all 30 items on the study guide have been answered. Follow the same procedures noted above.

8. Award up to 10 bonus points for "good tutoring": clear and accurate dictation of questions, appropriate use of the error correction procedure, contingent and accurate delivery of points, and use of praise and support statements. (To deliver these, the teacher should move about the classroom during the sessions.)

9. Ask students to total up the number of points they earned during the session and record that number at the top of their paper.

10. Schedule a "surprise day" when the teacher checks the students' papers and awards 10 bonus points for each team member who correctly totaled the points.

11. Post the students' scores on a laminated chart in front of the class.

12. Calculate the daily team totals.

13. Administer a weekly quiz on the study guide items and award students 5 points for each correct answer.

14. Calculate all the points for both teams following the weekly quiz and announce the winner.

15. Form a new set of teams for each 2-week period.

Modifications and Considerations

Data from Maheady et al.'s (1989) research indicated that most students, including those with learning disabilities, improved their scores on tests and corresponding grades as a result of the peer tutoring sessions. The authors noted that this program was carried out without disrupting other classroom features; however, it required considerable time to prepare adequate study guides. (Refer to Learning from Textbooks: Study Guides in Chapter 6 for a detailed outline on how to prepare study guides.)

Monitor

In Maheady et al.'s (1989) article, the students' weekly scores on the quizzes were charted in terms of percentages. These scores were charted for a few weeks during a baseline, when the peer tutoring intervention was not in effect, and for a few weeks while the tutoring was scheduled. In fact, the researchers set up a multiple baseline design across classrooms: The intervention was scheduled in one class, then in another, and finally in the third.

References

Allsopp, D. H. (1997). Using classwide peer tutoring to teach beginning algebra problem-solving skills in heterogeneous classrooms. *Remedial and Special Education, 18*(6), 367–379.

Maheady, L., Sacca, M. K., & Harper, G. F. (1989). Classwide peer tutoring with mildly handicapped high school students. *Exceptional Children, 55,* 52–59.

COOPERATIVE LEARNING: CIRCLES OF LEARNING

Background

According to Johnson, Johnson, Holubec, and Roy (1984), the essence of cooperative learning is positive interdependence—students recognize that they are in this together; they sink or swim as one. These situations are also characterized by individual accountability: Every student is accountable for both learning the assigned material and helping other group members learn.

Who Can Benefit

Johnson et al. (1984) maintain that, at best, cooperative learning experiences lead to the following: positive interactions, feelings of psychological acceptance, psychological success, self-acceptance and high self-esteem, and understandings of other students. They recommend that teachers resist the advice they may have been given as beginning teachers to isolate students who pester others; teachers should, instead, integrate those students into cooperative groups.

Procedures

Specify Objectives

Specify objectives of two types: those that pertain to academic expectations and those that detail which collaborative skills will be emphasized.

Teacher Decisions

Decide on the size of the groups (i.e., from two to six). Decide on how to assign students to groups and how long the groups will remain together (Johnson et al. recommended that the groups be as heterogeneous as possible, and stay together until some unit of work is finished). Decide how to arrange the room to facilitate the cooperative groups. Decide how the materials or information will be provided to the groups, and whether the members of the groups will be assigned roles (e.g., summarizer, checker, recorder). Goor and Schwenn (1993) offered a number of suggestions on the types of roles and their duties that may be involved in cooperative learning arrangements.

Explain the Academic Task

Explain the objectives of the lesson and relate the concepts and information to be studied to students' past experiences. In addition, explain the criteria for success on the academic task and inform students what is expected of them collaboratively.

Structure Positive Goal Interdependence

Inform students that they have a group goal and must work collaboratively. Ask the groups to produce a single product, report, or paper. When completed, each member should sign the paper to indicate that he or she agreed with the report and can summarize its content. Provide group rewards.

Structure Individual Accountability

Assess frequently the level of performance of each group member (e.g., give intermittent tests to each member, select at random one paper from the group to grade, ask members to explain answers, require members to edit each other's work).

Monitoring and Intervening

Roam about the room while the cooperative groups are functioning, and provide feedback and assistance as needed.

Modifications and Considerations

Johnson et al. (1984) noted that cooperative relationships are just as effective with teachers as they are with students; teachers are more effective when they have positive support from colleagues and can solve problems together. The enhanced product of collaborative groups has been supported in the context of teacher assistance teams by R. Beck (personal communication, 1990). When a group of teachers was asked to come up with a variety of interventions to arrange with academic and social concerns, the group identified about three times as many as did any single teacher.

Monitor

Johnson et al. (1984) recommended that teachers use a formal observation sheet to count the number of times they observe appropriate student behaviors in groups. At first teachers may simply record who talks in each group to get a notion of the participation patterns. Later, they could gather data on the following: contributing ideas, asking questions, actively listening, expressing support and acceptance, encouraging all members to participate, summarizing, checking for understanding, and giving direction to the group work. It is important also to acquire data on the product of the groups' efforts on the academic task, and to evaluate the extent to which the various groups worked together.

References

Goor, M. B., & Schwenn, J. O. (1993). Accommodating diversity and disability with cooperative learning. *Intervention in School and Clinic, 29*(1), 6–16.

Johnson, D. W., Johnson, R. T., Holubec, E. J., & Roy, P. (1984). *Circles of learning.* Alexandria, VA: Association for Supervision and Curriculum Development.

COOPERATIVE LEARNING: STUDENT TEAMS–ACHIEVEMENT DIVISIONS

Background

According to Slavin (1986), Student Teams–Achievement Divisions (STAD) is one of the simplest of all cooperative learning methods, and is a good model to begin with for teachers who want to get started with these arrangements. Moreover, STAD is one of the oldest and most extensively researched of the cooperative learning structures.

Who Can Benefit

Researchers (e.g., Slavin, 1986) have reported that this method leads to positive social outcomes, such as enhanced interpersonal relationships, for students in Grades 4 through 12. Increased acceptance of minorities, including racial minorities and individuals with disabilities, has been reported as a consequence of experiences with this cooperative learning structure (Nastasi & Clements, 1991).

Procedures

Preparation

- *Prepare materials*—Make a worksheet, answer sheet, and quiz for each unit. This could be in the form of a study guide or graphic organizer. (See Chapter 6 for details on developing those formats.)

- *Assign students to teams*—Organize students in groups of four or five who, to the extent possible, represent a cross-section of the class in terms of academic performance, gender, and race or ethnicity.

- *Determine initial base scores*—Calculate each student's average score on a number of past quizzes.

Schedule of Activities

- *Teach*—Tell students what they are about to learn and why it is important. Review any prerequisite skills or information. Stick close to the objectives that will be tested. Assess students' comprehension by asking questions. Require students to solve problems or in other ways become involved with the lesson. (This might take one or two class periods, depending on the amount of information to cover and other factors.)

- *Team study*—Students study the worksheets in their teams. They have two copies of the worksheets and one answer sheet. Teams study the sheets until everyone knows the items. Ask students to explain answers to one another instead of merely checking one another's answers. If someone has a question, he or she should ask all members for help. While the teams are working, the teacher should circulate among them to keep them on track, to praise those who are doing well, and to help those who have problems. (This could take one or two class periods.)

- *Test*—Distribute the quiz and inform students to work on it individually. When finished, ask students to exchange papers with members of other teams, or give them to you for scoring. (This might take up only a part of a period.)

Calculate Individual and Team Scores

- *Individual improvement scores*—Students earn points for their teams based on how much their quiz scores exceed their base scores. For example, a score of 10 points above = 10; a score of 20 points above = 20; and so on.

- *Team scores*—Record each team member's points on a team summary sheet; add them up and divide by the number of members on the team.

- *Recognize team accomplishments*—Give awards that indicate three levels: good team, great team, or super team. Those awards should be based on team averages.

- *Return quizzes*—When the first set of quizzes (with base scores, quiz scores, and improvement points) is returned, the scoring system should be explained.

Modifications and Considerations

Occasionally, recalculate the base scores. This should serve to gradually raise pupils' scores. After 6 weeks or so, change teams. This will give the students opportunities to know more of their classmates, and give them experiences in working with a wide range of individuals. Although the greatest proportion of a student's grade should be based on his or her actual quiz scores, or perhaps improvement scores, a student's team scores should make up a proportion of the grade.

Monitor

To evaluate the effects of this cooperative approach on academic performance, two phases could be arranged. During the first, or baseline, phase, pupils would work independently on their lessons, and in the next phase, they would be in cooperative groups. Data could be obtained during both conditions and studied to determine which youth did better during which condition. Furthermore, data would indicate which groups were generally productive and which ones were not.

References

Nastasi, B. K., & Clements, D. H. (1991). Research on cooperative learning: Implications for practice. *School Psychology Review, 20*(1), 110–131.

Slavin, R. E. (1986). *Using student team learning* (3rd ed.). Baltimore: Johns Hopkins University, Center for Research on Elementary and Middle Schools.

COOPERATIVE LEARNING: TEAMS–GAMES–TOURNAMENT

Background

Teams–Games–Tournament (TGT) is the same as Student Teams–Achievement Divisions, the previous tactic, in every respect but one: Instead of the quizzes and the individual improvement score system, TGT uses academic tournaments in which students compete as representatives of their teams with members of other teams who are at the same academic level (Devries & Slavin, 1978).

Who Can Benefit

A few studies have indicated that students in TGT groups gained significantly more friends outside their own racial group than did control students. Other studies have reported that more students in TGT groups believed it was important to do well in class than did control students, and that students in these groups named more friends than did youth in control situations.

Procedures

Preparation

Make a worksheet, a worksheet answer sheet, and a quiz for each unit you intend to teach. The worksheet could be a study guide or a graphic organizer (see Chapter 6 for details on those organizational formats). In addition, prepare a set of cards numbered from 1 to 30 for every three students, and write a question on each card.

Class Presentations

Initially, introduce material to the class in the form of direct instruction or with a lecture–discussion format.

Teams

Arrange teams of four or five students who represent a cross-section of the class in several respects. Nastasi and Clements (1991) offered considerable detail on forming cooperative learning groups. They addressed the following questions, among others: How can one ensure that all students participate? What kinds of interactions should be encouraged? Do students need to be taught prerequisite social skills?

Games

Design content-relevant questions, which are the bases of the games, to test students' knowledge from the class presentation and team practice. Games are carried out with numbered questions on a sheet. They are played at tables of three students, each of whom is from a different team. A student picks a numbered card and attempts to answer the corresponding question. Players are allowed to challenge one another's answers.

Tournaments

The tournament is the structure in which the games take place. For the first week, the teacher assigns students to tables on the basis of their past performance: the top three students to table 1, the next three to table 2, and so on. On following weeks, students change tables depending on their performance in the most recent tournament. The winner at each table is promoted to the next higher table; the second scorer stays at the same table; and the lowest scorer is moved to a lower table. This equal competition enables students of all levels to contribute to their team scores.

Team Recognition

Determine individual improvement scores and team scores. For individuals, give points on an arrangement such as the following: more than 10 points below base (initial test) score = 0 points; 10 points below to 1 point below base score = 10 points; base score to 10 points above base score = 20 points. To figure team scores, record each member's improvement points on a summary sheet, total the points, and divide the total by the number of members.

Schedule of Activities

Follow this cycle: Teach for one or two class periods, team study for one or two periods, and schedule tournaments for one class period.

Modifications and Considerations

After 5 or 6 weeks, assign students to new teams. For additional variety, use TGT for a few units of your instruction and other cooperative structures for other parts. For example, use TGT in combination with STAD, either by having quizzes one week and tournaments the next, or by having a quiz the day after each tournament and counting both the quiz score and the tournament score toward the team score.

Monitor

A major concern with this type of cooperative learning might be determining the best possible combinations of students in which to place youth with disabilities or those who are at risk. Try systematically assigning those boys and girls to a variety of groups and compare their data across each of them.

References

Devries, D. L., & Slavin, R. E. (1978). Teams–games–tournaments (TGT): Review of ten classroom experiments. *Journal of Research and Development in Education, 12,* 28–38.

Nastasi, B. K., & Clements, D. H. (1991). Research on cooperative learning: Implications for practice. *School Psychology Review, 20*(1), 110–131.

COOPERATIVE LEARNING: COOPERATIVE INTEGRATED READING AND COMPOSITION

Background

According to Stevens, Madden, Slavin, and Farnish (1987), a major objective of Cooperative Integrated Reading and Composition (CIRC) is to use cooperative teams to help students learn broadly applicable reading comprehension skills. Various aspects of instruction (e.g., story structures and reciprocal teaching) are incorporated in the approach and directed toward that objective.

Who Can Benefit

Although CIRC was designed as a comprehensive program for teaching reading, writing, and language arts in Grades 4 through 6, it would also be appropriate for youth who are at risk or remedial in middle school or high school. Harrell, Doelling, and Sasso (1997) recommended CIRC, as well as other related cooperative structures, as a way to promote social interactions in inclusive classrooms.

Procedures

Major Components of CIRC

- *Reading groups*—Assign students to reading groups according to their reading level.

- *Teams*—Assign students to pairs within their reading groups; then assign the pairs to teams composed of partners from two reading groups. Team members receive points based on their individual performances on quizzes, compositions, and book reports, and these points form a team score.

- *Textbook activities*—Assign a reading passage to the youth. This could be a story from literature or a section from a science or social studies text. Set the purpose for reading by introducing new vocabulary, reviewing old vocabulary, and discussing the material after students read it.

Reading Activities

- *Partner reading*—Students read the entire passage silently, then take turns reading it aloud with a partner, alternating paragraphs. Circulate about the room as this is going on.

- *Vocabulary study*—Give students a list of new, difficult, or important words from the passage. Ask them to look up and write the definitions of the words, and write sentences in which they are used.

- *Retell*—After reading the passage and discussing it in reading groups, students summarize the main points to their partner.

Subsequent Activities

- *Partner checking*—After students complete each of the above activities, their partners initial a form indicating that they completed the task.

- *Tests*—Give the students a comprehension test over the passage at the end of three class periods. Students work on their own.

- *Direct instruction in reading comprehension*—Provide direct instruction in specific reading comprehension skills (e.g., identifying main ideas, paragraph restatements) once a week.

- *Writing*—Students write paragraphs or letters on topics of their choice or on specific, teacher-directed lessons. Students submit drafts of their writing to their teammates and the teacher.

- *Independent reading and book reports*—Students are asked to read a trade book for at least 20 minutes every evening. Parents initial forms indicating that students read for the required time.

Modifications and Considerations

Other activities could be involved in the CIRC program, such as spelling, laboratory exercises, and special projects. Whereas classroom teachers could use the CIRC approach in a number of subjects, it would be especially appropriate for special education teachers to arrange that structure for students in resource rooms or in basic skills classes.

Monitor

There are a few natural features to measure in this program, since the main emphasis is on reading. It would be a good idea to keep track of the time youth spent reading, the number of books they read, and the rate at which they read orally and silently. Furthermore, data could be acquired on the rate at which students write or say facts (or other features) about the passage.

References

Harrell, L. G., Doelling, J. E., & Sasso, G. M. (1997). Recent developments in social interaction interventions to enhance inclusion. In P. Zionts (Ed.), *Inclusion strategies for students with learning and behavior problems* (pp. 273–295). Austin, TX: PRO-ED.

Stevens, R. J., Madden, N. A., Slavin, R. E., & Farnish, A. M. (1987). Cooperative integrated reading and composition: Two field experiments. *Reading Research Quarterly, 22,* 433–454.

COOPERATIVE LEARNING: JIGSAW II

Background

The original Jigsaw approach was developed by Aronson, Blaney, Stephan, Sikes, and Snapp (1978). A few words about it are included in the Modifications and Considerations section. A more practical and easily adopted form, Jigsaw II, developed by Slavin (1986), is described here.

Who Can Benefit

Jigsaw can be used whenever the material to be studied is in written form. It is appropriate for subjects such as social studies, literature, and science, in which it is important to learn facts and concepts and to relate them to one another. According to Kagan (1989–1990), Jigsaw II is designed to promote the following: acquisition and presentation of new material, review of old material, informed debate, interdependence, and status equalization.

Procedures

1. *Preparation*—Select several chapters, stories, or other units of print. Identify four topics within the first unit and make an expert sheet for each topic. On it, include a summary of important facts and concepts along with the definitions of necessary key words. To the extent possible, see that material on each topic appears throughout the unit. Develop a quiz for each unit comprising at least eight questions (two for each topic).

2. *Assign students to teams*—Assign four students to each team; teams should be as heterogeneous as possible.

3. *Assign students to expert groups*—Members of each team are assigned to expert groups. Each group is assigned a different topic within each unit. In this example, there would be four students in each of four expert groups.

4. *Reading*—Students receive expert topics and read assigned material to locate information on their topics (one class period).

5. *Expert-group discussions*—Students with the same topic meet in groups. They each appoint a leader who keeps the discussion going and sees to

it that everyone participates. While the expert groups are working, the teacher roams around the room and spends time with each group. These meetings should take half of a class period.

6. *Team report*—Experts return to their teams and take turns teaching their topics to the team members. Experts may question their mates after their report to see if they learned the material. This reporting takes half of a class period.

7. *Test*—Distribute quizzes. Students work alone on tests. When finished, they exchange them with members of other teams for scoring.

8. *Scoring*—Give points for individual improvement and for team averages.

Modifications and Considerations

In the original Jigsaw, each student within a team read material from different sources. This has the advantage of making the experts on each topic possessors of unique information. The drawback to that approach, however, is that the teacher would have to find four related but different passages for students to read. Another way to vary the Jigsaw approach pertains to evaluation. After the experts gave their reports, the students could write essays or give oral reports instead of taking written quizzes.

Monitor

If the major concern is to raise students' performance level, then measures of an academic activity should be acquired for a few sessions before introducing the Jigsaw procedure and for a few sessions while it is in operation. Likewise, if you believe that this cooperative learning structure might influence peer acceptance, locus of control, or something else, then gather measures pertaining to those attributes before and during the process.

References

Aronson, E., Blaney, N., Stephan, C., Sikes, J., & Snapp, M. (1978). *The jigsaw classroom.* Beverly Hills, CA: Sage.

Kagan, S. (1989–1990, December/January). The structural approach to cooperative learning. *Educational Leadership,* pp. 12–15.

Slavin, R. E. (1986). *Using student team learning* (3rd ed.). Baltimore: Johns Hopkins University, Center for Research on Elementary and Middle Schools.

COOPERATIVE LEARNING: GROUP INVESTIGATION

Background

Group Investigation has its origins in philosophical, ethical, and psychological writings from the early years of this century. John Dewey would have promoted this approach to learning, in that he viewed the classroom as a place to develop social skills for dealing with the complex problems of life.

Who Can Benefit

According to Slavin (1995), Group Investigation is appropriate for integrated study projects that deal with the acquisition, analysis, and synthesis of information to solve multifaceted problems. The task should allow for diverse contributions from group members, and not be designed simply to obtain answers to factual questions.

Procedures

In this approach, students progress through six stages:

1. *Identifying the topic and organizing pupils into groups*—Present a broad problem or issue to the students. Students meet in small groups and write down all the things they would like to learn about the topic. They then share those ideas in a class discussion. As ideas are presented, they are written on the board and then classified. The idea is to come up with one list. Students are grouped on the basis of their interest in any of the categories. You may want to limit the size of groups or subdivide some popular categories in an effort to have equal numbers of students in each group.

2. *Planning the investigation in groups*—After joining their respective groups, students select subtopics for themselves. They determine, as a group, which resources will be required to carry out their investigation. Each group comes up with a plan that details who is going to do what and how they will do it. The plans are posted.

3. *Carrying out the investigation*—While each group carries out its plan, you serve as a facilitator. When some individuals complete their tasks, they convene the group and present their findings. Other members discuss their work in progress. Summaries of the reports are written and collected by one of the group members.

4. *Preparing a final report*—During this stage, each group abstracts and combines the essential ideas of the various reports. Each group appoints a member to serve on a steering committee. Those individuals listen to the preliminary reports of all the groups and offer suggestions for drafting their final reports.

5. *Presenting the final report*—At this time, the class as a whole is convened and the groups present their reports.

6. *Evaluating achievement*—Evaluate students' higher level thinking about the subject they studied. Do this by asking students to tell or write about how they investigated certain aspects of the subject, how they applied their knowledge to the solution of new problems, how they used inferences from what they learned in discussing questions requiring analysis and judgment, and how they reached conclusions from sets of data.

Modifications and Considerations

The following are broad topics that would lend themselves to the Group Investigation approach: the Preconstruction era, the 30s and the Depression, chemistry and cosmetics, biology of the rain forests, natural disasters, the judicial system, U.S. Congress, and civil rights.

Monitor

If evaluative information beyond that detailed in Stage 6 of the Procedures section is desired, you could monitor pupils' affective experiences during the study, including their level of motivation and involvement. It might also be informative to interview the pupils, asking their opinions about the approach. You could reconvene the steering committee as a focus group to evaluate the process.

Reference

Slavin, R. E. (1995). *Cooperative learning: Theory, research, and practice* (2nd ed.). Needham Heights, MA: Allyn & Bacon.

COOPERATIVE LEARNING: CO-OP CO-OP

Background

The Co-op Co-op is a macro cooperative situation, that is, a combination of cooperative groups. For this approach, a few small groups are set up. The students in each group work together, and later, students from all the groups work together. They are dedicated to the same general theme.

Who Can Benefit

This cooperative learning structure would be most suitable for students who had participated in other, more basic cooperative arrangements, such as STAD or Jigsaw II, both discussed earlier in this chapter, and had acquired skills for working together (Kagan, 1994). The Co-op Co-op structure would benefit youth as they worked on large-scale academic projects. Prater, Bruhl, and Serna (1998) used this organization, along with teacher-directed instruction, to improve social skills of a group of youth with disabilities.

Procedures

The following are 10 steps for carrying out and evaluating Co-op Co-op.

1. *Student-centered class discussion*—Introduce a large theme to the class, one that is related to their lives, and hopefully one that will interest them. (The general topic I have chosen for this write-up is the timber industry in the Northwest.) Lead a discussion on the subject and attempt to find out what the students know about it. Encourage

students to express themselves freely on the subject, for the procedure's success is greatly dependent on the collective interest of the students.

2. *Selection of student learning teams and team building*—For this example, there are 30 youth in an 11th-grade geography class, divided into six groups with five students each. In assigning youth to groups, strive to make them as diverse as possible, while keeping in mind important social and academic factors.

3. *Team topic selection*—Encourage students in each group to select a specific topic to work on, one that is related to the central theme. Roam about the room while the students decide on their topics and provide assistance when needed. Help them keep in mind the major theme, the forest industry in the Northwest. Schedule a meeting or two with the entire class. During those sessions youth from all groups inform others about their themes. Students, as a class, will discuss how the small group themes relate to one another and to the large topic.

4. *Minitopic selection*—Each member of each cooperative group selects a topic within the group topic; it should cover one aspect of their collective subject. Although some students may be able to take on more complex assignments than others, every student should make a contribution.

5. *Minitopic preparation*—Students work individually on their assignments, but they should support and encourage one another. Their preparation might involve library or Internet searches, interviews or observations, surveys or questionnaires, or other means of gathering information.

6. *Minitopic presentation*—Students present their results to their small group. These presentations should be rather formal. Following those individual presentations, the team members discuss their group topic, and blend information from all the individual reports. During these presentations, one team member should take notes and another should serve as a critic, raising questions from time to time. Other students in the group could be assigned other roles. After this meeting (or series of meetings), students should continue working on their individual assignments. They should clarify points that were raised during the meeting or expand on certain comments or questions that were raised. Later, the students in each group should reconvene. (A group may need to meet several times before they are able to pull their topic together.)

7. *Preparation of team presentations*—Each team combines the individual reports into a common presentation. The form of the presentation would be determined by the content of the material, but nonlecture formats, such as displays, demonstrations, or team-led class discussions, are recommended.

8. *Team presentations*—Each team presents its report to the class as a whole. Based on the number of class sessions set aside for the reports, each team will have a designated amount of time to present information. Time should be allowed for comments and feedback. (It might be a good idea to select a timekeeper, to ensure that every group has a turn and none takes up too much time.)

9. *Total class presentation*—Representatives from each group assemble and develop a presentation that reflects information from all the groups. (That might require several sessions.) They will present their report to the entire class.

10. *Evaluation*—Consider evaluation of three types: (1) individual contributions to their team, to be evaluated by that person's teammates; (2) each group's write-up or presentation to the other groups, by the members of the other groups; or (3) presentation of the combined groups, to be evaluated by the teacher.

Modifications and Considerations

You might interview selected students following this exercise to determine techniques or strategies that might be considered when setting up Co-op Co-op situations in the future. When it comes to sources for gathering information, you might ask one group to rely on one source (e.g., the Internet) and others to use other, specified sources.

Monitor

In addition to the evaluations suggested in Step 10 of the Procedures section, the teacher should, as I suggested earlier, interview pupils regarding their impressions and opinions about the approach.

References

Kagan, S. (1994). *Cooperative learning*. San Clemente, CA: Kagan Cooperative Learning.

Prater, M. A., Bruhl, S., & Serna, L. A. (1998). Acquiring social skills through cooperative learning and teacher-directed instruction. *Remedial and Special Education, 19*(3), 160–172.

 # COOPERATIVE LEARNING: LEARNING TOGETHER

Background

Studies have demonstrated that the Learning Together structure has positive effects on interpersonal relations, and has enhanced students' motivation and attitudes toward learning (Johnson & Johnson, 1999).

To explain this structure, I have taken significant liberties with the original research to show how it might be set up in a 12th-grade English literature class. Although there are youth in this class characterized as at risk, most of the boys and girls are bright and motivated. Several, in fact, intend to be English majors in college. For this exercise, we also assume they have taken other literature classes and are somewhat familiar with the authors who are the topic of the upcoming unit. We assume further that these youth have had experiences in various cooperative learning structures. Related, we are aware that they have given mixed reviews of those engagements; some reported favorable experiences, whereas others were not so pleased.

Who Can Benefit

The Learning Together structure has been used primarily at the elementary level. As I will explain here, however, it can be adapted to subjects at the secondary level.

Procedures

This was a semester-long assignment for the class.

1. The teacher outlined the program. The general goal was to come away with an understanding of five contemporary English novelists: Iris Murdoch, Anthony Powell, Evelyn Waugh, Kingsley Amis, and Doris Lessing. The teacher offered a fair amount of information about the authors: their total oeuvre and most significant work, the consistent and general themes of their writing, their standing in contemporary literature and what other writers and reviewers thought of them, and their backgrounds and private lives.

2. The teacher informed the class that they were to learn about these authors through a cooperative learning structure. She went on to review, briefly, the essential ingredients of these situations: that students work together to accomplish certain objectives, that individuals are rewarded for group and individual work, and so forth. In so doing, the teacher was mindful that these students, based on their experiences, would have criticisms about these structures and opinions on how they should be set up.

3. Following these sessions in which the teacher explained the assignment and other matters, she informed the class that they were to make several decisions about the task, including these:

   • Which cooperative structure to use
   • How to define the assignment
   • How to carry out the assignment
   • How to evaluate their work

4. Students met as a class to deliberate and decide on these matters.

   • First, in this class of 20, the students decided to form four groups of five. They did this by simply drawing names from a hat; the first five made up one group, the next five another, and so forth.

   • Second, again as a total class, they decided on how to structure the assignment. They elected to read, as a group, a few chapters of one novel of each of the five authors, and asked the teacher for her opinion on which ones to read. She selected acclaimed and representative books by each author: Amis's *Lucky Jim,* Lessing's *The Fifth Child,* Waugh's *Brideshead Revisited,* Powell's *A Question of Upbringing,* and Murdoch's *Jackson's Dilemma.* After several discussions the students decided that each group would concentrate on one author and would read at least three of his or her books. The matches of groups and authors was done by lottery. (The students decided, also, that each class member would select one book of one of the other authors to read, their "extra" book.)

- Each group selected the three books of its author to read. For this, students relied on the teachers' suggestions, the reviews of the authors' works in readers guides, and opinions of others. Several group meetings were required to do this, during which the students voiced their opinions as to which books should be read. Other meetings of the entire class were scheduled, during which time students informed others about the "extra" book they had chosen to read. The students decided that each group would write a review and criticism of their author, and present their information to the others orally and in writing. Then, all the students would work together to develop an overall critique, one that would combine the efforts of all students. It would be a comparison and criticism of the five authors. For this, they would come up with a set of characteristics about which to discuss and compare the authors. In addition, each individual would write up a brief report on the extra author they read about.

- The students, along with the teacher, decided on several ways to evaluate this semester-long effort: (a) Each student would write a brief report of his or her impressions of the group activity itself and what he or she learned about the group's author; (b) each group would write an evaluation of the other groups' product; (c) each member would write an evaluation of the total group product; and (d) each individual would write a report on his or her extra reading. The students and teachers agreed on a plan for assigning grades; they decided to give a portion of the grade based on the group effort and another based on the individual effort.

Modifications and Considerations

Students may put summaries of their reports on the school's Web site. Data regarding the number of individuals who access them and offer comments could be gathered and studied. Some of the students may decide, based on what they learned from their readings and the reports of others, on the next books they intend to read.

An important feature of this approach is that students would be allowed, even encouraged, to disagree with one another. This project provides several opportunities for this "structured controversy," including the decision about which books to read. Researchers (e.g., Johnson & Johnson, 1999) have shown that these instances have increased motivation and involvement in learning, and enhanced self-efficacy.

In accord with the original design of the Learning Together structure, the following features were represented in this example: Members have responsibility for deciding on important features of the program. Individuals are responsible for their own learning. Everyone is responsible for assisting other members to learn important concepts. Individuals are asked to explain their points of view and those of the group. Individuals evaluate their efforts in working as a team. Members evaluate the work of others.

Monitor

Several comments on evaluating this program were offered under Item 4 in the Procedures section.

Reference

Johnson, D. W., & Johnson, R. T. (1999). *Learning together and alone: Cooperative, competitive, and individualistic learning* (5th ed.). Needham Heights, MA: Allyn & Bacon.

Chapter 12
SELF-ESTEEM

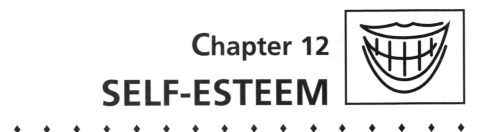

◆ ◆ ◆ ◆ ◆ ◆ ◆ ◆ ◆ ◆ ◆ ◆ ◆ ◆ ◆ ◆ ◆ ◆ ◆

Tactics in this chapter are designed to increase students' self-esteem. Many students are lacking in self-esteem, but youngsters who are at risk or who have disabilities are often especially lacking in this vital component.

Educators and citizens in general would agree that it is important to have adequate self-esteem. Although none of us knows exactly what that amount is, we acknowledge that, to succeed in school and later in life, a person needs enough self-esteem. Murray White, of *Magic Circle* fame (see the second tactic in this chapter), pointed out the importance of self-esteem when he said, "A person's judgment of self influences the kinds of friends he chooses, how he gets along with others, the kind of person he marries, and how productive he will be." That about covers it!

When it comes to improving one's self-esteem, I believe that it is generally best to go about it through a context—that is, to first develop reading, writing, trumpet playing, or something else, and the esteem part will follow. But there are times and cases in which it is desirable to attack the matter straight on.

There are six tactics in this chapter. The first three offer teachers suggestions for modifying students' self-esteem. It is important for teachers to convey the idea to youth that self-esteem can be raised. The last three techniques are designed for self-management by the youth themselves. Youth need to learn that to some extent it is up to them to elevate their self-esteem.

TEACHER MANAGEMENT: POSITIVE AND NEGATIVE STATEMENTS AND SELF-ESTEEM

Background

Teachers deal with adolescents who display a variety of emotional states. Some adolescents are more aware of their feelings and those of their mates than are others. One indication of sensitivity is when they begin to recognize that they and others express a number of negative statements. Once they become aware of their negative statements and those of others, they can begin responding to them with positive restatements.

Who Can Benefit

Adolescents, especially students with low self-esteem, will benefit from these exercises (Ellis & Harper, 1972). Indeed, most individuals, adolescents or otherwise, could do with a dose of this training.

Procedures

Take advantage of situations that arise in the classroom to counter negative statements. Following are seven exercises and four suggestions designed to increase students' self-esteem.

Seven Exercises

1. Instruct students to list the resources in their lives on which they can rely in difficult situations—friends, relatives, neighbors, clubs, agencies, churches, and so on. Ask them to list a few times they asked any of these resources for help and recieved it.

2. Encourage the students to plan to talk with someone they respect about a problem, and to picture beforehand how that person might react. Inform them to note how that person actually responded and how that affected them.

3. Explain to students that they should give themselves credit for all the roles they play in life: student, son or daughter, friend, grandson, neighbor, employee, and so on. Ask them to list the improvements they have made in their lives with respect to each of those roles.

4. Invite students to ask themselves this question: "In spite of everything you know about yourself, would you choose to be like yourself?" Ask them to think about the following as they respond to that question: "I don't want to be a superstar, and I don't want to be the wealthiest or most powerful person in the world. There are a lot of things about me that I like. Sure, there are a few things I might change, but I wouldn't trade my life with anyone." Hopefully, this will give them motivation to keep going in their present circumstances.

5. Encourage students to do the following:

   • Keep a calendar on which you note special activities for several days.

   • If you have a worry, write it down, and then think of other, more positive thoughts.

   • Listen to your favorite radio program or watch your favorite television show in the morning as you get ready for school. That might get you off to a good start.

   • Keep a book or diary in which you write a few positive thoughts for each day.

6. Identify the "pot shots" in their lives, and come up with counter measures to deal with them. Pot shots are those deflating remarks that come at us from teachers, peers, siblings, bosses, or parents. A few pot shots: "Why do you like to be with her?" "You wore that same sweater yesterday!" "How come you take a bus to school and don't drive a car?"

"You always seem to make low grades." A few defenses: "She's a good friend." "I like it." "I'm an ecologically sensitive kind of guy." "They're improving." Offer them suggestions for dealing with pot shots that they make at themselves. Tell them to learn to think, "That's not like me." Define themselves positively by saying, "I'm better than that."

7. Suggest to students that they end their day by thinking of three good things. Explain to them that, when they end the day on a positive note, they will sleep better and be better prepared to deal with life in the morning.

Four Suggestions

1. Ask students to write down, in private, the worst thing they ever did on a 3 × 5 card, then tear the card up and throw it away. This action should help them understand that they can get rid of bad memories and live for the present.

2. Create a corner in the classroom for selected pictures or clippings that are meaningful to students. Tell them that they should surround themselves at home and at school with positive messages. Suggest that they carry uplifting messages or photographs in their wallets and cars.

3. Post inspirational thoughts around the room and ask students to create posters of their favorite quotes:

   • "In the game of life, success isn't playing a good hand; it's playing well the hand you're dealt."

   • "How you spend your time is how you live your life."

   • "Opportunity is always knocking. It's here in the circumstances of your life. It's not something that always comes from others. It's something you have to discover."

   • "Remember you'll always do your best when you can shape the circumstances, so shape them carefully. When you can't shape the circumstances, you can shape yourself."

   • "Being obsessed with a wasted past wastes the present and surrenders the future. Don't dwell on the past and give it power. Celebrate the fact that you survived it. Dwell on selecting your best options now."

   • Consult *The Portable LIFE 101* (John-Roger & McWilliams, 1992) for quotes. One of my favorites: "While one person hesitates because he feels inferior, the other is busy making mistakes and becoming superior."

4. Consider playing some of the commercial tapes (of which there are zillions) that are intended to "pump up" individuals to achieve. They will at least stimulate discussions.

Modifications and Considerations

In setting up any of these exercises in attempts to elevate self-esteem, be familiar with the students' circumstances, and be prepared for emotional outbursts. Ask students to share their strategies for building themselves up.

Monitor

Instruct students to count, throughout the day or for a specified period of time, the number of positive thoughts they can generate about themselves and the number they think about others. It might be a particularly good idea to have them say or write as many positive things as they can about a person they are not too fond of.

References

Ellis, A., & Harper, R. (1972). *A guide to rational living.* North Hollywood, CA: Wilshire Book.

John-Roger, & McWilliams, P. (1992). *The portable LIFE 101.* Los Angeles: Prelude Press.

TEACHER MANAGEMENT: GROUP INTERACTIONS

Background

Most adolescents believe that no one else has ever experienced some of the events and circumstances that they are now dealing with. When they learn that others share some of their concerns, they may feel less alone or unique. Moreover, they might take the thoughts of others more seriously.

Who Can Benefit

Students of any ability level who feel alienated or isolated from other students should profit from this technique. The entire class could gain from confirming one another's concerns.

Procedures

The following are activities as described by Achterman (n.d.):

1. Set up chairs or desks in a circle.

2. Divide a chalkboard into as many sections as there are students.

3. Assign each participant a piece of the puzzle on the chalkboard. Tell the class that later each student will fill in his or her piece in the puzzle.

4. Ask the students to each draw a symbol of what is happening in the world right now. Tell them to make it their own symbol, one that represents their feelings about the world. The sign must be of something that has significance to them: a worry or concern, a like or dislike, something they hate or love. Alternatively, ask them to cut out images from magazines that convey one of their emotions or concerns.

5. Tell them to put their piece on the puzzle background when they are finished. You may need to establish a time limit for this activity.

6. Introduce the exercise as an experience in reflective listening, one in which all the students have an opportunity to express their feelings and to listen as others describe theirs.

7. Start the activity by asking if someone would like to know about one of the symbols. If someone asks about one, the designer explains it. Those interactions continue.

8. See that every student explains his or her drawing and tells the class why it has meaning. Before moving to the next person, get an affirmative answer from the students to one of these questions: "Do you think your feelings on this have been heard?" "Would you like to stop now even though your feelings may not have been completely heard?"

9. Plan follow-up activities that expand on the concerns of students. Allow them to suggest what they would like to do about their problems. Use that information to practice group decision making. For example, word lists of feelings can be written as having directions (e.g., pleasure or love in one direction, and pain or hate in the other). Students can hang word lists for these feelings on the wall and add to them when they desire.

Modifications and Considerations

Some students find it is easier to express their thoughts and feelings in small rather than large groups. The technique explained here could begin with small groups and eventually be scheduled with more and more students.

Students should be assigned to groups so as to avoid cliques and unnecessary disturbances. Counselors could be asked to recommend students for various groups, or even run some of the groups.

The Magic Circle routine explained by Murray White (n.d.) is much like the exercise just described. For that activity, ask students to sit in a circle on the floor. Start the process by offering an incomplete sentence, and give an example to finish it off. One sentence might be "What makes me laugh is . . . ." Then ask a student to repeat the phrase and put in his or her own ending. According to Murray, several serious and lively discussions come from these activities, where feelings are discovered, explored, and accepted. Students come to realize that if they understand themselves, it will help them better understand others.

Monitor

For this tactic, it is important to acquire data on students' reactions. It is informative not only to learn about the expressed concerns of the students, but to know about the reactions of others to those affairs. To gather data on the latter, students might be asked to write a few sentences occasionally that explain their feelings about certain points. Those data could be reviewed from time to time by each student to see if there is a pattern or trend to their thoughts. In some situations, where a teacher or counselor has established a feeling of trust among the students, some of those reactions might be shared with the group.

References

Achterman, E. (no date). *Self-enhancing education project.* Santa Clara, CA: Author. (For further information, write SEE, 1957 Pruneridge Avenue, Santa Clara, CA 95050)

White, M. (no date). *Magic circles—the benefits of circle time.* Murray White, 5 Ferry Path, Cambridge, England CB4 1HB (telephone and fax: 0223 65351).

 # TEACHER MANAGEMENT: THE POSITIVE SANDWICH APPROACH

Background

A positive approach to teaching is more effective than an aversive one. Although aversive comments may stimulate immediate results, their side-effects often include decreased enjoyment and increased fear of failure.

Aversive comments in a classroom can result in a power struggle between students and teacher. When that occurs, the negative behaviors from students increase. The approach recommended here relies on social reinforcement or praise to strengthen acceptable behaviors.

Who Can Benefit

Positive reinforcement creates a proper situation for learning skills and a positive environment for social interactions. The Positive Sandwich strategy was developed to deemphasize or temper the criticisms or grades regarding classroom behaviors and reinforce students' efforts and performances (Smith, Smoll, & Curtis, 1979). It is most effective with students with low self-esteem and those with newly formed skills. Students with the greatest need for this strategy are those who can accept only mild criticism, and not much of that.

Procedures

1. Identify students who have low self-esteem and a low tolerance for criticism, they may be high or low achievers. Look for signs of sensitivity to criticism, such as tears, face-hiding, or brash statements.

2. Implement a three-step strategy of sandwiching a constructive comment between two positive comments.

   - First, tell the student what he or she did well. Reinforce effort, which the student can control. Your goal is to prepare the student emotionally for a constructive comment.

   - Second, provide the student with specific directions about new behaviors to develop or about corrections to make. Gear the instruction to the needs of each student. Keep your expectations high.

   - Third, complete the interaction with a second positive comment to leave the student with a positive remark.

   Following is an example of this three-phase procedure. Joel is late to class for the fifth time. You make a constructive comment to him, such as, "The paper you handed in last Friday was excellent." Your next remark might be, "Joel, you need to show up regularly and on time in order to get the most out of this class and to get a good grade." Follow that with, "I'm sure that your next paper will be just as interesting and well written as your last one. If you would like to chat with me about the topic or the outline, please come in after school."

3. Over time, gradually increase your expectations for the student, while keeping them realistic and attainable.

4. To maintain a student's behavior, the scheduling of comments is crucial. Initially, offer a comment as close to the occurrence of the behavior as possible. Frequent reinforcement will strengthen the behavior and provide more feedback. Once behaviors have developed, they should persist longer with intermittent comments.

Modifications and Considerations

Following are a few suggestions for carrying out this technique:

1. Positive comments must be genuine. If they are phony, or perceived of as such, your credibility as a teacher will suffer.

2. Inform other teachers or counselors of your efforts, and involve them in the use of the Positive Sandwich treatment.

3. Discuss with students this strategy of sandwiching constructive comments with positive statements. Encourage them to make positive statements to others, particularly if they intend to criticize them for something.

4. Discuss the Positive Sandwich strategy with the class as a means to build better interactions with others by delivering sincere and constructive comments.

5. Do not overdo this technique; that is, do not feel that if you give a compliment, you must also deliver the other two elements of the sandwich. It is okay to simply pass out a good word now and then.

There are a number of Web sites that offer approaches for building self-esteem. One of them, Building Self-Esteem, is sponsored by the Ashland corporation (http://www.ashland.com).

Monitor

Keep a log of the times you use the three-phase procedure. Note what you said, to whom you said it, how they reacted at the time, and how they acted on your suggestions later.

Reference

Smith, R. E., Smoll, F. L., & Curtis, B. (1979). Coach effectiveness training: A cognitive-behavioral approach to enhancing relationship skills in youth sport coaches. *Journal of Sport Psychology, 1,* 59–75.

SELF-MANAGEMENT: ACCEPTING RESPONSIBILITY

Background

Students who are at risk sometimes fall into a mode of learned helplessness; they feel that outside forces control their lives, and that they have lost control. Teachers can intercept negative, blaming statements and teach students to replace them with more productive, self-controlling statements. Students can then attribute success to something they can manage. Attributing success to effort sets up a cycle of effort that breeds success and improved self-concept.

Who Can Benefit

Students of low ability tend to improve their school performance when they attribute success to effort. Students who believe they have lost control of their lives will benefit from the structure built into this lesson. The activities mentioned not only are useful for individuals in resource rooms, but can be arranged in regular classrooms as well (Stoker, 1980).

Procedures

1. Write on the board, overhead projector, or butcher paper, "I am the only person responsible for what I do."

2. Instruct students to think of times when other people seem to control what happens to them. Examples might include hiring for positions by employers, making rules by parents and teachers, and establishing laws by federal and state governments. Point out to students that, although they believe that others control them, *they* are actually in control because they make choices as to how to act when faced with expectations or rules. How they perform during a job interview, for instance, has a great deal to do with whether they are hired.

3. Instruct students to form small groups of four or five and appoint a "secretary" to write down all the tasks at home and school for which they are willing to accept responsibility. Students could list the consequences for not meeting each responsibility on a separate chart. (This applies to the next point as well.)

4. Complete a master list of accepted responsibilities in the classroom, and display it as a reminder to you and the students.

5. Assist students to organize what they have learned from this exercise by completing a responsibility chart (see example in Figure 12.1). Each pupil should complete one of these, and you should check off the activities.

Modifications and Considerations

Invite guests from the community to speak to the class on responsibility and self-control. It would be particularly interesting to bring in an employer and an

---

RESPONSIBILITY CHART

Name _____ Date _____

Teacher _____ Period _____

RESPONSIBILITIES FOR THIS CLASS:	Behavior/ Attendance	Materials	Assignments
	1.	1.	1.
	2.	2.	2.
	3.	3.	3.
	4.	4.	4.

Other classes:

1.
2.
3.
4.
5.

HOME:	Daily Jobs	Weekly	Occasional Jobs
	1.		
	2.		
	3.		
	4.		

Figure 12.1. Responsibility Chart for use in accepting responsibility. From *Grab H.O.L.D.: Help Overcome Learner Dropouts. Classroom guidance manual,* by J. Stoker, 1980, San Jose, CA: Resource Publications. Copyright 1980 by Resource Publications. Reprinted by permission.

employee, or a management person and an entry-level individual from the same business (perhaps not on the same day).

The idea of being in control is of supreme importance to youth. Goldhammer (1990) demonstrated that students were more effective (hence powerful) with respect to participating in planning when taught the I-PLAN strategy. That technique includes five steps:

1. <u>I</u>nventory your strengths, weaknesses, goals.
2. <u>P</u>rovide specific information on those points.
3. <u>L</u>isten to others and respond to them.
4. <u>A</u>sk questions during meetings.
5. <u>N</u>ame your goals specifically.

Monitor

Within the context of improving students' self-esteem and relating that to self-control, it would be informative if individuals took a few minutes once a week to write down the events or circumstances of their lives that were out of their control. Students could then write out a plan to either gain control or exercise more control over certain of those. The objective would not be to obtain total control over everything (no one has this or would probably want it), but to reach a level of command that elevates self-confidence.

Another way to monitor this technique would be to use a rating scale. A number of features that indicate the acceptance of responsibility could be listed on the vertical axis, and alongside them a set of numbers could be printed that refer to the degree those indicators were true. Periodically, the teacher or student could fill this out.

References

Goldhammer, R. (1990, Fall). I-PLAN: Implications for teaching self-advocacy skills to college students with learning disabilities. *Latest Developments,* pp. 2–5.

Stoker, J. (1980). *Grab H.O.L.D.: Help overcome learner dropouts. Classroom guidance manual.* San Jose, CA: Resource Publications.

SELF-MANAGEMENT: BUILDING SUCCESSES

Background

Although society does not provide many opportunities for individuals to express positive feelings about themselves, most individuals enjoy expressing pride in their accomplishments. Opportunities for positive self-expression can be incorporated into a classroom by providing a forum for disclosing positive and growth-promoting attributes about oneself. Shakespeare explained the philosophy behind these expressions in King Henry V when he wrote, "Self love, my liege, is not so vile a sin as self neglecting."

Who Can Benefit

Students who do not often identify successes in their lives will benefit from the following techniques. Elevating self-esteem is an especially important area on which to focus for students who are at risk or remedial.

Procedures

1. Decide how much class time you will spend on exercises to become acquainted with your students and to build their self-esteem.

2. Divide the class into groups of four or five students. Explain that the goal of these exercises is for them to get to know one another better and to share pride in each other's accomplishments.

3. Encourage students to react to the following items. They are listed in order of difficulty, with the easier ones listed first:

   - Things you have done for your parents
   - Things you have done for a friend
   - Your work at school, including extracurricular activities

- How you spend your free time
- Habits you have or something you do quite often
- About your religious beliefs
- How you earned some money
- How you usually spend your money
- Something you own or have purchased recently
- Something you have shared
- Something you tried hard to accomplish
- Thoughts about people who are different from you
- Something you have done in regard to racism
- Something you have done in regard to ecology

4. Encourage students to picture in their minds objects or circumstances that recall past successes or accomplishments, such as photographs, certificates, newspaper clippings, ticket stubs, and trophies. Instruct students to share their feelings and meanings connected with specific situations, as well as the successes they symbolize.

5. Ask students to share an accomplishment or achievement they experienced before they were 10 years old, then one between the ages of 10 and 15, and then one between the ages of 15 and the present time. (These age ranges can be revised.)

6. Ask students periodically to share a recent success or accomplishment: the past week, last month, over the weekend, during a vacation, over the summer.

7. Inform the students that each person has 5 minutes to boast about anything he or she wants to talk about: accomplishments, awards, skills, or personal characteristics. Require other group members to monitor their nonverbal signals as they listen, and to refrain from talking until they are asked to comment on the exercise.

8. Ask students to identify their greatest success for the day. This gives them an opportunity to review the day, and to become aware of day-to-day happenings. Some students will find this difficult at first, but as others begin to share their experiences, they may realize that they too have had a few successes. Encourage students to comment on the successes of their classmates.

9. Request students to write a paragraph or two to explain their successes, rather than reporting on them verbally. This type of exercise provides an ongoing record of accomplishments that students can review from time to time.

10. Encourage students to list five successful experiences they would like to have in the next year, 5 years, or longer period. This assignment could be scheduled in conjunction with goal-setting activities.

Modifications and Considerations

If some students report that they have no successes to share, remind them of instances you know about:

- You've been taking care of your younger brothers and sisters for 2 years; that's certainly an accomplishment.

- You helped Paul with some of his assignments when he missed several days of school.

- You were polite to the guest speaker last week, and asked some good questions.

- You reminded me to send home the letters to parents last week about the open house.

Canfield and associates have written several books that deal specifically with developing self-esteem and responsibility (e.g., Canfield & Siccone, 1994; Canfield & Wells, 1976). A suggestion in one of their books is to ask each student in a class to list the names of the other students and write the nicest thing they can think of about each one. The teacher collects those papers, summarizes all the responses, and gives each student a list of the nice things said about him or her.

Monitor

For a few minutes every day, students could be asked to list all the nice things about themselves, or others. Those data could be charted as frequency per session. Such data acquired for a few days before a self-esteem program, then for a period of time as the treatment was in effect, could help determine the effect of the intervention.

References

Canfield, J., & Siccone, F. (1994). *101 ways to develop student self-esteem and responsibility.* Needham Heights, MA: Allyn & Bacon.

Canfield, J., & Wells, H. C. (1976). *101 ways to enhance self-concept in the classroom.* Englewood Cliffs, NJ: Prentice-Hall.

SELF-MANAGEMENT: PROMPTING PRAISE

Background

Thinking positively about oneself cannot be overemphasized. Considerable research indicates that if individuals have proper estimates of themselves, they are better able to relate to others and are more able to learn skills in and out of school than are those with inadequate self-esteem. A prime contributor to self-esteem is praise and acknowledgment from others. Everybody needs recognition from peers, superiors, and elders, some people more than others. The technique explained by Baer and Wolf (1970) is designed to help pupils contact a sometimes dormant but readily available natural community of praise; that is, pupils can learn to seek reinforcement from their teachers.

Who Can Benefit

A characteristic of youngsters who are at risk and many others who have been in remedial or compensatory programs is that they have negative self-concepts.

Many of them have had so many experiences with failure that their self-concepts are fragile. This technique would be a suitable approach for them, particularly those who are reinforced by teacher praise yet rarely receive any.

Procedures

1. Inform students that you want them to evaluate their performance accurately in a specified area, such as physical science, U.S. history, math, or another subject.

2. Provide them with the necessary standards to do so; they must know what "good performance" is. Give them the necessary teachers' manuals, tape cassettes, or whatever else is needed for them to compare their performance to a standard.

3. Work with the students on the selected skills until they can discriminate good from poor performance, and until most of their efforts are first rate.

4. Obtain data regarding the extent to which students can accurately evaluate their performances. Depending on the skill, the evaluation of their performance could be more or less sophisticated. For some subjects, students could be required to provide a precise measure of frequency, percentage, or the like. For others, they might simply make a statement regarding quality: "That was great." "That wasn't too good." "That needs help, but it's better than it was."

5. Inform pupils to go to their teachers and prompt them for praise, if their work has improved or is of high quality.

6. Provide students with statements to use when they seek reinforcement from their teachers: "Look how much I've done." "I've improved since last week." "This work is neater (or better organized) than my work a week or so ago."

7. Assist students to determine the proper time to approach their teachers and the times they should not go to them to prompt reinforcement. Pupils should not, for example, go to teachers when it is obvious that teachers are busy or when they are having a bad day.

8. Keep data on the extent to which the pupils can go to teachers without becoming pests. Baer, Holman, Stokes, and Fowler (1981) suggested that youngsters in a large class should not approach their teacher for praise any more than four times a day.

Modifications and Considerations

The last point in the procedure must be kept in mind: an individual could ask for too much praise. People who constantly seek reinforcement can be very annoying. Perhaps another factor that should be blended into this technique is the rate at which the seeker of praise dispenses reinforcement. It may be that individuals can ask for as many praise statements as they give or, more likely, for one bit of praise for each four or five they pass out.

If a teacher believes that students' self-concepts are improving as a result of this technique and that they know when and how to seek praise from teachers, they might encourage students to do the same at home. There, instead of referring to their noteworthy schoolwork, students could make reference to their activities around the house: how they carried out assigned chores, how they voluntarily assisted in some way, how they remembered to pick up something. They should be reminded, as they seek reinforcement at home, to dispense praise to themselves and to keep their requests natural and under control. (Scan the tactics in Chapter 9, Participation, for ideas on how to initiate interactions.)

Monitor

Pupils should keep track of the number of times they "ask" for praise (see Item 8 in Procedures). Furthermore, they should keep data on whether they were, in fact, complimented or otherwise acknowledged when they asked for it, and on the circumstances of the interaction (e.g., time of day, what the teacher was doing when prompted). In other words, they should keep track of the antecedents and consequences that accompany their requests.

References

Baer, D. M., Holman, J., Stokes, T. F., & Fowler, S. A. (1981). Uses of self-control techniques in programming generalization. In S. W. Bijou & R. Ruiz (Eds.), *Behavior modification: Contributions to education* (pp. 39–61). Hillsdale, NJ: Erlbaum.

Baer, D. M., & Wolf, M. M. (1970). The entry into natural communities of reinforcement. In R. Ulrich, T. Stachnik, & J. Mabry (Eds.), *Control of human behavior* (Vol. 2, pp. 319–324). Glenview, IL: Scott, Foresman.

Chapter 13
CLASSROOM MANAGEMENT

The tactics in this chapter are designed to assist teachers to better control their classes. This is a major issue for many teachers, including some who have been in the business for a long time. Unfortunately, numerous teachers in training do not see classroom management as much of a problem. They believe that if they prepare exciting lessons, engage their students in those assignments, and periodically "reflect" on the few minor problems that do come up, there will be no management worries. In reality, regardless of how "relevant" and stimulating a class and its teacher happen to be, inevitably a student or two cause problems, some of which are more exasperating and challenging than others. So the teacher—old or young, experienced or inexperienced—is wise to accumulate a repertoire of proven management tactics, ones that cover a range of perplexing behaviors.

Eight tactics are described in this chapter. One write-up offers ideas for getting off to a good start at the beginning of the year. A couple of techniques deal with specific behaviors that are likely to come up in secondary classes. A few tactics demonstrate how various individuals—parents, peers, and pupils themselves—in addition to teachers can manage obstreperous behaviors. The final two tactics would be useful for dealing with youth who present serious behavior problems.

Several of the self-management tactics scattered throughout other chapters in this book relate to classroom management. Techniques in Chapter 8, Social Skills, are also related to classroom management.

BEGINNING THE SCHOOL YEAR

Background

The way a teacher begins the school year is crucial to instilling a classroom atmosphere conducive to learning. Although teachers should not let up during the year with respect to organization and preparation, it is absolutely necessary to establish firm and realistic expectations at the start of the term.

Who Can Benefit

The teacher and the majority of the students will profit if the class gets off to a good start at the beginning of the year or semester (Hutchins, 1988). This is particularly true for pupils who are remedial or at risk, or who have mild disabilities, for whom concise and firm expectations are requisites to their performance.

Procedures

Following are ideas to consider at the beginning of a new term.

Before Opening Day

1. Read your school's policy manual and reacquaint yourself with the rules and procedures: opening and closing hours, attendance policies, fire drill routines, cafeteria rules, and so on.

2. Plan for the first day to be a real day. Prepare written lesson plans and have necessary materials ready for students.

3. Plan the beginning and ending of class periods carefully. It is easy to lose control of students during these times.

4. Establish classroom rules. Select a few rules that establish an orderly environment and contribute to successful learning.

5. Set procedures for laboratory periods (i.e., cleanup of work areas or equipment, safety routines, distribution of supplies and materials).

6. Establish procedures for grading and for homework assignments.

Beginning Few Days

1. Identify your "standard operating procedures." Be sure that everyone knows the rules.

2. Closely monitor students' compliance with rules and standards for the first few days. Uniformly and fairly apply sanctions for failure to comply.

3. Recognize students' needs for breaks now and then.

4. Convince the students that they will be successful in your class. Tell them that you expect everyone to succeed and that you are there to help them.

5. Take it easy with respect to assignments the first few days. Arrange situations whereby all students succeed.

6. Become acquainted, to the extent possible, with each student's ability and motivational level.

7. Establish a system to help new students learn the rules. When a new pupil enters the class, ask a veteran student, one who knows the rules and procedures, to spend time teaching them to the newcomer.

8. Take advantage of every opportunity to meet the students' parents. Explain your goals and expectations to them. Suggest ways they can help their youth at home with assignments.

Modifications and Considerations

Use a checklist (see example in Figure 13.1) to identify procedures you follow in your class. Be aware of all the rules that have to do with security; secondary schools in recent years have become more conscious of this.

BEGINNING THE YEAR CHECKLIST

Use this checklist to identify procedures you follow in your classroom. Put a check mark in the space to the left of each item for which you <u>do</u> have a set procedure. Place an asterisk next to those items you <u>do not</u> have a procedure for but think you should. Circle items you think should be taught on the first day of school.

I. Beginning Class
_____ A. Roll Call, Absenteeism, Tardiness
_____ B. Academic Warm-ups
_____ C. Distributing Materials
_____ D. Class Opening

II. Room/School Areas
_____ A. Shared Materials
_____ B. Teacher's Desk
_____ C. Drinks, Bathroom, Pencil Sharpener
_____ D. Student Storage/Lockers
_____ E. Student Desks
_____ F. Learning Centers, Stations
_____ G. Playground, Schoolgrounds
_____ H. Lunchroom
_____ I. Halls

III. Setting up Independent Work
_____ A. Defining "Working Alone"
_____ B. Identifying Problems
_____ C. Identifying Resources
_____ D. Identifying Solutions
_____ E. Scheduling
_____ F. Interim Checkpoints

IV. Instructional Activities
_____ A. Teacher/Student Contacts
_____ B. Student Movement in the Room
_____ C. Signals for Students' Attention
_____ D. Signals for Teacher's Attention
_____ E. Student Talk During Seatwork
_____ F. Activities to Do When Work Is Done
_____ G. Student Participation
_____ H. Laboratory Procedures
_____ I. Movement In and Out of Small Groups
_____ J. Bringing Materials to School
_____ K. Expected Behavior in Group
_____ L. Behavior of Students Not in Group

V. Ending Class
_____ A. Putting Away Supplies, Equipment
_____ B. Cleaning Up
_____ C. Organizing Class Materials
_____ D. Dismissing Class

VI. Interruptions
_____ A. Rules
_____ B. Talk Among Students
_____ C. Conduct During Interruptions
_____ D. Passing Out Books, Supplies
_____ E. Turning In Work
_____ F. Handing Back Assignments
_____ G. Getting Back Assignments
_____ H. Out-of-Seat Policies

VII. Other Procedures
_____ A. Fire Drills
_____ B. Lunch Procedures
_____ C. Safety Procedures
_____ D. Peer or Cross-age Tutoring

VIII. Work Requirements
_____ A. Paper Headings
_____ B. Use of Pen or Pencil
_____ C. Writing on Back of Paper
_____ D. Neatness, Legibility
_____ E. Incomplete Work
_____ F. Late Work
_____ G. Missed Work
_____ H. Due Dates
_____ I. Makeup Work
_____ J. Supplies
_____ K. Coloring or Drawing on Paper
_____ L. Use of Printed or Cursive Writing

IX. Communicating Assignments
_____ A. Posting Assignments
_____ B. Oral Assignments
_____ C. Provisions for Absentees
_____ D. Long-term Assignments
_____ E. Returning Assignments
_____ F. Homework Assignments

X. Student Work
_____ A. In-class Participation
_____ B. In-class Assignments
_____ C. Homework
_____ D. Stages for Long-term Assignments

XI. Checking Assignments in Class
_____ A. Students Exchanging Papers
_____ B. Marking and Grading Assignments
_____ C. Turning in Assignments
_____ D. Students Correcting Errors

XII. Grading Procedures
_____ A. Determining Grades
_____ B. Recording Grades
_____ C. Grading Long Assignments
_____ D. Extra Credit Work
_____ E. Keeping Papers, Grades, Assignments
_____ F. Grading Criteria
_____ G. Contracting for Grades

XIII. Academic Feedback
_____ A. Rewards and Incentives
_____ B. Posting Student Work
_____ C. Communicating with Parents
_____ D. Students' Record of Grades
_____ E. Written Comment on Assignments

Figure 13.1. Sample checklist for beginning the school year. From *A+chieving Excellence: A Site-Based Management System for Efficiency, Effectiveness, Excellence* (p. 58), by C. L. Hutchins (Senior Author), 1988, Kansas City, MO: Mid-Continent Regional Educational Laboratory. Copyright 1990 by McREL Institute, Aurora, CO. Reprinted with permission.

Murdick and Petch-Hogan (1996) discussed alternative intervention strategies for educational problems in inclusive classrooms prior to evaluating a student for special education placement. Those techniques are arranged in six categories: physical setting, daily schedule, instructional delivery, reinforcement plan, classroom rules, and communication.

Monitor

One way to monitor this project would be to keep data, from one year to the next, on the number of rules and procedures that are instructed at the beginning of the year and how long it takes to put them in operation. The teacher also should keep data on the number of behavior problems, absences, late arrivals, and other concerns that are noted during the first few weeks of a term.

References

Hutchins, C. L. (Senior Author). (1988). *A+chieving excellence: A site-based management system for efficiency, effectiveness, excellence.* Kansas City, MO: The Mid-Continent Regional Educational Laboratory.

Murdick, N. L., & Petch-Hogan, B. (1996). Inclusive classroom management: Using preintervention strategies. *Intervention in School and Clinic, 31*(3), 172–176.

SCHOOL BEHAVIOR AFFECTS HOME PRIVILEGES

Background

When traditional school disciplinary measures have failed to curtail maladaptive behaviors of adolescents, involving parents in setting up contingencies in the home may be helpful. Daily reports on student behavior written by teachers, counselors, or school administrators are delivered to parents, who then institute the appropriate home reward or punishment, depending on the nature of the report.

Some benefits of this method are the following: (a) It does not demand much extra teacher time; (b) it involves parents positively in the educational process; and (c) it brings powerful home consequences (e.g., driving privileges, allowances, curfews) to bear on school behavior. In a study by Trice, Parker, Furrow, and Iwata (1986), a home and school program resulted in improved attendance, homework completion, compliance, class preparation, time on task, and weekly grades.

Who Can Benefit

Trice et al.'s (1986) study was conducted in a senior high school. Participants were four 16-year-old males who were enrolled in a 10th-grade support program for students who were disruptive and underachieving. Chronic serious misconduct was the basis for their placement. Although the boys had normal IQs, they were 2 to 4 years behind grade level in reading and math. They were all assigned to regular classes for about half of the school day. Each lived with a single mother who was employed during school hours. This tactic could be arranged for many students who were at risk or with learning or behavior problems.

Procedures

1. Ask the students' teachers to record the students' behaviors on a daily form (see example in Figure 13.2).

2. Give a satisfactory rating for the day if the student receives no more than two negative ratings from all the teachers. Make certain that students are aware of the rating criteria.

3. Contact parents by telephone to describe what they can do at home to help change their student's behavior at school. The following are some suggestions:

   - Impose a Friday curfew of 8:00 p.m. if less than four satisfactory daily reports are received in a week.

   - Give one fourth of the weekly allowance to the student for each good daily report.

   - Take away one fourth of the weekly allowance for each bad daily report.

4. Send home Good Day Cards bearing a single message: "Your (son/daughter) had a (good/bad) day today." Be sure each card is dated.

DAILY REPORT FORM

Student _____ Date _____

Behavior	Appropriate	Inappropriate
Attendance		
Prepared for Class		
Homework Complete		
On Task Throughout Period		
Classroom Behavior		
Compliant		

COMMENTS:

Weekly Average Grade _____ (Fridays only)

Figure 13.2. Example of daily student behavior report form.

5. Baseline measures taken prior to implementation of this procedure could provide verification of its effectiveness. A percentage of improvement over baseline rates could also be reported as part of the students' grades, or noted in the deportment section of their grade cards at the end of each grading period.

6. To determine levels of parent cooperation with the delivery of home-based contingencies, ask students each Monday how much allowance they received and whether they earned that amount.

7. At the end of each 9-week period, assess whether students are delivering reports to their parents by asking parents to return all Good Day Reports delivered to them during that time.

Modifications and Considerations

Trice et al. (1986) also tried three other interventions with varying degrees of success. The second most effective was comprehensive reports, followed by personal letters to parents, and then phone calls to parents. Because one of those methods might prove to be effective in other situations, they are briefly described.

Comprehensive Reports

Teachers prepared a summary of the daily five-item checklists and sent it home. Scores were tallied and either "satisfactory" or "unsatisfactory" was circled.

Personal Letters

Letters were sent to the parents, summarizing the student's day on the following points (computer programs may be available that can generate these data):

1. Statement of whether the day had been satisfactory

2. Summary of teacher ratings

3. Summary of teachers' unstructured comments

4. General statement of student progress, emphasizing the positive aspects of conduct and achievement

Phone Calls

Parents were called each day, following the same format as the personal letter.

Parents and teachers in the study liked the Good Day Cards technique best because it was the easiest to understand, and took the least amount of time to prepare and carry out. The telephone call condition was found to be the least effective, because it was often difficult to reach parents and there was a delay between the phone call and actual consequences. (This approach may be more effective now that more people have voice mail, answering machines, pagers, and cellular phones.) Another factor that may have bearing on the relative unpopularity of the phone call intervention was that it provided opportunities for lengthy conversations that conveyed more negative information.

Berdine and Cegelka (1995) offered a number of formal and informal strategies for developing home–school collaborations, one of which required students to earn "Good Student Reports," which they took to parents each week.

Monitor

See the comments regarding evaluation in points 5, 6, and 7 of the Procedures section. In addition, parents could be interviewed a time or two while this program is in effect. They could be asked about the procedures involved, how successful they were, and to comment on changes they might put into effect in the future.

References

Berdine, W. H., & Cegelka, P. T. (1995). Collaborative consultation: A key to effective educational delivery. In P. T. Cegelka & W. H. Berdine (Eds.), *Effective instruction for students with learning difficulties* pp. 19–46. Needham Heights, MA: Allyn & Bacon.

Trice, A. D., Parker, F. C., Furrow, F., & Iwata, M. M. (1986). An analysis of home contingencies to improve school behavior in disruptive adolescents. *Education and Treatment of Children, 6*(4), 389–399.

USING PEERS TO CONFRONT DISRUPTIVE BEHAVIORS

Background

Peer confrontation, in which peers notice discrepancies in behavior, call attention to those discrepancies, and indicate appropriate change for that behavior, has been effective in reducing maladaptive behaviors in problem students. Sandler, Arnold, Gable, and Strain (1987) designed this study to discover how beneficial the peer confrontation procedure is with adolescents with behavior disorders. They sought to determine whether peer confrontation would reduce two target behaviors in students: (a) off-task verbalizations (defined as a remark of a student not directly related to the task in which he or she is presently engaged) and (b) noncompliance (defined as the failure to follow a verbal command, given twice, within 10 seconds). The study also sought to discover how effective peer confrontation would be across several classroom situations: group discussions, independent work, and group–individualized instruction.

Who Can Benefit

Two boys, ages 9 and 11, and an 11-year-old girl, all special education students, participated in the study. They were said to have severe behavior disorders, including noncompliance, oppositional/disruptive behavior, and verbal/physical threats of aggression. The techniques, as described, also could be effective for youth with less severe behavior disorders.

Procedures

Interval One

1. Select a target behavior that is likely to have the most negative impact on students' performance (e.g., noncompliance).

2. Gather all students in one area of the classroom and seat them in a circle.

3. Ask one student to serve as the leader during group discussion. The leader may ask students questions about the weather, calendar, or current events, to which the others are to respond.

4. Observe and note the occurrence of the target behaviors during a 30-minute group discussion period.

5. Respond as usual with positive or negative consequences for behaviors displayed.

6. Initiate peer confrontation on the second day. Each time the problem student engages in a target behavior, ask the other students the following questions:

   • Can you tell Student X why that is a problem?

   • Who can tell Student X what he or she needs to do to solve the problem?

7. Record the number of target behaviors displayed during the peer confrontation intervention.

8. Schedule a group discussion the next day without peer confrontation.

9. Note the number of target behaviors that occur during the group talk.

10. Continue the steps in Interval One until every student has served as the group leader, including the problem students.

Interval Two

1. Engage the students in independent work. During this time, they are to remain seated, work independently, and raise their hands if they have questions.

2. Observe and record the number of target behaviors that occur during the first day, over the 30-minute interval.

3. Begin the peer-confrontation technique the next day during the independent work time. Follow procedures from Step 6 of Interval One.

4. Repeat observation of the target behaviors during the independent work time without peer confrontation on the next day.

5. Continue the same sequence over the next couple of days.

Interval Three

1. Conduct a group–individualized instruction activity. During this time, students are to remain at their desks while engaged in group games, worksheets, or videos.

2. Record the occurrences of target behaviors observed for a 30-minute block of time within the group–individualized instruction.

3. Begin the peer-confrontation intervention during the group–individualized activity on the following day. Follow the procedures from Step 6 of Interval One.

4. Note any target behaviors that occur the next day during the activity. Do not initiate peer confrontation.

5. Alternate peer confrontation with no peer confrontation during the activity over the next couple of days. Continue recording target behaviors.

Modifications and Considerations

Sandler et al. (1987) found that peer confrontation was an effective method for modifying disruptive behaviors of youth with behavior disorders. The intervention seemed to work best when implemented during individualized instruction. It appears that peer confrontation served as an aversive stimulus to students, in that they reduced the target behavior to avoid more confrontation. The students in the study gave favorable "reviews" of the intervention, and spontaneously confronted target youth without teacher assistance. (You need to watch this.) Moreover, target students sometimes approached other youth who displayed their target behaviors. (You need to watch this as well.)

A possible reason for the success of this procedure is that it instills in students a knowledge of the natural consequences of their behaviors—that of peer disapproval.

You may find initially that peer confrontation is somewhat threatening for the targeted student. It is important, therefore, to determine over the first few days of involvement if the intervention becomes less aversive for the student, or if there is a reduction in the target behaviors. If neither happens, temper the peer confrontation to a level that is more acceptable and effective for the youth.

According to Tierno (1991), the early adolescent's ability to think about the thoughts of others, including what others might be thinking about him or her, represents a primary cause of self-consciousness. Certainly, that must be taken into account when arranging peer support situations.

Monitor

In this project it is important to record the frequencies of the target behavior during each phase (i.e., group, independent, and group–individualized). The progression of events, as laid out here, may be necessary to assist some youth, but data over the three phases could also reveal that certain students are more influenced by one particular setting.

The interactions of the students in a group could be monitored by a tape recorder. Although that could be an intrusive and inhibiting factor, pupils might become accustomed to it if it were scheduled on a number of occasions. The playbacks from those sessions could be informative to pupils and teachers. Statements and interactions of several types could be counted.

References

Sandler, A. G., Arnold, L. B., Gable, R. A., & Strain, P. S. (1987). Effects of peer pressure on disruptive behavior of behaviorally disordered classmates. *Behavioral Disorders, 12,* 104–109.

Tierno, M. J. (1991). Responding to the socially motivated behaviors of early adolescents: Recommendations for classroom management. *Adolescence, 26*(103), 569–577.

SELF-OBSERVATION OF DISRUPTIVE BEHAVIORS

Background

The concept of modeling has been effective in encouraging the growth of social skills. One technique is to show videos that depict well-behaved students. In the research summarized here, students were shown videos of themselves as models of good behavior.

Who Can Benefit

The students who participated in McCurdy and Shapiro's (1988) research were between the ages of 9 and 11, and attended a school for individuals with social and emotional disturbances. Watching oneself on television is an entertaining activity for youth of all ages; therefore, this tactic is applicable for many students with behavior disorders from first grade through high school.

Procedures

This tactic requires the use of a video camera, as well as the help of an aide or volunteer.

1. Discuss with the targeted pupil which behaviors you consider inappropriate or disruptive. Then, make certain the youth is clear about the desired outcome of the tactic: to reduce the frequency of selected behaviors.

2. Ask the aide to monitor the student's behavior for one class period, marking down the number of times he or she displays any of the target behaviors. Do this for about 10 days. In addition, the aide could be asked to respond to a few items from a checklist prepared by the teacher having to do with the target individual.

3. Videotape the student for an entire period for 2 or 3 days during the second week of monitoring. (This will require the help of a second volunteer, perhaps an older student who is interested in video equipment.) Before the taping session begins, instruct the target student to be on his or her best behavior for the filming.

4. Edit the tape and delete any disruptive behaviors. The idea is to come up with at least one 10-minute video in which the student displays only acceptable behaviors.

5. Send the pupil to another room at the beginning of several class periods during the third and fourth weeks to view the 10-minute tape. (If

more than one 10-minute tape was made, alternate the tapes.) Continue to monitor the student's behavior for the remainder of the period.

6. Throughout this process, the pupil's daily misbehavior rates should be graphed so that he or she and the teacher can monitor the progress. It is desired that by the end of the fourth week the misbehaviors will have fallen to an acceptable rate.

Modifications and Considerations

Modifications can be made in the number of days or weeks the tactic is scheduled, as well as the way in which the students' behaviors are monitored and recorded. The focus students could be taught to monitor their own behaviors and graph the results themselves.

In addition to showing a video of the student behaving properly, it might be effective to show a video or two of the student behaving both inappropriately and appropriately. It would be up to the student to detect which behavior was appropriate.

Although all the students in McCurdy and Shapiro's (1988) research showed improvement as a result of the tactic, not all of them maintained their improvements in a follow-up study when the tactic was no longer in effect. With those students, the video approach could be arranged from time to time, or perhaps they should be encouraged to self-record certain of their behaviors.

Teachers or aides might consider using a checklist to identify behaviors of students they are monitoring. One such list is offered in the *Tough Kid Video Series* (1996). Following are three of its items: What do you like about this student? How many times in a day do you socially reward this student for good behavior? Is there a particular part of your schedule in which this student exhibits the most difficult behavior?

Monitor

A way to monitor this procedure has been referred to in item 6 in the Procedures section. If the youth watched a full unedited video of his or her actions, he could count and record instances of appropriate, inappropriate, and neutral behaviors.

References

McCurdy, B. L., & Shapiro, E. S. (1988). Self-observation and the reduction of inappropriate classroom behavior. *Journal of School Psychology, 26,* 371–378.

The tough kid video series. (1996). Longmont CO: Sopris West.

TALKING AND EXCESSIVE NOISE IN CLASS

Background

Talking out of turn, too often, and without permission is perhaps the number one behavior management concern of teachers. Sprick and Howard (1995) offered five plans to deal with this matter. Their Plan A is directed toward rather minor infractions, whereas Plans B through E are pointed toward more progressively serious concerns. Plan E, "for a situation in which the students simply aren't motivated to manage their excessive talking and noise," is summarized here.

Who Can Benefit

This plan is for an entire class that has fallen into a pattern of excessive talking and noise. Such a condition may come about when those behaviors become habitual and when a few influential students set a negative example for others.

Procedures

General Steps

1. Respond consistently to all instances of excessive talking and noise with a warning for the first incident per student, and announce time owed for each subsequent incident. For example, assign 1 minute after class for the first reminder after a warning and 10 minutes in detention for each subsequent reminder.

2. Monitor the number of incidents of excessive talking. Record each incident of excessive talking on a chart that shows each student's infractions and a total that represents the entire class. (You might display publicly the class data, but not that of individuals.)

3. Encourage the class to set a realistic daily performance goal for the target behaviors. This goal should be based on data gathered prior to this discussion and the involvement of the group reinforcement. One option would be to set the goal at 10% to 15% below the baseline, then to reduce it when the initial goal was reached for a few days, and so forth.

4. Set up a group reinforcement system. First, have the students come up with a list of rewards for the class, ones that are not too expensive and can be delivered (e.g., free time, time to socialize). Second, set up the requirements to earn points. For example, if there were more than 32 reminders (if that was the goal), then 0 points will be earned; if there were from 25 to 31, 1 point is earned; and so forth. Third, determine how many points each reward will cost. Some should be more valuable than others. Fourth, set up a time and place (if those are relevant) for the rewards to be given.

Steps for Developing and Implementing the Plan

1. Make sure you have enough information about the situation. You will need to explain precisely why a plan of some type is necessary and why you have settled on this particular plan. Give the students examples of noisy incidents (if that is necessary) and comment on the frequency of those disruptions.

2. Decide how to present the plan to the class. Wait for a time when you and the students are calm. (Do not spring this plan on them after a

blowup.) Give students the opportunity to ask questions and make comments. Encourage them to help establish the particulars of the plan.

3. Schedule a class meeting. Be certain you are prepared for the meeting. Develop an agenda and allow ample time for the meeting.

4. Decide on when and how to include parents in the plan.

5. Give the class regular feedback on their efforts to accomplish their goal.

Modifications and Considerations

If a classwide system such as this does not work or seems unlikely to be effective, an alternative strategy is to set up a team competition. Form two teams, and the one with the fewest infractions at the end of a period would gain the reward. Moreover, it is sometimes necessary to set up special arrangements with certain pupils.

Monitor

Ideas for monitoring were offered in points 2, 3, and 4 in General Steps in the Procedures section. Data should be kept on the class as a whole and on each individual student.

Reference

Sprick, R. S., & Howard, L. M. (1995). Talking/excessive noise in class. In *The teacher's encyclopedia of behavior management* (pp. 729–737). Longmont, CO: Sopris West.

 # FIGHTING OF ALL TYPES

Background

Fighting refers to a variety of disputes, ranging from verbal arguments to physical assault. The following plan is a general approach for dealing with students who have altercations of various types (Sprick & Howard, 1995).

Who Can Benefit

If proper interventions could be arranged to quell fights, most individuals would benefit, certainly the ones who get involved in them. Moreover, teachers and other students would profit from a fight-free environment. Possibly, adults who tend to fight would be less aggressive now had their teachers intervened in the past.

Procedures

1. Identify the specific behaviors that prompt you to say the pupil is fighting. For some students those behaviors are obvious, whereas for others

the behaviors are less apparent. Meanwhile, identify the times the fights take place, and whom the assailant fights with. Also, try to get a handle on the reasons for the fights, that is, the words or acts that initiated them. (Do not try too hard, however.)

2. Involve the students' parents(s) in your intervention plan. If they are supportive, work with them from the outset to set up consequences for each incident. Warn them that delivering physical consequences may make the fighting worse. If parents are not supportive, arrange school-based consequences such as in-school suspension, or assignment to other classes or areas. In addition, come up with a plan for working with the parents in the future; do not give up on them over the long haul.

3. Establish guidelines for dealing with physical fights if and when they occur.

   • Call for assistance or break up the fight. Establish procedures so that any adult can call for assistance from any location in the school. Interrupt the fight only if you are 100% certain that you can successfully do so without risk of injury to yourself or the students.

   • Disperse the audience. When a crowd is around the fighters, neither student can back down without being branded "the loser."

   • Verbally intervene; that is, tell the combatants to stop fighting. Identify yourself by name and position. Instruct one student to go to a specific location close by and the other one (or others) to go someplace else. If there appears to be a "winner," tell him or her to come stand by you. (That individual may be all too willing to resume the fracas.)

   • Physically intervene if necessary and prudent. When intervening with the assistance of another adult, coordinate your efforts so that you each pull off one student at the same time.

   • Once the immediate crisis has passed, send the students to the office. Alert someone there that "guests" will be arriving. (It may be necessary to escort them there.)

   • Document the incident immediately. Give one copy of your write-up to the building administrator and keep another.

Modifications and Considerations

School policies and guidelines for dealing with fights, even those of a rather benign nature, should be developed and communicated. In fact, it is a good idea for schools to have overall discipline plans, which deal with all sorts of infractions, not only fights. It is necessary also to have behavior plans in place for students in special education (see the next write-up for a reference on this matter).

Monitor

The obvious behavior to monitor would be the number of fights. Along with that, information should be kept on where the fights took place, with whom, and for what reason (if known).

Reference

Sprick, R. S., & Howard, L. M. (1995). Fighting. In *The teacher's encyclopedia of behavior management* (pp. 351–353). Longmont, CO: Sopris West.

SCHOOLWIDE INTERVENTIONS

Background

The purpose of this tactic is to explain and review schoolwide interventions that require the use of severe consequences. These interventions include expulsion and suspension (Bacon, 1990).

Who Can Benefit

Unfortunately, schools must be prepared to set up disciplinary interventions that are more punishing than other approaches discussed in this chapter, such as group contingencies, time-out, and response-cost. There will always be a number of students in every school for whom the following procedures must be involved.

Procedures

In-School Suspension

The in-school suspension (ISS) program requires that students be separated from others and sent to a special room to work. Teachers send assignments along with the students to ISS. While in the ISS program, students are not allowed to eat lunch with their peers or to participate in extracurricular activities. The following are guidelines for setting up and running ISS programs:

1. The age range among students in the program should be no more than three grades or years.

2. Maximum daily enrollment should be set. The number of students depends on the staff available to monitor the students, but should probably not exceed 15.

3. Criteria should be set for sending students to ISS. Those criteria should be the same for all students and understood by all teachers.

4. A placement in ISS should be for a set period of time, depending on the type of infraction, and should pertain to all students.

5. Students should return to regular classes contingent on their successfully participating in the program, and students and teachers should know what is meant by "successful."

6. If a student fails to meet the participation criteria, a meeting should be called to discuss the matter. At that time other options should be considered.

7. Students may be required to participate in a study skills or counseling program or some other scheduled activity while they are in ISS. (ISS programs that require students to take part in study skills or counseling programs have been more successful, with respect to recidivism, than those that do not.)

Short-Term Suspension

Disciplinary removal from school for fewer than 10 days is usually referred to as suspension. Before a student is suspended, he or she is entitled to the following:

1. Some kind of notice
2. Some kind of hearing
3. An opportunity to tell his or her side
4. A statement of the reasons for the disciplinary action

Parents are given a full statement of the reason for the suspension and a notice of their right to a due process hearing, at which the parents and student may discuss the suspension with a hearing officer who reports to the board, which in turn rules on the report. (Studies on the effectiveness of suspension have found its use to be questionable because the recidivism rate for suspended students is quite high.)

Long-Term Suspension and Expulsion

The terms *expulsion* and *long-term suspension* frequently overlap, but are generally defined as disciplinary removal from school for more than 10 days. In most schools there must be a formal hearing of the complaints before a student can be expelled. In *Wood v. Strikland* (1975) the Supreme Court ruled that students do not have a constitutional right to an education, but a student cannot be deprived of education without due process. (The effectiveness of this form of punishment is doubtful, especially if a measure of positive effects is that youth return to school and stay there. Too many students who are expelled once are expelled repeatedly, and ultimately drop out of school entirely.)

Modifications and Considerations

Special care must be taken in disciplining, suspending, and expelling students with disabilities. Prior to involving the interventions noted here or other rather severe procedures, a functional behavioral assessment must be carried out and a behavioral intervention plan developed. For details on doing this, see *Behavioral Intervention Planning* by Fad, Patton, and Polloway (1998).

Monitor

The types of data to keep on these radical forms of discipline should be obvious. (I doubt, however, if many schools bother to keep them.) Those data should reveal not only how many students were involved in the particular form of punishment or program, but how many of them repeated the offense and were involved again in a similar program. Also, data should be kept on the students who came back to school as good citizens and were not repeat offenders.

References

Bacon, E. H. (1990). Using negative consequences effectively. *Academic Therapy, 25,* 599–611.

Fad, K. M., Patton, J. R., & Polloway, E. A. (1998). *Behavioral intervention planning.* Austin, TX: PRO-ED.

Wood v. Strickland, 420 U.S. 308 (1975).

IMPLEMENTING A LEVEL SYSTEM WITH DIFFICULT YOUTH

Background

In a Level System students are placed on successively higher steps with increasing responsibility. As responsibility increases, so do privileges and rewards. Advancing from one level to another is dependent on meeting specified and increasingly stringent goals.

Who Can Benefit

The Level System is especially appropriate for students with moderate to serious behavior disorders, who have been difficult to manage. This procedure is commonly arranged in special classes for youth with behavior disorders. Certain features of the approach would be effective with students whose behaviors were less serious and chronic in general education classes.

Procedures

Following are characteristics of a Level System:

1. *Define steps clearly.* Level Systems are generally made up of three or four steps, moving from initial steps that are directed mostly by the teacher to later ones that are managed more by the student. Each step should be noticeably different from the others with respect to requirements and privileges.

2. *Define observable, specific desired behaviors.* Students should know exactly what is expected of them in order to advance from one level to the other, and be aware of the benefits that come to them when they advance. Teachers should follow their own guidelines carefully in advancing students from one step to the other.

3. *Clearly define undesirable behaviors.* Just as desirable behaviors should be defined and communicated to students, so should the unwanted behaviors. Behaviors of both types are taken into account in graduating from one step to another.

4. *Clearly define rewards.* Students should have a clear understanding of the privileges that will come to them at each of the levels. Obviously, those rewards should be reinforcing to the students involved in these programs.

5. *Determine measurable criteria.* Students should know just how many desirable behaviors they need to exhibit for how many days before they can move up a step. Related, they must know the extent they will be delayed in advancing a notch (or demoted) if they engage in undesirable behaviors.

6. *Measure and record student performance.* Records must be kept of the student's desirable and undesirable behaviors. For the initial steps the teacher should monitor those behaviors; as more steps are passed, the students should take on certain data gathering responsibilities.

7. *Communicate frequently.* Teachers should communicate often with students and their parents, daily at the beginning and less often as students move up the levels. Students should always know how they stand with respect to the levels and should know what it takes to advance, or possibly be demoted to a lower level.

See Figure 13.3 for the decision rules for transition in a three-level system.

Modifications and Considerations

Complementary systems may be included in a Level System. They may include token economies whereby merit is converted into tokens or points and students redeem those points for favorable rewards at another time. Contingency contracts may also accompany Level Systems. Those arrangements may be set up to be maintained at home or at school or in both locations.

Monitor

Monitoring the system was mentioned in number 6 in the Procedures section. Data should be kept on the extent the student displayed desirable and undesirable behaviors, and the time spent at the various levels.

Reference

Reisberg, L., Brodigan, D., & Williams, G. J. (1991). Classroom management: Implementing a system for students with BD. *Intervention in School and Clinic, 27*(1), 31–38.

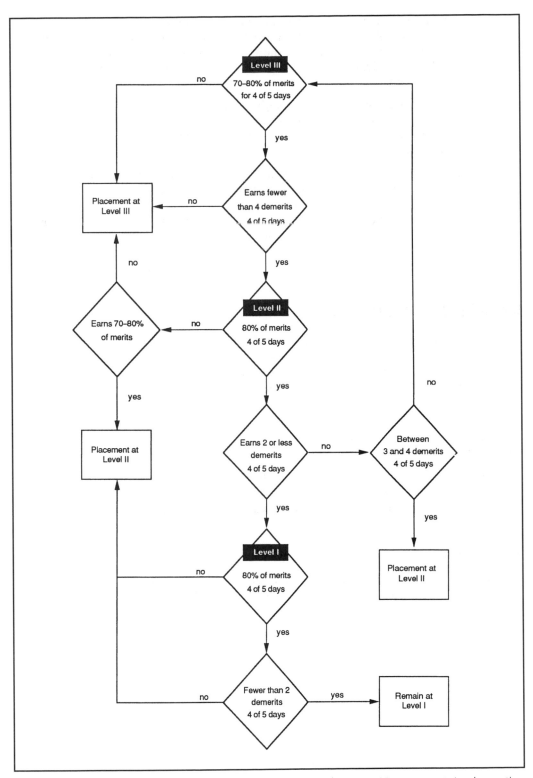

Figure 13.3. Decision rules flow chart for transitions. From "Classroom Management: Implementing a System for Students with BD," by L. Reisberg, D. Brodigan, and G. J. Williams, 1991, *Intervention in School and Clinic, 27*(1), p. 34. Copyright 1991 by PRO-ED, Inc. Reprinted with permission.

Chapter 14
SELF-MANAGEMENT

• •

Since about 1960 there has been an avalanche of research and commentary on the topic of self-management. The early work was carried out by researchers of a behavioral bent. After about 1980 individuals identified more with cognitive or constructivist approaches have taken considerable interest in self-management and renamed it self-determination. Fifteen self-management tactics have appeared previously in this book:

- One in the Attendance chapter—Self-Recording and Public Posting

- Three in the Motivation chapter—Increasing Interest in Schools: Immediate Applications; Self-Management: Identifying Antecedents and Consequences of Behavior; and Self-Management: Saving a Life

- Two in the Study Skills chapter—Managing Time: Being Prepared; and Taking Tests: Debriefing

- One in the Social Skills chapter—Getting Along with Others: Structured Learning with Self-Monitoring

- One in the Participation chapter—Participating in Discussions: Self-Monitoring

- Three in the Goals chapter—Setting Objectives: Self-Management; Arranging Contracts To Achieve Goals; and Setting Priorities

- Three in the Self-Esteem chapter—Self-Management: Accepting Responsibility; Self-Management: Building Successes; and Self-Management: Prompting Praise

- One in the Classroom Management chapter—Self-Observation of Disruptive Behaviors

I include only two tactics in this chapter; both are broader in scope than those in the other chapters. One is an outline of a program designed for youth who are at risk. The other is an inservice program that focuses on self-management, designed for secondary special education teachers.

A SELF-DETERMINATION PROGRAM FOR ADOLESCENCE

Background

According to Field, Hoffman, and Posch (1997), adolescence is a critical time for the development and expression of self-determination, and for embracing identity exploration and learned independence, which lead to self-awareness. They defined self-determination as the ability to identify and achieve goals based on a foundation of knowing and valuing oneself.

Who Can Benefit

Adolescents of all types would benefit from this program, but individuals with disabilities or who are at risk would especially profit, for a number of confounding factors are often associated with their development: (a) physical, cognitive, or behavioral issues; (b) social relationship issues; (c) heightened concerns of parents; and (d) inability of systems to adequately accommodate their needs.

Procedures

The model of Field and Hoffman's (1994) self-determination curriculum has five major components (see Figure 14.1). The first two—know yourself and value yourself—are internal processes that create a foundation for behaving in a self-determined manner. The next two—plan and act—delineate skills needed to interact with this foundation. The last step is to experience outcomes and to learn. The authors intend for this curriculum to be delivered over the course of one 55-minute orientation session, one 6-hour workshop session, and 16 topical sessions of approximately 55 minutes each. Although each session has a topical focus, several components weave throughout each one and topics are not considered discrete entities.

Orientation

1. Review the purpose and structure of the curriculum. Participants learn about themselves, their strengths and weaknesses, and what is important to them. They learn more about decision making, goal setting, and communicating with others.

2. Students discuss the meaning of self-determination and identify individuals who are self-directed.

3. Students discuss what it means to be self-directed.

4. Class discusses the advantages of being self-directed.

5. Participants select a parent or friend (a sponsor) to participate in the workshop with them, help them with homework, and generally support them throughout the curriculum.

6. Students identify the characteristics of such a person.

7. They write a letter of invitation to the chosen individual.

Workshop

1. Students (and teacher) become acquainted with one other.

2. Students demonstrate an understanding of self-determination. They talk about it and write about it.

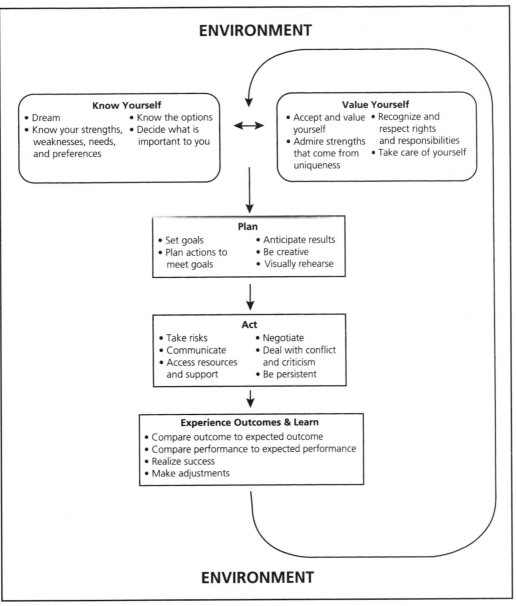

Figure 14.1. Model of self-determination. From "Development of a Model for Self-Determination," by S. Field and A. Hoffman, 1994, *Career Development for Exceptional Individuals, 17*(2), p. 165. Copyright 1994 by Council for Exceptional Children Division on Career Development. Reprinted with permission.

3. Students identify two of their strengths and one weakness in the following five areas: physical, mental, emotional, social, and beliefs.

4. Students identify strengths they have developed in response to a perceived weakness.

5. Students list traits associated with their ideal self and discuss how those traits relate to their current self.

6. Group discusses and discriminates between rights and responsibilities.

7. Students identify their need for support from others and identify ways in which they can obtain that support. (The teacher offers several examples.)

8. Selected sponsors identify ways in which to support their student.

Session 1: Dreaming to open possibilities

1. The teacher offers several examples of others' hopes and dreams.

2. Students think about and verbalize their dreams.

3. Students listen attentively as others talk about their dreams.

Session 2: What is important to me?

1. Students comment on how their dreams might be used to decide what they want.

2. Students write a statement identifying what is important to them.

3. They attempt to relate their dreams with those things that are important to them. (During this session and those to follow, students review the previous session and discuss matters of the current session as a class. Moreover, each student discusses the exercise with his or her sponsor.)

Sessions 3 and 4: Creating options for long-term goals

1. Students identify their personal needs for taking care of themselves.

2. Students, based on their perceived needs, generate a number of goals. (Inform students that some goals can be accomplished in a few days, whereas others take several days or weeks to accomplish. Inform them also that many of these long-term goals should be broken into goals that can be attained in short periods, and when they are achieved the long-term goal will be attained.)

3. Students write observable, measurable, and achievable short-term goals.

Sessions 5 and 6: Choosing short-term goals

1. Students identify one short-term goal that is related to their long-term goal.

2. Students identify what they need to do in a few days to make progress toward that goal.

3. Students discuss example student's steps to short-term goals (see Figure 14.2).

Session 7: Planning activities

1. Students identify activities to help them reach their short-term goals.

2. Students identify what they can do in the next few days to make progress toward their goals.

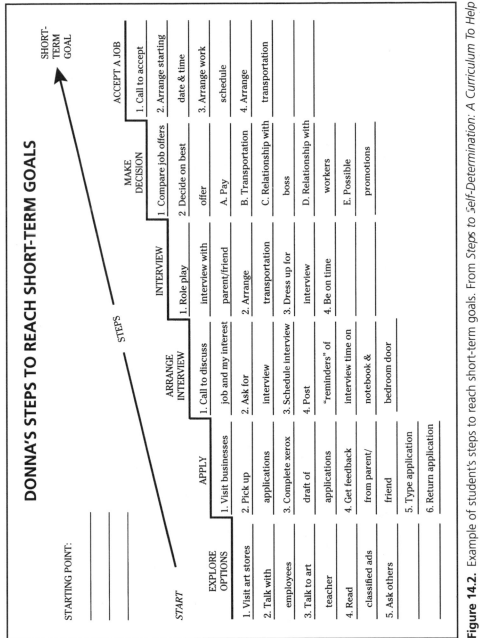

Figure 14.2. Example of student's steps to reach short-term goals. From *Steps to Self-Determination: A Curriculum To Help Adolescents Learn To Achieve Their Goals* (p. 115), by S. Field and A. Hoffman, 1996, Austin, TX: PRO-ED. Copyright 1996 by PRO-ED, Inc. Reprinted with permission.

3. They demonstrate their ability to "brainstorm" in coming up with possibilities.

Session 8: Taking the first step

1. Students identify the first action they intend to take toward reaching their short-term goals.

2. Students individually identify anticipated results of their planned actions. In so doing, they fill out a worksheet (see example in Figure 14.3).

3. Introduce the "Act" and "Experience Outcomes and Learn" components of the model (See Figure 14.1).

Session 9: Creative barrier breaking

1. Students demonstrate awareness of the concepts of *barriers* and *creativity*.

2. Students discuss the barriers that are likely to come up in a variety of circumstances.

3. Students identify individuals they believe are creative and explain why.

Session 10: A little help from my friends

Teacher emphasizes that a group is usually more powerful in creatively solving problems than are individuals. Several exercises are carried out to demonstrate this.

Session 11: A journey to self-determination

Students meet and talk with a person who has a disability about the process of becoming self-determined.

Session 12: Assertive communication I

Students learn that assertive communication is more effective than aggressive or passive communication to get them what they want.

Session 13: Assertive communication II

1. Students continue learning to distinguish between aggressive, assertive, and passive communication and to use assertive communication appropriately.

2. Students role-play the various communication styles.

Session 14: Negotiation

Students learn to negotiate in pairs, permitting both people to "win."

Session 15: Conflict resolution

Students learn to apply skills in negotiation, assertive communication, and the use of "I" statements to a "win–win" resolution of conflicts.

ANTICIPATING RESULTS

Planned action:

Possible results:

After thinking about the possible results, which of the following do you want to do?

____ Modify the plan
What would you change?

____ Discard the plan

____ Go for it, without any changes

Figure 14.3. Worksheet for anticipating results of planned action toward reaching short-term goal. From *Steps to Self-Determination: A Curriculum To Help Adolescents Learn To Achieve Their Goals* (p. 148), by S. Field and A. Hoffman, 1996, Austin, TX: PRO-ED. Copyright 1996 by PRO-ED, Inc. Reprinted with permission.

Session 16: Where do we go from here?

Students bring conclusion to the course through review and by planning how to continue the lifelong process of becoming more self-determined.

Monitor

One way to evaluate the effects of such a program would be to administer the Self-Determination Knowledge Scale that Hoffman, Field, and Sawilowsky developed (available as part of Field & Hoffman's, 1996, program). A less formal way would be to develop a checklist that covers the attributes the program intended to teach, and to administer it before, during, or after the program.

References

Field, S., & Hoffman, A. (1994). Development of a model for self-determination. *Career Development for Exceptional Individuals, 17*(2), 159–169.

Field, S., & Hoffman, A. (1996). *Steps to self-determination: A curriculum to help adolescents learn to achieve their goals.* Austin, TX: PRO-ED.

Field, S., Hoffman, A., & Posch, M. (1997). Self-determination during adolescence: A developmental perspective. *Remedial and Special Education, 18*(5), 285–293.

A SELF-MANAGEMENT PROGRAM FOR SECONDARY TEACHERS

Background

The inservice program described here was designed to instruct teachers to carry out self-management projects with their students (Lovitt & Higgins, 1996). The program relied on features of the Consumer-Validated Research Approach designed by Eaker and Huffman (1984).

Who Can Benefit

The participants in this program were 10 secondary special education resource room teachers from three school districts in the Seattle area (Lovitt & Higgins, 1996).

Procedures

The program has five steps.

1. *Identify a Topic*—The topic we selected was self-management. We believed that many youth with learning disabilities and others were lacking in these skills. Related, considerable research had been carried out on this theme.

2. *Present and Interpret Research*—We met with the 10 teachers on the university campus for the following purposes:

   - *Define self-management*—We defined it as the ability to plan, organize and prepare; to know oneself; to self-evaluate; and to understand relationships between cause and effect.

   - *Offer reasons for teachers to promote self-management with their students*—Reasons included increased time for teaching; it is emphasized in most instruction programs, is likely to improve performances of students, and may elevate students' self-confidence; and it increases chances of generalization.

   - *Discuss reasons for students to become better self-managers*—They would be more likely to stay in general education classes, have a better chance of graduating, make better grades, and be more popular; and the skills would help in finding a job.

   - *Give teachers their assignment*—Select one or more students to work with; pinpoint behaviors to address; assist students to carry out the project; and gather data on the selected behaviors.

   - *Present examples*—Several self-management projects were described that dealt with secondary-age students. They focused on self-recording, self-evaluating, and self-specifying contingencies. Copies of a few studies were handed out.

   - *Outline phases of the program*—Teachers were instructed to begin a self-management project in their classes; call university staff for help (as needed); schedule their visits to the classes; and return to the university for a group meeting in 4 months.

3. *Follow-up*—Between the two meetings, university personnel phoned each teacher at least four times and visited them at least three times. The purposes of those contacts were to check up on the teachers' progress and to offer help.

4. *Reconvene*—At this meeting, also held at the university, each teacher described her project, showed data to illustrate outcomes, and presented plans for future self-management instruction. Staff presented information from other self-management projects that dealt with adolescents.

5. *Continue with One Teacher and District*—We selected one teacher to continue working with. She and her director had agreed to train other teachers in the district to increase their students' self-management skills.

Table 14.1 shows information from the 10 teachers in this project. Figure 14.4 shows the steps teachers followed in assisting students to be self-managers.

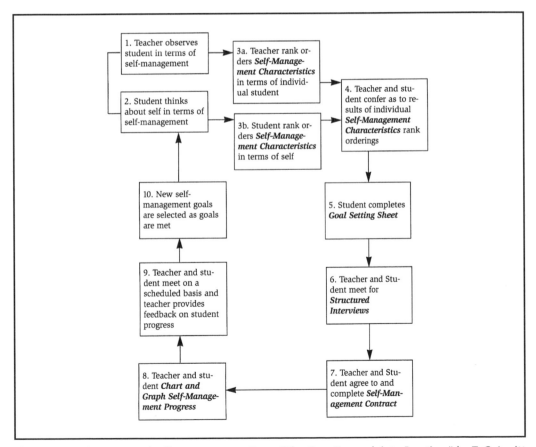

Figure 14.4. Steps toward self-management. From "The Gap: Research into Practice," by T. C. Lovitt and A. K. Higgins, 1996, *Teaching Exceptional Children, 28*(2), p. 68. Copyright 1996 by The Council for Exceptional Children. Reprinted with permission.

Table 14.1. Self-Management Projects

Teacher	Goal	Student	Class	Procedures	Results	Teacher Thoughts
Cyndy	Develop positive attitude	Male high school student with behavior disorders.	Structured study skills class.	Teacher recorded student behavior and attitude for 5 minutes; gave student feedback; charted results.	Student improved slightly in his interactions with others.	1. Student needs to be ready to accept self-management. 2. Classroom-based research was helpful because "I was going nowhere."
Roby	Complete tasks.	Male high school student with health impairments.	Language arts assignments.	Student carried an assignment sheet to be filled in by his classroom teacher; main responsibility was on the student; student earned points for returning assignment sheet.	Student completed more work and improved grades in language arts.	1. Self-management is a prime concern of special education. 2. Sharing between teachers is essential. 3. Process should begin before high school. 4. Cooperation between university and public schools is essential. 5. Continue focus of sharing research ideas with teachers.
Chris	Complete tasks.	Entire class of students with learning disabilities.	Project Access (study skills).	Students completed pie chart of daily activities to enable them to visualize how little time was spent studying.	Students have a much better idea as to how their time is spent.	1. Teacher found it difficult to help the student self-manage. 2. Students were amazed at how much time they wasted.
Sherry	Complete tasks.	Three high school males with learning disabilities.	Project Access (study skills).	Goal sheets kept for tasks completed (100%).	Students, as they recorded, completed more work.	1. Begin small and make it measurable. 2. Classroom-based research is more realistic than clinical research, but frustrating with a mobile population.
Terri	Turn in assignments.	Male ninth-grader with learning disabilities.	Earth science, math, language arts, Washington State history, and study skills.	Study skills teacher and general class teacher checked daily on assignments; if work was completed, student earned computer time.	Number of assignments turned in increased when student monitored progress.	1. A self-manager is reliable, consistent, and prompt. 2. Self-managers can work well.

Table 14.1. *(continued)*

Teacher	Goal	Student	Class	Procedures	Results	Teacher Thoughts
Cheryl	Spend time on homework.	Female high school senior with learning disabilities.	Peer tutoring class.	Time spent working on book reports was recorded daily.	Four book reports were completed by due dates.	Plans to continue working with self-management in peer tutoring situations.
Mary	Reduce talkouts.	16-year-old male with learning disabilities.	English class.	Teacher discussed problem with student; teacher recorded talkouts during baseline; teacher and student recorded talkouts during next phase.	Initial, dramatic drop during second phase; frequency of talkouts increased following winter break; when home reward was combined with self-recording, talkout rate quickly dropped.	Necessary to establish a firm reward system with youngsters of this type.
Kathleen	Come to class on time, complete homework, bring materials to class.	20-year-old male with learning disabilities	Economics class.	Teacher approached the student with tardiness problem; teacher and student outlined morning routine of student behaviors; devised a checklist.	Noticed carryover in another class with respect to being on time, doing homework, and bringing materials.	1. Important that student see or feel that there is a problem. 2. Maturity may be a contributing factor to self-management.
Lynn	Arrive on time for school.	17-year-old high school male.	First period class (study skills).	Teacher approached the student with tardiness problem; teacher and student outlined morning routine of student behaviors; devised a checklist.	Student arrived on time for school for two consecutive weeks.	Key factor in self-management is motivation of student.
Christine	Reduce assaultive behaviors, return student to full-day middle school program, increase compliance with adult requests, and decrease inappropriate off-task behaviors.	Two middle school males with learning disabilities and behavior disorders.	District treatment center and middle school program.	Students targeted behaviors interfering with school success; teacher collected counts on targeted behaviors; student collected counts on targeted behaviors; journal on behaviors kept by students.	Significant decrease in assaultive behaviors and not complying with adults' directions.	1. Self-management is key to student success. 2. Student must acknowledge a need for change.

Note. From "The Gap: Research into Practice," by T. C. Lovitt and A. K. Higgins, 1996, *Teaching Exceptional Children, 28*(2), p. 66. Copyright 1996 by The Council for Exceptional Children. Reprinted with permission.

Modifications and Considerations

This model of implementing research into practice through inservice sessions could be arranged for a variety of topics important to secondary-age students, such as adapting materials, study skills, and social skills training.

Monitor

Information on monitoring is included in Table 14.1: the number of teachers involved, the number of students with whom they worked, and the degree of their success.

References

Eaker, R., & Huffman, J. (1984). Linking research and practice: The consumer validation approach. *Roeper Review, 6,* 236–237.

Lovitt, T. C., & Higgins, A. K. (1996). The gap: Research into practice. *Teaching Exceptional Children, 28*(2), 65–68.

Chapter 15
HEALTH

◆ ◆ ◆ ◆ ◆ ◆ ◆ ◆ ◆ ◆ ◆ ◆ ◆ ◆ ◆ ◆ ◆ ◆ ◆

I t may seem presumptuous of me to delve into the business of health and the teenager. There are numerous programs available having to do with matters of diet (losing and gaining weight), physical fitness, sexual activity, smoking, drinking, and doing drugs. Newspapers offer all sorts of suggestions and statistics, and many devote several pages weekly to matters of health. There are countless books on dieting, smoking, alcohol, and drugs. Many hospitals provide group counseling in those matters, and some have teen centers that focus on special health needs and concerns. There are even television stations devoted to food and exercise. Knowing all that, I tackle the topic anyway because these affairs of health are especially relevant to youth who are at risk. Some educators would make the case that it is more important to deal with health concerns for students at risk than it is to teach facts and concepts of science and social studies.

Tactics in this chapter focus on the six categories of health-risk behaviors among youth and young adults that are monitored by the Youth Risk Behavior Surveillance System. They are behaviors that contribute to unintentional and intentional injuries; tobacco use; alcohol and other drug use; sexual behaviors that contribute to unintended pregnancy and sexually transmitted disease; unhealthy dietary behaviors; and physical inactivity.

Reference

Youth Risk Behavior Surveillance System (CDC Surveillance Summaries), <http://www.cdc.gov/epo/mmur/preview/ss4703.html>

ACCIDENTS AND HOMICIDES

Background

The following are a few alarming statistics relevant to youth:

- For youth ages 15 to 24, there were 59 motor vehicle deaths per 100,000 of population per year and 34 deaths per 100,000 from firearms. (From 1995 Web site statistics from the Centers for Disease Control and Prevention.)

- According to the 1997 Youth Risk Behavior Surveillance System survey, 19.3% of young adults rarely or never wear seat belts, and 30% of their deaths were caused by motor vehicle crashes.

- Washington State taxpayers pay $5 million per year for motorcycle trauma (Harborview Injury Prevention and Research Center, n.d.).

- Injury is the most costly of all major health problems facing our nation. Trauma costs taxpayers $130 billion per year, more than cancer and heart disease combined (Rivara & Grossman, 1996).

- About one third of the injuries to pedestrians occur in marked crosswalks (Rivara & Grossman, 1996).

Who Can Benefit

Youth would benefit from programs that prompted them to take fewer risks and to be more careful. Great numbers of youth believe they are not subject to the consequences that befall the rest of us. Likewise, those poor souls who get in the way of reckless youth would benefit.

Procedures

Preventing Vehicular Accidents

In addition to teaching youth to drive with skill and care, other things that should be considered to prevent them from killing so many of themselves and others in the process.

- The campaign should be constantly waged (and the law enforced) for passengers and drivers to wear seat belts and for motorcycle drivers to wear helmets. Although more and more states have laws requiring people to wear them, many drivers and passengers do not, and as a result, many have been killed or seriously injured. *Activity:* Students could contact insurance companies, hospitals, and trauma centers about these matters.

- Consider raising the legal age at which youth can obtain a driver's license, or set up a trial period between the 16th and perhaps the 18th year. Depending on how the youth performed between those years, he or she would or would not be granted a permanent license. This recommendation and the next are likely to prompt spirited discussions among youth.

- Require youth under the age of 18 to include a responsible parent in the car if they intend to have other youth ride with them.

- Encourage youth to come up with ways to assert their power other than driving fast and recklessly.

- Show youth pictures and videos of other youths' accidents, the gorier the better.

- As for motorcycles (and bicycles), safety programs should be fostered to promote wearing helmets. Data from the Harborview Injury Prevention and Research Center in Seattle revealed that bicycle helmets reduced the risk of head injury by 77% and brain injury by 81%.

Preventing Other Accidents

Instead of complacently accepting the fact that "accidents will happen," we should do all that is possible to prevent them.

- Have class discussions that focus on aspects of home safety, including fire; electricity; radon, asbestos, and other such materials; and the keeping of firearms in the home. *Activity:* Students could survey their homes with regard to safety issues.

- Other safety programs that merit discussion deal with sports and recreation: swimming, boating, surfing, scuba diving, mountain climbing, hiking, and camping out.

- Encourage better law enforcement and programs aimed at violations against (and by) pedestrians. Educate youth to be safer pedestrians: (a) Never cross a street without looking both ways simply because the light is green, the pedestrian light is on, or it is a crosswalk; (b) always run or walk facing the traffic, and be prepared to jump off the road at any moment; (c) be extremely careful of cars filled with young people coming from behind or approaching you; (d) never wear a radio with headphones as you run or walk (one must listen as well as look); and (e) be extremely careful of individuals driving "hot" cars, 4×4 pickups, sports utility vehicles, and individuals driving station wagons filled with children. In short, pedestrians should view all vehicles (including motorcycles and bicycles) as predators.

Cutting the Rate of Homicides

Data from the Harborview Center comparing the homicide rates in Seattle with those in Vancouver, British Columbia (which has stricter laws against handgun ownership), showed that, although the chances of being assaulted were the same in both cities, the chances of an assault with a firearm were seven times greater in Seattle. According to a 1998 survey, violence in schools is the number one fear of many students (Knutson, 1998). What to do:

- Set up an absolute no-weapons policy. Anyone who brings a weapon to school should be suspended indefinitely, if not forever.

- Youth should visit the emergency rooms of local hospitals and see first hand the victims of gunshots.

Modifications and Considerations

Rivara and Grossman (1996) reviewed statistics on traumatic deaths to children in the United States and determined that although deaths in several categories decreased in the past decade, the decline would be greater if available prevention strategies were more involved. Those strategies include airbags, lap and shoulder harnesses, helmets for bicycle riders, swimming pool fencing, smoke detectors, poison packaging, window bars, and elimination or secure storage of handguns in the home.

References

Centers for Disease Control and Prevention. (1995). Available: http://www.cdc.gov

Harborview Injury Prevention and Research Center. (no date). Contact: 325 Ninth Avenue, Seattle, WA 98104-2499

Knutson, L. L. (1998, August 12). Students worry about violence and crime. *The Seattle Times*, p. A3.

Rivara, F. P., & Grossman, D. C. (1996). Prevention of traumatic deaths to children in the United States: How far have we come and where do we need to go? *Pediatrics, 97*(6), 791–797.

Youth Risk Behavior Surveillance System (CDC Surveillance Summaries), http://www.cdc.gov/epo/mmur/preview/ss4703.html

STRESS, DEPRESSION, AND SUICIDE

Background

It is just as important to attend to adolescents' mental health as their physical health. Thankfully, a number of approaches and programs are available for dealing with this important matter. Although most secondary schools do not offer courses that deal specifically with emotional health, teachers in home living, home economics classes, and a few others often touch on this issue. All teachers should attend to these matters as opportunities arise.

Who Can Benefit

Many youth who are at risk show signs of stress, suffer from periods of depression, and may attempt suicide. Hopefully, the suggestions offered here for observing youth and the exercises for alleviating certain debilitating symptoms will be of assistance to teachers, parents, and students.

Procedures

In this section, comments are offered on three related topics as they pertain to youth: stress, depression, and suicide.

Stress

It is necessary for a person to be able to identify when he or she is under stress, to know what situations and conditions promote stress, and to understand how to deal with it.

Causes. It is important to point out and discuss the following:

- About half of the uninjured survivors of natural and manmade disasters experience acute emotional, physical, or psychosomatic consequences. *Activity:* Students keep track of worldwide disasters.

- Personality type can affect the risk for heart attack; that is, those characterized by high levels of achievement, striving, competitiveness, time consciousness, and impatience have been shown to have a high risk of developing coronary heart disease.

- Social isolation has been observed to put people at special risk for unexpected mortality and morbidity.

Implications. Theories about the effects of stress should be discussed (*Medicine for the Layman,* 1985):

- Stress can affect the cardiovascular system by increasing blood pressure and accelerating the atherosclerotic process.

- Stressful situations can impair the mechanisms involved in immunity, particularly the body's ability to fight disease via cellular immunity.

- Stress can cause peptic ulcers by stimulating hypersecretion of gastric acid.

Prevention. Following are a few suggestions from a publication by Overlake-Hospital Medical Center (n.d.):

- Although you cannot control the external circumstances of your life, you can control your reactions to them.

- Maintain good health: exercise, eat properly, and get enough sleep.

- Do not try to keep everything the same, and do not try to "fix" everything.

- Practice meditation. Go to a comfortable, private place without distractions. Close your eyes and focus on one peaceful word or image.

- Autogenic suggestion can relieve stress. With this technique, individuals tell themselves how they want to feel.

- Breathe deeply and slowing; this can interrupt stress responses and help one relax.

- Practice relaxing muscles deeply; this helps one to relax the entire body from head to toe by first tensing, then relaxing various muscle groups.

- Practice stretching and exercising to reduce stress. Some examples are the head and neck roll, back stretch, leg stretch, arm stretch, and most forms of aerobic exercise.

Depression

According to Sullivan and Engin (1986), over 30% of students in schools reported moderate or severe levels of depression symptoms. Shaffer and Fisher (1981) maintained there is a frequent association between depressive symptoms and suicidal behavior in adolescents.

Disposition. Following are eight signs and symptoms of depression in children and adolescents, according to Wright-Strawderman, Lindsey, Navarette, and Flippo (1996): depressed mood, withdrawal, poor concentration, appetite changes, increased or decreased energy, indicators of suicidal ideation, any significant change in child or adolescent, and poor self-esteem.

Prevention. Following are a few responses to forestall or mitigate depression (Turner, 1987):

- Don't push your worries behind you, out of sight, where they can heckle you. Bring them out front and look them over. Decide which ones you can do something about and which ones you have to live with.

- Strive to turn a minus into a plus. If life hands you a lemon, make lemonade. A positive outlook sees some good even in unpromising situations. *Activity:* Students could comment on the times in their lives this has happened, or might have happened.

- Do something each day for someone else at some cost to yourself. In caring for the needs of others, we are less likely to concentrate on our own problems.

- Live one day at a time. Will Rogers's motto on this score was, "Never let yesterday use up too much of today."

- Nurture a sense of humor. Being able to laugh at ourselves is a sign of wholeness and wholesomeness.

Suicide

According to Neiger and Hopkins (1988), suicide rates increased 200% for girls and 300% for boys aged 15 to 24 over the previous 25 years. According to the Centers for Disease Control and Prevention (1995), there were 26 suicides per 100,000 youth aged 15 to 24 in 1995. The numbers would be even higher if other forms of self-destruction, such as fatal one-car accidents, drug overdoses, and self-administered poisonings, were taken into account.

Disposition. Although no one particular type of teenager commits suicide, certain characteristics (Neiger & Hopkins, 1988) tend to increase the risk of suicide, and every teacher, counselor, administrator, and parent should be aware of them:

- *Age*—Generally risk increases with age, between the ages of 15 and 24.

- *Gender*—Women attempt suicide three times more often than men, but twice as many men actually succeed in committing suicide.

- *Race*—Blacks attempt suicide more often than members of other races, but whites complete suicide more often.

- *Geographic patterns*—There is a high rate of youthful suicide concentrated in the Western United States, especially in the intermountain region. Some research has related suicide to densely and sparsely populated areas.

- *Depression*—As many as half of all teenagers suffer from regular bouts of depression.

- *Acute suicidal behavior*—Indicators of suicidal ideation are actual suicide attempts, frequent discussions of death, making plans for death, purchasing or carrying deadly weapons, and taking deadly risks.

- *Poor family relationships*—Feelings of helplessness and vulnerability make teenagers more prone to suicide, and factors such as family violence, intense marital discord, and loss of a parent through divorce or death can significantly increase this sense of helplessness.

- *Alcohol/drug use*—There appears to be a direct relationship between the use of drugs and alcohol and suicide attempts by adolescents.

- *Precipitating circumstances*—Often, a precipitating circumstance will push the teenager "over the edge": rejection by an important person, unwanted pregnancy, family crisis, poor performance in school, a fight with a peer, dispute with a close friend, fight with a parent, or mimicking another suicide.

- *Other characteristics*—Suicidal adolescents are usually dependent, accident prone, restless or bored, obnoxious, easily fatigued, experiencing notable changes in sleeping habits, or prone to frequent mood swings.

Prevention. Garland and Zigler's (1993) recommendations regarding suicide prevention include support for integrated primary prevention efforts; suicide prevention education for professionals; education and policies on firearm management; education for the media about adolescent suicide; more efficient identification and treatment of at-risk youth, including those exposed to suicidal behavior; crisis intervention; and treatment for those who attempt suicide.

Modifications and Considerations

Several resources are available for treating youth who are depressed and are possible candidates for suicide: hot lines, psychiatrists and therapists, school psychologists, mental health agencies, school-based support groups, psychiatric hospital units, and dozens of Internet sites.

Monitor

Teachers, parents, and others should be sensitive to the moods and behaviors of teenagers and, if danger signs are noted, intensify their observations and actions and inform others of their concern. Checklists that indicate critical behaviors of youth could be developed for this purpose.

References

Centers for Disease Control and Prevention. (1995). Available: http://www.cdc.gov

Garland, A. F., & Zigler, E. (1993). Adolescent suicide prevention: Current research and social policy implications. *American Psychologist, 48*(2), 169–182.

Medicine for the layman: Behavior patterns and health. (1985). Washington, DC: U.S. Department of Health and Human Services, Public Health Service, National Institutes of Health.

Neiger, B. L., & Hopkins, R. W. (1988). Adolescent suicide: Character traits of high-risk teenagers. *Adolescence, 23*(90), 469–475.

Overlake Hospital Medical Center. (no date). Available from 1035 116th Avenue NE, Bellevue, WA 98004.

Shaffer, D., & Fisher, P. (1981). The epidemiology of suicide in children and young adolescents. *Journal of the American Academy of Child Psychiatry, 20,* 544–565.

Sullivan, W. O., & Engin, A. W. (1986). Adolescent depression: Its prevalence in high school students. *Journal of School Psychology, 24,* 103–109.

Turner, D. (1987, May 30). Rx for depression: See the good that lies at hand, and "rejoice and be glad in it." *The Seattle Times,* p. C8.

Wright-Strawderman, C., Lindsey, P., Navarette, L., & Flippo, J. R. (1996). Depression in students with disabilities: Recognition and intervention strategies. *Intervention in School and Clinic, 31*(5), 261–275.

🩺 SMOKING, ALCOHOL, AND SUBSTANCE ABUSE

Background

Offered here are a few ideas for teachers to consider as they attempt to persuade youth not to smoke, drink alcohol, or use drugs.

Procedures

For the three habits or addictions, I first identify risks that are involved and then offer ideas for breaking the habit.

Smoking

Risks. The following risks are involved in smoking (*The Providence Stop Smoking Handbook,* 1988):

- *Shortened life expectancy*—The risk is proportional to the number of packs smoked and the length of time one smoked.

- *Heart disease*—Smokers are twice as likely to have a heart attack as nonsmokers, and five times more likely to die suddenly from a heart attack.

- *Peripheral vascular disease*—Because smoking accelerates "hardening of the arteries" and encourages platelet adhesion, it can negatively affect blood circulation in the legs, which can lead to gangrene and amputation.

- *Lung cancer*—Smoking is responsible for over 80% of all lung cancers. This type of cancer is the leading cause of cancer deaths among men and will soon be for women.

- *Laryngeal cancer*—Smoking increases the risk of this cancer by about 3 to 18 times.

- *Mouth cancer*— Smokers have 3 to 10 times as many oral cancers as nonsmokers.

- *Cancer of esophagus, bladder, and pancreas, and chronic bronchitis and emphysema.*

- *Stillbirth, prematurity, low birth weight, and sudden infant death syndrome*—All these conditions are increased if a woman smoked during pregnancy.

- *Effects on nonsmokers*—Breathing smoke-laden air can cause elevated heart rate and blood pressure in nonsmokers.

Quitting. Ten to 15 years after a person has quit, exsmokers' mortality rates approach those of persons who never smoked. The increased risk of heart disease decreases sharply after 1 year of nonsmoking. The following six steps to quitting the habit are from *The Providence Stop Smoking Handbook* (1988):

1. *Fear of quitting*—Write down some of your past successes to indicate the power and sense of control and competence you had. Eliminate cliché beliefs such as, "I'm afraid I'll gain weight if I stop smoking," "I've been smoking too long to stop," or "Cigarettes relieve my tension."

2. *Create commitment*—List several reasons to stop smoking, considering the following: It will reduce my chances of getting lung cancer. It will reduce my chances of developing heart trouble. I'll have more endurance when I exercise or participate in a sport. I'll be less likely to catch colds, flu, and other diseases.

3. *Begin healthy activities*—Begin a regular program of exercise. Practice relaxation techniques and visualization.

4. *Plan pleasure activities*—List a number of things that you like to do, and make sure you do them as much as possible. Plan rewards for quitting smoking.

5. *Plan your quit day*—Set a date for quitting 3 or 4 weeks from today. Plan special rewards for yourself in the short and long term. Sign a contract that you are quitting with your physician or other significant person. In preparing for your quit day, do not carry cigarettes, put away all ashtrays, go to places where you cannot smoke, go to bed earlier, keep your hands occupied, take frequent showers, and drink nonalcoholic beverages.

6. *Quit day*—Get rid of all cigarettes, ashtrays, lighters, and matches. Tell your friends, your family, and your coworkers that you have quit. Remind yourself repeatedly that the strange feelings you have when you quit will go away in 2 to 4 weeks.

Alcohol

Facts. The following facts, noted by Hawkins and Catalano (1988) and Elmquist (1991), should be pointed out and discussed.

- Almost 91% of high school seniors reported having used alcohol. One third of them reported drinking heavily at least once in the previous 2 weeks, and 60% reported having a drink in the previous 30 days.

- Alcohol accounts for roughly 75,000 deaths annually in the United States. About two thirds of these are caused by accidents, suicide, and homicide, and one third by acute and chronic alcohol-related illnesses.

- Alcohol is a factor in half of all serious motor vehicle accidents.

- Frequent alcohol use has been shown to increase risk for a variety of chronic illnesses, particularly cancers and liver disease.

- Alcohol appears to act with tobacco to multiply the risk of esophageal cancer.

- Evidence links heavy alcohol consumption to fatty liver disease, alcoholic hepatitis, and cirrhosis.

- Acute pancreatitis has been associated with long-term alcohol abuse.

- Nervous system disorders are a common, yet less widely recognized problem associated with long-term alcoholism.

- Alcohol has an effect on the endocrine system and is implicated in sexual dysfunction.

- Alcohol has been shown to produce special risk to the developing fetus. Alcoholic mothers are twice as likely as nonalcoholic mothers to suffer habitual spontaneous abortion and to produce low birth weight babies. Drinking 1 ounce of alcohol per day in early pregnancy results in fetal alcohol syndrome rates between 1% and 10%.

- Suicide has been reported to occur 30 times more frequently among alcoholics than among the general population.

Prevention. Teachers and parents should set out to dispel prevalent myths about alcohol, such as: "Alcohol improves my mood and alters my mental state," "Alcohol makes me perform better," and "Alcohol helps me socialize better."

For another, avoid the following if you want to find out more about students' possible drinking: cornering them aggressively, threatening, lecturing, and offering absurd or inaccurate "information."

Substance Abuse

Characteristics or Possible Causes. Hawkins and Catalano (1988) provided the following information:

- Delinquents are more likely than nondelinquents to have depressed levels of autonomic and central nervous system arousal, and low arousal may contribute to sensation-seeking behaviors such as substance use among adolescents.

- Youth characterized by withdrawal responses to new stimuli, biological irregularity, slow adaptability to change, frequent negative mood expressions, and high intensity of positive and negative expressions of affect more often become regular users of alcohol, tobacco, and marijuana in adulthood than those who evidenced greater adaptability and positive outlook early in life.

- Researchers have found a higher prevalence of substance abuse disorders in late adolescence among youth diagnosed as hyperactive in childhood.

- Poor parenting, high levels of family conflict, and a low degree of bonding between children and parents appear to increase the risk of adolescent problems generally, including the abuse of alcohol and other drugs.

- Lack of maternal involvement in children's activities, lack of parental discipline, and low parental educational aspirations for children are associated with drug use.

- Children from homes broken by marital discord are at higher risk of delinquency and drug use.

- Parent–child interactions characterized by lack of closeness and lack of maternal involvement in activities with children appear to be related to initiation of drug use.

- Poor school performance is a common antecedent of initiation into drugs and has been found to predict subsequent frequency and levels of use of illicit drugs.

- A low degree of commitment to education appears to be related to adolescent drug use. Data show that the use of hallucinogens, cocaine, heroin, stimulants, sedatives, or nonmedically prescribed tranquilizers is lower among students who plan to enter college than among those who do not.

- Peer use of substances has been found to be among the strongest predictors of substance use among youth.

- Alienation from the dominant values of society, low respect for religion, and rebelliousness are positively related to drug use and delinquent behavior.

- High tolerance of deviance, resistance to traditional authority, a strong need for independence, and normlessness have all been linked with drug use.

- Earlier onset of drug use seems to signal the later extent to which drugs are used.

Prevention. According to Miksic (1987) the following are requirements of successful substance abuse education programs:

- Establish clear, well-defined policies for teachers and students; detail how apparent or substantiated drug use or possession will be dealt with.

- Encourage teachers to establish basic drug education curricula for their grade levels. Programs should be simple, brief, and nonjudgmental, and emphasize teachers' concerns for students' welfare.

- Provide an atmosphere in which teachers can develop skills for resolving classroom and individual problems and for leading discussions about topics such as adolescent development and drug use.

- Develop an intervention program that involves families as well as students by offering both one-on-one and group counseling and by making use of community resources.

- Develop peer group approaches with positive role models for group or individual support.

- Promote understanding of the emotional structure and perceptions that often accompany drug use. For example, drug-using students who feel they are incompetent and unreasonably rejected by adults and peers need a sympathetic approach rather than a disciplinary and judgmental attitude that confirms their belief that teachers and administrators are concerned only about keeping order, not about helping them.

Modifications and Considerations

Data from a survey on addiction and substance abuse sponsored by Columbia University, as reported in *The Seattle Times* (Meckler, 1998), indicated that age 13 is the critical time in the antidrug fight.

Monitor

Schools should keep up with data regarding the numbers and types of students who smoke, drink, or abuse substances as reported by various agencies, and be in touch with successful programs that have been reported. In addition, schools should, to the extent possible, keep data on their own students, and be particularly conscious of any changes and effects from the programs they set up to deal with those matters.

References

Elmquist, D. L. (1991). School-based alcohol and other drug prevention programs: Guidelines for the special educator. *Intervention in School and Clinic, 27*(1), 10–19.

Hawkins, J. D., & Catalano, R. F. (1988). *Risk and protective factors for alcohol and other drug problems in adolescence and early adulthood: Implications for substance abuse prevention.* Unpublished manuscript, Social Development Research Group, University of Washington, Seattle.

Meckler, L. (1998, September 1). Age 13 critical time in anti-drug fight. *The Seattle Times,* p. A3.

Miksic, S. (1987). Drug abuse management in adolescent special education. In M. M. Kerr, C. M. Nelson, & D. L. Lambert (Eds.), *Helping adolescents with learning and behavior problems* (pp. 225–253). Columbus, OH: Merrill.

The Providence stop smoking handbook: A step-by-step guide to smoke-free living. (1988). Available from Providence Respiratory Care Center, Providence Medical Center, 500 17th Avenue, P.O. Box C-34008, Seattle, WA 98124.

SEX EDUCATION AND BEYOND

Background

Even though the adolescents with whom we are dealing, those who are at risk and others, are likely to know something about the penis, testicles, vagina, ovaries, and other vital sexual parts, and about masturbation, intercourse, and all the ways to "do it," it would be a mistake for educators to presume that many adolescents were aware of the consequences, especially the long-term consequences, of having sex with someone of the same or opposite gender. Many students act unaware of the fact, for example, that a baby can result from their sexual involvement, or that serious diseases are transmitted through sexual activity.

Procedures

Teachers may choose to engage youth in discussions on several topics related to sex, but two *critical* topics are rearing children and acquiring sexually transmitted diseases.

Raising Children

Discussions about the responsibility of women while pregnant should be encouraged. Emphasize the importance of not smoking, of exercising, of prenatal care, and of not drinking alcohol or doing drugs during pregnancy. Other discussions should focus on the man's and woman's responsibilities insofar as preparing for the baby: attending birthing classes, buying necessary clothes and supplies, preparing the home generally, and preparing others in the home for the baby's arrival. Talk about the many initial responsibilities when the baby arrives: feeding, changing, and interacting. Emphasize the fact that what occurs early in children's lives is of vital importance, that what happens in the first weeks, months, and years sets the stage for children's development throughout their lives.

Invite young mothers and fathers to the class to talk about their baby. Have them bring the baby. They will probably tell the group that the care and nurturing of a baby takes considerable time, not merely an hour or two before going on to another activity. It is a day-after-day, night-after-night responsibility. They will undoubtedly inform the class that they get tired of this constant care, that they would like to meet with their old school chums, or do almost anything but tend the baby. They will most certainly tell the group that they get irritated, even mad, some nights when the baby wakes them up and they are tired. Hopefully they will say that, regardless, the baby must still be given constant love and affection and tender and knowledgeable care.

Talk about situations that have not worked out, ones in which the woman or the man was too irresponsible, too immature, or too selfish to properly care for the baby, and ones in which one parent was left to raise the child alone. Unfortunately, we all know of several instances like this.

Sexually Transmitted Diseases

Students should be taught about sexually transmitted diseases, including AIDS, gonorrhea, syphilis, and herpes.

Acquired Immune Deficiency Syndrome (AIDS) (Bartlett, 1995)

What are AIDS and HIV?

AIDS is the last, fully developed stage of HIV disease, a long-term chronic illness caused by the Human Immunodeficiency Virus (HIV). Over a period of years, HIV damages the infected ("HIV-positive") person's immune system, leaving him or her vulnerable to unusual infections and cancers which may be fatal.

Why should I be concerned about HIV and AIDS?

There is no cure for HIV infection, nor is there a vaccine. AIDS is a significant cause of death, especially among younger people.

Who is at risk for getting HIV?

Anyone who is sexually active in unsafe ways or shares drug needles may be at risk for HIV infection.

How is HIV transmitted?

HIV is found in the blood, semen, and vaginal secretions of an infected person and may be transmitted to others through two risk behaviors: unprotected sexual intercourse (no condom) or shared drug needles. Also, a pregnant woman may pass the virus to her baby. HIV is not transmitted through saliva, sweat, tears, urine or other bodily fluids and so is not passed through casual contact of any kind.

How can HIV infection be detected?

If infected, a person's immune system responds by making protein "soldiers" called antibodies to fight the infection. A test for these HIV antibodies can accurately detect the presence or absence of HIV infection.

For reliable results, present testing technology requires a 3-month wait between the last possible exposure and HIV antibody screening.

What are the symptoms of HIV disease and AIDS?

After several years with no symtoms, most HIV-positive people begin to experience symptoms which are common to viral diseases, but which are unusually long-lasting or recurrent (fatigue, fever, shills, appetite loss, diarrhea, weight loss, muscle aches, swollen lymph nodes).

In the AIDS stage, the most common "opportunistic" illnesses are infections and lymphatic cancers not typically a problem for immune-healthy people. It is these illnesses which often cause death from AIDS, not HIV itself.

Is there any treatment for HIV?

Treatment has improved significantly, especially if begun early, but there is no cure.

How can HIV be prevented?

The guarantee for prevention is to abstain from the risk behaviors, unprotected sexual intercourse and shared drug needles. Outside of a long-term monogamous relationship, correct and consistent condom use will reduce sexual risk significantly.

Gonorrhea. Gonorrhea, one of the most common sexually transmitted diseases, is caused by the bacterium gonococcus (*Sexually Transmitted Diseases*, 1989).

What are the symptoms?

A woman may have a discharge from the vaginal area or a slight burning sensation when urinating. As the disease progresses, she may develop a pelvic inflammatory disease, a serious infection of the pelvic organs. If the woman is pregnant, she can transmit the disease to the child during birth. The most common symptoms for a man are the discharge of pus from the penis and a burning sensation when urinating.

What is the treatment?

Penicillin and tetracycline are the two most commonly used drugs. Although gonorrhea can be completely cured, it can be caught again. Untreated gonorrhea can lead to complications such as sterility, arthritis, meningitis, or heart problems.

Syphilis. Syphilis is a disease caused by a bacterium known as treponema pallidum that spreads throughout the body.

What are the symptoms?

The first symptom is usually a small, painless sore on the penis or vagina. Later, a rash, swollen glands, fever, or tiredness may be noticed. It may then appear to be dormant for a time, perhaps several years. When syphilis reemerges, it may damage the brain, spinal cord, heart, or other organs. If a woman is pregnant and has syphilis, she can transmit the disease to the unborn child through the bloodstream.

What is the treatment?

The most common treatments are penicillin injections or tetracycline pills. Syphilis can be cured, but it can be caught again.

Genital Herpes. Genital Herpes is a disease caused by the virus herpes simplex. There are two types: Type I causes fever blisters near the mouth, and Type II causes genital herpes infections.

What are the symptoms?

Blisters appear on the penis, vagina, or other infected areas typically from 2 to 12 days after sexual contact with an infected person. The sores break open and become painful. Later, there may be swollen lymph glands, fever, and aching muscles or joints. The time between the first infection and later eruptions may be months or even years. A woman with herpes can have a normal, healthy child if precautions are taken by her doctor.

What is the treatment?

Although there is no cure for genital herpes, some relief from the sores is possible. Washing with mild soap and water helps. A woman who has had herpes should have a Pap smear every year, because she may have a greater likelihood of getting cervical cancer.

There are a number of other sexually transmitted diseases such as nongonococcal urethritis, bacterial vaginosis, candidiasis, scabies, trichomonas, nonspecific vaginitis, pelvic inflammatory disease, molluscum contagiosum, and mucopurulent cervicitis. To keep up with medical advances regarding sexually transmitted diseases, consult Web sites of health care organizations. One exceptional site is the Virtual Hospital site (www.vh.org).

Modifications and Considerations

It seems that education programs about having sex are having some effect. According to data from the Centers for Disease Control and Prevention's Division of Adolescent and School Health, the percentage of high school students who reported having engaged in sexual intercourse declined from 1991 to 1997 ("Fewer High School Students," 1998).

Formal sex education programs must be continued and must be updated as new data and procedures come to light. As pointed out earlier, matters about sex and other important health issues, should be handled as occasions arise.

Monitor

Schools should keep data on the number of students who have children while still in school and, if known, the number who have contracted sexually transmitted diseases.

References

Bartlett, J. S. (1995). *The AIDS primer.* AIDS Services of Austin: Austin, TX.

Fewer high school students having sex, poll shows. (1998, September 19). *The New York Times,* p. A18.

Sexually transmitted diseases. (1989). Available from Division of Health, Sexually Transmitted Disease Section, LP-13, Olympia, WA 98504.

EATING DISORDERS

Background

Information is provided here on eating disorders of three types: obesity, anorexia, and bulimia. Hundreds of adolescents are too heavy, if not obese. Some are academically at risk and others are not, but unless something is done to assist these youth to lose weight, they are in for a lifetime of rejection, from themselves and others. Whether we like it or not, the slim body is prized, in fact oversold. Although anorexia and bulimia are not as prevalent as obesity, they are just as serious.

Procedures

Obesity

Following are a few ways to lose weight (National Dairy Council, 1987):

- Do not waste time and money on fad diets, diet pills, or other methods that promise quick weight loss.

- Keep records of how much you eat, when and where you eat, what you are doing while you eat, and your mood. Go over your records and look for patterns or bad habits.

- Attack one bad eating habit at a time. Do not take on another until you are sure you have the first problem licked.

- Eat your meals at the same time each day. Condition your body to expect food only at certain times.

- Eat breakfast. You will not save calories by skipping breakfast and snacking later.

- Do not eat while watching TV or reading.

- Do not shovel food into your mouth. Enjoy each mouthful.

- Do not leave serving bowls and plates of food on the table while eating.

- Remember, although no single food is fattening, too much of anything can be.

- If you are possessed with an uncontrollable desire to eat something, take a walk, or drink a glass of water.

- If you must snack, keep food around that involves some work, like unpopped popcorn or an orange that has to be peeled.

- As an incentive to maintaining a diet, put a photo of a thinner you or of someone else on the refrigerator or mirror.

- Generally, the slower you take off weight, the longer you keep it off. Aim for a weight loss of 1 or 2 pounds a week.

Anorexia

Anorexia is a complex illness in which individuals (mostly women) starve themselves. Research indicates that 1 in 100 women aged 12 to 25 suffers from anorexia, or 280,000 American women (Life Skills Education, 1983). Anorexia and other eating disorders are more likely to occur during periods in a person's life that require adjustment to or acknowledgment of significant changes: the beginning of menstruation, leaving home, divorce, the death of a loved one. Following are a few indicators of anorexia:

- A weight loss of 25% or more is often a sign that something is wrong, particularly if the person was of normal weight when he or she began the diet.

- Dry, flaking skin. Because of a lack of necessary nutrients, the skin becomes rough and cracked, and scalp hair may fall out.

- Cold extremities. Loss of weight means loss of the body's protective layer of fat. Many individuals with anorexia are cold in warm weather and wear unusual amounts of clothing.

- Body hair. A fine growth of hair may cover much of the body.

- Menstruation often stops before any loss of weight because the person's highly charged emotional state causes a physical reaction.

- Thinking is often disorganized and unrealistic as a result of the body's disorganization.

- Individuals may exercise to excess in an effort to lose weight or justify the food they do eat.

- Hyperactivity. Their bodies are off balance, irritated, and keep them on the move.

- Individuals often chew their food excessively; a mouthful could last 5 or 10 minutes before being swallowed.

- Anorexia not only gives the victim the illusion of self-control; it allows the individual to control others.

- Individuals with anorexia often see other people, who are in reality much heavier than they are, as being thinner than themselves.

- They may see their illness as an expression of strength, believing that average people could not do what they are doing.

- Parents of many anorexics are very demanding. They want and expect their children to be successful, and often their children do not feel that enough affection and support are provided.

- Some anorexic females do not like being female. They believe that society gives males more opportunities to feel worthwhile and valuable.

Bulimia

Bulimia refers to a cycle of behavior of consuming food and then eliminating it through vomiting or the use of laxatives and diuretics. Research indicates that as many as 1 million Americans have bulimia, mostly women (Life Skills Education, 1984). Bulimia usually develops around age 18, but can appear at any age. The intensity of the disorder ranges from those who have only an ice cream cone and vomit, to those who eat 55,000 calories in one day and purge themselves. Among the problems the bulimic may face as a result of the eating and purging cycle are onset of diabetes, malnutrition, erosion of tooth enamel and subsequent cavities, gum disease, digestive problems, intestinal problems, rectal bleeding, rupture of the esophagus, hernias, bleeding and infection of the throat, enlargement of lymph or salivary glands, and potassium depletion.

The following are some general characteristics of individuals with bulimia:

- They appear to be normal, healthy, happy, attractive, and successful.

- They learn that eating and then vomiting reduces stress, for a time. Over time and with repeated bulimic behavior, however, that period of stress-free feeling decreases. Therefore, to increase the amount of time the person feels free of anxiety, the only option is to increase the frequency of vomiting.

- Because they want to be liked so desperately, they often overcommit themselves to people and projects.

- They often overexercise, hoard food, are irritable or depressed, take numerous trips to the bathroom, and eat all they want but never seem to gain weight.

- They often complain about stomach cramps, severe constipation, loss of menstrual cycle, insomnia, muscle fatigue, feeling faint, weakness, dizziness, chills, headaches, bloodshot eyes, numbness of hands or feet, muscle spasms, and erratic heartbeat.

Modifications and Considerations

A number of excellent Web sites are available that offer information on eating disorders. One is the National Eating Disorders Organization, which can be accessed from the Laureate site. On this site, data, comments, and suggestions are available on the following topics, among others: anorexia, bulimia, binge eating, and information for families and schools. Other Web sites enable parents, educators, and youth to stay abreast of theories and practices on these topics. Two excellent sites are The University of Pittsburgh's www.upmc.edu and the Mayo Clinic's www.mayohealth.org.

Monitor

School personnel should keep up with regional and national statistics on eating disorders and should be especially on the alert for youth in their schools who appear to have a problem.

References

Life Skills Education. (1983). *Anorexia: A lonely starvation.* Weymouth, MA: Author.

Life Skills Education. (1984). *Bulimia: Eating yourself sick.* Weymouth, MA: Author.

National Dairy Council. (1987). *You: A guide to food, exercise, and nutrition.* Rosemont, IL: Author.

National Eating Disorders Organization. Available: http://www.laureate.com/nedointro.html

PHYSICAL FITNESS

Background

Good physical fitness is a familiar term meaning that the heart, lungs, and muscles are working to the best of their ability. A combination of flexibility, muscle strength and endurance, and cardiovascular endurance is involved.

Flexibility refers to the ability to move muscles to their full extent. It is achieved through stretching, which can prevent injury and muscle soreness by loosening the muscles and getting the blood circulating.

Muscle strength is the ability to apply force, and *endurance* is the ability of the muscles to apply force for an extended period of time. Exercises that fatigue muscles can increase one's muscle strength.

Cardiovascular endurance refers to the extent the heart and lungs are able to supply oxygen to the working muscles. Adequate aerobic capacity enables one to perform activities over longer periods of time, and is believed to prolong life.

Who Can Benefit

It is important for all individuals to come up with an exercise program that they can maintain. It is particularly important for youth who are at risk to set up an exercise program, because one common characteristic of these individuals is that they are not physically fit.

Procedures

The Benefits of Daily Physical Activity (from American Heart Association, 1998, Web site: http://www.amhrt.org)

- Reduces the risk of heart disease by improving blood circulation throughout the body
- Keep weight under control
- Improves blood cholesterol levels

- Prevents and manages high blood pressure

- Prevents bone loss

- Boosts energy level

- Helps manage stress

- Releases tension

- Improves the ability to fall asleep quickly and sleep well

- Improves self-image

- Counters anxiety and depression and increases enthusiasm and optimism

- Increases muscle strength, giving greater capacity for other physical activities

- Provides a way to share an activity with family and friends

- Establishes heart-healthy habits in children and counters the conditions (obesity, high blood pressure, poor cholesterol levels, poor lifestyle habits, etc.) that lead to heart attack and stroke later in life

- In older people, helps delay or prevent chronic illnesses and diseases associated with aging and maintains quality of life and independence longer.

Key Points for the Beginner (Overlake Hospital Medical Center, n.d.):

- It generally takes 3 to 6 weeks to go from a sedentary lifestyle to being minimally fit.

- Exercise should be increased by about 10% per week.

- Maintain an exercise program. Use it or lose it!

- Pain is your body's way of telling you that you are injured. Pay attention to it!

- An exercise program consisting of 1 hour per day three to four times a week is sufficient.

Warm-Up and Stretching

- Schedule at least 1 minute of easy jumping jacks, jogging, or aerobic movement.

- Follow with 5 to 10 minutes of nonbouncing stretching exercises.

- Choose an aerobic activity you like to do at home: biking, jogging, swimming, or aerobic dancing (slowly, for about 5 to 10 minutes).

Aerobic Exercise

- Calculate your threshold heart rate (number of heartbeats per minute during exercise). To figure this, subtract your age from 220 and multiply by .65. The threshold heart rate for most teenagers is about 135 to 140 beats per minute.

- Conduct the aerobic activity so that you maintain your threshold heart rate for 20 minutes.

- Stop, and take your pulse at rest by counting beats per minute from the wrist or neck.

- Walk about the room for 5 minutes, take your pulse, and compare that rate to your target heart rate.

- You should be able to carry on a conversation without panting, but slow down if you cannot.

- Try to do a bit more every time.

Modifications and Considerations

Everyone should come up with an exercise program that fits them. Toward that end, individuals should sample a wide range of activities before they buy expensive equipment for the first program they consider. Not only is it important for individuals to identify a type of exercise they like, but they should select at least one alternative. It can become boring to do the same thing day after day.

When discussing exercise and weight control, it is not a bad idea to point out some relationships between various exercises and the time it takes to burn off calories. Start by informing students that the recommended daily allowance is 2,700 calories a day for a 150-pound man, and 2,000 for a 120-pound woman. Some informative discussions, leading to assignments, can be carried out regarding the amount of energy required to burn off calories from certain foods. A male, at the weight just noted, would have to play tennis for about 33 minutes to burn off the 233 calories in 20 french fries, walk 59 minutes to burn off the 307 calories in a cheeseburger, and run for 28 minutes to take care of the 354 calories in a slice of cheese pizza. A woman would have to bicycle for 6 minutes to burn off the 21 calories in a carrot, play tennis for 26 minutes to burn off the 150 calories in a half-pint of whole milk, and play basketball for 89 minutes to dispose of the 643 calories in a chicken dinner.

Monitor

Keep a chart posted in the classroom that shows each student's progress in the physical fitness program. At the end of each week, discuss the progress they have made.

Reference

Overlake Hospital Medical Center. (no date). Available from 1035 116th Avenue NE, Bellevue, WA 98004.

Chapter 16
PARENTS

According to a study reported in *The New York Times* (Tabor, 1996), the most critical influences on teenagers' performance in school are their parents and peers. It was pointed out that although school-oriented reformers have dominated the debate about schools, and have seen to it that billions of dollars were poured into reconfiguring schools and retraining teachers, the major contributors to children's school success are mom, dad, and friends.

Nine tactics that have to do with parents have appeared previously in the book:

- Three in the Attendance chapter—Three Techniques To Reduce Tardiness; Parental Involvement and Suggestions for Substitute Teachers; and Praise and Rewards for Attending

- Four in the Homework chapter—Homework and Self-Monitoring; Homework Target and Homework Teams; Homework Folders and Tracking Charts; and Parents Helping Youth With Homework

- One in the Social Skills chapter—Learning To Compromise: The Art of Negotiation

- One in the Classroom Management chapter—School Behavior Affects Home Privileges

In this chapter I include only two reports. The first has a dozen suggestions for parents, and the second has a dozen suggestions for teachers. In extending these suggestions, I relied on research of adolescent specialists and educators.

Reference

Tabor, M. B. W. (1996, August 7). Comprehensive study finds parents and peers are most crucial influences on students. *The New York Times*, p. A12.

 ## FOR PARENTS: BASICS FOR RAISING CHILDREN

Background

Most parents are excited when their child begins school and they continue to be engaged in their child's education throughout the elementary grades. By the time their boy or girl reaches middle school, junior high, or high school, however, many parents are discouraged and weary of the whole business: the schools, the teachers, the meetings, and even their children. This is unfortunate because the period of adolescence is the time when parents are most needed. The following are a dozen fundamental suggestions for them as they support their youth.

Suggestions

1. Nourish and shelter them. See to it that they exercise and have a proper diet, and have a comfortable and safe place to live. (Keep guns out of the house.) Encourage them to eat their meals with the family, and during those times talk about their hopes, fears, accomplishments, and responsibilities.

2. Provide good (nonhypocritical) examples. Do not drink, smoke, or use drugs. Read and study; demonstrate that you too are a learner. Be nice to one another. Keep up with current events, and discuss issues sensibly, calmly, and without haranguing. Go to libraries, museums, and concert halls, as well as athletic fields and stadiums. Be honest; do not cheat; do not boast. Consider taking the family to religious services.

3. Learn about schools. Tap into the school's Web sites; many of them are very informative. Visit the schools and possibly volunteer. Read the school's and district's newsletters. Support your student's teachers. If your child comes home with a concern, listen and discuss it; do not be too quick to judge either the youth or the school. If you are concerned about a school issue such as year-round schooling, read up on it; stay abreast of the topic.

4. Help them study and deal with school. Keep up with your youth with respect to their assignments. You should know what the teachers require. Dial in to the homework hotlines and find out what is going on. Set up some policies (if not rules) regarding homework. Reinforce your child for studying. Help the youth set up a time and place to work. Make sure that he or she has the necessary equipment and books to carry out the work. Encourage participation in co-curricular activities. (Arrive at a proper balance between athletics, musical activities, and academics.)

5. Help them find good friends. Peers are powerful! Some professionals say they are more influential than parents. Although you cannot always control whom your youth spends time with, provide ample opportunities for your child to interact with decent, upstanding companions. Music and church groups are often good places to start.

6. Know about resources other than schools. If you are unable to help your child with school work such as calculus, chemistry, and other subjects, find knowledgeable people to help. There might be a neighbor or two who can "tutor" your child. Certainly the local library will lend a hand. Scads of resources are available from the Internet.

7. Know about children's rights and the legal system. You need to know when the youth is responsible for actions, and what the consequences for those actions are at various ages. The youth need to know that if they do certain things, dad or mom cannot always bail them out. According to a piece in *The New York Times* ("Young Offender Faces Death," 1998), 24 states permit execution of offenders under age 18 at the time of the crime.

8. Help with future plans. Do not assume that youth will get all the help needed with respect to future plans from high school counselors, who are often too busy to help everybody. Use the Internet for assistance with educational matters; dozens of sites offer suggestions on scholarships and financial aid. Every 2- and 4-year college and university has a Web site. The Internet is also a valuable resource for vocational, military, and other postschool options. The local library also has resources available.

9. Require youth to help at home and in the community. Convey the idea that, although your child is important and you love him or her a great deal, other people also inhabit the planet. See to it that your child not only helps out at home with chores, but contributes to the community. (The idea of helping others should begin much earlier than adolescence.)

10. Be supportive and forgiving. Do not yell and scream when your youth does something stupid, or kick your child out of the house for coming home drunk or being caught shoplifting. However, do not be too complacent about these matters, either; see to it that your child owns up to the transgressions. (Supporting your child means more than simply attending a few soccer matches.)

11. Be knowledgeable about adolescents. Read about adolescence, a magnificent but troubling time of life. Do not be too influenced by folk wisdom. According to Eccles and Harold (1993), "Adolescence is one of the most fascinating periods of development. Other than infancy, there is no other time in life when the individual experiences such rapid and dramatic change" (p. 568).

12. The parent of a child with disabilities. Know about your rights and those of your child. Be especially informed about IEPs and due process. See the booklet, "Special Education: Common Questions—Common-Sense Answers" (Lovitt, 1997), which provides straightforward answers to important and often perplexing questions about special education.

References

Eccles, J. S., & Harold, R. D. (1993). Parent–school involvement during the early adolescent years. *Teachers College Record, 94*(3), 568–587.

Lovitt, T. C. (1997). *Special education: Common questions—common-sense answers.* Longmont, CO: Sopris West.

Young offender faces death, and state is urged to halt it. (1998, October 14). *The New York Times,* p. A18.

 # FOR TEACHERS: WAYS TO COMMUNICATE WITH PARENTS

Background

Many secondary teachers work with as many as 150 children a day, whereas their elementary colleagues deal with only 20 or so. Therein lies one reason that secondary teachers communicate with parents less than do teachers at the elementary level. However, it is probably as important to stay in contact with parents at this stage regarding the development of their youth as it was in their children's early years. Toward that end, I offer a dozen suggestions.

Suggestions

1. Use e-mail and voice mail. Provide your e-mail address and voice mail extension to parents, and encourage them to use them. When they communicate with you, get back with them quickly. Keep a directory of their email addresses.

2. Send messages home. Messages about assignments and upcoming events can be sent home with students. Some parents will never see them, but keep trying. Occasionally, leave space on the messages for parents to comment and return them to you.

3. Videotape your class. Have one of your students videotape a few class sessions, possibly ones that feature a special happening. Parents could check these out and view them at their leisure, or they could be shown on "back to school" nights.

4. Phone parents. Keep a list of the parents' phone numbers (including cellular numbers) at your desk. Call them when things come up. Keep in mind that some youth have parents or guardians with different addresses and phone numbers.

5. Schedule times to meet parents. Set up a couple of times each week for parents to stop by without making appointments, perhaps one in late afternoon and another in early morning. For the afternoon time, you might set up your "office" at a coffee shop in the neighborhood.

6. Use parent volunteers. Use parents to help out with certain classes or with field trips. Take advantage of their special areas of interest and expertise. Keep in mind, however, that many secondary students do not want their parents to help out at school ("High Schools Gear Up," 1994).

7. Update the school Web site and phone hotline. Keep your part of the Web site and the phone service up to date. Students, their parents, and citizens at large can tap into these resources.

8. Hold special meetings. Schedule meetings on certain topics for parents (e.g., study skills, helping with homework, using the Web). These could be with only your class or with your department. Some meetings could be for only one session, whereas others could be for several meetings.

9. Survey parents. Send home a survey once in a while. This is a quick way to find out what they are concerned about, and what they would like to chat with you about.

10. Be prepared for the angry parents. There will be times when a parent, or a group of parents, comes after you. They could be furious about your grading policy, the books you have selected, the homework assignments you give (or do not give), the way you interacted with a youth. Sometimes a parent will schedule an appointment to vent grief, but at other times they will arrive unannounced. Be prepared.

11. Communicate with the parents of a child with disabilities. Make sure that these parents know their rights and privileges. Be especially knowledgeable about IEPs, due process, and discipline policies. A number of resources are available. See, for example, the U.S. Department of Education Web site having to do with youth with disabilities.

12. Be a referral agent. Keep up with current trends, both the goofy and the authentic. Parents will want your advice about attention deficit disorder and dyslexia, about various therapies and interventions, about private schools and tutoring agencies, about a new diet or type of exercise. Do not make a referral or recommendation unless you know what you are talking about. Keep a list of trusted professionals to whom you can send parents.

References

High schools gear up to create effective school and family partnerships. (1994). *Research and Development Report,* Center on Families, Communities, Schools & Children's Learning No. 5.

U.S. Department of Education, http:www.ed.gov

Author Index

Subject Index

I Found a Solution program, 243–244
IEP grading, 194, 195
IEPs, 263, 272–274, 371, 373
Imagery. *See* Mental imagery
Index Card NoteTaker, 188
Individualized Education Plans (IEPs), 194, 195, 263, 272–274, 371, 373
Individuals with Disabilities Education Act, 151
In-school suspension (ISS), 329–330
Instruction. *See also* Peer-mediated instruction; Teachers
  advance organizers for lectures, 98–99
  notetaking and, 94
Internet
  eating disorders Web sites, 364
  educational resources on, 150–151, 155–157
  homework help from, 155–157
  National Parent Information Network (NPIN), 150
  physical fitness Web site, 365
  school Web site, 370, 372
  self-esteem Web sites, 307
  U.S. Department of Education Web site, 373
  writing and, 132–133
Interpersonal relationships. *See* Peers; Social skills
Intrinsic motivation, 41
Iowa Tests of Basic Skills, 202
Iowa Tests of Educational Development, 202
ISS (in-school suspension), 329–330

Jigsaw II, 292–293
Job design, 63
Job interviews, 130
Journal writing, 87–91

Kent School District (Wash.), 156
Keyboarding instruction, 134
Keywords for mnemonics, 107–109

Landscaping of schools, 44
Learning
  motivation for, 39–43
  real-world learning, 59–60
  relevancy of, 71
Learning logs, 87–91
Learning Together structure, 297–300
Legal system, 370
Lesson plans, 199, 200
Level System, 331–333
Lighting of classrooms, 45
Listening and responding to criticism, 237–238
Long-term suspension and expulsion, 330
Lotteries, for attendance, 25–27

Magic Circle, 226, 228, 305
Management
  behavior modification and, 63
  communication and, 63
  job design, 63
  Likert's management system, 61–63
  theory X–theory Y, 63
  types of management systems, 61–63
Mastery-level system of grading, 194, 195
Matching questions on tests, 100–101, 102
Math awareness, 126
Mathematics
  assessment of, 124
  calculators for, 125
  computation skills, 124–125
  estimation skills, 125
  RIDGES strategy, 127
  story problems in, 126–128
  use of, in daily lives, 126–128
Mayo Clinic Web site, 364
Memorization, 106–110
Memory questions, 253
Mental imagery and reading, 82–85, 123
Message writing, 129
Metacognition, 253
Middle school, transition to high school from, 16–18
Minimum competency tests, 202
Mnemonics, 106–110
Modeling for social skills training, 211, 223
Modified diplomas, 204
Monitoring. *See* Cognitive monitoring
Motivation
  aesthetics and renovating urban schools, 43–44
  boredom and, 63–67
  classroom modifications and, 45–47
  contingent socialization and, 68–69
  extrinsic incentives and, 40–41
  and increasing student interest in course content, 50–51
  intrinsic motivation, 41
  for learning, 39–43
  Likert's management system, 61–63
  peer forums for, 47–49
  preconditions for, 40
  pupil governance and, 70
  real-world learning, 59–60
  and relevant learning opportunities, 71
  and school upkeep and maintenance by students, 70
  schoolwide changes for, 69–72
  self-management and, 52–58
  stimulating student motivation, 41–42
  and student help at school, 69–72
  success expectations and, 40

About the Author

◆ ◆ ◆ ◆ ◆ ◆ ◆ ◆ ◆ ◆ ◆ ◆ ◆ ◆ ◆ ◆ ◆ ◆ ◆

Thomas C. Lovitt is a professor emeritus at the University of Washington. He joined the faculty in special education in 1966, after spending countless years at the University of Kansas. Although he retired in 1997, he still teaches a class now and then and works with a couple of doctoral students. In addition, he visits a few elementary and secondary schools in the Seattle area. In his spare time he copes with his six grandchildren, reads, writes, and watches too many sports events on television.